Systems Simulation
for Regional Analysis
An Application to
River-Basin Planning

Systems Simulation
for Regional Analysis
An Application to
River-Basin Planning

H. R. Hamilton
S. E. Goldstone
J. W. Milliman
A. L. Pugh III
E. B. Roberts
A. Zellner

The M.I.T. Press
Massachusetts Institute of Technology
Cambridge, Massachusetts, and London, England

Preface and Acknowledgments

This book is a study of the application of systems simulation to regional analysis. It is an outgrowth of a series of reports dealing with economic growth in the Susquehanna River Basin prepared by the Battelle Memorial Institute–Columbus Laboratories for a group of utility companies. The decision to write this book was based upon the premise that the methodology developed was unique and that significant progress had been made in terms of advancing the state of the art in regional science. In August 1962, Battelle was approached by a group of electric utility companies with an interest in the economic development of the Susquehanna River Basin. The utility companies subsequently sponsored a series of three studies[1] designed to develop new methodology for the better understanding of regional and water resource phenomena within the basin. The first study or phase of the over-all program was aimed at defining the problem and selecting a methodology. The second phase developed a computer simulation model that was extended and modified in phase three.

The following utility companies have sponsored the three Susquehanna studies:

Baltimore Gas and Electric

Delmarva Power and Light

Luzerne Electric Division of
   United Gas Improvement

Metropolitan Edison

New York State Electric and Gas

Pennsylvania Electric

Pennsylvania Power and Light

Philadelphia Electric

Public Service Electric and Gas

West Penn Power

[1] "Estimating the Economic Impact of Systems of Works on the Susquehanna River Basin Through Computer Simulation," W. L. Swager, H. R. Hamilton, D. C. Sweet, S. E. Goldstone, N. Kamrany, and A. L. Pugh III, Battelle Memorial Institute, February 11, 1964.

"A Dynamic Model of the Economy of the Susquehanna River Basin," H. R. Hamilton, S. E. Goldstone, D. C. Sweet, N. M. Kamrany, R. D. Shultz, J. W. Duncan, D. E. Boyce, A. L. Pugh III, and E. B. Roberts, Battelle Memorial Institute, November 13, 1964.

"A Dynamic Model of the Economy of the Susquehanna River Basin," H. R. Hamilton, S. E. Goldstone, F. J. Cesario, D. C. Sweet, D. E. Boyce, and A. L. Pugh III, Battelle Memorial Institute, August 1, 1966.

The authors of the book are either members of the Battelle staff or consultants to Battelle. Each of the authors participated in the earlier studies. Although the book represents the work of the six authors, it should be stated that a number of other Battelle staff members contributed to the research program.[2]

Battelle Memorial Institute is the world's largest independent not-for-profit research institute.[3] It conducts physical and social science research at four major centers located in Columbus, Ohio; Richland, Washington; Geneva, Switzerland; and Frankfurt, Germany. The research discussed in this book was conducted at the Battelle-Columbus facilities.

The list of people and organizations to whom the authors are indebted for help is a long one, reflecting the size of the undertaking, the complexity of the task, and the financial support needed to sustain the research over a four-year period. We wish to thank the utility companies for their encouragement and financial support of the original research program. A special note of appreciation is extended to George S. Wallace, Jr., who, as executive secretary of the sponsor group, provided guidance and coordinated the ever-necessary communication between sponsors and researchers. The authors wish to thank the management of Battelle-Columbus for providing financial support to the authors during writing of the book and also for showing a great deal of patience during periods when drafts were slow in forthcoming. We are particularly grateful, in this regard, to David C. Minton, Jr., Director, David D. Moore, Manager of the Department of Economics and Information Research, and to William L. Swager, Associate Manager. Many others deserve thanks, including staff members and former staff members and the many secretaries who spent long hours typing many drafts.

Despite the generous help supplied by all these organizations and people,

[2] These staff members are Joseph W. Duncan, David C. Sweet, Frank J. Cesario, Dr. David E. Boyce, Dr. Robert D. Schultz, and Dr. Nake M. Kamrany. The latter three are now associated with various other institutions.

[3] For further descriptions of Battelle, see "A Fast-Growing Lab Regroups on the Run," *Business Week*, February 6, 1965; and "Research Worldwide," Battelle Memorial Institute, Columbus, Ohio, May 1965.

the authors accept full responsibility for any errors of fact or interpretation that still remain. Although the views we express are not necessarily endorsed by the utility companies nor by Battelle, we can faithfully report that the six of us have achieved a consensus. Perhaps this, too, is an application of systems simulation.

November 1, 1967
H. R. Hamilton
S. E. Goldstone
Battelle Memorial Institute
J. W. Milliman
Indiana University
A. L. Pugh III
E. B. Roberts
Massachusetts Institute of Technology
A. Zellner
University of Chicago

Contents

Systems Simulation
for Regional Analysis
An Application to
River-Basin Planning

Chapter 1
Introduction
and Summary

Since the end of World War II, problems, policies, and programs with a regional orientation have received increasing emphasis in the United States. The Federal Government has spent millions of dollars in attempts to encourage greater economic development in regions that have lagged the nation with respect to growth and prosperity. In response to the flow of resources toward regional programs, the ranks of those engaged in regional analysis and planning have swollen. Regional economics has become a well-recognized profession.

Concurrent with the rise in importance of regional analysis, the digital computer has grown in usefulness and availability. With the computer has come a host of computer-oriented techniques valuable for analysis and planning purposes. The utility of these techniques has been enhanced by the development of so-called computer software—generally available computer programs and compilers. Of special note has been the rapid acceptance of large-scale computer simulation as a technique with widespread applicability for gaining insight into complex problems.

Despite the obvious complexities involved in regional analysis and the apparently unique capability of large-scale computer simulation to deal with many of these complexities, simulation has received much less attention by regional analysts than have many other techniques. The purpose of this book is to explore how systems simulation may be applied to regional analysis. Although the actual model presented has been developed within the context of river-basin analysis and planning, the presentation is more than a case study. The findings of the research and the model developed are suggestive of other applications and should serve as a starting point for the construction of other regional simulation models.

This book is an outgrowth of a series of research programs dealing with the economic growth of the Susquehanna River Basin conducted by Battelle Memorial Institute—Columbus Laboratories. These studies were aimed at developing and refining new methodology for the better understanding of regional and water resource phenomena in that basin. During these studies a computer simulation model of the Susquehanna River Basin was developed.

This chapter summarizes some of the major research findings stemming from the construction of the Susquehanna model and lays out the plan for the chapters that follow. The conclusions that are presented in fairly dogmatic fashion here are defended and developed in these succeeding chapters. We have intentionally adopted a normative posture to suggest how systems simulation can be applied to regional analysis and to highlight the sorts of relationships that need further emphasis and study. We recognize, however, that additional studies in the future will, in turn, suggest new avenues of research and new approaches to regional models.

The Problem and How It Was Approached

The problem presented by the Susquehanna River Basin Utility Group to the research team at Battelle Memorial Institute had numerous aspects. Essentially, Battelle was asked to analyze the economy of the Susquehanna River Basin and to define the role the basin's water resources would or could play in the future development of this economy. However, another goal was to develop improved techniques for accomplishing this type of analysis. In particular, the need for incorporating the normally considered regional economic variables and those directly relating to the water resources of the region within the same analytic framework was recognized from the inception of the research.

The research program was carried out in three major steps: a problem definition and technique selection phase, model development phase, and a model refinement phase. The latter two phases each saw evolutionary changes in the model as the research progressed, but an operational model was always kept available. While undergoing modification, the model was continually simulated and the simulation results used as a guide to the direction that future research should take.

The first phase of the study defined a large, complex system requiring analysis. Because demands on the water resource would be largely determined by population levels and by the levels of economic activity in the region, it was necessary to consider these variables. The demographic features of the population which were the major causal factors producing population change—births, deaths, and migration—had to be treated in appropriate detail. Those factors shaping the development of the region's economy also needed explicit treatment and included variables relating to employment by appropriate industry groups, unemployment, regional advantages and disadvantages, and similar elements. Because they are causally related, the demographic or supply of labor variables needed to be tied to the economic variables depicting the demand for labor such that these two major classes of variables would tend to maintain a reasonable relationship to one another. Finally, water quality and quantity variables were also required. These water-related variables had to be tied to those demographic and economic factors that are relevant in terms of shaping water demands and influencing water quality.

With the exception of the emphasis on water resources, the preceding paragraph describes a system that is characteristic of those encountered in many regional studies. This system has a number of very important features. First, it contains many variables. For instance, in relation to population alone, age-specific birth rates, death rates, labor-force-participation rates, and migration characteristics, as well as the age structure of the population itself, must be considered. Second, a great many of the variables in the system are interrelated in the form of feedback relationships. For instance, population levels affect unemployment rates that, in turn, affect population through migration. Third, such a system often contains time lags, nonlinearities, and sometimes even discontinuities. The many kinds of equations needed to describe such a system will usually not yield to analytic solutions. Thus, a dynamic analysis employing computer simulation seems the most effective approach to model manipulation and use.

At this point in time, the contribution that models can make to regional analysis is widely recognized. First, the explicit nature of such models facilitates communication of what has been studied and the weighting of the factors involved. Second, models can be used to test the impact of alternative policies, a factor extremely important to regional analysis and planning. However, a third advantage of models that is often overlooked concerns their usefulness in terms of guiding the research studies that spawn them. This advantage is gained by using the model in various stages of refinement to specify critical relationships requiring further research effort.

The last contribution of modeling to a research effort suggests some very important elements of good model-building research strategy. The first of these elements involves assembling a preliminary version of a model as rapidly as is reasonable during the early parts of a research program. Then, observations of how model output responds to systematic changes in the values of parameters, and in the form of the relationships themselves, will provide valuable guidance as to where further research effort is needed. This approach indicates that the research should be what might be termed "balanced and iterative" in nature. "Balance" will be obtained by allocating research effort to the segments of an over-all problem in relation to their importance. The research program will proceed in an "iterative" fashion because a first model will suggest further research resulting in a modified model, which may, in turn, indicate the need for additional effort along new paths. This iterative process will continue, within the practicalities of research resource limitations, until a model that is judged satisfactory for its intended use is developed.

Another important element in research strategy and, for that matter, in regional analysis and planning is that modeling research should not be "one-shot" in nature. Rather, a model should be constructed to be used. The model seldom if ever should be considered as the output of a study. This means that a set of regional projections should not be viewed as a "once and for all" input to planning and policy-making. Rather, the model should be used to generate different sets of projections under alternative assumptions regarding data and functional relationships. Further, if the alternative policies being studied are felt to have important and measurable regional impact, the model itself should be used to test the implications of the policy choices available. This research process should continue over time, and as new facts and ideas become available, they should be used to modify and update the model.

Despite the apparent reasonableness of the statements in the preceding paragraph, regional planning often proceeds from what is often termed an "economic base study" and one set of projections. The effects of the policies being evaluated on the projections are usually not examined explicitly. Perhaps river-basin planning and transportation planning are outstanding examples of fields where the one-shot approach is common.

The tendency toward one-shot projections can possibly be explained by the inability of conventional techniques (1) to generate easily alternative sets of projections, and (2) to incorporate policies within the framework used for projection so as to test their potential impact. In addition, there is a tendency to view research as a completed product and not as a continuing process. One of the purposes of this book is to indicate how computer simulation, accompanied by empirical research, can be used to make regional planning a more cohesive and continuing process, rather than a group of separate inputs concerning an over-all problem that are often difficult to integrate. The proposed key to a cohesive planning effort is a model that can serve as a central focus to a study by relating the parts of the study and tending to keep them in balanced perspective. A model also provides the framework for monitoring the region's economic health over time and for revising forecasts and planning strategy in the light of new developments.

River-Basin Analysis and the Susquehanna Model

It is generally accepted that comprehensive river-basin planning must be regional in character, although the relevant region is not always easily defined. Changing water-use patterns in one part of a basin often influence the quantity and quality of water available downstream. Similarly, water-oriented developments planned for one segment of a basin may conflict with those planned in other areas. Such conflicts may not be clearly recognized if water development plans are formulated on a strictly local basis.

While river-basin planning should be accomplished within an integrated, basin-wide framework, a gross, aggregative basin-wide analysis is of little value. For instance, total basin water withdrawal is normally a useless statistic for planning purposes because most water withdrawn from a water course is returned. Therefore total withdrawal may exceed river flow many times over. A worthwhile basin analysis must consider the supply of, and demand for, water in relation to many specific geographical areas within the basin.

The model of the Susquehanna River Basin which is described in several of the chapters that follow has been shaped by (1) the nature of the problem in general, and (2) the nature of the Susquehanna Basin and its economic regions in particular. Thus while certain aspects of river-basin planning and regional analysis have been studied and modeled in some detail, others may have received much less attention because, after preliminary study, they did not seem relevant in the Susquehanna River Basin.

The planning region relevant to the study of the Susquehanna River Basin is shown in Figure 1.1. It includes portions of Maryland (specifically the Baltimore economic region), central Pennsylvania, and the southern tier of counties in upper New York State.

Figure 1.1 also depicts several of the economic subregions that lie within this area. These subregions are quite diverse in many ways. For instance, they have had widely differing patterns of economic development in the 1950's and 1960's. The southernmost subregions, G (Harrisburg) and H (Baltimore), have experienced a relatively healthy pattern of economic growth. On the other hand, subregions where coal mining once was a predominant factor in the employment mix, for instance, Subregion E (Wilkes-Barre–Scranton), have suffered declining employment with associated high unemployment rates and outmigration. While most of the basin is only sparsely populated, a few of the regions have relatively large urban populations. Of course, the Baltimore Subregion (H) is predominantly urban in character. Because of these differing characteristics, different growth patterns among the subregions should not be unexpected a priori, and for this reason aggregation of the subregions depicted to form larger regional units seems unjustified for our purposes. Further, the subregional breakouts provide one means for relating water demands to specific river segments or tributaries.

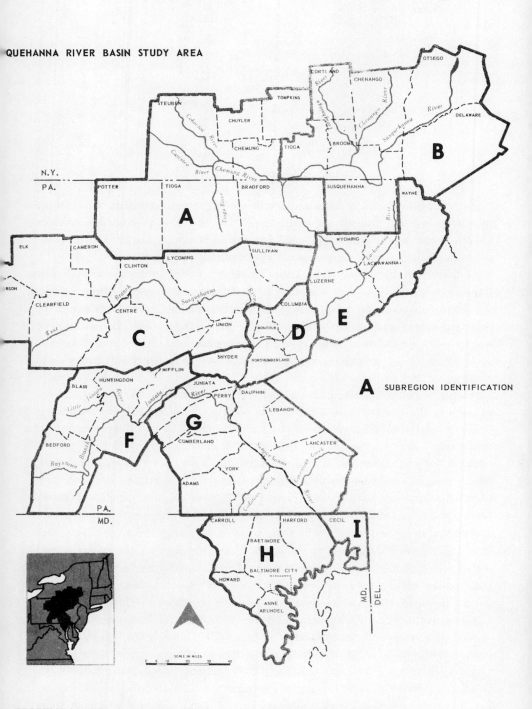

QUEHANNA RIVER BASIN STUDY AREA

FIGURE 1.1. The Susquehanna River Basin and its economic subregions.

The relationship of the Susquehanna River to the economy of its basin appears somewhat unique even for the relatively humid eastern United States. In general, the Susquehanna is a large river, and the demands placed upon it by the sparsely populated subregions of the basin are characteristically less than those placed upon smaller rivers in more developed basins. This unique relationship is probably most significant in terms of the relationship between the water sector of the model and the demographic and employment sectors. In the Susquehanna model, most potential feedbacks from the water sector to the demographic and employment sectors were judged to be inoperative. That is, while growth of population and industry obviously affects the river in terms of water quantity and quality, it was judged that the resultant changes in the river will not be of sufficient magnitude and kind significantly to alter industrial and population growth patterns except in some special instances as in the case of certain recreational developments.

The model outlined here in concept and in detail in some of the chapters that follow has several important features. The model is relatively unique in the manner in which it combines these features. First, the model ties the "economic base," that is, the employment and demographic sectors, and a water sector together within the framework of one model. Second, it interrelates and projects the demographic and employment variables simultaneously, rather than independently as is done in many regional models. Third, the model is operational. It is programmed for computer simulation rendering inexpensive experiments on the effects of changes in parameter values. The computer running times are short, making the model useful in the sense that the cost of performing such experiments is small. Fourth, the model is largely data based. Significant effort was devoted to obtaining subregional, regional, and national data shedding light on the variables treated. Fifth, examination of the data led to a model with a relatively high degree of disaggregation. As a result, the model yields information specific to the various subregions of the basin and to particular geographic points within these subregions. Within a subregion, information is also available concerning employment by industry group, unemployment rates, labor-force-participation rates, migration, births, deaths, and concerning population levels by age groupings as well as other variables.

An important point should be borne in mind as the reader examines the details of the model presented. The research findings and the model are, in many ways, the result of a synthesis of the ideas and work of others. One of the contributions of the study is the formulation of the means by which these previously conceived ideas and findings could be combined into an over-all analysis.

Although the features mentioned are felt to be desirable elements in regional models to be applied under a wide variety of circumstances, no claim is made that *the* Susquehanna model presented in this book is applicable to other regions or river basins without substantial alterations, additions, or deletions. With regard to river-basin analysis, some elements of comprehensive basin planning are not included in the Susquehanna model. For instance, those elements having a large engineering input, such as flood control, are not embodied. Also, navigation and irrigation did not seem important enough in the Susquehanna River Basin to warrant inclusion. Nevertheless, many of the model's features, as well as the research strategy employed, are felt to be applicable to many problems in regional analysis. Certainly, systems analysis and computer simulation seem to have wide applicability to many regional problems.

Plan of the Book

This book is comprised of thirteen chapters. Each chapter is primarily the work of one author. Although an attempt has been made to reduce these individual efforts to one style of writing or approach, we recognize that considerable differences in approach among the chapters still remain. Four technical appendices have been added to include material too detailed for the general reader.

This first chapter introduces the book and summarizes a number of its salient features.

Chapter 2 presents some relevant "Perspectives on Mathematical Models in the Social Sciences." The purpose of Chapter 2 is to give some insight into the problems and issues surrounding model-building research in the social sciences in general and in economics in particular. The chapter maintains that the role of mathematical models in the social sciences is practically the same as their role in the natural sciences. Also presented are comments on progress made in the state of the art of mathematical modeling in economics and a review of some of the problems and pitfalls that have been encountered.

Chapter 3, "Regional Economic Analysis and River-Basin Planning," helps to set the stage for the presentation of the Susquehanna model. First, a brief review of the state of the art in regional analysis is presented. Pertinent problems regarding data availability, conflicts in planning goals, institutions for regional development, and other matters are discussed. Particular emphasis is placed on those issues which relate to river-basin analysis and planning.

While regional data have been improving because of increasing interest in problems and analysis with a regional focus, the chapter concludes that the data about small, open, regional economies will continue as a major, or perhaps the major, problem in regional studies. However, the problem is deeper because, in terms of analysis and planning, regional goals are seldom clear. What is clear is that it is difficult to imagine a one-dimensional goal for regional development, such as income maximization or unemployment-rate minimization, as being satisfactory. Such one-dimensional analyses may not even be meaningful given the wide variety of national, local, political, and private interests that must be considered. Therefore techniques that utilize a single objective function are probably of small value. Another major problem in regional analysis is the institutional framework available for carrying out regional plans; political and economic jurisdictions seldom coincide with physical (e.g., hydrologic) boundaries. All these problems are potentially present in comprehensive river-basin analysis and planning.

In Chapter 4, the general features of the Susquehanna model are compared to a number of other regional-economic and river-basin models. Those analyzed are the New York Metropolitan Study, the Upper-Midwest Study, the Ohio River

Basin Study, the California Development model, the Hawaii model, and the Lehigh Basin simulation model, and, of course, the Susquehanna model itself. The chapter concludes that, among these models, the Susquehanna model is unique in several respects. First, it includes the demographic and employment sectors within the scope of one model. Second, the Susquehanna model is dynamic in nature, incorporating explicit feedbacks and lagged relationships among sectors and variables. Third, because the model is of the simulation type, it allows for convenient model use particularly in terms of extensive sensitivity analysis. Finally, and perhaps most important from a river-basin point of view, the Susquehanna model is the only one of the river-basin models published to date to incorporate an explicit water sector within the regional economic model itself.

Chapter 5 presents "The Philosophy and Methodology of Approach." Relying on the background material outlined in Chapter 3, Chapter 5 analyzes the characteristics of a regional economy from the point of view of systems analysis. The chapter concludes that the most effective technique for handling large, nonlinear feedback systems such as regional economies is dynamic computer simulation. The chapter then outlines some of the features of the specific method of computer simulation selected for use in the Susquehanna research project. Problems and techniques of model construction and model validation are discussed, and a simplified regional model is developed to illustrate the method of approach utilized.

Chapter 6 presents the "Regional Setting" of the Susquehanna study itself. The methodology for devising economic subregions within the basin is spelled out, and each of these economic subregions is discussed briefly. The general characteristics of the Susquehanna River and its major tributaries in each of the subregions are outlined.

Chapter 7 presents a brief "Overview of the Model." The purpose of this chapter is to give the reader perspective as to how the individual sections of the model are interrelated. The nature of the model's major links between its three principal sectors—demographic, employment, and water—is spelled out. Then the major features of each of these sectors are explained. Because the chapters that follow Chapter 7 discuss each of the three main model sectors almost as if they were separate entities, one of the major purposes of Chapter 7 is to give the reader an understanding as to how the sectors are tied together, so that they can then be viewed in proper perspective.

Chapter 8 presents the "Demographic Sector" of the model. The chapter contends that while regional demographic factors obviously play a major role in shaping the future of an area, these factors have often been relatively neglected in earlier regional studies. The chapter outlines a generalized model structure for the demographic sector of a regional simulation model and then specifies how this general structure was adapted to the needs of the Susquehanna River Basin study. The latter part of the chapter goes into some detail as to how the dynamics of birth, death, migration, and labor-force-participation rates were analyzed and incorporated into the model structure. The chapter concludes with a description of some preliminary research on the impact of education, training, and skills on regional demography.

Chapters 9 and 10 discuss the "Employment Sector" of the model. Chapter 9 presents the basis for sectoring the employment structure and for identifying endogenous and exogenous forces shaping the regional economy. Chapter 10 concentrates on export industries. A mechanism for relating internal changes within the region to industry location and growth is specified. Particular attention is paid to changes in regional wage patterns as a determinant of regional costs. Finally, the method by which regional attractiveness is updated by the model during simulation is outlined.

Chapter 11 discusses the "Water Sector." This chapter begins with a discussion of the methodology by which significant water-related variables were ferreted out and inserted in the model. The "critical point" concept is used to identify potential problem locations. The influence of changing economic patterns and different treatment levels is tied to water quantities and qualities or critical points.

The economic impact on the various subregions of several levels of river works construction is simulated. The chapter concludes with a section showing that water is only one kind of technical variable or sector that might be considered in a regional simulation model. An example of how a region's growth might be tied to forestry and forest management variables is shown.

Chapter 12, "Simulation of the Model," presents a number of the more interesting model simulations that were conducted. The results of these simulations show the sensitivity of the model's output to changes in parameter values, function forms, and specific model inputs. As a result of these simulations, a number of model refinements are suggested.

Chapter 13, "Implications of the Model-Building Effort for Future Research," concludes the body of the book by summarizing some of the lessons learned and principles applied during the research. This chapter stresses the need for a model-building strategy and points out the advantages of what is termed the "balanced and iterative" approach, and it concludes with a discussion of some of the future potential uses of regional simulation models.

The book includes a series of appendices. Appendix A discusses the role of management in a multidisciplinary study such as the Susquehanna program. This appendix points out some of the difficulties that are encountered in multiperson, multidisciplinary studies and outlines some of the methods that were used in attempting to overcome problems during the Susquehanna program. Appendix A concludes that, while the management problems of such studies are obviously important, they have received little mention in the literature. The management function is largely ignored in many research programs of this kind.

Appendix B, "Industrial Classification," discusses the details of the separation of the industries into the local-serving and nonlocal-serving categories. Appendix C, "Determining Access Factors," describes the method by which a region's relative transportation costs were derived. Appendix D provides a technical description of model.

A Final Perspective

As can be seen by the preceding chapter-by-chapter description, the book leads the reader from the very general—the role of models in the social sciences—to the specific—individual sectors of a specific model of a specific river basin. The author have not attempted to be exhaustive in treating the subject. Instead, only those topics that seem particularly important in terms of showing that systems analysis and computer simulation are useful techniques for regional analysis receive attention. Admittedly, what may seem important may vary considerably with the background of the reader or the goals of a particular piece of research. For example, what may seem unimportant to an economist may be new information to a demographer or operations research analyst. Moreover, different agencies, public and private, and different kinds of regions may have considerably different demands for regional analysis.

The resulting book is not long and, in large measure, puts forth ideas more than the mechanics of implementing these ideas. When the mechanics are presented, particularly in relation to the Susquehanna model, they are intended to demonstrate that implementation can be achieved rather than to suggest that there is only one way of achieving satisfactory application or reaching a given modeling goal.

The dividing line between describing what "we did" and stating what a regional simulation model "ought to be" is obviously somewhat nebulous, particularly from the standpoint of the authors who, of course, find it difficult to take a detached point of view with regard to their own work. We believe quite strongly that systems simulation has a great deal of promise for regional analysis. We also believe that the particular model described here represents a significant advancement in the state of the art. The Susquehanna model breaks new ground in tying together the employment, demographic, and water sectors of a large region in one model, that is, within a systems simulation framework. Yet, it is recognized that the model was designed to meet a specific set of goals and, therefore, may not be fully adequate for a different set of demands or goals.

fact, there can be no such thing as a "general purpose" regional model. addition, all model-builders must work within constraints of budgets, data ailability, and computer and software capacities. Finally, theories of regional owth and development are not fully developed.

We fully expect that further refinements and advances in the field of regional odel-building will appear in the next few years. Certainly, as computer capacities e increased, as more regional data become available, as more research funds e provided, and as our knowledge of regional development is advanced, the ontiers of regional science will continue to move outward.

The purpose of this chapter is to give readers some insight into the problems and issues surrounding the role of mathematical models in the social sciences. By having these problems and issues explicitly stated, it will be possible to appreciate and assess the work on the development of the Susquehanna model in a broader perspective and to relate it to the general, continuing research on the problems of producing useful models of social systems. Although special attention will be given to developments in economics, it is thought that many of the issues and problems that have arisen in economics and that are mentioned here have important implications for work in other areas.

The Role of Mathematical Models in the Social Sciences

It is maintained that the role of mathematical models in the social sciences is almost the same as the role of mathematical models in the natural sciences. That is, in the social sciences we have a number of social phenomena that we want to understand and explain; for example, why do certain regional economies grow while others stagnate, or why do individuals migrate from a given region to other regions? Usually, we have data pertaining to these social phenomena, say, data relating to regional economies or to past migration. Mathematical models are the constructed in an effort to explain and understand the variation in our data, that is, changes in migration rates, income, employment, and so on. As in the physical sciences, it is assumed that if our models are useful in explaining variation in our given data, then we shall be better able to predict data as yet unobserved and to institute changes that will affect as yet unobserved phenomena, say, future region economic growth, in a predictable manner. Of course, the inference from past given data to as yet unobserved data may not turn out to be correct. However, this eventuality is not peculiar to inferences about social phenomena because the possibility for error in making inferences about as yet unobserved data is present in all of science. For example, Newtonian physics was found wanting with regard to its predictions about many phenomena studied in modern atomic physics.

Thus, while the possibility for error in our predictions is always with us, it is not necessarily associated uniquely with mathematical models in the social sciences. The usefulness of mathematical models in the social sciences is pretty much an empirical issue that can only be settled by experience with the construction and use of these models.

In the preceding paragraph, the position was taken that the role of mathematical models in the social sciences is not much different from that in the physical sciences. A similar position on the unity of scientific method was eloquently expressed by Karl Pearson many years ago as follows:

Now this is the peculiarity of scientific method, that when once it has become a habit of mind, that mind converts all facts whatsoever into science. The field of science is unlimited; its material is endless, every group of natural phenomena, every phase of social life, every stage of past or present development is material for science. *The unity of all science consists alone in its method, not in its material.* The man who classifies facts of any kind whatever, who sees their mutual relation, and describes their sequences, is applying the scientific method and is a man of science. The facts may belong to the past history of mankind, to the social statistics of our great cities, to the atmosphere of the most distant stars, to the digestive organs of a worm, or to the life of a scarcely visible bacillus. It is not the facts themselves which form science, but the methods by which they are dealt with.[1]

Thus, for Pearson, as well as for others, the simple fact that social and economic phenomena constitute an investigator's subject matter does not preclude his being scientific if this term is understood as meaning using scientific methods in dealing with the analysis of observational data. The position taken here, and it is thought to be far from revolutionary or novel, is that the use of mathematical models is a key element in the scientific method and thus the use of mathematical models in the analysis of social phenomena is part and parcel of the scientific approach to the analysis of social phenomena.

The last remark may seem trite or obvious. However this may be *at present*, it is the case that many heated discussions regarding the appropriateness of the

[1] K. Pearson, *The Grammar of Science* (Everyman Edition, 1938), p. 16.

use of mathematical methods in the social sciences have appeared in the literature. While no attempt will be made here to analyze all the issues that have been raised in these discussions, a few of fundamental importance will be considered briefly.

First, it is obvious that mathematical formulation is no insurance that a model will necessarily be a good one. Clearly, it is possible that a mathematically formulated model may be at variance with known facts and may also yield predictions far from the mark. The same can be said about nonmathematical models. However, mathematically formulated models do have the advantage that, in general, their logical consistency can be checked using the available operations of mathematics. While this task is not always easy, it does appear easier than that associated with checking the logical consistency of many nonmathematical models.

Second, it is sometimes argued that mathematical models in the social sciences involve precisely defined mathematical variables that have no counterpart in the "real world." This is undoubtedly true of a wide range of mathematical models in the social sciences which have been put forward with little or no emphasis on empirical implementation and use and thus depart from the general scientific method which lays great emphasis on the relation of mathematical models to observed data. In cases in which mathematical models have been formulated in such a way as to be implemented with empirical data, there can be no question that important conceptual measurement problems arise as, for example, in the case of measuring human skills or regional income. Similar problems arise in nonmathematical discussions of variables of this kind. The very process of having to define and measure these variables, as required in a serious mathematical approach, is a fundamental source of progress in scientific work in the social sciences as well as in other sciences. In the former case, the development of very useful systems of national income accounts was in part prompted by efforts of

2 See, e.g., D. Novick, "Mathematics: Logic, Quality and Method," *Review of Economics and Statistics*, 36 (1954), 357–358, and the discussion following his paper.

researchers to implement mathematical models involving such variables as national income, gross national product, unemployment, consumption, and similar variables. In the physical sciences, attempts to measure illusive quantities such as the "ether wind," the electric charge of an electron, the velocity of light, and other such complex quantities were important steps in the development of science. Similarly, it is to be expected that continuing to face up to difficult measurement problems in the social sciences is the way to make progress rather than by bypassing them as "hopeless." In fact, some of the most promising and important research in economics has recently been aimed at measuring such complex variables as permanent income, human capital, technological change, and the rate of return on education.

Third, it is sometimes argued that mathematical models in the social sciences are not likely to be successful because the social scientist cannot perform controlled experiments. There can be no question but that experimentation in the social sciences is difficult and expensive, particularly because such experiments generally involve human beings in a fundamental way. Still, the fact that limited experimentation with humans has been, and probably will be, the case for some time does not preclude success in applying scientific principles to the nonexperimental data that are, and will be, available. There are other areas of science, for instance, astronomy, geophysics, meteorology, and cosmology, which are faced with difficulties in generating controlled experimental data but which have progressed considerably in spite of this difficulty. It does not seem overly optimistic to predict that similar progress will be experienced in the social sciences. Further, a more important role for controlled experimentation in the social sciences in the near future seems likely.

Fourth, some point to the complexity of social systems as a reason for not being optimistic about the success of a scientific approach in the social sciences. It seems pertinent to point out that similar complexity is a feature of many physical and biological systems. In recent decades, nuclear physics has delved into the complexities of matter producing a large number of new particles including pi, kappa, and tau mesons, neutrinos, positrons, and so on, which have not been very well integrated into any general theory of matter. Couple this with the well-known dual wave-particle view of matter, and it appears that the situation in nuclear physics is every bit as complex and unsettled as is the case in areas of the social sciences. Also, with respect to biological systems, particularly human systems, it is the case that the complexity extends even to include the problem of what life is itself in some areas. These problems too are far from simple and appear to be complex. To a certain extent, saying that a problem is complex is saying nothing more than that ignorance exists. More observational evidence and additional thought leading to appropriate concepts and models are needed. Hopefully in the social sciences, as in other sciences, such an attack on complex problems will provide a payoff. This has been true in the past and is likely to be true in the future.

Fifth, there is the problem that the social scientist interacts with the social system and may thus be unable to apply the scientific method in the study of social phenomena. At the technical level, it is also true that the atomic or nuclear physicist interacts with the systems that he studies, the fundamental point of the famous Heisenberg Uncertainty Principle. This interaction sets limits on the accuracy with which certain physical quantities can be determined but does not preclude production of generally useful results. It may be argued in a similar vein that while the social scientist interacts with the systems which he studies, this does not logically imply that he will be unable to produce useful scientific results. Perhaps it may be more difficult to separate an investigator's value judgments from his scientific work in the social sciences than in the physical sciences, and on many occasions this mixture is still encountered. However, more and more in the social sciences, the distinction between "positive" social science, that is the question of "what is," is sharply distinguished from "normative" social science, the question of "what ought to be," and recognition of this distinction has resulted in there being fewer obstacles to making progress in the social sciences.[3]

Last, in connection with applying mathematical models in the analysis of social phenomena, it is sometimes asserted that this is a hopeless task because human behavior is random and unpredictable. In this regard, the same remark may be and has been made with respect to the weather. Yet remarkable progress has been made in predicting future weather. This is not to say that weather predictions are deterministic or 100 percent accurate. In fact, current weather forecasts are often couched in probabilistic terms. Here intensive observation and analysis of past observations, coupled with theories of meteorological systems, have resulted in very useful results. Similarly, with respect to voting behavior, business conditions, consumers' behavior, etc., a similar approach seems to be leading to very encouraging results. Naturally, random elements, just as with the weather, can lead to poor predictions of social phenomena. Still, the prospect of being "right" in a high proportion of predictions is a goal, among others, that does not seem out of the reach of social scientists in a number of areas.

The considerations just discussed provide some basis for thinking that a scientific approach to the analysis of social phenomena using mathematical models and empirical data is possible and potentially valuable. To show that this proposition is not merely speculative and to delve into other issues and problems, a brief account of the development and use of mathematical models in the area of economics will now be presented. This account will feature developments that have a close connection with a number of the methodological underpinnings of the Susquehanna regional economic model.

Mathematical Models in Economics

Mathematics and mathematical models have been used in economics for a long time. For example, among others, Cournot, Marshall, Edgeworth, Walras, and Keynes all relied heavily on mathematical models of economic systems in their

---

[3] In economics, M. Friedman's important essay "The Methodology of Positive Economics," in his book *Essays in Positive Economics* (Chicago: University of Chicago Press, 1953) helped to emphasize the difference between "positive economics" and "normative economics" and to suggest that progress in the area of positive economics would be of great value in resolving problems in normative economics.

works.[4] However, what distinguishes this early work with mathematical models from more recent work is the fact that observational evidence was not systematically and formally brought to bear on the earlier models. The reasons for this are that good economic data were not generally available, and further, even if they were, the statistical techniques and concepts required to analyze observational evidence within the context of mathematical models of economic systems were not available. Also, the computational facilities available to the early mathematical economists were rather inadequate. Thus, even if they had large bodies of good economic data and modern multivariate statistical techniques, these would have been of little value without adequate computing facilities. In addition, the lack of good computing facilities meant that the earlier workers were precluded from using computers to explore properties of the mathematical models that they developed.

It was not until the twentieth century that the movement toward developing empirically implemented mathematical economic models acquired considerable momentum. The reasons for the recency of this movement are not hard to discover. The movement had to wait for the appearance of such pioneers as H. Moore, H. Schultz, and J. Tinbergen, among others, as well as for the development of appropriate methodological tools, before it could assume major proportions. It is no accident that the major movement toward the use of empirically implemented economic models took place just about the time that substantial progress was being made in the field of statistics on problems of statistical estimation and testing procedures for multivariate models.[5] These developments, coupled with a growing availability of data, better computing facilities, and a distinct tendency on the part of economists to formulate their

[4] In some of these works, particularly Marshall's, the exposition is in large part nonmathematical. However, it appears that many important results were obtained using mathematics and then verbalized with the mathematics sometimes presented in appendices.

[5] Note that much of the path-breaking work in statistics was done in the 1920's, 1930's and 1940's by R. A. Fisher, J. Neyman, E. S. Pearson, A. Wald, H. Jeffreys, and others.

models so that they can be empirically implemented, are the main elements in the movement toward more widespread use of mathematical models in the field of economics.

J. Tinbergen is often regarded as the father of the movement toward the use of empirically implemented mathematical models for the analysis of economies. His pioneering work,[6] prompted to some extent by the depressed conditions of the 1930's, involved construction of multiequation dynamic models of the Dutch, U.S., and British economies which were designed to be useful in furthering our understanding of, and possibly in controlling, an important economic phenomenon, fluctuations in the general level of economic activity. His model for the United States, a 50-equation linear stochastic difference equation model, included 32 behavioral, technological and institutional equations and 18 definitional equations. Among the former group, Tinbergen included equations purporting to explain how consumers and investors behave. In addition, he formulated and estimated equations representing the operation of banks, corporations, and several important markets including the bond, stock, and labor markets, among others. Remembering that this work was done in the 1930's, it is indeed a remarkable achievement, one that showed that modeling economies was possible.

As might be expected, Tinbergen's pioneering work raised many important issues, many of which are still with us today. In Keynes's review[7] of Tinbergen's work and Tinbergen's reply,[8] a good deal of attention is devoted to the role of economic theory in model-building, the conditions required for statistical methods to be applicable to economic data, the causal interpretation of Tinbergen's model, determination of functional forms and lag structures for economic relationships,

[6] J. Tinbergen, *An Econometric Approach to Business Cycle Problems* (Paris: Herman et Cie., 1937) and *Statistical Testing of Business Cycle Theories* (2 volumes; Geneva: League of Nations, 1939).

[7] J. M. Keynes, "Professor Tinbergen's Method," *Economic Journal, 49* (1939), p. 558–568.

[8] J. Tinbergen, "On a Method of Statistical Business-Cycle Research: A Reply," *Economic Journal, 50* (1940), 141–154.

and the appraisal of the economic implications of certain of Tinbergen's results. These are indeed relevant issues, and much work in economics has appeared since the 1930's dealing with them.

Particularly noteworthy in this respect was the work of Haavelmo[9] and of the group at the Cowles Commission at the University of Chicago in the 1940's and 1950's.[10] This work covered a wide variety of important topics and produced many fundamental concepts and techniques. On the side of model construction, Anderson, Haavelmo, Hurwicz, Koopmans, Rubin, and others developed the concept of a complete model, provided basic results on the identification problem, and developed new statistical techniques for estimating coefficients and other parameters of economic models and for testing hypotheses.[11] Much of this research was performed in connection with analyses of the "simultaneous equation" economic model, a special multivariate model that is flexible and general enough to permit lagged and unlagged or instantaneous feedback effects. Simon[12] provided an interesting causal interpretation of simultaneous equation models while Klein,[13] building on the work of Tinbergen, constructed and estimated multiequation dynamic models of the American economy, models in the "simultaneous equation" or "interdependent" form. Klein's early work represented an interesting example of an effort to use existing economic theories to derive the relations of his models of the American economy. Since Klein's early contributions, he and others have continued work on the development of models of economies.[14]

[9] T. Haavelmo, "The Probability Approach in Econometrics," *Econometrica, 12* (Supplement), 1944.

[10] Some of the main work of the Cowles Commission group appears in T. C. Koopmans (ed.), *Statistical Inference in Dynamic Economic Models* (New York: John Wiley & Sons, 1950) and Wm. C. Hood and T. C. Koopmans (eds.) *Studies in Econometric Method* (New York: John Wiley & Sons, Inc., 1953).

[11] See the references cited in footnote above for a report of some of this work.

[12] H. A. Simon, "Causal Ordering and Identifiability," in W. C. Hood and T. C. Koopmans (eds.) *Studies in Econometric Method, op. cit.*, pp. 49–74.

[13] L. R. Klein, *Economic Fluctuations in the United States, 1921–1941* (New York: John Wiley & Sons, Inc., 1950).

The reaction of the economics profession to the work of Tinbergen, Haavlemo, and the Cowles Commission group was mixed. As usual with a new movement, there was a group of enthusiastic supporters who, in varying degrees, began work on the task of filling in and extending this line of research. However, a much more numerous group expressed skepticism and pointed to serious problems. In this group there were many who lacked the mathematical and statistical background needed to understand and appraise the highly technical and complex contributions of Tinbergen, Haavelmo, and the Cowles Commission group. Their skepticism appears to have been founded on feelings of insecurity and/or a feeling that, in general, very complicated methods and models were probably not going to work very well. However, some others who had the required technical background to appraise this body of work were also skeptical. A review of some of the main critical points follows.

First and foremost, there was a feeling that economists did not know enough about the workings of the over-all economic system to produce serious and useful dynamic models of national economies. In this connection, it has to be remembered that Keynes's contribution to macroeconomics involved formulation of a comparative *static* model, a model that was not completely understood or accepted by many.[15] The dynamics of consumer and investor behavior as well as the dynamic behavior of markets were relatively unexplored areas in the 1940's and early 1950's. The role of money and prices in influencing aggregate economic activity was not well understood. Given these shortcomings in our economic knowledge, it was difficult for many to see how the early economic model-building efforts could be successful.

Second, even in terms of the models that were put forward, many felt uneasy because they could not understand how they worked and what they implied.

[14] M. Nerlove, "A Tabular Survey of Macro-Econometric Models," *International Economic Review*, 7 (1966), 127–175. Models of a number of national economies are described in this paper.

[15] J. M. Keynes, *The General Theory of Employment, Interest and Money* (New York: Harcourt, Brace & Co., 1935).

It is, of course, no easy matter to understand the mathematical and economic implications of multiequation dynamic models involving many variables and relationships whose functional forms were often chosen with an eye toward ease of mathematical and statistical analysis and not on solidly based subject matter considerations. And the producers of the early models rarely provided the mathematical analysis or the results of simulation experiments which would aid in understanding the properties of their models. Therefore, it is accurate to say that many who produced large-scale models did not know very much about their properties. In fact, this important aspect of model analysis was relatively slighted in favor of a heavy emphasis on the problems of statistical estimation.

Third, with respect to statistical problems, it was pointed out that models containing literally hundreds of parameters had been estimated from very small samples of highly autocorrelated observations using complicated techniques that have only a *large sample* justification *given that the models were correctly formulated and that the data contained no measurement error.* Clearly, there was uneasiness on these technical grounds alone.

Fourth, there were serious aggregation problems connected with these economic models. For example, many of the earlier models designed for business cycle analysis were formulated and empirically implemented with the unit of time being a year. Many dynamic responses are of much shorter duration than a year, and it was not apparent to what extent these were appropriately represented in models in which the unit of time was taken to be one year. Other aggregation problems arose from the fact that aggregate relationships were used which were supposed to represent the behavior of groups of individuals who were not very similar. Also, aggregate variables included many different components. For example, the consumption expenditure variable in many models included auto expenditures, food expenditures, and educational expenditures, and other items. Many felt that work at this level of aggregation was not satisfactory.

Fifth, some of the early models omitted entirely or dealt inadequately with sectors of the economy which some considered to be extremely important. For example, some models neglected to treat money markets. Others gave no attention to the agricultural sector, the housing market, the stock market, and the foreign trade sector. Needless to say, these deficiencies served as another basis for criticism. In fact, it appears that much interest in Leontief's "input-output" models[16] was due to the fact that such models incorporated many industrial sectors and provided a means, albeit a rough one, of taking account of intersectoral interactions.

Sixth, it was not clear how the early models were to be used in formulating economic policies designed to achieve such objectives as economic stabilization, full employment, and adequate economic growth. To some extent this problem arose because the early economic models did not incorporate a well-developed governmental sector. No allowance was made for the operation of state and local governmental units, and even the federal government's activities were not adequately represented in the early models. Perhaps more fundamentally, however, the basic methodology of control theory was not available. Therefore, it is no surprise that the important problem of how models were to be used in controlling economic activity was not adequately treated.

While some of the early model-builders were overly enthusiastic and claimed too much, many were acutely aware of the many vexing problems raised by the critics; and in fact much of the work since the discussions of the 1940's and early 1950's has contributed toward making progress on these issues and problems. In this connection, the following developments should be noted.

Since the early 1950's, there has been a tremendous growth in the volume and quality of empirical work in economics. In large part this is the result of having more economists who are trained in mathematics and statistics, the growing availability of more and better data, and the widespread use of high-speed electronic computers, which facilitates the application of statistical techniques in the analysis of data. The experience and knowledge gained from these empirical

[16] On input-output models, which are mainly due to the efforts of W. W. Leontief and others at Harvard University, see, W. W. Leontief, *Structure of the American Economy, 1919–1929* (2nd ed.; New York: Oxford University Press, 1951).

studies, coupled with advances in economic theory, have resulted in a fuller understanding of economic phenomena, a precondition for the construction of good economic models.

The importance of the appearance of more and better economic data cannot be overemphasized. Among other things, this has helped enormously in connection with problems of aggregation. Recently, dynamic economic models using quarterly data have been constructed. This means that the problem of temporal aggregation may not be as serious as with annual data. Thus the dynamic responses of the economic system can be better approximated. Further, a greater richness in our data permits a greater degree of disaggregation with respect to commodities and economic groups and sectors, thereby avoiding to some extent other aggregation problems.

Finally, the acquisition of data pertaining to shorter time periods and the formulation of models with an eye to shorter time periods have resulted in simplified forms for the structure of economic models. That is, instead of having to deal with models incorporating instantaneous feedback effects, it becomes possible to have large parts of models or even entire models in a form involving lagged feedback effects alone.[17] Because this is a somewhat simpler form, it is easier to understand how models work and to perform mathematical and computer operations with them. Our discussion in Chapter 5 emphasizes the importance of feedback relationships in modeling a dynamic economy.

Since the early 1950's, continuing research on statistical methods for analyzing economic data has yielded a whole new set of techniques for estimating parameters of economic models. Such new techniques as two-stage least squares[18] and

[17] T. C. Liu has recently formulated a monthly model having just lagged feedback effects which he discussed at a seminar at the University of Chicago in 1967.

[18] This method of estimation appeared first in H. Theil, "Estimation and Simultaneous Correlation in Complete Equation Systems" (The Hague: Centraal Planbureau, 1953), and has been and is frequently used in econometric work. It is clearly described in A. S. Goldberger, *Econometric Theory* (New York: John Wiley & Sons, 1964), p. 329 ff.

hree-stage least squares[19] are much simpler than the Cowles Commission maximum
ikelihood estimation techniques, and yet they yield estimators with the same large
ample properties. Many Monte Carlo experiments have been performed in an effort
o establish the small sample properties of these estimation techniques.[20] Further
›rogress has been made on obtaining analytical results for this problem.[21] More
‑ecently, considerable progress has been made in developing and applying
3ayesian techniques in the statistical analysis of economic models.[22] Because
hese techniques provide finite sample results and a means for introducing prior
nformation conveniently, it is thought that their use will contribute to obtaining
›etter results in work with economic models.

On the problems associated with the use of models for policy purposes, there
1ave been some significant contributions. The problem of maximizing the
nathematical expectation of a criterion function involving variables of an economic
nodel, with the equations of the model as constraints, has received a good deal

[19] A. Zellner and H. Theil, "Three-Stage Least Squares: Simultaneous Estimation of
5imultaneous Equations," *Econometrica*, *30* (1962), 54–78.

[20] See J. Johnston, *Econometric Methods* (New York: McGraw-Hill Book Co., 1963),
›p. 275–295, for a review of the results of several Monte Carlo experiments designed to
nvestigate the finite sample properties of alternative estimators.

[21] See R. L. Basmann, "A Note on the Exact Finite Sample Frequency Functions of
3eneralized Classical Linear Estimators in Two Leading Overidentified Cases," *J. Amer.
5tat. Assoc.*, *56* (1961), 619–636, and D. G. Kabe, "On the Exact Distribution of the GCL
Istimators in a Leading Three-Equation Case," *J. Amer. Stat. Assoc.*, *59* (1964), 881–894.

[22] For general treatment of Bayesian methods and principles, see H. Jeffreys, *Theory of
Probability* (3rd ed.; Oxford: Clarendon Press, 1961) and D. V. Lindley, *Introduction to
Probability and Statistics from a Bayesian Viewpoint, Part 2. Inference* (Cambridge, England:
University Press, 1965). Quite a few papers have appeared since about 1961 in which
3ayesian methods have been developed for the analysis of statistical models used in
:conomics. A few of these are: J. Dreze, "The Bayesian Approach to Simultaneous Equations
Istimation," ONR Research Memo No. 67, The Technological Institute, Northwestern
University, 1962: T. J. Rothenberg, "A Bayesian Analysis of Simultaneous Equation
5ystems," Report 6315, Econometric Institute Rotterdam, 1963; and A. Zellner and G. C.
Tiao, "Bayesian Analysis of the Regression Model with Autocorrelated Errors," *J. Am.
5tat. Assoc.*, *59* (1964), 763–778.

of attention.[23] Briefly, this problem can be explained as follows. In models of economies there are certain variables that have great policy importance. For example, one of these is the unemployment rate. If the unemployment rate is high, society suffers a loss in welfare. On the other hand, if the unemployment rate is extremely low, society may suffer a loss in welfare due to the effects of inflation. In this simple example, as a first approximation, social welfare W may be considered as a function of the unemployment rate U, say $W = W(U)$, an example of a criterion function. In actual cases, W would depend not only on U but on other variables as well. Now the variable U appears not only in the criterion function $W(U)$ but also in an economic model of the economy, and thus its movement is conditioned by the economic laws embodied in the model. However, also appearing in the economic model are policy control variables such as government spending, tax rates, the supply of money, etc., which can be varied by policy-makers to affect U, again subject to the economic laws embodied in the model. The problem then, is to set the policy control variables so as to achieve maximum welfare. Because U is usually treated as a random variable in economic models, the policy problem has been formulated as determining the settings of the policy control variables so as to maximize the mathematical expectation of $W(U)$. In actual cases, as just stated, W will depend not just on one variable U but on a number of variables. Also, because there may be costs involved in changing policy control variables, the criterion function W has usually been formulated to allow for this possibility. Last, the function W has been formulated in the literature to take account of the fact that it depends on current *and* future values of variables. The optimization problem in this case becomes more complicated.

[23] Some interesting references are J. Tinbergen, *On the Theory of Economic Policy* (Amsterdam: North-Holland Publishing Co., 1952); H. A. Simon, "Dynamic Programming under Uncertainty with a Quadratic Criterion Function," *Econometrica*, 24 (1956), 74–81; H. Theil, "A Note on Certainty Equivalence in Dynamic Planning," *Econometrica*, 25 (1957), 346–349; C. J. van Eijk and J. Sandee, "Quantitative Determination of an Optimum Economic Policy," *Econometrica*, 27 (1959), 1–13; H. Theil, *Optimal Decision Rules for Government and Industry* (Chicago: Rand McNally & Co., 1964); and K. A. Fox, J. K. Sengupta, and E. Thorbecke, *The Theory of Quantitative Economic Policy* (Chicago: Rand McNally & Co., 1966).

Results, obtained for the case of quadratic criterion functions, have been applied in several very interesting applications.[24] While problems exist with respect to formulation of appropriate criterion functions and the question of how to handle uncertainty about the values of parameters and other features of economic models, it is the case that the fundamental methodology has been created and work is under way to improve and extend it. Further, given that quite a few countries employ economic models as an aid in formulating economic policies, considerable practical experience has accumulated with respect to the use of economic models for policy purposes.

Another important development is work on checking the accuracy of forecasts yielded by economic models.[25] Because models are modified from time to time, data are revised and improved, and forecasts often are made that incorporate judgmental elements, it is indeed difficult to separate out the contribution of the economic model in evaluating forecasting performance. While this is a problem in interpreting forecasting records, the very fact that these records are being kept and analyzed is indeed a significant step forward in the methodology of model verification and contributes to efforts to improve economic models.

Finally, some progress has been made in the study of the dynamic properties of economic models. Mathematical techniques for analyzing models' dynamic properties have been developed and applied in certain instances.[26] In some cases, simulation techniques have been used to study dynamic properties of economic

[24] One example is P. J. M. van den Bogaard and H. Theil, "Macrodynamic Policy-Making: An Application of Strategy and Certainty Equivalence Concepts to the Economy of the United States, 1933–1936," *Metroeconomica, 11* (1959), 149–167.

[25] See D. B. Suits, "Forecasting and Analysis with an Econometric Model," *American Economic Review, 52* (1962), 104–132, and H. Theil, *Economic Forecasts and Policy* (2nd ed.; Amsterdam: North-Holland Publishing Co., 1961) for some comparisons of predictions with actual outcomes. Suits considers some results for the U.S. economy, while Theil reviews results for European economies.

[26] Two good examples are A. S. Goldberger, *Impact Multipliers and Dynamic Properties of the Klein-Goldberger Model* (Amsterdam: North-Holland Publishing Co., 1959) and H. Theil and J. C. G. Boot, "The Final Form of Econometric Equation Systems," *Review of the International Statistical Institute, 30* (1962), 136–152.

models.[27] However, this area appears to be one of the underdeveloped areas in the analysis of economic models.[28] This is indeed unfortunate because knowing the dynamic properties of an economic model is essential for understanding what the model implies about dynamic economic phenomena. Also, it is extremely important that the dynamic responses of a model to changes in policy variables be appreciated before a model is used as an aid in formulating and evaluating alternative policies. To some extent, the failure to study dynamic properties of models has arisen because large complex models are difficult, if not impossible, to analyze mathematically. In view of this, it is to be expected that simulation techniques will be used much more extensively in the future. In this connection, however, the complexity of certain economic models appears to put severe demands on some currently available simulation computer programs. Then too, some further work on the planning and design of simulation experiments would be valuable.

In closing this review of some of the current and recent trends in research on economic models, it must be pointed out that an extremely difficult, but most important, area is receiving very little attention. This is the area of model formulation and the organization of model-building efforts. The methodology for finding and developing good models is hardly existent except, perhaps, in the form of an art at which some individuals seem particularly gifted. Such general prescriptions as "use economic theory in constructing models," or "keep models simple," while useful as guides, hardly seem adequate in view of the multidimensional activities involved in formulating and developing a serious economic model.[29]

[27] See, e.g., I. Adelman and F. L. Adelman, "The Dynamic Properties of the Klein-Goldberger Model," *Econometrica*, 27 (1959), 569–625, and T. C. Liu, "An Exploratory Quarterly Model of Effective Demand in the Postwar U.S. Economy," *Econometrica*, 31 (1963), 301–348.

[28] Some progress has been made in studying dynamic models in the field of systems analysis and the results of much of this work is finding its way into the social science. See, for instance, J. W. Forrester, *Industrial Dynamics* (Cambridge, Mass.: The M.I.T. Press, 1961).

[29] Appendix A describes the management problems of organizing and carrying out a large-scale model-building effort and makes some suggestions for dealing with these problems.

In Chapter 5, attention is devoted to the philosophy and methodology of the systems simulation approach employed in the Susquehanna model-building effort. In the concluding chapter of this book, we then return to the general perspective of model-building efforts in which we contrast this approach with other economic model-building approaches. We, therefore, provide an explicit statement of an approach to model-building that may be of interest to others and perhaps take its place in the evolution of mathematical models in economics.

Chapter 3
Regional
Economic
Analysis and
River-Basin
Planning

The general purpose of this chapter is to show the interrelationships between regional economic analysis and river-basin planning. The literature in both fields is substantial, yet an intimate relationship between the two types of analyses has never been fully established. The Susquehanna model represents an attempt to bridge this gap.

This chapter first describes the nature of regional analysis and the difficulties involved. Next, attention is devoted to the matter of specifying goals for regional development. We conclude that the inability to specify clear-cut goals may require the regional model-builder to turn toward simulation techniques. The last sections of the chapter deal with the need to devise better institutions for the planning and management of water resources.

The Emergence of Regional Analysis

The study of national economies has always had first claim on the attention of economists. In contrast, the study of regions, which are parts of an over-all national economy, has not been in the main stream of policy, research, and theorizing although regional economic studies of natural resources, agriculture, and state and local public finance have had a long and respected tradition. In the last fifteen years, however, we have witnessed accelerated development of the theory and practice of regional economic analysis. In the academic world, an increasing number of economists have turned to regional economics, and for the first time regional economics has become a recognized specialty within the field of economics.[1] At the same time, public policy has become more and more concerned with problems of a regional nature. Area redevelopment, regional

[1] For an excellent overview of the field, see John R. Meyer, "Regional Economics: A Survey," *American Economic Review*, Vol. LIII, No. L, Part I (March 1965), pp. 19–54. A large part of the credit for the development of regional analysis as a recognized field of study must be given to Walter Isard. See his classic textbook, *Methods of Regional Analysis* (New York: John Wiley & Sons, 1960).

transport systems, metropolitan-urban planning, and natural resource development are all examples of public concern for small area or regional analysis.

River-basin planning, on the other hand, has a more or less separate development. Strangely enough, although a river basin is a region par excellence, the need to deal with the whole river as a *system* of hydrologic interrelationships has kept river-basin planning largely outside the main stream of regional economics. On the surface, it would seem that river-basin planning, with its earlier antecedents at the public policy level in Columbia River Basin projects, in the Tennessee Valley Authority, and on the Colorado River, would be one of the most fertile sources of theoretical inspiration for regional economics. The facts of the matter seem to be that river-basin planning has not been responsible for new developments in regional economic theory, nor has river-basin planning achieved its earlier promise of being truly regional in character.[2]

With the possible exception of the Tennessee Valley Authority, water resource investment in the United States has not been focused either on the entire river per se or upon the regional economic system encompassing the river. This thought will be developed at greater length later in this chapter, but it is important to stress at this point that public investment in water resources in the United States has generally been *project* oriented. That is to say, the analysis and policies have been concerned with the benefits and costs stemming from a particular public investment at a particular place on a stream and not upon placing the project within the context of a regional economic system.

However, the project orientation of water resource investment in the United States, with its concentration on benefit-cost analysis, can be credited in large part for significant advances in public investment theory.

Although great strides have been made in the theory of public investment decision-making, e.g., the selection of discount rates, handling of risk and

[2] An illustration of this point is provided in the bibliography contained in the Meyer article cited in Ftn. 1. Meyer lists 130 separate references but does not include a single reference to river-basin planning or regional water resource development.

uncertainty, measurement of secondary benefits, it is clear that two major strands
of analysis have not been given sufficient emphasis. First, the project orientation
of public water resource investment has tended to underplay the management of
the entire river as a system, and second, the projects have not been placed
within a model context incorporating the regional economy as a whole. As the
level of public investment in water resource development increases and as increased
attention is devoted to river management to encompass water quality standards,
it is apparent that river-basin planning and regional economic analysis must be
employed jointly. We believe the analysis of public investments in the water
resource field should take place within the framework provided by an over-all
regional model.

Difficulties of Regional Economic Analysis

The purpose of this section is to discuss some of the general problems of regional
analysis so that the reader can place regional models in a better perspective.
Most of these difficulties show that theories of regional income generation are not
as yet well developed.

It is generally admitted that theory and practice of national income and
employment analysis is considerably advanced over the state of the art for regional
economic analysis. The discrepancy between the two types of analyses is attributable
to a number of basic differences, not the least of which is the obvious fact that the
objectives of regional economic development may be very different from those
existing at the national level. As we shall point out in the next section, it is not
obvious that an increase in regional employment will always be consistent with an
attempt to increase national welfare. Moreover, the political institutions for
carrying out regional economic objectives do not possess the same arsenal of
weapons that is available to policy makers at the national level of government;
therefore the kinds of problems to be dealt with may not coincide.

Among the most common difficulties that plague regional analysis is the fact
that there can be no such thing as a common set of regions which might be

suitable for various kinds of regional analysis. Clearly, this problem will always be with us because a region can be defined in many different ways depending upon the types of questions we ask and the problems we attempt to solve.

In the past, three major approaches have been used in defining regions:

1. Regions based upon common or homogeneous sets of physical, economic, or social characteristics, e.g., a coal mining region, a river-basin region, or a region of French-speaking peoples.
2. Regions based upon polarization around some central place, e.g., Cleveland metropolitan area.
3. Regions based upon some administrative or political area, e.g., the State of California.

However, as John Meyer points out, all these attempts at regional definition are simply variations on some sort of homogeneity criterion, and the important question always must be "homogeneity with respect to what." [3] It is also evident that the three classification schemes are not mutually exclusive. In fact, from a pragmatic point of view, the homogeneity sought for may be determined with respect to the availability of data.

Regional analysis is often at the mercy of the availability of data. For obvious reasons, regional data collection will always lag behind national data collection. Nevertheless, the increased availability in the future of data on a county-by-county basis will make it easier for analysts to build and to reconstitute sets of counties for various types of regional analysis.[4]

But the question of data on a regional basis is more difficult than one of just defining or agreeing on a common set of regions. It is always going to be difficult, perhaps impossible, to identify transactions by region when the region is part of a

[3] John R. Meyer, *op. cit.*, p. 22.

[4] For an example of the recent efforts to make data available for regional analysis, see *Small-Area Data Activities*, issued occasionally by the U.S. Bureau of the Census with the assistance of the Small-Area Data Advisory Group, Bureau of the Census, Department of Commerce, Washington, D.C.

national economy. Business firms and households cannot be expected to distinguish between purchases and sales to and from specific geographic regions within an over-all economy. Equally troublesome are such questions as how to allocate corporation profits and capital consumption allowances of national firms among regions. In addition, it is clear that a region may not be a small-scale replica of a nation. This means that the set of accounts used in measuring national income may not be the ones relevant for measuring regional income and product. In other words, "standard" national income and product accounts may tend to suppress important differences and needs at the regional level.

On the other hand, data collection is made incredibly more complicated if standard regional accounts are not employed. Moreover, comparisons between regions will be difficult to make if regional accounts are not more or less uniform.[5] In practice, some of these difficulties will have to be glossed over because many regional accounts will probably have to be derived from national income series instead of having regional accounts built up from the local level.

Closely related to the problems of regional definition and data collection is another factor that makes regional analyses very tricky. This stems from the fact that most regional analyses deal with regions that are very "open." This is in contrast with national income theory, which deals with relatively "closed" economies. At the regional level, there is a fairly easy flow of goods, services, and people across regional lines.[6] These tendencies may be accentuated when the

[5] For more discussion of the problem of regional income estimation, see Walter Isard, *op. cit.*, pp. 86–90 and Werner Hochwald, "Conceptual Issues of Regional Income Estimation," *Regional Income*, National Bureau of Economic Research Studies in Income and Wealth, Vol. 21, Princeton, N.J., 1957, pp. 9–26.

[6] It could be argued that if resource mobility were complete, regional analysts would have little to do because regional difficulties often stem from the fact that resources, particularly labor, are not mobile among regions. In fact, to some writers, regional economics can be thought of as the "economics of resource immobility." As a practical matter, resource mobility can never be complete as long as transportation and communication costs are nonzero and as long as differential locational patterns of natural resources exist. Even with complete mobility, however, it would still be important to understand the forces influencing the spatial location of economic activities.

region is part of an over-all economy with a common language, common political institutions, and a common monetary system.

The "openness" of a region and its smallness mean that trade with other areas is not only easier to facilitate but is also more necessary because regions are usually less able to rely on internal production to meet their needs than are national economies. For a regional economy, exports and imports will constitute a large part of total economic activity. Also, we are just as concerned with *where* spending takes place as with type and level of spending. For example, on a national basis we can often assume that an increase in consumption spending following an increase in income may have certain multiplier effects on income and employment in the economy. But from a regional standpoint, it is important to know where the spatial incidence of any spending actually takes place. That is to say, an increase in spending in region A may cause imports to increase so that the multiplier effects take place in other regions. It is also quite possible that the construction of a dam or a highway in a given region may generate very little immediate income within the region if most of the labor and construction materials are purchased from other regions.

This discussion is designed to suggest that we do not have a well-constructed theory of regional income generation. In contrast, the theory of national income generation, in the post-Keynesian period, has received a great deal of scrutiny and is now relatively sophisticated and well developed. Actually, national income theory has tended to go hand in hand with the development of national income accounting. If regional income theory is to advance further, it is clear that we must develop better regional accounting and certainly better regional data.

In many ways, regional income and employment theory is a good deal like international trade theory with its emphasis on imports and exports. Nevertheless, it differs from trade theory in the degree of mobility of resources across boundaries and by the use of a common monetary system. For one thing, data availability is greatly simplified for international trade analysis by the almost universal recording of transactions across national boundaries. By contrast, measures of exports and imports at the regional level are extremely crude. Much of this suggests the regional income-employment theory must be a "blend" of national income theory and international trade theory, with special reference to spatial separation and regional boundaries.

Goals for Regional Planning and Development

On the surface, it might appear that the matter of specifying goals for regional planning and development should be a rather simple and obvious matter. Poor regions need to grow to escape poverty, and rich regions desire to become richer. Growth of the region in terms of employment and income would seem to be a rather straightforward strategy for increasing the aggregate economic welfare of a region.

The purpose of this section is to explore the complexity of the problem of setting forth goals for regional planning. We shall argue first that one-dimensional views of regional goals may be shortsighted. It will be shown that a number of regional goals may exist and that they may not be compatible with one another. Second, it is also possible (perhaps likely) that there may not be a consensus on the ranking of goals among the various groups within a region. Third, pursuit of regional goals may not result in optimal development for the nation as a whole.[7] The discussion of the difficulties that arise because of a lack of congruency between the region or regional problem and the political institutions for dealing with the problem is taken up in the following section.

This discussion of goals will have a direct bearing, not just upon regional economic planning for river basins but also upon the choice of economic models for projecting future economic activity. In particular, many mathematical models used in regional analysis employ a mathematical programming framework, which requires the specification of an objective function to be maximized, i.e., the specification of a theoretical optimum. If goals cannot be uniquely specified,

[7] The discussion in this section reflects some of the earlier ideas of Charles L. Leven, "Establishing Goals for Regional Economic Development," *Journal of the American Institute of Planners*, Vol. XXX, No. 2 (May 1964), pp. 100–110.

an objective function may be difficult or impossible to construct. In addition, the complexity of the economic and social systems being analyzed may be so great that an optimal situation, even if it could be specified, could not be solved by present analytical techniques. Under these situations, regional models of the simulation type would seem to offer promise.[8]

From the viewpoint of the region itself, putting aside for the moment questions of national welfare and migration of population, the expansion of a region's employment base is often taken as the overriding objective for regional development. At first blush this would not be a serious shortcoming if it is realized that total jobs are only a first approximation for total community purchasing power or income. Total income per capita is usually a better index of regional welfare than employment. Specifically, maximizing the number of jobs may cause the planners to overlook such important factors affecting regional incomes as the level of income earned per employee, the hourly wage rates for different types of work, the regional earnings of factors other than labor, nonwage and salary payments received by regional residents from abroad, and tax levies and transfer payments to and from nonlocal governments. Clearly there are many factors that could influence the level of regional income in regions with identical levels of employment.

Even with income there are a number of ambiguities such as total income versus income per capita, average income versus marginal income, and the distribution of income. In addition, questions of distribution of income can be further subdivided into the distribution relative to income classes, relative to occupations, relative to age groups, and relative to geographical and political areas or to racial composition.

However, we are not interested in the level of employment or even of income in just the current period. Equally important may be such economic objectives as the stability of income and employment over time, the possible sacrifice of more desirable employment at a later date for immediate gains, the size distribution of

[8] See the useful symposium on simulation with articles by G. H. Orcutt, M. Shubik, G. P. E. Clarkson, and H. A. Simon in the *American Economic Review*, Vol. L., No. 5 (December 1960), pp. 893–932. Further elaboration of the point is provided in Chapter 5.

incomes, and the effect of economic expansion upon the regional cost of living. It is not difficult to visualize situations where myopic efforts to increase the number of available jobs in a region could increase cyclical instability, sacrifice valuable plant locations for more productive employment at a later date, adversely affect the distribution of incomes, raise the level of prices, or even substitute jobs of low productivity for jobs of higher productivity. Also to be considered are the possible adverse effects of industrial expansion upon the regional environment and urban amenities.

When the possibilities of in- and out-migration are admitted to the realm of policy variables, the question of how to specify regional welfare becomes a great deal more complex. It may now be necessary to look at people and households directly and not to "fix" them in a particular region. In a dynamic economy, mobility of resources, including labor, may be the best way of facilitating and easing the problems of change and transition. If a region's job opportunities are not sufficient to absorb the regional labor force, there is the policy question of whether it is more desirable to move labor to jobs in other regions or to increase job opportunities within the region. Here are possibilities for several sorts of conflict. From the viewpoint of public authorities within the region, and also perhaps from local merchants, the out-migration usually would not be a favored policy alternative. The loss of regional prestige, the reduction in political constituents, and the possible drop in retail sales would be difficult to digest.

Out-migration of the younger age groups in the labor force and the heavy welfare load of the groups remaining behind would impose fiscal burdens on local communities at the very time local tax revenues were falling. By contrast, from a national point of view and often for the out-migrant, migration may be the better alternative in light of all of gains and costs even though the region may seem to bear a disproportionate share of the costs. Who is the "community" in this case? Should regions, just as business firms in a capitalistic economy, be forced to bear losses on original investment decisions when reductions in market demand or technological obsolescence occur? What is the proper role for regional planning? How far should we go in preserving regional institutions in the face of apparent forces for mobility?

Sources of goal conflict may even arise when job opportunities increase faster than the growth of the local labor force. Higher wages may often bring on higher costs of living for local residents and increase costs of production for firms selling local products in outside markets. Increased job opportunities may attract new residents to the region. Some economic groups within the region would be likely to gain from this growth in population. Yet these new residents may require expansion of capacity in local public works, e.g., water and sewer systems, roads and streets, schools, and other forms of expensive social overhead capital. It is also possible that an inflow of people could lead to a significant increase in residential and commuting densities. Because of congestion, the marginal social costs to the community as a whole may well exceed the private costs seen by the in-migrants. This tendency will be accentuated if user charges and taxes fail to reflect incremental costs of social overhead services. Failure to equalize private and social costs can lead to excessive in-migration with the burden of costs borne by those older residents who may not profit directly from sales of goods and services to the newer residents.

These sources of conflict are raised to show that goals of community or regional development are multidimensional, that there may be important conflicts within the region with respect to each goal, and that the goals themselves may be in conflict with each other. Not only is there a chance that goals themselves will be difficult to order in consistent fashion, but there is even greater likelihood that the preference patterns of the various regions will order goals in different fashion. Not only does this make it difficult for a national government to attempt to apply uniform policies between regions, but it also leads to the possibility that policies pursued at the regional level may be of the "beggar thy neighbor" variety, i.e., policies by various regions may be mutually antagonistic.

It is not obvious just what the national interest in regional development ought to be. Regional gains may not be in the national interest, if they come about at the expense of growth elsewhere. This is especially true if increased capital formation in one region involves transfers of resources from other regions. On the other hand, it is unlikely that balanced growth among all regions in a dynamic world, with the various regions possessing nonhomogeneous sets of resources, would provide maximum output and growth from a national point of view. Under such circumstances, maximum national growth could call for different growth rates among regions and perhaps even declining production in some areas when labor and capital resources should be transferred to new lines of activity elsewhere.

Because of the difficulties of reconciling various goals for required development and because of the complexities of regional growth models, we believe that criterion functions that attempt to specify optimal policies are to be viewed with skepticism. Maximization in an operational sense is an empty gesture unless one can specify the technical properties of the system under consideration. We believe that the difficulties of formulating an acceptable criterion function for long time horizons, for changing regional populations, and for the multitude of importan policy variables and instruments is overwhelming. Even if this could be done, there would be the difficulty of deriving a "solution" (if it is unique). Our strategy in constructing the Susquehanna model was to simulate a limited range of policies and to try to show their likely impact on regional trends. The aim was to further our understanding of the complex interrelationships among variables in a regional economy, not to specify optimal policies for regional development.

In light of these considerations, it is not clear to us just what sort of regional planning really "ought" to be carried out. Presumably, the national interest would be served if spatial arrangements and regional development promoted such generalized objectives as (1) efficient allocation of resources; (2) provision for full employment, economic growth, and price level stability; and (3) establishment of a distribution of income and wealth having social sanction and acceptability. However, these objectives are so general in scope that they do not offer much help devising concrete policies. In the real world, there are all sorts of conflicting

olicies and objectives. Moreover, there is no one kind of "maximizing unit."
ather, there is a hodge-podge of federal, state, regional, and local governmental
nits involved in policy-making affecting regional economies. The multiplicity
 units and their interactions with each other do a great deal to complicate our
nderstanding of regional economic development.

Yet despite problems of goal conflicts and the complexities of regional growth
eory, various kinds and degrees of regional planning are, in fact, undertaken.
ur position is to view policy-making as a sequential search for improvement,
ot as a search for a maximizing solution. We do endorse changes in present
gional policies which promise to deal with obvious inefficiencies and when new
atial arrangements and regional development can be expected to promote
ch general goals as efficiency, equity, growth, and stability. It is clear, for
ample, that the present management of our river basins leaves a great deal to be
sired in the reconciliation of upstream and downstream uses of water. As we
ggest here, the establishment of improved institutional arrangements for the
anagement of river basins is probably our most serious "water problem."
owever, new management needs to be viewed *within* the context of a regional
onomy. Again, we come back to the problems of regional economic development
d the need to simulate a regional economy.

stitutions for Regional Development and River-Basin Planning

Regional development, when attempted, must be related to the institutional
amework for carrying out regional policies. One of the first questions is the locus
 power for the planning agency. Should the agency be a national one designed
 administer to a special set of needs for a given region (or perhaps a national
ency designed to administer a function for a set of regions)? On the other hand,
ould regional planning be undertaken by local or regional political authorities
 deal with the needs of the region? The latter kind of institutional framework
ould appear desirable when regional policies do not have important spillover
fects upon other regions. For example, a regional plan for water supply would

not seem to call for a national agency to act as sponsor but, instead, could be negotiated at the regional level. No easy answers can be given to these questions. Their importance is clear-cut, yet many discussions of regional planning tend to ignore them.

It needs to be recognized, however, that the locus of power and the extent of power to be exercised are not abstract matters because of the existing framework of public institutions and the system of federal, state, and local governments already established. If the planning is to be done by an existing public agency, the kind of planning will depend to a large extent upon the legal powers and jurisdiction of that agency. Therefore, we may not have complete freedom to establish an "optimal" planning agency consistent with our view of the "correct" region and the "proper" definition of the regional problem. The Corps of Engineers, for example, has certain specific missions defined by law, and the Corp is limited to certain types of federal financing. For example, the Corps may evaluate only certain restricted engineering alternatives to provide flood control protection under situations where the local beneficiaries are required to bear only a small percentage of the costs of protection. This means the important management and technical alternatives for dealing with flood protection are not admitted to the set of alternatives to be evaluated.

The controversy over development of the Potomac River is illustrative of the need to see that institutional alternatives be broadened so that many alternatives in regard to objectives, management, and engineering can be evaluated before a fu development plan is constituted.[9] The difficulties of achieving interstate cooperatic over common problems through the device of the interstate compact are well known. Often the planning process at the regional level will operate in an institutional framework that may hamper lines of action and limit the range of alternatives to be considered.

This problem of institutional framework is relevant to our earlier discussion

[9] National Academy of Sciences—National Research Council, *Alternatives in Water Management*, Washington, D. C., 1966, pp. 9–13.

f specifying the relevant "region" and identifying various regional problems. We argued then that the relevant region depends upon some degree of homogeneity with respect to a problem that has spatial or areal dimensions. Our position was that each problem must be analyzed in its own terms, and there are many sets of regions for different kinds of regional problems. However, to deal with a problem requires an institutional framework or mechanism with powers and jurisdiction for action. The dilemma is now clearly posed: if we redefine the spatial boundaries of a region for every kind of regional problem, we must face the possibility of having to devise a separate set of institutions for each set of problems. Can we tolerate such a proliferation of "regions" and of regional planning institutions?

The boundaries for the relevant region for metropolitan transportation planning clearly may not coincide with the logical ones for regional air pollution, regional water pollution, regional economic development, or for a regional school system. Obviously, some compromises need to be made to fit regional problems to existing regional institutions and to limit excessive proliferation. On the other hand, the flexibility and pluralism of planning agencies and the experimental character of planning are probably characteristics of regional planning that are to be preserved and not condemned.

In the United States there are a large number of institutions dealing with various aspects of regional development. Perloff has identified nineteen types of organizations, involving thousands of separate agencies, engaged in regional planning and development.[10] Some of the more prominent types of public organizations are official city planning agencies, official metropolitan planning commissions, metropolitan special districts, rural special districts, federal regional authorities, state planning agencies, federal governmental agencies, and state departmental agencies.

To some observers this multiplicity of regional planning organizations would constitute a contradiction in terms. Planning to many social scientists would mean

[10] Harvey S. Perloff, *Education for Planning: City, State, and Regional* (Baltimore, Md.: The Johns Hopkins Press, 1957), pp. 101–103.

setting forth a "plan" to integrate and coordinate all policies in a "comprehensive
fashion. Presumably, "comprehensiveness" should be carried up to the top level
of government and give rise to a "master plan." A multiplicity of planning
organizations with overlapping areal dimensions would seem to be the antithesis
of "planning." Ylvisaker has argued, for example, that the optimum number of
levels among which to share areal (spatial) power to govern is three and that the
assignment of powers to regions or component areas should be a general one
covering the entire range of governmental functions, not a partial one covering
only special functions.[11] He reasoned that broad grants of power to component
regions would limit the need for the "pathological" tendency toward special
devices. The argument for three levels of powers seems to be largely based upon
intuition and custom. Also, it is not clear why the formation of special districts is
pathological in character.

It could be asked, why is it necessary in all cases to coordinate or to integrate
actions of various public and private agencies through the device of a plan?
Economists have long argued that the price system, where applicable, can play
an important role in coordinating intelligence and decisions among many scattered
producers and workers in the chain of production leading to the final consumption
of goods and services. Similarly, citizen voting through the ballot box and through
elected representatives can achieve a remarkable degree of coordination of the
wishes of the electorate on various matters. Explicit coordination through a plan
is needed if there are important spillover effects that are not taken into account
by alternative means for integrating intelligence or for reconciling differences.
Obviously, it is wise to "lay the sewers before we pave the streets," and a river
with hydrologic interdependencies should not be developed in piecemeal fashion.
Yet it is not evident that one central, regional agency need be responsible for all
of the various "regional" problems within a geographic area or between areas.

[11] Paul Ylvisaker, "Some Criteria for a 'Proper' Areal Division of Governmental Powers,"
reprinted in John Friedmann and William Alonso, editors, *Regional Development and Planning
A Reader* (Cambridge, Mass.: The M.I.T. Press, Massachusetts Institute of Technology,
1964), pp. 526–528.

It is sometimes claimed that the Tennessee Valley Authority is one of the few regional river authorities empowered to carry out a comprehensive development program and that it should serve as a model for other kinds of economic development agencies. However, river-basin authorities naturally take the river (and water) as their major point of focus. Even if they succeed in breaking out of the narrow mold of managing water per se and relating water to the economy of the region, it is not clear that all or most of the economic activities within the basin are river-related. More important, the basin itself may not be the proper spatial focus for the region from other standpoints, e.g., the airshed, the transportation system, or the development of new industry. It would probably be unwise, for example, to approach the economic development of the Midwest or of Appalachia by using the major rivers in these areas as the basis for regional definition.

Although regional planning in the United States has evolved in large part as a way to use natural resource development as a means of economic development, it is probable that regional planning in the future will become more oriented toward the city or metropolitan area as the developmental region. Friedmann writes that "The basic spatial relations in an economy are found (1) between a central city and its surrounding region and (2) between one city region and another." [12] To Friedmann, planning at the national level will shift to increasing concern with the relations between city regions. City regions will constitute the nerve centers of economic life" and will serve as functional regions for planning purposes.

We have stressed that it is not very satisfactory to analyze the proper definition and scope of a planning region without relating planning to the special sorts of regional problems that seem to require explicit public planning action. Many kinds of decisions are best left to the discretion of private firms, households, and to lower levels of government. In turn, the problems and planning region must be directly related to the legal powers, jurisdiction, and financial resources of the

[12] John Friedmann, "The Concept of a Planning Region—The Evolution of an Idea in the United States," in Friedmann and Alonso, *op. cit.*, pp. 514–515.

public agencies involved. Not only are we concerned with "planning for what" but also "planning with what."

Persuasive as they are, neither Friedmann nor Ylvisaker seems to achieve the necessary synthesis. Ylvisaker, on the one hand, gives relatively little attention to the kinds of problems with which the regional authorities should deal. He seems to neglect completely the fact that the regions or spatial boundaries for various kinds of problems may be quite different, and his three-part level of areal government may be far too inflexible a framework of the wide spectrum of "regional" problems. We should not ignore the attributes of spatial separation nor the characteristics of spatial homogeneity.

On the other hand, Friedmann seems to underplay the need for consideration of the legal and institutional framework within which the planning must take place. For example, his discussion of the city region and the relations between city regions is carried out without any direct consideration of the kind of political-legal structure necessary to implement the regional planning implied by this two-layer spatial world. The widespread unpopularity of recent attempts to establish metropolitan government in the United States raises some real questions about the ease of establishing the city region as an effective planning unit. Willber believes that "a new metropolitan-wide, self-governing community is likely to be a will-o'-the-wisp in most circumstances, beckoning the crusader, but rarely if ever attained." [13] Instead he sees that future urban political marketplace as a maze of complex overlapping governmental arrangements of territorial units, corporate units, special districts, cooperative agreements, and mechanisms for state and federal participation. Perhaps we should not be frightened by the prospect of the pluralistic model, but we need to bear in mind that kind of regional planning which results will be governed by the special missions and jurisdictions of the governmental units involved.

[13] York Willbern, *The Withering Away of the City* (University, Ala.: University of Alabama Press, 1964), p. 122. A similar position is also taken by Robert Warren, "A Municipal Services Market Model of Metropolitan Organization," *Journal American Institute of Planners*, Vol. 30, No. 3 (August 1964), pp. 193–204.

esign of Water Institutions

The roots of the management problem in water resources go back to the fact that water is usually a fugitive, migratory resource which is variable in distribution over time and space. These features make it very difficult to develop property rights in water. There is no such thing as federal water law; federal power over river basins and inland navigation are derived instead from the commerce and proprietary powers. Each state has been permitted to adopt its own system of water law.

The situation has two important features that are responsible in large part for the current poor management of water resources. First, existing water laws usually fail to deal with the obvious externalities that develop from multiple use of common interrelated supplies across state boundaries and even within individual states. Serial uses of river flows and the mining of ground water are inadequately taken into account by existing water laws and by existing federal and state agencies. Second, the operation of water law in most states has prevented the development of a market system for water resources which might help with the problem of transferring water supplies to new uses in response to changing economic relationships. In some states, water rights are actually tied to specific lands. This means that the transport of water to new uses, particularly to growing urban areas, is sharply restricted.

We believe that more concern should be devoted to devising institutions to provide efficient management of water resources that are used in common, which have to be subject to a balancing of gains and costs as the demand for water grows in the future. It appears that two different sorts of solutions need to be followed in different combinations in different sections of the United States.

One procedure is to establish regional systems of water management;[14] the other solution lies in the development of systems of water law applicable across

[14] The Water Resources Planning Act of 1965 marks an important step forward in meeting these problems. It provides for the establishment of the Water Resources Council to coordinate the work of federal agencies. It also provides for the development of river-basin commissions that can develop joint state-federal action.

state boundaries to establish property rights in water so that water markets can help allocate water to its most productive uses. Most clearly, these two solutions are at opposite poles. One involves centralized decision-making by public authorities; the other involves greater use of the market and decision-making by private individuals and groups. Yet, it appears that a set of efficient institutions and processes for the management, allocation, and development of our water resources will involve some combinations of both kinds of solutions.[15]

Despite the skepticism expressed earlier regarding the tendency to think of river basins or watersheds as major regions for planning for economic development, it is important to stress that the river basin *is* the proper perspective or "region" for investments, public and private, that are water related. Localized development on a river should be fitted into an integrated water resources development plan equal to the task of taking into account interdependencies between upstream and downstream use and be capable of balancing the economic and social returns of all of the various uses of the river. The individual projects on the river should be related to each other, and these in turn should be viewed within the over-all economic development of the region. Too often in the past master plans for watersheds have tended to emphasize hydrology and not the appropriate social, political, and economic regions within which society functions.

Currently, the federal government spends about two billion dollars annually for water resources development, and nonfederal spending totals about ten billion dollars. Federal water resource investment has been focused on river basins for over three decades. Despite this experience, the mechanisms for effective river planning are rudimentary. Apparently, in the United States, only the Tennessee Valley Authority and the newly established Delaware River Basin Commission have the broad authority to combine water resources development and management in a single regional agency. All of this suggests that regional analysis and regional

[15] For a further discussion of these points, see Jerome W. Milliman, "Economic Considerations for the Design of Water Institutions," *Public Administration Review*, Vol. XXV, No. 4 (December 1965), pp. 284–289.

development need to give a great deal of consideration to the neglected questions of mechanisms and institutions.

These cautions are well recognized in the literature. The point to add at this juncture is that effective river-basin planning *also* requires a suitable analytical framework for placing the river system and the water variables *within* a regional economic context. It is true that many of the principles for water resource management are well understood and also that we have been slow in devising suitable institutions for managing our water resources; it is *not* well recognized, however, particularly in the "water" literature, that water management and river-basin planning need to be viewed as part of a regional economic system.

Chapter 4
Contemporary
Regional
Projection
Models

This chapter first discusses the general nature of regional economic projections and then concentrates upon methodological developments in regional model-building. A survey of six important regional models is presented so that the reader may place the Susquehanna model in better perspective.

Regional Economic Projections

Regional economic projections are useful to all sorts of groups, public and private who need to have a better understanding of the likely course of future events. Yet is it very difficult to specify the exact relationship between regional planning and regional forecasting. On the one hand, regional economic forecasts must be tailored to meet the special needs of various kinds of regional planning agencies. On the other hand, we do not have a clear understanding of the various planning processes in terms of goals, scope, and institutional framework.

Undoubtedly a certain amount of circularity and ambiguity will always condition relationship between regional planning and regional forecasting. The planner cannot plan without having some sort of projections in mind. It is also true that the projector cannot forecast without making some assumptions about the plans and their estimated effectiveness. Moreover, the type of projections to be made, the extent of detail required, and the underlying policy assumptions employed will depend upon needs of the planning agency. In other words, projections must be related to the objectives and mission of the planning unit and to the policy instruments which that unit can employ.

There are no generally accepted procedures or rules of conduct for the forecasting and planning process except to suggest that both activities should be mutually supporting and they must proceed in joint fashion. As a practical matter, initial planning guidelines must be established, and then a preliminary forecast model may be constructed. Preliminary projections often will reveal the need for information about additional variables that in turn may modify the planning assumptions. The refinement of plans and forecasts is usually the result of an iterative nature of the process. However, this refinement may be hampered by the ever-present possibility of conflicts among objectives and by the sheer inability to assume a well-defined social welfare function.

In such cases, it is often desirable to construct a projection model in mathematical form that can be manipulated on a computer in order to illustrate the effects of alternative assumptions about goals, plans, and projections. The mathematical formulation serves to make alternative assumptions explicit, and it provides a systematic framework for quantitative analysis. The technique of computer simulation is particularly well suited to this iterative relationship between planning and projection. We can simulate the consequences of alternative forecasts upon a given plan; we can simulate the consequences of various plans embodying different instruments and objectives upon future projections; and we can highlight important feedbacks between sectors. The model, then, is not a device for producing optimal or single-valued projections. Instead, it can be a means of facilitating understanding of complicated systems of relationships relevant to policy-making. In general, an optimal set of values can be specified only with an oversimplified model using one-dimensional goals. Simulation allows the planner to visualize sets of consequences likely to arise under many different assumptions about goals, plans, and the nature of the economy.

Regional forecasting techniques may be classified as being sophisticated or less sophisticated. In the latter classification we find such techniques as (1) trend extrapolation, (2) share analysis, and (3) simple economic base studies. Under the heading of sophisticated techniques are all of the various kinds of mathematical models that make use of such tools as linear programming, input-output analysis, and complex regional accounting models.[1]

[1] The general reference is Walter Isard, *Methods of Regional Analysis: An Introduction to Regional Science* (Cambridge, Mass.: The M.I.T. Press, Massachusetts Institute of Technology, 1960). For a discussion of economic base analysis, both simple and complex, see Charles M. Tiebout, *The Community Economic Base Study*, Supplementary Paper No. 16, Committee for Economic Development, New York, December 1962. Meyer discusses theoretical foundations and types of approach to regional studies. See also John R. Meyer, "Regional Economics: A Survey," *American Economic Review*, Vol. LIII, No. 1, part 1 (March 1963), pp. 29–45.

All of the various methods of regional economic forecasting have a number of similarities. Moreover, they all have different sorts of strengths and weaknesses. The best technique to use depends to a large extent upon the need for completeness in the forecast and the budget and technical personnel available. For many kinds of purposes, the less-sophisticated techniques are quite adequate.[2]

The sophisticated techniques generally involve the construction of complex economic models and the use of computers. Such models are costly in terms of time, talent, and data. Also, many of the less-sophisticated techniques have been incorporated to some degree in these ambitious attempts to build regional economic models. For example, one might attempt to forecast future income and employment for the State of Indiana by taking a simple percentage or "share" of the gross national product and deriving an Indiana forecast from a more or less standard national forecast. The sophisticated model-builder would probably attempt to formulate a complete model of the Indiana economy with all of its linkages and interdependencies. Yet at several places in the model the analyst might resort to "share" analysis to derive some of the coefficients or parameters for his equations.

It is also possible that the projections yielded by sophisticated models may not differ a great deal from those derived by less costly means. In fact, it is possible that simple straight-line projections of regional economic trends may yield more accurate or more plausible results than a highly specified model taking into account interdependencies and various economic hypotheses.[3]

In contrast, our ability to understand how an economy works is advanced by the attempt to explain relationships between variables within a framework designed to encourage consistency between complex relationships in line with our theories. Not only do we wish to avoid inconsistency, but we wish to advance our

[2] Charles Tiebout, *op. cit.*, p. 23, suggests that a community of 25,000 could carry out a simple economic base study using published data and indirect measures of the economic base at a cost in the $2,000 to $5,000 range.

[3] It would be interesting to compare the forecasts of the sophisticated projection models discussed later with ones that might have been derived by "naïve" methods to see what variations in forecasting ability might be found.

understanding of regional economic phenomena. In fact, we emphasize that the forecasts or actual levels projected are often not as important as the ability to permit the planner and model-builder to see the impact of alternative hypotheses or policies. Projections then are properly regarded as conditional, subject to change with the changes in information and changes in policies.

Regional Projection Models

During the past ten years, a number of large-scale regional projection models have been developed. Each of these efforts has involved large budgets and sophisticated analysis. We will discuss the general features of six of these regional models to illustrate the general state of the art. This survey is not comprehensive either in terms of coverage or depth, although a comprehensive appraisal of *all* the various regional forecasting models is greatly needed. Our purpose here is to set the stage for the model of the Susquehanna River Basin so that the reader can see the Susquehanna model in perspective among the growing array of regional economic models.

The six regional models discussed are (1) the New York Metropolitan Region Study by the Graduate School of Public Administration, Harvard University, for the Regional Plan Association, (2) the Upper Midwest Economic Study jointly undertaken by the Upper Midwest Research and Development Council and the University of Minnesota, (3) the Ohio River Basin Study by Arthur D. Little for the Corps of Engineers, (4) the California Development model for the State of California, (5) the Oahu, Hawaii, model for the State of Hawaii, and (6) the Lehigh Basin simulation model. In addition, brief attention will be given to the National Planning Association's study of the Susquehanna River Basin.

We believe that these six regional models are generally representative of current thinking. They offer a coverage that is sufficiently broad in scope in terms of the type of region analyzed and the particular study techniques employed to provide general background to the reader. Some of the major regional models not covered in this survey are the Stockholm model, the Pittsburgh regional model, the

Chicago Area Transportation Study, the Penn-Jersey model and the Philadelphia region input-output study.[4] A number of other state and local economic models are under construction.

The New York Metropolitan Region Study. In 1956, the Regional Plan Association requested the Graduate School of Public Administration of Harvard University to undertake a three-year study of the New York Metropolitan Region, a 22-county expanse covering 7,000 square miles (in parts of three states) and constituting the most populous metropolitan area in the United States.[5] The study analyzed the major economic and demographic features of the region and made projections for 1965, 1975, and 1985. The results of the study were made public in ten separate volumes, but reference here will be confined to the summary volume and to the technical supplement dealing with methodology.[6] Many scholars view this study as the "grandfather" of large-scale regional models in the United States.

The New York Metropolitan Region model, as do all of the models considered

[4] References for the major regional models not covered in our survey are (1) the Stockholm model, Roland Artle, *The Structure of the Stockholm Economy*, American edition (Ithaca, N.Y.: Cornell University Press, 1965); (2) the Chicago Area Transportation Study, Irving Hoch, *Economic Activity Forecast, Final Report*, Chicago, 1959; (3) the Pittsburgh Regional Model, Pittsburgh Regional Planning Association, *Region with a Future* (Pittsburgh, Pa.: University of Pittsburgh Press, 1963); (4) the Penn-Jersey model, Henry Fagin, "The Penn-Jersey Transportation Study: the Launching of a Permanent Regional Planning Process," *Journal of the American Institute of Planners*, Vol. XXIX, No. 1 (February 1963); and (5) the Philadelphia Input-Output study, Walter Isard, Thomas W. Langford, Jr., and Eliahu Romanoff, *Philadelphia Region Input-Output Working Papers*, Vols. I and II, Regional Science Research Institute, Philadelphia, Pa., March 1967. References to a number of European regional models can be found in H. Theil, *Economic Forecasts and Policy* (Amsterdam, Holland: North-Holland Publishing Company, Second Printing, 1965). Estimates of U.S. regional export balances and regional incomes may be found in J. Thomas Romans, *Capital Exports and Growth Among U.S. Regions* (Middletown, Conn.: Wesleyan University Press, 1965).

[5] Nine counties in New Jersey, twelve counties in New York, and one county in Connecticut.

[6] Raymond Vernon, *Metropolis 1985; An Interpretation of the Findings of the New York Metropolitan Region Study* (Cambridge, Mass.: Harvard University Press, 1960); Barbara R. Berman, Benjamin Chinitz, and Edgar M. Hoover, *Projection of A Metropolis: Technical Supplement to the New York Metropolitan Study* (Cambridge, Mass.: Harvard University Press, 1961).

here except the Susquehanna model, makes two independent projections of population and the labor force. Population projections were first made with standard demographic techniques taking into account birth rates, deaths, and migration by age groups. Employment and population projections then were derived from a separate model of economic activity. Comparisons showed that the employment and population projections implied by the economic model were *higher* than those generated by demographic techniques. Reconciliation was achieved by allowing the economic projections to stand and increasing the degree of response of in-migration in the demographic model. This "reconciliation," by changing the demographic projection to conform to the employment projections, was followed for each of the three projection years, 1965, 1975, and 1985.

The New York model is designed to forecast employment, output, and value added for 43 industrial groups for the years 1965, 1975, and 1985. It also generates estimates of employment for domestic servants and government employees, as well as for disposable personal income and population. The complete system contains 47 linear equations in 47 variables (outputs of 43 industries, total population, disposable personal income, domestic servants, and government employees).

It should be noted that the formal economic model now being described was not put together until after eight earlier book-length studies of the New York region were completed. The projection model, then, was designed to utilize the data and incorporate the many special projections derived earlier and if possible to harmonize them and to make them consistent. This means that there was little opportunity to have the partial projections fitted into an over-all model *before* they were made. Not all of these separate studies used the same background assumptions so that
This necessarily resulted in the employment of rough adaptation of material developed by others. Furthermore, some of the ingredients for the model presented here simply were not developed in other parts of the study and had to be fabricated from scratch. Thus, some of the bricks were made with remarkably little straw. This is not to deny that the over-all projections are of value. It may be, however,

that the refinement of the method is somewhat in excess of the refinement of the data.[7]

The relation of data-gathering to model-building followed in the New York model is emphasized at this point to make the reader sympathetic to the difficult process of model construction and also to alert him to the thinking that went into the Susquehanna model, which stressed initial model formulation *before* data gathering was started and *before* partial projections were developed.

The conceptual design of the New York model divides firms or industries into two groups: (*a*) those who sell on the "national market" and thus export goods and services outside the region, (*b*) all other firms, which are labeled as "local market" firms. These industries include those that sell exclusively to the local population and some who sell to the national market firms. In all, 43 industry groups were selected; 10 were completely local market and 25 industries served both markets. Total employment was conceived as the sum of employment in the 43 industry sectors plus employment in government and as domestic servants.

Essentially, what was done was to project total employment in the United States by industrial industry groups for 1965, 1975, and 1985.[8] Employment in national industries in the region was assumed then to be some constant "share" of the total U.S. employment in that industry. These exogenously derived employment demands for the national industries were then used to drive an input-output matrix for the region. The matrix multiplied the exogenously determined employment into total employment through the implied multipliers in the matrix based upon assumed local input demands, local consumption patterns, and local labor-force-participation rates. Once total employment was found, then the output and employment for each industry was derived as well as estimates of disposable personal income and total population.

Before analyzing some of the individual features of the input-output matrix, it should be noted that the factors influencing the location of the national market

[7] *Projection of a Metropolis, ibid.*, p. 3.

[8] This work was done separately by Robert M. Lichtenberg, *One-Tenth of a Nation* (Cambridge, Mass.: Harvard University Press, 1960).

ndustries in the New York area were assumed to be *outside* the projection model. There were no internal devices *within* the model to generate changes in the ocational advantages of the region relative to other areas in the United States. In other words, the local firms serving national markets were assumed to have national market shares relatively unaffected by internal factors within the region or by the rise of competitive location sites elsewhere in the national economy. Price evels within the region therefore were assumed to retain a constant relationship o national price levels so that substantial changes in the import-export mix were uled out.[9]

Conceptually, the input-output framework divided the local market into three groups of buyers: business purchasers, consumers or households, and governmental units. Business purchases were subdivided into inputs for current production and purchases for investment to expand capacity. The interindustry coefficients were derived from the 1947 input-output table compiled by the Bureau of Labor Statistics for the U.S. economy. Straight-line growth projections were made for purchases of capital goods.

The problems with fixed input-output coefficients over time are well recognized, out it deserves emphasis that the use of national coefficients at the regional level s even more perilous. There is usually little reason to expect regional and national production coefficients to be the same. Moreover, the use of national coefficients t the regional level involves specifying not only amount of inputs per unit of output but also the regional source.[10] In view of the data limitations involved, the builders of the New York model had no other choice but to use national coefficients once they chose to use a regional input-output framework.

[9] These difficulties were recognized by the builders of the model. See *Projection of a Metropolis*, *op. cit.*, p. 32. The reader may see how these matters were handled in the Susquehanna model in Chapter 10.

[10] For further discussions on the limitations of regional input-output models, see Leon N. Moses, "The Stability of Interregional Trading Patterns and Input-Output Analysis," *American Economic Review*, Vol. XLV, No. 5 (December 1955) and Charles M. Tiebout, Regional and Interregional Input-Output Models: An Appraisal," *Southern Economic Journal*, Vol. XXII, No. 2 (October 1957).

In fairness, we must state that several of the models reviewed here also employ regional input-output analysis and were forced to use national coefficients at the regional level. A central preoccupation with each of these studies has been to adopt simplifications designed to reduce some of the difficulties associated with regional input-output models.

Consumption purchases from each of the 43 industry sectors were computed by a simple linear consumption function based upon population and disposable personal income. Parameters were derived from a least-squares fit to time-series data on national consumption expenditures for the period 1929–1956. Apparently, family interview data were used to modify estimates in some categories when consumption patterns in the New York area did not appear to follow estimates based upon national consumption patterns.

Government expenditures were treated as a linear function of the region's population. Purchases from each local market industry were considered to be a fixed proportion of total government expenditure. Equally simple formulations were used to derive disposable personal income and total population. Disposable personal income was taken as a direct function of total employment; total population was derived from total employment by single parameter. In both cases, the single parameters were used to approximate a whole host of economic relations that would affect the level of population and disposable personal income as a function of total employment. For example, the relation of disposable personal income to employment is affected by such variables as wage rates, productivity of labor, personal tax rates, transfer payments, indirect taxes, undistributed corporate profits of firms in the region, salaries of governmental employments, depreciation on capital equipment, and nonwage and salary incomes. All of these complex factors and relationships were expressed in a single constant.

Perhaps this survey of the New York Metropolitan Region model will serve to illustrate some of the difficulties and anomalies which face a regional model-builder. This model, a pioneer when constructed, has a number of strengths and weaknesses; model-building can seldom be satisfying on all counts. Parts of the model seem ncredibly simple and nonrigorous; other features employed the most rigorous techniques then available. We can do little better at this point than to quote the final reactions of the study director, Raymond Vernon, who stated that

This is the insubstantial stuff that our projection—that practically any economic projection—is made of. No projection of the economic and demographic characteristics of a metropolitan area can be free of the risk of error; no public or private planner can afford to assume that the potential error is small. From a policy standpoint, this may suggest that planners and investors should regard the preservation of flexibility as a virtue in itself, a virtue worth paying for at the seeming sacrifice of other standards of performance.[11]

The Upper Midwest Economic Study. The Upper Midwest regional study was designed to develop basic data for 1960 and to make projections of employment, income, population, and migration for 1975. The study was begun in 1960 as a joint venture between the Upper Midwest Research and Development Council and the University of Minnesota. The Upper Midwest region was taken as being coincident with the Ninth Federal Reserve District which includes Montana, North Dakota, South Dakota, Minnesota, and 26 counties in northwestern Wisconsin and the Upper Peninsula of Michigan. In 1960 the region had a population of 6.3 million people and a land area of 411,000 square miles.

The component states have shared many similar growth experiences with employment closely tied to the processing of natural resources. Employment and growth rates were below the national trends, and this also held true for per capita income. The homogeneity criterion for "regionality" of the six states was derived from its common Federal Reserve District affiliation and apparently from a moderate degree of economic interdependence of the economic activities in the area.

The institutional framework for undertaking common regional policies in the Upper Midwest region would seem to depend upon cooperation between the various state and local governments and collateral help from the Federal Reserve Bank and private companies with developmental interests. *It would not seem that extensive*

11 Vernon, *op. cit.*, p. 196.

region-wide policies could be implemented based upon this sort of loose-knit institutional base,
although this sort of cooperative regional action to influence economic developmen
was assumed by the research team. However, the economic understanding of
the problems and prospects of the region developed in the study can help the
fragmented mix of public and private decision-makers to deal more effectively
with their own individual, localized problems. The final study report was
published in 1965.[12]

In common with most of the large-scale regional studies, the projections of the
Upper Midwest group are not the product of one large over-all model, the major
exception being the Susquehanna model. Instead, the formal model is of the
interregional multiplier type[13] designed to provide estimates of income and
employment under various exogenous or independent assumptions about populatio
increase, migration, and unemployment.

The assumptions and the determination of the demographic variables do not
come out of the economic model itself.[14] Instead, the model took as an input
certain basic assumptions about population levels in 1975, i.e., zero out-migration

[12] A number of technical and study papers issued earlier by the Upper Midwest Econom
Study are also available. Most of the discussion in this section is based upon the final repor
See James M. Henderson and Anne O. Krueger, *National Growth and Economic Change in the
Upper Midwest* (Minneapolis, Minn.: University of Minnesota Press, 1965).

[13] The major formulation was by Lloyd Metzler, "A Multiple-Region Theory of Income
and Trade," *Econometrica*, Vol. 18 (October 1950). A discussion of the interregional trade
multiplier may also be found in Isard, *op. cit.*, pp. 205–213. In simple formulations, exports
of the various regions are considered autonomous magnitudes. Multiple regional incomes a
a sum of regional investment and exports. The multiplier shows the change in regional
income resulting from changes in regional investment and exports, i.e., $\Delta Y = k\Delta(I + E)$
where Y = regional income, k = the multiplier, I = investment, and E = exports.

[14] We do not wish to suggest that the Upper Midwest Study did not seriously study
migration, population, and employment. In fact, some excellent work on these matters was
done in two study papers by Larry A. Sjaastad. Migration and population projections were
made for 13 age groups for 31 state economic areas. Rural migration projections were base
upon multiple-regression relationships between age, farm income, farm structure, and rural
migration in the 1950–1960 period. Urban populations were projected separately. However
there were no feedback relationships between the demographic and the employment and
income sectors.

or enough out-migration to maintain 1960 unemployment rates in 1975, and then it projected the kind and level of employment needed to be consistent with the 1975 "targets." In this sense, the projections are partial ones *not* designed to predict the future course of the variables but to show instead what economic trends are implied by certain exogeneously derived assumptions about terminal (1975) unemployment and migration rates.

The basic set of projections for 1975 are labeled as "neutral" projections and are based upon five major planning assumptions:

1. That projection made by the National Planning Association for regions outside the Upper Midwest will be realized,
2. That Upper Midwest sectors will maintain their 1960 shares of the regional and national markets that they serve,
3. That Upper Midwest sectors will realize labor productivity increases at nationally projected rates,
4. That Upper Midwest sectors will realize income increases at nationally projected rates, and
5. That the labor force in each Upper Midwest state will increase at the same rate as total employment.[15]

We will comment upon some of the implications of these assumptions although the reader can note that many of the relationships assumed at the outset are often the very things that many regional models attempt to project. For example, assumption number 5 says that the unemployment rate for each state in 1975 will remain at its 1960 level.[16] Given this "neutral" assumption, the economic projections of the model are then used to derive population estimates based upon the amount of out-migration needed to reconcile natural population growth with the assumed 1975 unemployment rates. In other words, the problem of unemployment in 1975

[15] Henderson and Krueger, *op. cit.*, p. 21.

[16] The 1960 unemployment rates were as follows: Montana 6.8%, North Dakota 5.6%, South Dakota 4.1%, Minnesota 5.0%, N.W. Wisconsin 6.1%, and Upper Michigan 10.4%. The corresponding national rate for 1960 was 5.0%.

is abstracted at the beginning and the projection concentrates upon predicting out-migration.[17]

It should be evident that the Upper Midwest model is one of the partial equilibrium variety, as well as being relatively static in its structural makeup. It projects economic activity with independent demographic variables affecting the size of the labor force determined outside the model. In addition, a large element of dynamic realism is lost when it is assumed (number 2), for example, that regional industries will maintain in 1975 the same national market shares they held in 1960.

The authors caution that if the assumptions underlying these "neutral" projections are violated, the projections will not be accurate. On the other hand, there is no discussion of the "accuracy" of the five planning assumptions themselves. This position of "neutrality" is rationalized by stating, "Accurate predictors, however, would not be of much use for regional policy analysis since they could imply nothing much could be done about the future course of economic development." [18] One might respond that attempts to be more dynamic, perhaps by developing changes in unemployment rates within the model or by systematically looking at variables likely to affect national market shares, might also be useful for the design of regional policy. It is not clear why attempts to introduce accuracy, realism, or dynamic factors would necessarily imply that nothing could be done about the course of economic development. It is conceivable that policy actions would have a chance for greater effectiveness with more accurate predictions rather than with those known to be less accurate. A more important test of a regional model is its ability to predict the impacts or outcomes of various regional policies.

The economic model itself is a variation on the interregional multiplier

[17] Some attention was also paid to alternative employment projections needed to employ the labor force under various assumptions about the degree of out-migration. The less the amount of out-migration, the greater the needed increase in nonagricultural employment designed to maintain 1960 unemployment rates. Henderson and Krueger, *op. cit.*, pp. 27–28,

[18] *Ibid*, p. 21.

framework. The input-output approach is to set up an interindustry matrix for the region. Influences from the outside would operate on the region either through an import-export sector[19] or through estimates of shares of national demands operating on specific industries which then drive a regional input-output matrix.[20] In contrast, the Upper Midwest model concentrates upon interregional trade flows to specific regions instead of interindustry sales to specific industries. This means that the questions of the stability and size of interindustry coefficients needed for other types of input-output models can be put aside. However, the assumed size and stability of the flow coefficients governing trade flows to the various regions is now crucial, and we see the need for assumption number 2.[21]

The formal model uses 38 income-generating sectors or "industries" plus exogeneous estimates for agricultural and military income. Sales for each of the 38 sectors are computed for each of the 6 states and for 9 regions (7 in the United States) encompassing the rest of the world, making a total of 15 regions. Income for each state and for each industrial sector is derived from total sales by a parameter specifying the proportion of sales accruing as income payments.

The flow of sales to the various regions was estimated from data in the 1958 Census of Manufactures. These sales formed the basis for estimates of flow coefficients tying the sectors and states to their various regional markets.[22] The flow coefficients were assumed to remain constant to 1975. Other coefficients were then used to convert sales estimates by sector and by state to employment categories. Levels of national demands for 1975 were computed exogenously. For example, national and foreign demands for 1975 were derived from projected

[19] See the Stockholm model in Artle, *op. cit.*

[20] See the New York Metropolitan Regional Study discussed in the preceding section.

[21] The income level of each Upper Midwest state is expressed in terms of a matrix of multipliers plus the external income components of each state. The six Upper Midwest states are endogenous; all other regions are exogenous. Different multiplier values were calculated for the 1960 and the 1975 neutral projections. See Henderson and Krueger, *op. cit.*, p. 161.

[22] Sales are assumed equal to output, implying no inventory increases or decreases. Henderson and Krueger, *op. cit.*, p. 162.

values for personal income, population, and total sales of industries as developed by the National Planning Association. With demand or purchase levels given, the interregional trade matrix was able to develop sales, employment, and income projections for each of the sectors and for each of the Upper Midwest states for 1975.

The formal model contained 690 equations, 921 variables, and 2,784 parameters which was said to be "far too large for convenient projection." [23] Therefore, a greatly simplified model using only 6 equations (684 equations were collapsed) was used to get total state incomes expressed as direct functions of purchase levels (demands by external regions). Once total income levels by states were computed, reference was then made to the expanded model to derive incomes and employments for each of the employment sectors.

Much of the validity of the model, from a conceptual point of view, hinges upon the stability of the coefficients describing interregional trade patterns, particularly the assumption that the Upper Midwest sectors will have the same shares of regional and national markets in 1975 that they had in 1960. Some of our observations on the New York regional model also apply here. Stability of market shares implies either that all of the many factors affecting relative price levels between regions, and the other locational attributes affecting the ability of 38 sectors to sell in 15 regions, must remain relatively unchanged or that changes offset each other. These are heroic assumptions, especially when historical regional growth trends in the United States seem to show all sorts of dynamic shifts and changes.[24] On this same point, constant market shares would seem to imply that as other regions (the rest of the world) grow, they would continue to import from the Upper Midwest the same percentage of all of the various products over time. This would seem to deny the influence of import substitution and agglomeration economies in other regions outside of the Upper Midwest. These factors are important in explaining past shifts in the distribution of manufacturing activities.

[23] Henderson and Krueger, *op. cit.*, p. 160.

[24] See Harvey S. Perloff, Edgar S. Dunn, Jr., Eric E. Lampard, and Richard E. Muth, *Regions, Resources and Economic Growth* (Baltimore, Md.: The Johns Hopkins Press, 1960), especially Part IV.

The Upper Midwest model also seems to imply that the imports into the Midwest from the rest of the world will not increase relatively as this region grows. In other words, the "neutral" projection allows manufacturing employment to increase equally with the increased demands for manufactured goods in the local markets as well as in the outside markets—and this despite the fact that some of the 6 states lost or failed to maintain market shares for manufacturing during the 1950–1960 decade.

Ohio River Basin Study. The Ohio River Basin projections were developed by Arthur D. Little, Inc., for the Corps of Engineers as part of a comprehensive study of water-development activities in the basin. The model was designed to provide 50-year projections (1960 through 2010) of employment and income for the entire Ohio River basin.[25] This area covered parts of 10 states and 400 counties. It included 163,000 square miles and $\frac{1}{10}$ of the nation's population, second in size only to the Upper Midwest study. Because the drainage basin did not conform to state lines, it was necessary to rely upon the county as the basic political unit for purposes of data sources. This feature along with the size of the area imposed difficult constraints upon data availability.

There is some question as to whether such a large area, defined in watershed terms, actually represents an economic region or integrated economy. With the exception of a few industries having direct dependence upon the river, e.g., access to water transportation or water supply, it seems likely that much of the economy of the area is not tied in any important way to the Ohio River. It is even doubtful that some of the large cities located directly on the river, e.g., Pittsburgh, Cincinnati, and Louisville, have many economic activities that are interdependent. In other words, river basins may not be good regions for dealing with economic development even though rivers themselves may be "correct" regions for water-related activities and for dealing with water problems.[26]

[25] Arthur D. Little, Inc., *Projective Economic Study of the Ohio River Basin*, Appendix B. Ohio River Comprehensive Survey, Volume III. Prepared for the Corps of Engineers, U.S. Government Printing Office, 1964.

[26] However, as we note later, this model does not contain a water sector.

The Ohio River study concentrated on developing equilibrium estimates of the supply of and the demand for labor by decades over a 50-year period. The supply of labor was projected separately in a standard demographic model based upon cohort-survival techniques involving estimates of births, deaths, and migration. Assumptions were then made concerning labor-force-participation rates and unemployment rates to determine the supply of labor.

The demand for labor was based upon a modified input-output model using 29 separate sectors. There were 27 major industry groups, one government sector, and one nonclassified sector. The demands for each industrial sector were derived in turn from final demands for consumption, for capital formation, government, defense, net exports, and for interindustry demand. The total demand for labor was achieved by solving a set of simultaneous linear equations describing the demand sectors.

It was decided that reconciliation of the separate supply and demand for labor forecasts would not be undertaken unless the two estimates differed by more than 10 percent. This was not the case, and the differences ranged from a +6.42 percent to a −5.54 percent.[27] A consensus was achieved by simply averaging the two sets of projections for each preceding projection year and checking back to make all of the numbers consistent with the "equilibrium" projections.

Total output in the basin was taken as the sum of demands for 29 sectors derived from 6 sources of demand: the 5 final demand sectors were (1) consumption expenditures, (2) investment expenditures, (3) government expenditures, (4) defense expenditures, and (5) net exports—plus the interindustry demands. Consumption and interindustry demands were derived endogenously within the model. The estimates of demands for investment, government spending, net trade balances, and for defense expenditures in the basin were derived exogenously from

[27] The discrepancy was computed as a demand/supply projection ratio. For 1980 demand-based projections exceeded supply-based projections by 6.42 percent; for 2,010 demand-based projections fell short of supply-based projections by 5.54 percent. Arthur D. Little, *op. cit.*, p. 118.

national projections. These exogeneous demands were used to drive a modified input-output matrix to generate interindustry demand and consumption employment and thus finally arrive at total employment.

For the modified input-output framework, Arthur D. Little used only 81 interindustry coefficients instead of the 729 that would have been required by a full 27-industry matrix. It had been hoped that the data from the 1958 input-output study would be available for use in constructing the model. The 1958 study was not published until the fall of 1964,[28] so Little had to "up-date" coefficients from the 1947 input-output study. This is to say that the Ohio River study was not only forced to use national coefficients at the regional level, a somewhat shaky procedure itself, but the coefficients used were seriously out of date. The "up-dating" of the 1947 coefficients proved to be a difficult task. As a short-cut, Little used the region's share of national employment at the one-digit level of the Standard Industry Classification Code to modify the 1947 interindustry coefficients. The use of 81 coefficients (27×3) also was a short-cut device that allowed for substitution among inputs *within* each subtotal as long as the *sum* of inputs remained a fixed proportion of total output.

In the Ohio River study, the basin's investment demands were derived from national projections for investment by assuming the basin's share of investment to be the same as its share of total national output. Net exports demands for 7 industries, which were large exporters, were related directly to national growth trend projections. For the other 21 industrial sectors, Little estimated net trade balances by assuming them to be a constant share of total output for each of the industries. Consumption functions for the Ohio River basin were derived by assuming that the consumption expenditures were the same functions of disposable personal income in the region as they were for the national economy.

In some ways this model is a clear example of the general tendency among

[28] Morris R. Goldman, Martin L. Marimont, and Beatrice N. Vaccara, "The Interindustry Structure of the United States: A Report on the 1958 Input-Output Study," *Survey of Current Business*, Vol. 44, No. 11 (November 1964).

regional models employing input-output frameworks to spend a great deal of care in devising frameworks depicting fairly sophisticated structural relationships within the region. By contrast, relatively little time was spent in assessing the exogenous or independent variables that are assumed to drive the matrix to generate total employment. This is not just a matter of attempting to secure data for elusive regional coefficients of intermediate demands, it is also a matter of philosophy concerning model-building. Leven pointed toward this apparent inconsistency when he argued:

Even so it seems fair to ask whether it is easier to predict the independent variables in a system than to predict directly these dependent variables in which one is specifically interested. It is not clear that the independent variables can be predicted more easily. And if not, the moral should be clear: there is a legitimate basis for skepticism about the use of sophisticated analytical systems simply for the purpose of obtaining more accurate predictions of such major regional economic aggregates as employment, population or income.[29]

It is quite correct to respond to this argument that the use of a sophisticated system, such as a regional input-output matrix, is probably justified when we wish to predict a fine detail and to describe complex interrelationships between sectors. However, the smaller the region and the more "open" the economy, the less important will be the internal interindustry relationships, and the more important will be interregional trade flows of imports and exports to the rest of the world. Nevertheless, the point seems well taken that accurate predictors depend equally upon the derivation of valid exogenous estimates as well as sophisticated structural frameworks.[30]

Separate projections were also provided for 19 subareas in the basin. These were done by fitting least-squares regression equations to each subarea's share of total

[29] Charles L. Leven, "Establishing Goals for Regional Economic Development," *Journal of the American Institute of Planners*, Vol. XXX, No. 2 (May 1964) p. 101.

[30] The sophisticated structural framework in the Ohio study, however, is limited to the economic sector. As we indicated earlier, no attempt was made to tie the demographic and economic sectors together explicitly.

employment for each of the 29 employment sectors from 6 historical observations. A lag of time was employed to damp the effect on growth implied by historical trends. This means that the projections for individual subareas were not made independently of the projections for the basin as a whole and therefore did not take into account internal factors influencing subarea growth.

Ostensibly, the purpose of the Ohio River projections was to provide guidelines and backup data to the Corps of Engineers and to public agencies interested in various kinds of water resource-related investments in the region. However, the projections that were developed did *not* consider water qualities or water quantities for any of the activities specified. This is a river-basin model that does not contain a water sector! In fact, the Corps instructed Arthur D. Little to make its projections on the explicit assumption that *water would be available at all times in sufficient quantities and qualities to support the projected economy.*[31]

Perhaps we should point out some of the implications of this assumption. The major implication is that the threshold cost of water in terms of quantities and qualities will *not* rise in the future despite growth of population and production in the basin. This, in turn, implies *either* that there are not likely to be future water shortages *or* that possible water constraints in terms of qualities or quantities would be modified or removed in such a way as not to affect the water costs in the basin. The first alternative is a possibility, of course, but it is not one which the Corps of Engineers usually endorses. The second possibility would mean that additional investments on the river (public and private) would be made at *no cost* to the region. This possibility does not seem very plausible despite the fact that river works construction by the Corps of Engineers is largely subsidized in relation to the regions in which the works are built.

Moreover, it is likely that river works construction *itself* would have some feedbacks on the economy and thereby affect employment and income projections. As we point out in the Susquehanna model, river works construction may generate employment during the actual period of construction. A second feedback may occur

[31] Arthur D. Little, *op. cit.*, p. 3.

if the projects themselves generate *new* employment opportunities in the long run in the region, e.g., employment stemming from recreation. Therefore, as a general policy it would seem desirable for river-basin projection models to build a water sector into the model in the beginning to take into account possible feedbacks from the economy on the water and possible feedbacks from the water sector back on the economy. Otherwise it may be difficult to formulate valid regional employment projections and even more difficult to determine the economic feasibility of prospective water investments in the basin.

The California Development Model. The California Development model was designed to forecast personal income and employment on a quarterly basis by major industry groups for the State of California from 1960 to 1975. The projections were commissioned by the State Office of Planning in connection with the preparation of a State Development Plan. The study was financed jointly by the State of California and by a 701 Planning Grant from the Housing and Home Finance Agency.[32]

The California model has two different versions. The Phase I model was developed by Arthur D. Little under contract with the Office of Planning. This model was widely anticipated in the profession, but references to it have largely been confined to one journal article because the final report describing the model was never made public.[33]

Subsequently, a Phase II model was constructed under contract with the Institute for Urban and Regional Development at the University of California at Berkeley. This second model was completed in January 1966.[34] Model

[32] By 1963 planning efforts in 22 states and 3 territories were being supported by 701 Grants. For a discussion of California planning see John W. Dyckman, "State Development Planning: The California Case," *Journal of the American Institute of Planners*, Vol. XXX, No. 2 (May 1964), pp. 144–152.

[33] The Phase I report by Arthur D. Little to the State Department of Finance in 1964 was not made available for public distribution. For a general account of the model, see John W. Dyckman and Richard P. Burton, "The Role of Defense Expenditures in Forecast of California's Economic Growth," *Western Economic Journal*, Vol. III, No. 2 (Spring 1965), pp. 133–141.

construction for each version was directed by John W. Dyckman and Richard P. Burton. Widespread rumors of difficulties in the Phase I model were partially confirmed by publication of the Phase II report, which described some serious conceptual and statistical problems in the earlier formulation.

The Phase I model projected personal income and employment for 53 industry sectors by quarters (60 quarters) for the period 1960 through 1975. The basic economic framework was in the tradition of the quarterly econometric models developed earlier for the Netherlands by Tinbergen, for Norway by Frisch, and for the United Kingdom by Klein.[35] Yet the model also combined elements of input-output analysis coupled with an export base theory of regional growth. This amalgamation of model concepts created difficulties in defining the role of the interindustry sectors. The Phase I model apparently was an uneasy compromise between features requiring simultaneous solutions and procedures requiring sequential or recursive solutions.

Wages and salaries served as proxy variables for output. Multiple regressions for income and employment for each of the sectors were derived from a sample of 40 quarterly observations for the period 1950 to 1960. Explanation of patterns of trade flows for the demand sectors was thus inferred from correlative changes in wages and salaries. Constant ratios between the industry demand sectors and total output were assumed in estimating interindustry demands.

Three types of demand sectors were used: export demands, interindustry demands and local final demands. Exports for 7 categories were determined from national economic projections prepared by the National Planning Association. Once these were determined, interindustry and local final demands were developed endogenously. Local final demands were made up of local consumption demands,

[34] Richard P. Burton and John W. Dyckman, *A Quarterly Economic Forecasting Model for the State of California*, Center for Planning and Development Research: Institute of Urban and Regional Development, University of California, January 1966.

[35] Jan Tinbergen, *An Econometric Approach to Business Cycle Problems* (Paris: Hermann et Cie., 1937); Ragnar Frisch, *Statistical Confluence Analysis by Means of Complete Regression Systems*, University Economics Institute, Oslo, Norway, 1934; and L. R. Klein et al., *An Econometric Model of the United Kingdom* (Oxford, England: Basil Blackwell, 1961).

local investment demands, and local government demands. The model first produced estimates of wages and salaries for the various demand sectors, and from these estimates employment figures were derived. Simultaneous equations were used in the Phase I system. It was claimed that the model yielded "highly reliable individual industry and total industry forecasts" based upon forecast results for 1960–1962.[36]

When work on the Phase II model began in 1964, it was reported that the Phase I model would be expanded to develop an interregional model. The first phase was essentially a one-region model depicting California and the rest of the world without feedback from California to the rest of the world. California exports to the rest of the world were the generator of state economic growth. The Phase II model, as originally proposed, was to divide California into 4 regions so there would be a 4-region model plus the rest of the world. Again, as in Phase I, the primary driving force for the California economy would come from the rest of the world through the influence of exports, but the interregional model would then generate local final demands, interindustry, and interregional demands for each of the regions. If successful, this would have been the first operational interregional model developed for use in regional economic forecasting.

In order to secure data for this ambitious attempt, a comprehensive survey of California firms was carried out. Each enterprise was asked to apportion its sales by 5 geographical regions (4 California regions and the rest of the world) and also by industry classification. The survey was actually conducted, but apparently the difficulties of constructing the interregional model proved to be too great because the Phase II model that actually appeared is largely a reconstruction of the Phase I one-region model and not an interregional one.[37]

[36] Dyckman and Burton, *Western Economic Journal, op. cit.* p. 136.

[37] The promise of delivery of an interregional model was given by John W. Dyckman and Richard P. Burton, "Some Interregional (Intra-State) Problems in the California State Development Studies," mimeographed paper presented to the Regional Science Association, Ann Arbor, Michigan, November 1964, 17 pp.
The Phase II report makes no mention of the failure to produce an interregional model except to indicate that such a model was given some trial runs that seemed promising. *A Quarterly Forecasting Model, op. cit.,* p. 9.

The Phase II model both expanded the scope of the Phase I effort and introduced important changes in statistical methodology. On the expansion side, the period of observation was lengthened to 52 quarters (13 years); the personal income section was expanded to 59 industries; some of the predetermined variables influencing the volume of exports were disaggregated; and forecasts were now provided for some miscellaneous categories, e.g., types of taxable sales, which are important for estimating state revenues.

The methodological changes involved in the Phase II effort centered around attempts to reduce serial correlation and multicolinearity, which plagued the structural equations of the Phase I model. A second modification was the removal of triangularity in the interindustry sector.[38]

The Phase II model abandoned the triangular ordering. This model is largely recursive; i.e., the structural relations are not decided simultaneously but are expressed in lags that are unidirectional with respect to time. The Phase II model was expanded to 130 equations.

In most other aspects, the Phase II model retained Phase I features:

1. It is linear in variables and in coefficients,
2. It forecasts to 1975 by quarters,
3. It continues to use NPA projections to forecast export variables, and
4. Wage and salaries as used are proxy measures of industry output.

The summary forecast results for the Phase II model are presented for 1963–1964 using actual values for the exogenous variables. Comparison of actual versus forecast values for the 8 quarters (1963–1964) shows apparently low-percentage deviations for such aggregate classifications as total wage and salary disbursements, personal income, and total employment. However, no comparisons were presented for individual industry figures (actual versus forecast values). In addition, the report describing the model does not apply sensitivity analysis to important assumptions of the model, nor is there any discussion of the "reasonableness" and meaning of the forecast results beyond 1964 to 1975.

[38] For an extended discussion of these modifications, see *A Quarterly Forecasting Model*, *op. cit.*, pp. 36–47.

The Oahu, Hawaii, Planning Model. In cooperation with the University of Hawaii and with the assistance of a 701 Planning Grant from the Housing and Home Finance Agency, a team of economists developed a model for economic planning and growth for the island of Oahu, Hawaii. The study began in 1963 and the first phase of the program was completed in 1965. At that time it was decided to extend the model to the State of Hawaii as a whole, i.e., Oahu and the Neighbor Islands, and the model was taken over by Department of Planning and Economic Development for the State of Hawaii. In March 1966, a report of the model containing projections of the Hawaiian economy to 1985 was submitted to the Hawaii State Legislature.[39] The report was given only limited circulation and is now out of print. As a result, general knowledge of the model is limited to one journal article describing the early Oahu model and to several very general nontechnical articles on the complete model.[40] The discussion here will be confined to the Oahu model. No major structural changes were made in the extended model.

The novel feature of the Oahu model was the attempt to quantify and integrate planning goals *within* the model itself. In other words, the model projected the economic growth and the types and levels of certain kinds of exogenous spending necessary to achieve four planning goals. These goals, specified in quantitative terms, were related to the shape of income distribution, to desired levels of population, to external payments outside the island, and to combined budgets of state and local governmental agencies. For example, not only did the model

[39] Department of Planning and Economic Development, *The Hawaiian Economy: Problems and Projects, A Report on the Economic Foundations of the General Plan Revision*, Honolulu, Hawaii, March 1966, 100 pp.

[40] The Oahu model was described by its principal designer. See Roland Artle, "External Trade, Industrial Structure, Employment Mix, and the Distribution of Incomes: A Simple Model of Planning and Growth," *The Swedish Journal of Economics*, 1965, pp. 1–23. General articles on the complete model may be found in the *Hawaii Economic Review* published by the Department of Planning and Economic Development, State of Hawaii, Honolulu, Hawaii, for Spring 1966 and Summer 1966.

predict total incomes but it distributed these incomes among three household categories—low-income, middle-income, and high-income households. Labor demands from the industrial, household, and government sectors were also divided into three groups—demands for unskilled, medium-skilled, and skilled labor—with income used as a proxy measure of skill levels. No discussion was provided on how the planning goals themselves were to be derived. The report describing the second-phase model for the entire state indicates that primary attention was given to the achievement of certain levels of population in 1985 and the ability of the economy to produce a sufficient number of jobs.

In conceptual makeup, the Oahu model was quite simple. The local economy was conceived as a household sector plus 16 industry sectors that included a service sector and state and local expenditures (excluding public investment spending). The relatively isolated nature of the island economy enabled the model builders to have more data on exports and imports than would be expected in most "open" regions. The local economy was viewed as being driven by exogenous spending divided into four categories: (1) federal defense spending in Oahu, (2) tourist expenditure in Oahu, (3) research and development expenditures in Oahu, and (4) public and private investment in Oahu. However, the usual orientation for regional projections was reversed. Instead of assuming certain levels of exogenous spending to drive the local economy, this model assumed certain planning goals to begin with and then derived as an output the levels of exogenous spending in these four categories necessary to achieve the planning goals. Apparently, possible trade-offs between types of exogenous spending and between types of goals were not considered.

In contrast with many other regional models, exports of goods to the rest of the world were given a rather minor role. Exports of sugar and pineapples were predetermined outside the model based upon trend projections over the past two decades on the plausible assumption that these sales were not likely to change much over time. The values of other exports were generated endogenously within the model under the assumption that given proportions of total outputs would be exported. Initially, import coefficients for each household and industry were assumed to remain at their 1960 levels. Apparently, future model runs were to employ sensitivity analysis on this assumption.

Coefficients for most of the equations were determined on the basis of time-series estimates. Weights assigned to variables were often allowed to vary with time using shift variables that allowed for some nonlinearities, e.g., scale economies and relative price changes. Business taxes and business savings were viewed as linear functions in time. For industries where products were used widely among the 16 industry sectors, e.g., public utilities, sales and outputs were viewed as fixed proportions of total interindustry demand, relaxing the assumption of fixed input-output coefficients for individual demand sectors. For other industries, ordinary input-output coefficients were estimated on the basis of local sales data. Noncapital expenditures for state and local governments were viewed as a linear function of total household incomes earned locally.

Total population in Oahu was derived from a sum of total employment adjusted by coefficients measuring unemployment (4 percent was used) and labor-force-participation rates. This population estimate was viewed as an "artificial" one, i.e., a parametric constant, to be compared with side assumptions and calculations dealing with such demographic factors as birth rates, deaths, and net migration.

In contrast to many, perhaps most, regional studies, the Hawaii model apparently will not be "put on the shelf" nor will its initial projections be kept intact. The Department of Planning and Economic Development of the State of Hawaii hopes to use the model as a planning tool and a learning device. Plans are under way to keep the model in operation and to see that it is revised and updated in the light of new information. In addition, the model will be used to test the likely effects of alternative hypotheses and programs relating to such things as changes in tax rates, growth of exports, and fluctuations of public expenditures. If the model is used in this way, it may improve the understanding of the Hawaiian economy and pinpoint crucial areas for further study.

The Lehigh Basin Simulation Model. The Lehigh model is included in this survey of regional models for two reasons. First, it is a river-basin model. In contrast to the Ohio River study, this model emphasizes the river and its hydrology. The study recommends procedures for planning, designing, and operating a system of river works to meet various kinds of economic demands. Second, the model relies upon simulation techniques. It will be important, therefore, to contrast the simulation attempted in the Lehigh model with the systems simulated in the Susquehanna model. Because the Lehigh model is an outgrowth of the Harvard Water Program and the earlier study, *Design of Water-Resource Systems*,[41] we will first present a brief overview of the earlier study before turning to the Lehigh model.

Design of Water-Resource Systems was an ambitious attempt to integrate economic, engineering, and governmental planning and to devise new techniques for designing multipurpose, multiunit water systems. Probably the most important contribution of the book was the development of two techniques of system design—the simulation of a simplified river basin on a digital computer and the development of mathematical models for programming river systems.

The hypothetical river system involved twelve design variables consisting of reservoirs, power plants, irrigation works, target outputs for irrigation water and hydroelectric power, and specified allocations of reservoir capacity for active, dead, and flood storage. The study used monthly hydrological data on normal inflows and six-hour data for floods. These flows were then routed through the reservoirs, power plants, and irrigation systems for various periods of stream flows. The basic hydrologic data were for a 32-year period. A separate computer model was employed, however, to synthesize flows for longer periods of time, and these synthetic flows were also routed through the model. Fixed operating procedures, in conjunction with *predetermined benefit and loss functions*, were used to generate outputs and the resulting net benefits.

[41] Arthur Maass et al., *Design of Water-Resource Systems: New Techniques for Relating Economic Objectives, Engineering Analysis, and Governmental Planning* (Cambridge, Mass.: Harvard University Press, 1962).

Although the Harvard study is an important milestone in river-basin planning, it contains a number of limitations, most of which are also found in the Lehigh basin model. For one thing, despite the emphasis on simulation, the study attempted to specify optimal design and optimizing procedures. The optimizing procedures were based in large part upon linear programming techniques and specified objective functions. These programming techniques necessarily required considerable simplification of the original problem. For the sake of simplicity, target outputs and benefit functions were highly restricted and simplified, and a rigid system of priorities had to be imposed. Operating procedures for facilities were fixed, and many sorts of dynamic feedbacks had to be omitted.

The attempt to find optimal solutions, then, forced the problem into channels that could be solved by linear programming techniques. Therefore, the study was limited even within its own framework of how to design a water system. More important, however, was the fact that the model was one of hydrology and engineering design that took the regional economy as given. All regional economic variables were fed into the model from the outside. The emphasis was on engineering and water management, not upon regional growth and development.

The Lehigh basin simulation extends and refines the methodology developed in the earlier Harvard study to a real world situation, namely the Lehigh River Basin in Pennsylvania. The model is later extended to the entire Delaware River Basin. It is described in a book by Maynard M. Hufschmidt and Myron B. Fiering, two of the authors of the first study.[42] The project was financed largely by the Corps of Engineers under a contract with the Harvard Water Program. The book contains detailed reports on the steps and procedures used. It is intended, then, to serve as a guide to others who wish to design water resource systems.

The simulation analysis described in the book is designed primarily "to utilize

[42] Maynard M. Hufschmidt and Myron B. Fiering, *Simulation Techniques for Design of Water Resource Systems* (Cambridge, Mass.: Harvard University Press, 1966).

long synthetic streamflow traces derived by statistical analysis of parameters of the historical record." [43] The planning problem is viewed as a detailed analysis of engineering and management alternatives leading to the identification of an optimal design or designs. Only four water demands were studied—water supply, hydroelectric power, flood control, and recreation—although in theory the model could be modified to deal with other purposes. The model simulates mean monthly flows and three-hour flows at flood peaks measured at six reservoir sites.[44] The major construction elements in the system are six reservoirs and nine hydroelectric power plants.

With each system design there is an associated unique optimal operation policy: in terms of priorities for the use of minimum flows, first priority is given to minimum flows for flood storage space at each reservoir; minimum recreation storage is given second priority; water supply output is given third priority; and fourth priority is given to hydroenergy production. Given certain initial conditions—inflows to the system and a set of targets—the essence of the simulation is to trace the behavior of the system over time.

Economic benefit functions associated with the targets for water supply, flood control, recreation, and power are then used to evaluate the results and point toward the optimal design. Benefit functions used in the model in theory combine two elements: (1) benefits that result when the system *exactly* meets a predetermined target, and (2) losses associated with undershooting or overfulfillment of targets in any time period. In theory, the program can handle different types of investment programs (static and dynamic), different methods of discounting benefit streams, and differing lengths of simulation periods.

We say "in theory," because the actual model produced does not deal with many of the complexities and variables discussed in its theoretical chapters. Even

---

[43] *Ibid.*, p. 14.

[44] In contrast, the Susquehanna model deals with water supplies, water qualities (primarily dissolved oxygen), and recreation. The Susquehanna model uses 7-day-5-year low flows and computes water qualities and quantities at various "critical points" in relation to changing economic growth patterns generated by the model. See Chapter 11.

with simplification and short cuts, the Lehigh model represents "an enormous coding effort" and computer program (FORTRAN):

It consists of a main routine and 22 sub-routines, and the compiled or binary object program occupies 32,744 memory locations, leaving a scant 24 registers of the IBM 70904 computer unused.[44]

Apart from the need for simplications and short cuts[45] that plague all model builders, there is an important question of philosophy regarding planning for river-basin development.[46] We think the Lehigh simulation model does an excellent job in tackling the problem of optimal design and optimal management of a river system under highly specified external conditions (especially output targets and benefit-cost functions) and when the system is only moderately complex. If the model is placed within this perspective, it represents a very useful piece of work.

However, we wish to highlight two major points of difference in philosophy regarding river-basin planning efforts in particular and simulation analysis in general. Turning to the latter point first, we believe that the use of optimizing and programming techniques limits the researcher in the complexities of problems he can tackle. The mathematics for programming under many complex situations simply does not exist.[47] In addition, there are basic difficulties of public policy stemming from a lack of congruency of goals for development and the inability to specify social welfare functions.[48]

Second, with regard to regional model-building and river-basin planning we feel that the two strands of analysis—regional economic growth and river works construction—are inextricably part of the same general system. We have stressed

[45] Hufschmidt and Fiering, *op. cit.*, p. 89.

[46] A short cut of interest to water economists is the case of point estimates of the "requirements" for water made by the Corps of Engineers for the years 1965, 1980, and 2010. For example, the Corps estimated that flow requirements at Bethlehem, Pennsylvania will be 570,000 acre-feet in 2010. Also, unit costs for alternative water supplies are assumed to remain constant ($88,000 per cubic feet per second) over the entire 50-year period. See Hufschmidt and Fiering, *op. cit.*, pp. 35, 61.

[47] The reader is referred to the discussion in Chapter 5.

[48] See Chapter 3.

that regional economic analysis of river basins should take into account the effects of the economy upon the water and the possible feedbacks from the water sector back upon the economy. In our view, it would be incorrect to plunge into river-basin planning by designing optimal management systems for the water variables without first having a general regional economic model of the basin which includes a water sector. In many ways, models of the Lehigh basin type should follow, not precede, the more general approach. It is in this spirit that we hope that planning organizations do not make use of the guidelines offered by the Lehigh simulation model until they develop the proper framework within which to approach the question of optimal design.

Another Susquehanna Model. Throughout this book we refer to the Susquehanna model as the one constructed by Battelle Memorial Institute. Actually, another attempt has been under way since 1963 to develop a separate set of economic projections for the Susquehanna River Basin. The second model is (or was) being constructed by National Planning Association under joint contract for the Corps of Engineers and the U.S. Public Health Service. The final report describing the NPA model for the Susquehanna basin has not yet been made available to the public. Our knowledge of the model is limited to two short reports that were issued by the NPA when the model construction first began.[49] The discussion of the NPA model is confined to its apparent outline circa 1964.

The NPA model projects both income and employment for the basin by 10-year periods to the year 2010. It recognizes the close relation between the demographic and economic sectors, and the reconciliation of the two sectors is accomplished at each 10-year period. If the two separate projections of labor force and employment seem to be at variance with each other, modification is made and the projections

---

[49] National Planning Association, "Projection Procedure for the Susquehanna Area Economic Base Study," February 28, 1964, Washington, D.C., mimeographed paper, 18 pp.; National Planning Association, "A Comparison of Proposed Procedures Used for Making Economic Projections for the Susquehanna River Basin Area" by the National Planning Association and Battelle Memorial Institute, Washington, D.C., no date, mimeographed paper, 19 pp.

are rerun for that decade. Once reconciliation is achieved, these values become the basis for starting projections for the next decade or so.

The NPA model is a modification of the export base theory of regional growth. That is to say, exports are viewed as the generator of economic activity and are influenced by the cost of production and by transport costs vis-à-vis other areas in the economy. Changes in regional locational advantages are described by a version of the "differential shift" technique developed by Dunn and Perloff.[50] This shift technique does not specify individual location factors but describes instead the impact of all of these factors in an aggregative sense.

Total employment is divided into export employment and "residentiary" employment. Residentiary employment is broken down into employment for local consumption and employment for intermediate goods and services. Intermediate employment is a function of total employment and consumption employment is a function of personal income in the area. Personal income is derived by relating projected employment to projected wages and to projected nonwage income.

Perspectives on Regional Models

In the chapters that follow, the Susquehanna model will be discussed in detail. Some of the points that the reader should look for in appraising this model and in seeing the differences between the Susquehanna model and the other regional models are surveyed here.

First, the reader should understand that the Susquehanna model has some strengths and some points of weakness, as do all regional models. Perhaps we should say that it does some things very well and that it does not cover other items. Models of course reflect the specific purposes for which they were designed and the particular techniques selected. There is no such thing as a general regional model.

Second, although the Susquehanna model represents (we believe) a significant advance in the state of the art, it still has considerable room for improvement,

50 Perloff et al., *op. cit.*, Chapter III.

and there is a great deal of scope for future modification. Even though some parts of the model employ complex formulations, other parts of the model use rather "standard" or conventional formulations. For this reason, we stress that the model itself is better judged from an over-all point of view and in its entirety, rather than by scrutiny of its individual parts. We think that the importance of the model stems in large part from its attempt to tie important regional variables together in a general model.

Third, the reader should consider these differences between the Susquehanna model and the six regional models just surveyed in this chapter. (1) The Susquehanna model is the only one to tie the demographic and economic sectors together in one model. (2) The Susquehanna model is of a simulation type that makes it possible to insert a wide variety of assumptions and parameters and to employ sensitivity analysis. (3) The Susquehanna model is of a dynamic type. There are explicit feedbacks and lagged variables within the various sectors and between the sectors. (4) Finally, it is the only river-basin model to combine the economic and water sectors. Projections of water quantities and water qualities are derived along with the usual economic projections. In addition, the model shows the employment feedbacks on the economy that results from the construction of various systems of river works.

Chapter 5
Philosophy and
Methodology
of Approach

Chapter 2 described the role of mathematical models in the social sciences, and Chapter 3 pointed up many of the problems that complicate regional analysis. The purpose of this chapter is to describe how these general perspectives and the particular objectives of the Susquehanna study led to the selection of our mathematical approach.

The chapter begins with a description of the factors influencing the choice of methodology. After concluding that continuous computer simulation seems to be the best way to model the region, a discussion of specific simulation methodology is presented. This discussion of modeling is illustrated by the step-by-step development of a simple, hypothetical regional model.

Over-All Considerations

The approach that should be selected for any analysis depends largely upon two over-all considerations: the problem or the situation to be investigated, and the purpose of the study. Many problems preclude choice of certain analytical approaches. For example, an extremely complex multifaceted problem denies the possibility of using intuitive methods; formal models are required. A situation embodying significant behavioral variations over long periods of time questions the appropriateness of numerous static approaches; a dynamic framework is called for. A situation in which empirical data are severely lacking may preclude selection of a statistically based modeling approach that demands extensive data analysis for determination of model form and estimation of parameters.

In a similar vein, a variety of purposes suggests a variety of approaches even to the same problem setting. As Chapter 3 pointed out, analysis of a region may be undertaken for different purposes that often demand different philosophies and methodologies of approach. For example, a desire to compare several specific public investment proposals on the basis of benefit-cost analysis may lead to an approach to regional research quite different from what would be chosen to engage in long-term forecasting of the region's growth. Or the goal of determining optimal

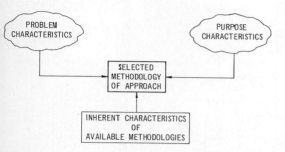

FIGURE 5.1. Influences on methodology selection.

allocation of plant sites will demand an approach different from that chosen if the objective were limited to description of evolving land utilization patterns.

The problem and the purpose of the study therefore highlight priorities for taking advantage of different inherent characteristics of the various methods of analysis that are potentially applicable. This interplay is suggested in Figure 5.1.

Attributes of Regional Economies

In undertaking analysis of a regional economy, selection of the research approach will thus be strongly influenced by the nature of regional economies in general and by consideration of special characteristics of the region under investigation. Chapter 3 reviewed the problems of regional analysis in comparison with national economic analysis. In this chapter our concern is with how regional characteristics affect research methodology.

Large Number of Variables. The first characteristic that comes to mind as one considers a regional economy is that there may be many complex relationships. It is likely that a region as large as the Susquehanna River Basin will not possess a homogeneous economic base—some areas may be highly influenced by manufacturing, others by mining, while still others may have more than normal employment in government. Similar differences may be found in cultural and demographic patterns. Such a diversified region cannot be accurately described by a few aggregate variables but must be divided into subregions and subsectors, each with its own set of variables and parameters.

Within each subregion there are a large number of considerations that are both economic and noneconomic. Our primary focus is on the impact of a system of river works. This means that, at a minimum, we must consider the river, the local economy, and the population. The river involves the questions both of water quantity and water quality. The economy includes employment and the growth of employment in a number of industrial and service categories. The population determination requires the consideration of births, deaths, and migration.

After considering the number of subregions and the number of variables within

FIGURE 5.2. A positive feedback loop.

a single subregion, one concludes that such a study will involve a large number of both economic and noneconomic variables. (The final model contained about 1800 variables.)

Feedback Nature of Regions. After consideration of the number of variables, the next question is how they interact. The study treats the impact of river works on the region. But that is not the end of the story as the population and the economy also have an impact on the quantity and quality of the water in the river. More generally we are concerned with the feedback of any variable on itself. Unemployment affects migration, which in turn affects labor force and thereby affects unemployment. Unemployment also affects wages, but these affect the growth of job opportunities and finally feed back upon the unemployment level.

The preservation of the dynamic feedback nature of the economy is a significant difference between this study and earlier mathematical studies of regional economies. Feedback exists in an economy when chains of causes and effects loop back upon themselves. For example, earlier regional models projected population and employment separately. Feedback was recognized to a limited degree when the extrapolated trends presented unlikely or divergent results. Previously "independent" projections were then adjusted or reconciled on an ad hoc basis "outside" the model to give more reasonable results. But feedback phenomena deserve more explicit treatment.

Feedback loops can be found almost everywhere. Closed feedback loops include linkages such as exist between room thermostats, furnaces, and room temperatures; the amount of carbon dioxide in the blood and the respiration rate; and the amount of an item in inventory and the production rate. Such loops exhibit behavior that can only be analyzed by studying the complete system; analyzing the separate components of the loop in isolation from one another often does not even hint at the sorts of behavior that might arise.

Feedback loops can be broken into two classifications—positive and negative.

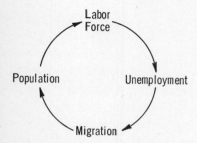

FIGURE 5.3. A negative feedback loop.

Positive feedback loops involve relationships that build on themselves. For example, the loop shown in Figure 5.2 from population to birth rate back to population is a positive loop. Given appropriate time lags (and other factors), the population creates births that add to the population. In due time, allowing for aging, maturation, and family formation delays, these new births will create still more births. If no other factors influenced population size and birth rate, this positive feedback loop would be self-amplifying on a continuing basis, with no tendency for population growth to halt. Of course, other factors from other feedback loops do intervene in this process.

The more common type of feedback loop, found in biological, electromechanical, and economic control processes, is the negative feedback loop. Figure 5.3 illustrates, in simple form, one of the basic feedback loops affecting regional dynamics. All other influences being ignored for the moment, an increase in population leads to an increased labor force; the higher labor force effects an increase in unemployment; this influences further outward migration from the region, which decreases population. The closed negative loop acts in the direction of opposing any initial change in one of its linkages. Although such a negative feedback loop is therefore referred to as self-correcting, it may really do much more or less than merely "correct." Even in the simple illustration shown in Figure 5.3, given the time required for information flow and action taking, and the further complications caused by differing responses by the aggregates of individuals and firms, the ultimate results are not readily predictable. The negative feedback loops that permeate economic systems may cause problems to shift over time from one direction of effect to another, causing economic fluctuations, business cycles, or various cobweb patterns of behavior. From these perspectives it appears important for formulation adequacy that such feedback loops be included in a regional model looking toward long-term analysis.

Dynamic Nature. The feedback relationships described in the previous section are dynamic; time is required for the chains of causes and effects to close. High regional unemployment in 1967 results in lower relative wages by perhaps 1970 that, in turn, may mean more jobs sometime during the 1970's and later. A dynamic approach recognizes the possibility that the situation may never be in static equilibrium. If we are studying a region over a fifty-year period, the region will in all probability begin the period out of equilibrium. Over the fifty-year period, it will grope toward equilibrium, but factors like changing death rates, technological shifts, and changes in the national economy will prevent it from ever reaching equilibrium. A regional simulation model that is dynamic may better reflect the levels of activity at the end of various time periods, but it may also better portray the patterns of adjustment in reaching the various levels. As we point out in the following sections, simulation models can illuminate the various patterns or paths regional economic variables may take over time in response to dynamic changes. Very often regional analysis requires not only a forecast of future levels of activity but also an understanding of the time patterns of adjustment.

Nonlinear Relationships. Another characteristic of the relationship between real world variables is that these relationships are not always linear.[1] The unemployment rate is one example of a nonlinear relationship as it involves the *ratio* of the unemployed to the total labor force. This ratio can be approximated by a linear function for small variations in either the unemployed or the total labor force, but large variations in this index must be expected over a fifty-year period. Restricting ourselves to linear approximations would force us to make many more compromises than we currently are making. The effect of these additional compromises on model adequacy would be difficult to evaluate.

Summary—Problem Characteristics. In summary, the problem characteristics arising in regional analysis and planning situations will often demand methodologies of approach that

1. Contain the capacity to treat a large number of variables,
2. Have the flexibility for handling wide variations in data types and functional relationships,

[1] A linear relationship is one of the form

$$A(t) \times (t) + B(t) \frac{dx(t)}{dt} + C(t) \frac{d^2x(t)}{dt^2} \cdots = f(t).$$

That such relationships can be solved analytically is, in some instances, a very desirable quality.

3. Are oriented toward dynamic considerations (as opposed to static analysis) including consideration of time-varying factors, and
4. Permit inclusion of feedback relationships.

Techniques of Regional Analysis

Given the problem characteristics and the demands upon the method of regional analysis just enumerated, let us consider in a general fashion what techniques are available. A simple classification includes quantitative and nonquantitative methods of regional analysis.

Nonquantitative Methods. Prior to the development of quantitative economics for regional science, analyses for economic projection and/or policy purposes were carried out in a largely descriptive or nonquantitative manner. It is reasonable to suggest that nonquantitative analysts in fact had mental models of the problem settings they analyzed. However, only the bare outlines of such models are often detectable from their writings and, many times, much controversy has ensued from attempts to quantify these earlier theories.[2]

Although the insights of these nonquantitative analysts were often brilliantly predictive, a number of problems arose in attempting to use the nonquantitative approach. First was the difficulty of explicitly treating the many variables of importance. The more complex the problem setting, the larger the number of factors needing consideration and the more entangled the factor relationships. With time and feedback phenomena included in the problem situation, intuitive analysis becomes nearly impossible to carry out.

Whether or not an initial analysis can be structured, additional problems arise in the lack of verifiability, reliability, and repeatability of such analyses. Without

[2] Largely qualitative works regarding national economic analysis that fall in this category are
J. M. Keynes, *The General Theory of Employment, Interest, and Money* (New York: Harcourt Brace, 1936).
J. A. Schumpeter, *The Theory of Economic Development; An Inquiry Into Profits, Capital, Credit, Interest, and the Business Cycle,* translated by Redversopie (New York: Oxford University Press, 1961).
W. W. Rostow, *The Stages of Economic Growth, A Non-Communist Manifesto* (Cambridge, England: University Press, 1962).

explicit quantitative statements of assumptions and relationships, checking any basis for the analysis, or redoing or updating it independently, becomes tortuous if not impossible. The only check seems to be an after-the-fact assessment of prediction accuracy, a rather undesirable assurance measure when actions based on long-term analyses or projections are being contemplated.

Without diminishing the important contributions of possible nonquantitative methods of regional analysis, explicit quantitative techniques seem preferable in most circumstances.

Quantitative Methods. Quantitative methods involve fitting the problems to some mathematical procedure that can be exercised without too much difficulty. The results of applying these quantitative approaches generally depend on how well the procedure fits the problem rather than on the execution of the procedure. The procedures that have been tried in regional analysis studies include trend extrapolation, input-output analysis, mathematical programming (especially linear programming), dynamic simulation, and others.

Because the objective of this book is to explain and put forth dynamic simulation and is not to analyze the comparative advantages of other methods of regional analysis, we shall discuss only the method of interest.[3]

Dynamic Simulation

Of the quantitative methods available in general, the simulation approach place the least restrictions on problem representation. Practically the only requirement is that the variables be quantifiable and the relationships between variables be defined.

[3] For a discussion of these other techniques see John R. Meyer, "Regional Economics: A Survey," *American Economic Review*, Vol. LIII, No. 1, Part 1 (March 1963), pp. 19–54, and Walter Isard, *Methods of Regional Analysis* (Cambridge, Mass.: The M.I.T. Press, 1961).

[4] Good background on the use of simulation models is provided in a series of three articles published in the *American Economic Review*, Volume L, No. 5, December 1960: G. H. Orcutt, "Simulation of Economic Systems," pp. 893–907; M. Shubik, "Simulation of Industry and Firm," pp. 908–919; and G. P. E. Clarkson and H. A. Simon, "Simulation of Group Behavior," pp. 920–932.

Broad philosophical and methodological treatment of the dynamic systems simulation approach used in the study presented in this book is contained in Jay W. Forrester, *Industrial Dynamics* (Cambridge, Mass.: The M.I.T. Press, 1961).

For many years, engineers have built physical models to aid in their designs. Wind tunnels, shiptowing tanks, scale models, and pilot plants have been used to check technical plans and ideas for flaws that might otherwise produce expensive failures. More recently, mathematical models have also come into vogue. A mathematical model differs from a physical model in that the latter obeys (hopefully) the same laws as the object being modeled because it is physically similar, while the builder of the mathematical model tries explicitly to identify and express in mathematical form the laws obeyed by the object he is modeling.

Once there is a precise mathematical statement of the situation, there are two ways to determine how the model will behave:

1. The equations can be solved analytically, and or
2. The equations can be simulated.

In general, if the model is to be solved analytically, it will have to be linear and relatively simple. If these conditions are met, then a number of calculations are possible, such as deriving maximum or minimum values for given variables under certain assumptions relating to the other variables. In addition to the simplifications required to make optimizing models mathematically tractable, their use requires the specification of objective functions. As we pointed out in Chapters 3 and 4, regional analysis may often have to face situations where objective functions cannot be specified because of the conflicts between goals and because of lack of consensus between various groups within and between regions.

If the manipulations necessary to get an analytic solution are not possible (or too expensive), then the model can be simulated. If the conditions are known at one point in time, the equations can be used to compute the conditions at the next point in time. By repeating this process, one can move step by step through time.[5] Thus one is able to calculate the course of the variables over any time interval

---

[5] If an analogue rather than a digital computer is used, the model moves continuously rather than step by step through simulated time—a difference that is inconsequential for this discussion.

desired and produce various patterns of regional adjustment corresponding to various assumptions about dynamic change.

The difficulty of the simulation approach is that all parameters must be fixed before the calculations (simulation) are made, and that the only way to measure the impact of alternative parameter values on the results is, therefore, to change the parameter and recalculate the results—that is, to conduct the simulation again.

Fortunately, there are several significant advantages to simulation:

1. Simulation can be inexpensive. In particular, the type of simulation used for the Susquehanna River Basin model is a low-cost approach.
2. Minor changes (such as investigating alternative formulations and parameter values) can be easily made.
3. The model is not restricted to linear formulations.
4. The model can contain many variables.

There are several types of simulation.

1. *Microanalytic or event simulation.* In this technique the microstructure of the system being simulated is carefully reproduced in the model.[6] When simulating a company, for instance, individual orders are traced through each step of production. However, in the case of a broad economic study such detail is obviously impossible if the modeler attempts to include every event associated with every individual and company in the economy under examination. Using a sample population in lieu of the total population provides most of the advantages of this technique without the prohibitive computer cost. Nevertheless, the costs are often still large.[7]

[6] So-called "discrete change" simulation languages such as SIMSCRIPT or GPSS are often associated with microanalytic or event simulation.

[7] Orcutt states that it required 1 hour of IBM 704 time to simulate 1 year of a model including only a demographic sector that excluded economic factors such as labor-force participation, migration, etc. He estimates that the more modern IBM 7090 would require 5 minutes to do the same task. See Guy Orcutt *et al.*, *Microanalysis of Socioeconomic Systems* (New York: Harper & Brothers, 1961), pp. 311–312. In contrast, the continuous simulation approach adopted for the Susquehanna River Basin Study used only 1 minute of IBM 7090 time to simulate 50 years of the total model's operation.

2. *Simulation of econometric models.* In this approach a difference equation model is first built by econometric methods, and then the resultant model is simulated. Econometricians have only recently started to simulate their models, and the techniques are still in the process of being developed. The primary obstacle lies in the difficulty of solving large sets of nonlinear simultaneous equations.[8]

3. *Continuous simulation.* While the study described in this book is the first example known to the authors of continuous simulation applied to regional economics, this technique has been used extensively by engineers. With this technique, the real world is described by a set of simultaneous differential equations. The model can be simulated on an analogue computer or, more recently, on a digital computer. The analogue computer does not lend itself as easily as the digital computer to the simulation of large models. With the digital computer the set of simultaneous differential equations is approximated by a set of nonsimultaneous difference equations.[9]

Continuous simulation was chosen for our problem because the costs were reasonable, the numerical methods for approximating simultaneous differential equations were developed, and because a computer program was available to reduce significantly the cost of programming and running the model. The program, which is called DYNAMO, is a special-purpose compiler.[10] It translates a model

[8] For examples, see Irma Adelman and Frank L. Adelman, "The Dynamic Properties of the Klein-Goldberger Model," *Econometrica*, 27 (October 1959), 596–625; *Brookings Quarterly Econometric Model of the United States*, edited by J. S. Dusenberry, G. Fromm, L. R. Klein, and E. Kuh (Chicago, Ill.: Rand McNally & Co., 1965).

[9] The analog and digital approaches are described, respectively, in Arnold Tustin, *The Mechanism of Economic Systems* (Cambridge, Mass.: Harvard University Press, 1953); and Jay W. Forrester, *Industrial Dynamics* (Cambridge, Mass.: The M.I.T. Press, 1961).

[10] See *DYNAMO User's Manual, Second Edition*, by Alexander L. Pugh III (Cambridge, Mass.: The M.I.T. Press, 1963). DYNAMO is available for the IBM 7090, 7094, 7040, and 7044 computers. Slightly modified versions of DYNAMO are also available on the Burroughs B-5000 and the Hitachi 5020 computers. A new version (DYNAMO II) is currently being written for the new generation of computers.

from an easily understood equation language using simple mnemonics to machine language, runs the model, and produces tabulated and plotted results.

General-purpose program compilers like FORTRAN might be used for the same purpose as DYNAMO. In fact, a DYNAMO-type model is well within their capability.[11] Unfortunately, a general-purpose program must require the user to spell out the computational procedure exactly. It cannot make assumptions about what the programmer intends. It cannot even check whether the computational procedure is a reasonable one. Methods of data input and output are very general and therefore require elaborate specifications. Furthermore, the general-purpose compilers and computer program loaders are relatively slow, adding to the cost of computation. Finally, the error remarks used to assist the analyst in finding errors in his model that are produced by these general-purpose compilers are frequently quite obscure. The net result is that professional programmers are almost a requirement when one is using a general-purpose language.

In summary, the use of DYNAMO offers the following advantages:

1. More easily understood model statements,
2. Easily specified outputs in both tabular and plot formats,
3. Automatic ordering of equations for computation of results,
4. Thorough error checking (debugging) and easily understood error remarks,
5. Faster compilation and faster simulation operations.

DYNAMO carries out the translation of the complete Susquehanna model from equation form to final computer instructions in about 60 seconds.[12] The efficiency of continuous simulation when used in conjunction with the DYNAMO compiler

[11] A modified version of the Susquehanna model programmed in FORTRAN has been developed by the University of Alabama in relation to a study of the economy of the Coosa-Mobile-Alabama River Basin.

[12] When all the subregions of the Susquehanna were being studied in a single simulation run, a sector expansion program was used as a preprocessor. This permitted the reduction in physical size of the model from 3,000 cards to 1,000 cards and added another 3 minutes to the time required to translate the model.

can be seen in the fact that the computer rental budget was less than 5 percent of the total research budget.

Specific Methodology

While there are four clearly definable steps to our methodology, one aspect underlies all the steps—the iterative approach.[13] Any step in the research may suggest that an earlier step can be improved upon and, in fact, is worth improving given the goals of the research. The fact that an earlier step is being reviewed does not necessarily imply that work accomplished in earlier steps must be discarded.

This iterative approach is perhaps most easily understood in the context of model improvement. For example, a particular formulation for migration is suggested by real world considerations. This formulation requires several parameters that are determined by careful study of census data. The formulation is tried in several model runs using various parameter estimates. The results of these runs indicate that migration is a sensitive part of the model. This suggests that further research, both into the basic formulation and the parameters, is in order. The additional research may yield a formulation that includes more factors than the original, different factors, and different parameter estimates.

During the time the model is being used, it is kept operative and subject to revision. In our experience, less than 1 percent of the model was altered between runs after the initial debugging period. Several potential revisions may be under study simultaneously. There is no reason to consider the model final or complete even though it is viewed as usable.

The four steps that form the framework of our methodology are

1. Problem definition,
2. Model construction,
3. Model simulation, and
4. Model validation.

[13] This iterative approach is discussed in detail in Chapter 13, and further aspects are mentioned in Appendix A.

Each of these steps is described in the sections that follow. To explain our views on model construction more fully, a small, hypothetical model is specified, and the results of simulating this model are shown. Under the section on "model simulation," we discuss our philosophy on "how to use" a model.

Problem Definition

The careful definition of a problem may seem like an obvious first step, but the failure to do so can lead to much difficulty. If there is no specific problem, there is no bench mark against which to make any of the many judgments that must be a part of such a research undertaking. For instance, how can one decide what to include or exclude in a model? What level of aggregation is tolerable? While answers to such questions are not always obvious even when one has a specific goal, there is no basis for making them without a goal.

Within any region, such as the Susquehanna River Basin, a variety of study objectives are possible, and these objectives will often imply different methodological requirements. In the case of the Susquehanna study, the sponsors were interested in determining the future adequacy of water resources in the region and what factors might alter the need for water. They wanted to assess the extent of future needs for dams and other facilities affecting the quantity and quality of water available. Furthermore, they wished to be able to estimate the impact that various proposed systems of river works might have on the economy of the Susquehanna River Basin. Traditional analyses of federal water resource development programs are based upon long-term projections of fifty or more years. Therefore, a long-term orientation appeared to be required in order to assure comparability with any federal analyses.

Many examples of specific problem delineation decisions with implications on our model-building effort could be cited. For instance, the decision that the questions under study were not closely related to the business cycle allowed the model-builders to avoid short-term national economic considerations and focus on the long term. It was further decided that the geographic limits of the model were not to include the Chesapeake Bay, despite the fact that the control of the flow of the Susquehanna River might affect several physical and economic factors in and around the Bay.[14]

In this same spirit, one must be careful not to just "build a model of a region" without an end in mind. A model is a means to an end; it is not an end in itself. This is not to say that goals cannot be broad, however, as long as all concerned realize the broad scope involved. For instance, a broad, worthwhile goal might be to build a model to enhance understanding of certain behavior within a system. Here again, the goal is understanding of the prespecified phenomena, and not the model itself.

Model Construction

The development of a model can be divided into the problems of (1) what to model and (2) how to model.

What to Model

BREADTH. The first problem in building a model is deciding what should be included and what can safely be excluded. The obvious answer is to include what is important relative to the problem and to exclude everything else. Given that there is an explicit problem, this is a start, but we are left with the problem of ferreting out important relationships and measuring them.

The importance of some variables is obvious. In a regional model, variables such as population, labor force, and employment will require treatment at various levels of detail. (The question of level of aggregation is discussed later.) The need to study certain other variables is not nearly as obvious. For instance, there is the

[14] Exclusion of the Chesapeake Bay from the model was possible because it was doubtful that effects on the bay caused by activity in the basin would feed back on the basin. The relevant question was, therefore, how interested were we in the bay and the effects of the Susquehanna's flows on it in relation to the scope of the research? Curiously, this interest grew during the study, until it finally reached the point where the sponsor group was actively considering research on this problem when this book was submitted to the publisher.

question of studying the skill level of the labor force, whose significance is often ignored because it is difficult to measure. However, when one notices the number of feedback loops in which skills participate, he becomes suspicious that this factor merits careful investigation.[15] The fact that there is only a limited amount of data available on skills is not sufficient reason to ignore the information completely, even though it may be difficult to place a high degree of faith in the results. In certain instances we know that there is a definite relationship and, if we choose to ignore skills, we are in effect saying that there is no relationship.

The next consideration after deciding to include a variable is whether it should be included exogenously or endogenously. Feedback considerations answer this question primarily. If the variable is a part of a significant feedback loop, it must be included endogenously; otherwise exogenous treatment will probably suffice. For example, the nation's economy plays a significant role in the level of activity of the basin's economy, but the basin's economy is sufficiently small so that it does not significantly affect the economy of the nation as a whole. Thus national economic changes can be handled as exogenous factors. On the other hand, the population is affected by the availability of jobs, both through its long-term influence on the birth rate and by its shorter-term effect on the migration rate. Consequently, job availability must be treated as endogenous.

DEPTH. Once it has been decided to include a quantity and to treat it endogenously or exogenously, we are still left with the question of what level of aggregation is appropriate. Use of aggregates tends to keep things simpler, and on this basis alone is preferable wherever their use does not interfere with the objectives of the study. If one disaggregates too extensively, he finds himself adding complexity without adding to the explanatory value of the model. For instance, in a region, if one disaggregates industry into all the four-digit SIC codes, he could easily end up attempting to predict the future of a number of individual companies or even, in some instances, the birth of the industry in the subregion. Such detail must be carefully considered both in the light of the problem under attack and the detail level of the balance of the model.

[15] The skills analysis is discussed in the latter portion of Chapter 8 and in Chapter 12.

In general, the desirability of modeling aggregate relations depends on (1) whether questions being asked of the model can be answered with information about aggregates and (2) the extent to which meaningful, stable relations between aggregates exist in the real world system being modeled. It is fairly obvious how the level of aggregation may depend on the first criterion. For example, if we are interested in the number of people in different age groups rather than in total population only, then we would have to disaggregate into the age groups of interest. However, even if we are interested only in total population, as we are in this study, it still might be desirable to disaggregate by age. This would be the case if meaningful stable relationships could not be established between the total population aggregate and other related variables in the model. If we do not disaggregate population into a number of age classes, we must assume either (1) that a fixed percentage of the total is and will remain in each of the age classes, or (2) that there is a *linear* relationship between age and the behaviors such as migration, child bearing, and labor-force participation.[16] An examination of the data very quickly reveals that the relationships between age and the other demographic variables of interest are all extremely nonlinear (see Tables 7.1, 7.2, 7.3, and 7.4) so that the latter assumption is definitely not tenable. The former assumption, that the percentage of people in each age class will remain fixed, is, on examination, equally untenable. If one considers an area with a high unemployment rate, he would expect to find that many of the young adults have emigrated. This is an important fact because this is the group that produces the most children. Consequently, one would expect a lower-than-normal percentage in the young adult age classes and a birth rate based on the total population that is lower than normal. Failing to disaggregate population by age class would ignore this consideration and leave one on shaky grounds.

In the light of these considerations, population in the Susquehanna model was disaggregated into six groups. As described in Chapter 8, the age classification

[16] If we could assume a linear relationship between these variables and age, then age effects could be incorporated into the model by means of an aggregate linear relationship such as: migration $= a + b$ (average age). This, of course, would entail the additional problem of modeling changes in the "average age" variable.

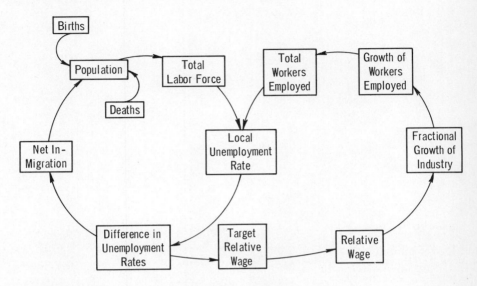

FIGURE 5.4. A flow chart of a simplified subregional model.

procedure was devised to yield age groups that either (1) were so small, as in the case of the 14–19 year old group, that it became reasonable to assume a fixed percentage intragroup distribution, or (2) showed such little variation over the age range included within the group, as in the case of the 45–64 year old group, that it was not necessary to assume a fixed percentage intragroup distribution.[17]

How To Model

EQUATION WRITING. The details of writing the equations for a model will be explained by actually building a *highly* simplified and hypothetical model of a subregional economy. A diagram of this economy is given in Figure 5.4.

There has been no effort to disaggregate the population by age or employment. The population depends on births, deaths, and migration. Birth and deaths in turn depend on the population. The labor force is simply a fraction of the population. The local unemployment rate depends on the labor force and the number of workers employed. The difference between local and national unemployment rates determines the migration rate that when multiplied by the population determines the number of people migrating.

On the employment side of the model, the difference in unemployment rates determines a target relative wage, which after a delay becomes the actual wage relative to the rest of the country. The wage in turn determines the growth rate of employment that, when multiplied by the number of people currently employed becomes the number of new jobs added each year.

As was explained earlier, we are constructing a model with differential equations

[17] If all ages within a particular age group exhibit the same responses for behaviors of interest, then we may conclude that age will not help explain or predict intragroup variation in these behaviors. Thus, once population is classified into such homogeneous groups, age distribution within each group can be ignored.

1at will be approximated by a set of difference equations. The model is then
ompiled and simulated on the computer using the DYNAMO system. As with
very programming system, the input must be in the language that goes with the
/stem.

The DYNAMO language, rather than emphasizing the differential form of
1e equation, stresses the difference equation approximation. Each variable will
ave a time subscript indicating the point in time for which it is being calculated
r at which it was calculated. Variables are calculated for time K; depending on
1e type of variable, they are calculated either from variables calculated at time
or from other variables calculated previously at time K.

"Level" variables, which correspond to stocks in economic terms and to
1tegrals in mathematical terms, are calculated for time K from their value at
me J and from the flows into or out of the level. The flows also are calculated
r time J. The equation for population is an example of a level relationship.

$$L \quad POP.K = POP.J + (DT)(BRTH.J + NIM.J - DTHS.J)$$

s can be seen, the time subscripts are set off from the variable name by a period.
he equation for the population POP at time K (the current time) is equal to its
alue at time J (the last instant of time for which values were calculated) plus
T, the increment of time between J and K (delta time), times the sum of the
umber of births per year $BRTH$ and the net inflow of migrants per year NIM
ss the number of deaths per year $DTHS$, all calculated earlier at time J.

The other type of variable, which is called an auxiliary, is calculated at time
from other variables that were calculated earlier at time K. DYNAMO
1tomatically reorders equations so that the order of computation is proper.
should no amount of reordering satisfy the condition that all variables are
1lculated for time K before they are used during time K, DYNAMO prints an
ror statement; simultaneous equations are not permitted.) An example of an
1xiliary equation is the one for the number of births.[18]

[18] DYNAMO recognizes a third class of equation, rates. Rates have the same mathematical
rm as auxiliaries, and consequently auxiliaries can be used in their place. Although most
dustrial dynamics models use all three equation types, the Susquehanna model has been
:veloped using only levels and auxiliaries.

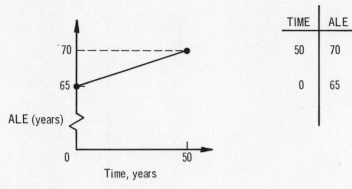

TIME	ALE
50	70
0	65

FIGURE 5.5. Average life expectancy.

$A \quad BRTH.K = (BRTHR.K)(POP.K)$

The number of births $BRTH$, measured in units of men per year, is the product of the birth rate $BRTHR$ (men per year per man) and the population POP (men) In this simple model, the birth rate will be assumed constant:

$C \quad BRTHR = .04 \qquad$ men/year/man

The number of deaths is another auxiliary. In this case the death rate will be stated in terms of the life expectancy: the number of deaths per year $DTHS$ is equal to the population POP divided by the average life expectancy ALE.

$A \quad DTHS.K = POP.K/ALE.K$

While this simple formulation does give the proper average life expectancy, the population variable ignores the problem of the distribution of ages. Because this model is intended to be demonstration of an equation-writing technique rather than an accurate representation of reality, the problem will be ignored.

The average life expectancy ALE increases with time as shown in Figure 5.5. A very convenient way to incorporate this into the model is to use a special DYNAMO form called a Table function. The range of the independent variable $TIME$ is given as two of the function arguments, while the values of the dependent variable are given on a special constant (C) card.

$A \quad ALE.K = TABLE\ (TALE,\ TIME.K,\ 0,\ 50,\ 50)$

The arguments of the DYNAMO table function are
1. The table of values (in this case, $TALE$),
2. The independent variable ($TIME.K$),
3. The value of the independent variable corresponding to the first value in the table (here equal to $TIME = 0$),
4. The value of the independent variable corresponding to the last value in the table (shown as $TIME = 50$), and
5. The increment in the independent variable corresponding to adjacent values in the table (here shown also as 50).

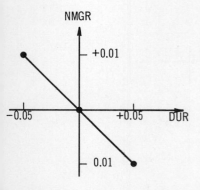

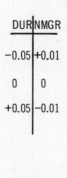

FIGURE 5.6. Net migration and unemployment rates.

The table in this rather simple case contains but two values corresponding to life expectancy values at $TIME = 0$ and $TIME = 50$ years. This assumes a linear improvement in life expectancy over the 50-year simulation period.[19]

$C \quad TALE^* = 65/70$

The auxiliary for number of people migrating into the region per year NIM is the product of the size of the region in terms of its population POP and the rate of migration $NMGR$. Negative in-migration will be considered as out-migration.

$A \quad NIM.K = (NMGR.K)(POP.K)$

The migration rate $NMGR$ (expressed in men per year per man) can also be conveniently expressed as a table function of the difference between local and national unemployment rates DUR. This is shown in Figure 5.6. The fact that the differences between adjacent values of the dependent variable $NMGR$ are equal is a result of our choice here to have a straight line and is *not* a requirement of the table function.

$A \quad NMGR.K = TABLE \ (TNMGR, DUR.K, -.05, .05, .05)$

$C \quad TNMGR^* = .01/0/-.01$

The difference between local and national unemployment rates is calculated as one would expect.

$A \quad DUR.K = LUR.K - NUR.K$

For simplicity, the national unemployment rate NUR is assumed to be constant.

$C \quad NUR = .05$

The local unemployment rate LUR is computed from the total labor force TLF and the total workers employed TWE.

$A \quad LUR.K = (1/TLF.K)(TLF.K - TWE.K)$

---

[19] In the equation the asterisk indicates that $TALE$ is a table of values rather than a simple constant.

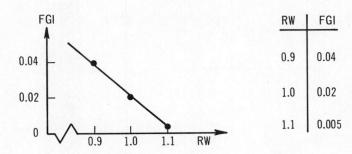

FIGURE 5.7. Fractional growth rate and relative wages.

The total labor force TLF is assumed to be a fixed fraction FPE of the population POP.

A $TLF.K = (FPE)(POP.K)$

C $FPE = .4$

Industrial activity in the region is measured by the number of workers employed. This is computed by a level relating the total workers employed TWE to the growth rate of the workers employed GWE.

L $TWE.K = TWE.J + (DT)(GWE.J)$

The growth rate of workers employed GWE is the product of the fractional growth rate of industry FGI and the total workers currently employed TWE.

A $GWE.K = (FGI.K)(TWE.K)$

In our simple model, the fractional growth rate of industry will depend only on the region's wages relative to the rest of the nation. Again we will use a table function. See Figure 5.7.

A $FGI.K = TABLE\ (TFGI, RW.K, .9, 1.1, .1)$

C $TFGI* = .04/.02/.005$

After a delay, the relative wage RW responds to the relative unemployment rate. If the relative unemployment rate goes up, the wage relative to the rest of the nation will fall after a period of time. The transformation of relative unemployment rate to wage rate and the delay will be done in separate steps. The order of the two steps is unimportant; here we will first transform unemployment to a target relative wage TRW and then delay the target value to form the relative wage. The transformation is again a table function. See Figure 5.8.

A $TRW.K = TABLE\ (TTRW, DUR.K, -.05, .05, .05)$

C $TTRW* = 1.05/1/.9$

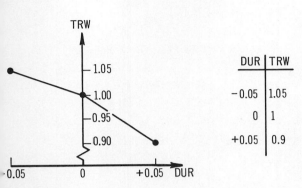

FIGURE 5.8. Target relative wage and unemployment.

Up to this point there has been little discussion of time subscripts. The rules are mechanical: .K on the left of the =, and .J on the right if the equation is a level equation, or .K on the right if it is an auxiliary. One does not get a historical value by using .G or .F. Instead, one writes an explicit equation to delay a value. One of the simplest equations to form a delay or to average a variable is the following:

L $RW.K = RW.J + (DT)(1/DRW)(TRW.J - RW.J)$

The equation both delays TRW by DRW years and smooths TRW. It is the DYNAMO form of the exponential smoothing equation frequently written in the form

$$RW_t = (1 - \alpha)(RW_{t-1}) + (\alpha)(TRW_{t-1})$$

where α is equal to $1/DRW$ if the time step between t and $t - 1$ is one year.[20] This equation states that the relative wage RW is the target relative wage TRW delayed by DRW years.

C $DRW = 10$ years

All the active equations have been specified; it is necessary to specify the initial values for the level equations. Because this is a model of a hypothetical region, we shall not defend the choice of values.

N $POP = 1000$

N $TWE = 360$

N $RW = .92$

The only tasks remaining are to indicate which variables are to be tabulated and which are to be plotted and to specify the length of the run, the size of DT,

[20] This can be seen in the equation for RW by setting DT equal 1 (year) and α equal $1/DRW$) and then regrouping terms. For a discussion of exponential smoothing, see Jay W. Forrester, *Industrial Dynamics* (Cambridge, Mass.: The M.I.T. Press 1961), Appendix E.

```
PAGE 2        SUS-1        SIMPLE SUSQUEHANNA MØDEL    06/28/67    2149.1

PØP=P, BRTH=B, NIW=I, LUR=U, RW=W

       0              0.03              0.06              0.09            0.12    U
     0.91             0.93              0.95              0.97            0.99    W
     -50              0                 50                100             150     IB
       0              1000              2000              3000            4000    P
    0- - - - W - I -P- - - - - -B- - - - - - - - - - - U - - - -        .
    •          W     I P           B  •          U    •                 .
    •            W   I .P          B  •    U          •                 .
    •            W IP              UB •                •                 .
    •             IP  W    U       B •                •                 .
    •             .IP   U   W      B •                •                 .
    •             .IPU            B•                  •            . BW
    •             .I UP           B •   W             •                 .
    •             .I UP           B         W         •                 .
    •             .IU P           B                W  •                 .
   10 - - - - - - .I  UP- - - - - B- - - - - - - - W - - - - -          .
    •             .I    UP        .B              W   •             . PU
    •             .I     P        .B             W    •             . PU
    •             .I       P      . B                W•                 .
    •             .I      PU      . B              W  •                 .
    •              I       P  U   . B                 •  W              .
    •              I       P  U   . B                 •  W .            .
    •              I        P  U  . B                 •  W.             .
    •              I        P  U  . B                 •  W.             .
    •              I.       P   U . B                 •  W.             .
   20 - - - - - - I.- - - - -P- -U- - B- - - - - - - .- - - - -W- - -   .
    •             I.         P   U.   B              •         W.        .
    •             I.         P    U   B              •         W.        .
    •             I.         P    U    B             •         W .       .
    •             I.         P    U   . B            •         W .       .
    •             I.         P    U     B            •         W         .
    •             I.         P    U     B            •         W         .
    •             I.          PU        B            •         W         .
    •             I.          P         B            •         W    . PU
    •             I.          UP         B           •        W          .
   30 - - - - - - I.- - - - - UP- - - B - -.- - - - W- - •- -            .
    •             I.          U P       B       •       W                .
    •             I.          U  P      B       •       W                .
    •             I.          U   P     B       •       W                .
    •             I.          U    P    B       •       W                .
    •             I.          U     P   B  •            W                .
    •             I.          U      P   B•             W                .
    •             I.          U       P  B.             W                .
    •             I.          U        P  B             W                .
    •             I.          U         P   .B          W                .
   40 - - - - - - I.- - - - - U- - - -P- - -.B- - - W- - - -             .
    •              I •        U          P  . B      W                   .
    •              I •        U           P  . B     W                   .
    •              I .        U            P  . B    W                   .
    •                I .      U             P . B    W                   .
    •                I  .     U             P.  B    W                   .
    •                I  .     U              P.  B   W                   .
    •                I   .    U               P  B   W                   .
    •                I   .    U               . P  B W                   .
    •                I    .   U                . P  BW             . BW
   50 - - - - - - - I -.- - - U- - - - - - - -.- - P - WB- - -
```

EXHIBIT 5.2. Subregion-plotted results.

GE 1   SUS-1   SIMPLE SUSQUEHANNA MODEL   06/28/67   2149.1

TIME	POP	BRTH	DTHS	NIM	LUR	TWE	GWE	RW	TRW
E+00	E+00	E+00	E+00	E+00	E+00	E+00	E+00	E+00	E+00
.000	1000.0	40.00	15.385	-10.000	.10000	360.0	12.960	.92000	.9000
5.000	1114.1	44.56	17.009	2.350	.03945	428.1	13.597	.94118	1.0105
0.000	1280.0	51.20	19.393	3.786	.03521	494.0	12.772	.97071	1.0148
5.000	1462.5	58.50	21.993	.755	.04742	557.3	12.726	.98582	1.0026
0.000	1652.3	66.09	24.662	-2.446	.05740	623.0	13.845	.9888Y	.9852
5.000	1855.2	74.21	27.485	-4.006	.06080	697.0	15.941	.98564	.9784
0.000	2081.5	83.26	30.610	-4.328	.06040	782.3	18.336	.98281	.9792
5.000	2338.6	93.54	34.140	-4.429	.0594W	879.8	20.801	.98179	.9811
0.000	2630.6	105.22	38.124	-4.827	.05917	990.0	23.429	.98167	.9817
5.000	2960.6	118.42	42.599	-5.540	.05936	1114.0	26.378	.98160	.9813
0.000	3332.9	133.32	47.613	-6.429	.05964	1253.7	29.747	.98136	.9807

EXHIBIT 5.1. Simple subregional model. Tabular results.

and the frequency with which output printing and plotting will be done.

PRINT   1)POP/2)BRTH/3)DTHS/4)NIM/5)LUR/6)TWE/7)-GWE/8)
         RW/9)TRW

PLOT   POP = P/BRTH = B, NIM = I/LUR = U/RW = W

SPEC   DT = .25/LENGTH = 50/PRTPER = 5/PLTPER = 1 YR

The tabular results are shown in Exhibit 5.1 and the plotted results in 5.2.

How To Use the Model. Broadly, there are two ways to use model results or simulations—individually as projections and in groups as sensitivity measures. Use of the model simply to make projections is fraught with dangers. Some projections will be good for one purpose and not others. Many potential users will not understand how the projections were derived and will expect unreasonable accuracy. Some people may use the results without even reading the report that accompanies them. Major plans may be made as though the numbers were god-given.

Sometimes a more basic difficulty evolves when a model is used to generate projections as an input to policy-related decision-making. Often, *one* set of projections is selected and then various policies are analyzed using *the* projection as an input. Two kinds of difficulties arise here. First, the projections are derived independently of the policy considerations when, in fact, alternative policies may affect the projections differently. Thus, feedback from policy to the economy is ignored, often even when such feedback is claimed as justification for the policy. Second, while it is conceivable that one could test a policy under a variety of alternative projections, in fact, this is often so difficult to do as a practical matter that it is not done. If it is done, the number of alternative projections tested is usually very restricted. Therefore, a better designed study will incorporate the policy considerations of interest within the over-all economic "projection" model and will employ extensive sensitivity analysis to evaluate a range of policies under a range of conditions.

Sensitivity analysis can also be used to aid in directing model development.

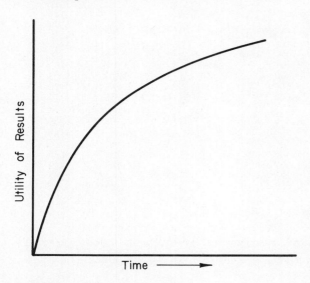

FIGURE 5.9. Utility of results with time.

All studies are made with limited budgets, and it is important to allocate research dollars and manpower to those subject areas with the greatest payoff. By developing a working model early in the research program, it is possible to start to develop results in line with research objectives very quickly. Iteration between model simulation and additional data collection and analysis often leads to enhancement of the results in the manner suggested in Figure 5.9. As indicated in the figure, we believe that large gains can often be made relatively quickly.

Nevertheless, the continuing use of sensitivity analysis will indicate those areas of the model in which reasonable changes in parameter values or formulations have significant impact on model results. This process identifies the principal areas of model uncertainty, providing clues to the appropriate cautions that should be applied to the model results at any stage in model development. Additionally, the sensitivity analysis indicates those portions of the model that deserve the greatest additional research. Dollars can be saved by not studying parameters that have little or no effect on the results.

Model Validation

Debate on the subject of model validation has generated much heat and little light. It is little understood and could be the subject of much useful research. A few thoughts of the authors are presented.

"Model validity" is a bad choice of words in that the words carry the connotation of a simple dichotomy—the model is valid or not valid. In practice, the problem is never that simple. The real issue is, "Is the model good enough to answer my questions?" Here also, the answer is almost always clouded. At present there are few objective tests that can be applied. Especially there are none that can give an answer relative to a specific use of the model. So the question

comes one of whether the builder has confidence in his model for the use to
hich he plans to apply it—admittedly a subjective evaluation. This being so, he
annot prove the validity to anyone else, but he can answer the question for
imself.[21]

Attention to three areas can contribute to the model-builder's confidence in
is model.

Microstructure. Is the microstructure of the model reasonable? Have the
appropriate variables been included and is their dependency on other
variables sensible? Is the form of the dependency reasonable? Is the direction
of cause and effect correct?

Statistical fit. Have the sensitive parameters been carefully derived from data?
Have the residuals been carefully studied for signs of missing variables?

Over-all model behavior. Is the over-all model behavior reasonable? Are there
peculiar biases toward special modes of behavior that one would not
reasonably expect? If the model is run over a period of time for which there
is historical data, does it reproduce history reasonably well?

The last point, attempting to reproduce historical values, merits additional
mment. It is the one technique that most people think of when faced with the
lidity issue. The principal problems encountered here are expense and meaning
 the results. In order to make such analyses, additional data must be gathered
ncerning the historical period of interest and must be carefully checked for
nsistency with the more current data used in constructing the model. As methods
 reporting data often change with time, the problem of consistency is a serious
e, often rendering this type of model test an almost impossible task.

The results of historical simulations are also difficult to interpret. The results
ill never agree perfectly with historical data. What errors are acceptable? Are
 e results good for the wrong reasons? Does a representation of the past guarantee
ceptable projections for the future?

[21] Of course, if model results are to be used, it is often necessary for the model-builder
 impart his faith in the model to others who must take action.

While historical analysis will seldom establish validity, there are other benefits to be gained from such an effort. In studying the results of a simulation which are generally judged as reasonable, those portions of the model that performed the poorest are obvious nominees for additional research. Furthermore, an unsatisfactor historical run does suggest that substantial additional work may be necessary. Our experiences with historical runs of the Susquehanna model are described in Chapter 12.

Summary

This chapter has spelled out the principal features of our methodology and the reasoning that led us to it. The core of our approach is the preservation of the dynamic feedback loops that influence regional economic behavior. Because the system we are dealing with is large and nonlinear and features feedback as well, dynamic simulation was the only practical tool to use in studying the problem. After defining the problem, we endeavored to build a model of sufficient breadth to include important feedback loops and with sufficient depth to represent the variables of interest in an adequate fashion.

Previous chapters have described the philosophy within which the authors believe a regional economic model for river-basin analysis and planning should be assembled. This chapter describes the Susquehanna River and the economy of its drainage basin so as to give perspective to the chapters that follow and outline the Susquehanna model in some detail.

The Susquehanna River and Its Drainage Basin

The Susquehanna River shown in Figure 6.1 is formed near Cooperstown, New York, at Lake Otsego and flows 450 miles to the Chesapeake Bay. The river has a drainage area of about 27,500 square miles, of which about 6,450 are in New York, about 21,000 are in Pennsylvania, and about 250 are in Maryland. The West Branch, its principal tributary, drains an area of approximately 7,000 square miles and flows some 240 miles through the center of Pennsylvania. The second largest tributary, the Juniata, drains an area of about 3,400 square miles. Table 6.1. presents information concerning the river and its tributaries.

The precipitation in the Susquehanna basin is generally characteristic of the humid eastern United States, averaging annually about 40 inches over the entire basin. Runoff is greatest during March, April, and May and is least during the fall months.

Delimiting the Study Area

Chapter 3 discussed the general problem of selecting the proper geographic units for regional analysis. In terms of selecting the study area for the Susquehanna program, the following factors were emphasized:

1. *The hydrologic entity.* Because much of the focus of the study was upon water, the physical drainage basin of the Susquehanna was the major factor considered in selecting the over-all study area.

2. *Regional economic considerations.* Because the study was regional and economic in nature, it was necessary to ensure that the boundaries of existing economic

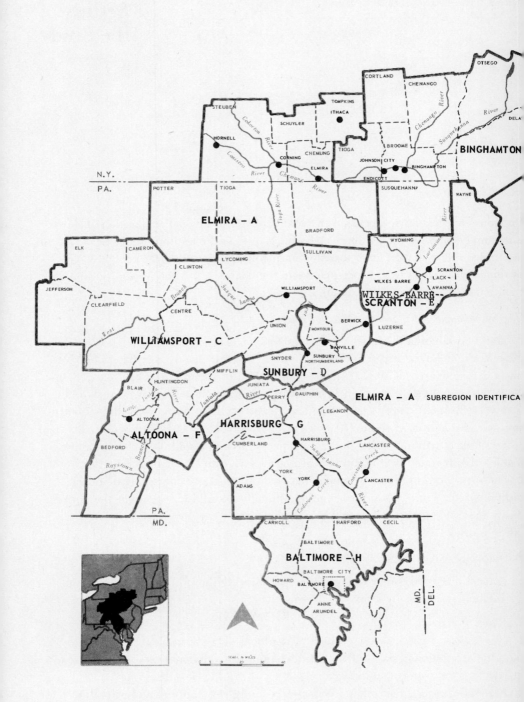

FIGURE 6.1. The Susquehanna River Basin and its economic subregions.

TABLE 6.1
Stream Data—Susquehanna River Basin

	Drainage Area (square miles)	Length (miles)	Average Slope (feet/mile)
Susquehanna	27,501*	450	2.7
West Branch to Juniata	1,441	38	2.4
Juniata to mouth	4,355	85	3.9
Unadilla	556	55	3.4
Chenango	1,621	78	3.9
Lackawanna	346	40	26.0
Chemung	2,596	46	4.4
Tioga	1,378	43	10.6
Cohocton	608	41	8.8
West Branch	6,990	240	6.5
Clearfield	392	62	13.2
Sinnemahoning	1,044	53	2.6
Bald Eagle	779	51	11.2
Pine	991	72	13.2
Loyalsock	506	50	24.0
Juniata	3,409	90	2.7
Frankstown	188	56	10.4
Raystown	963	110	3.9

* Total of entire basin.
Source: *Susquehanna River Basin and Chesapeake Bay Area*, Planning Status Report, Federal Power Commission, 1967.

regions were not unduly distorted in the process of selecting the study area. For instance, areas tied to the economy of the basin were not arbitrarily excluded from the study area merely because they were not in the drainage basin.

3. *Data considerations.* The "facts of life" regarding regional data availability dictate that the county be the basic building block of study areas selected for most regional analysis purposes.

In light of these considerations, the study area selected was composed of whole county units. In the majority of cases where a county is partly within the physical drainage basin, this county was included in the study area. An exception to this general rule occurred when only a tiny portion of the county was in the basin, or when the economy of the county was tied to regions outside the basin and the county did not place heavy demands on the river for its water. For example, Cecil County, Maryland, fell in this latter category because its economy is tied to counties in Delaware and its demands on the river are small. For this reason, Cecil County was never incorporated into the model although it received preliminary study to determine its water use patterns and general economic characteristics. On the other hand, Subregion H, Baltimore, was included in the study area and was modeled because it presently draws water from the basin and might draw more water from this source in the future.

Once the study area was defined, it was then necessary to divide it into economic subregions. This was necessary for two reasons. First, the various economies within the study area were developing at grossly different rates. Some, in fact, declined in population and employment from 1950 to 1960. The second reason for subregionalization related to the water orientation of the study. Gross, basin-wide demands on the water resource mean very little. Subregionalization was the first step in terms of localizing the various water needs.

Subregionalization was accomplished within the context of defined labor markets and retail and wholesale trading areas. Labor markets were defined on the basis of commuting patterns.[1] Subregions were selected that minimized commuting from one subregion to another. By selecting subregions in this way, the growth of economic activity (employment) in one subregion has a minimum effect on that of other subregions. This effect is further minimized by attempting to assure that the subregions selected are also retail and wholesale trading areas.[2] This ensures that income earned by an employee working and residing within one subregion is not largely spent in another. Thus, the subregionalization procedure was designed to yield fairly autonomous economic areas with a minimum of economic interdependence.[3]

The process of study area delimitation and subregionalization has been discussed as if it were entirely sequential in nature. Actually, it is iterative, with continual adjustments being made to the subregional and study area boundaries, as additional

[1] U.S. Bureau of the Census, *U.S. Census of Population; 1960*, Vol. 2, Part 6, "Journey to Work," U.S. Government Printing Office, Washington, D.C.

[2] *Rand McNally Commercial Atlas and Marketing Guide* (New York: Rand McNally & Co. An annual publication).

[3] The great advantage from a modeling point of view of subregions defined in this manner is that they can be modeled separately. This allows model experimentation (simulation) of single subregions for many purposes. However, it certainly is not difficult to imagine circumstances where it may be desirable to link the economies of two or more subregions. This should in no way be considered a modeling problem of great magnitude. In fact, the water sector of the Susquehanna model links all the subregions. However, simulations relating to many regional economic factors can be conducted on a single subregion model for the purposes of preliminarily exploring the nature and impact of specific variables.

criteria for delimitation are examined. For instance, the first outline of the study area was drawn basically in line with hydrologic- and county-boundary considerations. However, regional economic considerations led to a reconsideration of the original boundaries selected with subsequent expansion or contraction of the over-all study area.

Figure 6.1 shows the study area and the economic subregions finally selected for the study. It should be noted that political entities were not a primary basis for selecting either the over-all area or the subregions except when the political entities also had data implications as in the case of the county units. In particular, Subregions A and B are combinations of counties in both Pennsylvania and New York.[4]

Figure 6.1 also illustrates that the river flows through most of the subregions rather than providing a boundary between them. This fact allowed demands upon the river at most geographical points to be related to the economy of a single subregion rather than two. While this desirable subregional configuration was recognized early in the study, it was not allowed to warp the subregionalization process.

In general, the Susquehanna River Basin is not densely populated. The entire drainage basin (27,500) had a 1960 population of about 3,267,000, of which 2,630,000 were in Pensylvania. The study area's population in 1960 was 5,220,800, the difference being accounted for principally by the presence of Baltimore in the study area but not in the basin. The best agricultural areas are in the northeastern part of the New York portion of the basin and in the southern part of the Pennsylvania portion. Mineral production consists mostly of bituminous and anthracite coal and lime and limestone products. A wide variety of manufacturing industries are located in the basin.

The following sections describe each of the subregions included in the basin. These brief descriptions are followed by a comparison of several of the more interesting economic and population variables relating to the regions.

---

[4] It should be recognized that ignoring state and other political boundaries may not be valid from the point of view of plan implementation.

Subregion A—Elmira. This area includes 7 counties, 4 in New York State and 3 in Pennsylvania. Economic activity is centered about several medium-sized cities in the New York counties. The nonelectrical machinery and stone, clay, and glass industries were leading manufacturing employers.

The area gained in population during the 1950–1960 decade, increasing from approximately 356,000 to 386,000. The unemployment rate was approximately 4½ percent in 1960. Per capita income levels, approximately $1,900, were about average for the study area. The rivers found in this subregion are major tributaries of the Susquehanna. These are the Chemung, Cohocton, Canisteo, and Tioga Rivers.

Subregion B—Binghamton. This area consists of 6 counties in New York State and 1 in Pennsylvania. The region's economic activity is focused on the metropolitan area of Binghamton, which also includes the satellite cities of Endicott and Johnson City. Most of the manufacturing activity in the subregion is located in this area. The electrical equipment, machinery, fabricated metals, and leather industries are important employers. The region gained in population during the 1950–1960 decade, increasing from about 418,000 to 463,000 people. Income levels, approximately $2,100, were above average for the basin, and the unemployment rate approximated 4.4 percent in 1960.

The headwaters of the Susquehanna River are found in this area. The main stem of the river is used about as intensively in this subregion as anywhere in the basin.

Subregion C—Williamsport. Subregion C consists of 9 counties in Pennsylvania, which are relatively sparsely settled.

Population grew very slowly during the 1950–1960 decade, increasing from about 410,000 in 1950 to about 431,000 in 1960. Per capita income levels, approximately $1,600, were below average for the basin in 1960, while unemployment was very high in that year, approximating 7.4 percent. In large measure, the unfavorable unemployment situation was due to the decline of the bituminous coal industry as a source of employment.

The West Branch of the Susquehanna River flows through Subregion C. Acid pollution of the river by drainage from abandoned coal mines is common in this subregion.

Subregion D—Sunbury. Subregion D is the smallest of the subregions and is composed of 4 counties in Pennsylvania. A number of small communities exist in the area, but no large cities have developed. The subregion declined in population during the 1950–1960 decade, falling to a population level of about 200,000 in 1960 from a 1950 level of 209,000. The region had a per capita income of about $1,500, which was below average in relation to the study area in 1960. The unemployment rate in 1960 was about 6.9 percent. The garment industry is a major employer.

The confluence of the West and North Branches of the river occurs in this subregion.

Subregion E—Wilkes-Barre–Scranton. Subregion E is one of the more urbanized subregions. It consists of 4 Pennsylvania counties, and the cities of Wilkes-Barre and Scranton are both located there.

The region had a marked decline in population during the 1950–1960 decade, falling from about 695,000 people in 1950 to about 627,000 in 1960. The region had a per capita income of about $1,600 in 1960, which was below average relative to the study area. The unemployment rate in that year was the highest among the subregions, about 9.2 percent. This high rate of unemployment is largely attributable to the decline of the anthracite coal industry during the 1950's. At the date of writing, the garment industry is a major employer.

The North Branch of the river flows through the region. The Lackawanna is a major tributary that was characterized by both organic and acid pollution in 1960.

Subregion F—Altoona. Subregion F consists of 5 Pennsylvania counties. Altoona is the largest city and has long been a center for the railroad industry. The 1960 unemployment rate of about 6.0 percent is a partial reflection of the decline of this industry. It also had the lowest labor-force-participation rate. The per capita

TABLE 6.2
Subregional Population by Age Groups in 1960

Age Group	Subregions A Number	% of Total	B Number	%	C Number	%	D Number	%
0–13	113,588	29.5	135,116	29.2	120,551	28.0	52,671	26.3
14–19	37,670	9.6	41,136	8.9	42,647	9.9	18,195	9.1
20–24	24,966	6.5	24,923	5.4	30,632	7.1	10,730	5.4
25–44	93,026	24.2	115,227	24.9	108,793	25.3	50,314	25.1
45–64	74,382	19.3	96,445	20.8	84,396	19.6	45,636	22.8
65+	41,995	10.9	50,591	10.9	43,684	10.1	22,733	11.4
Total	385,627	100.0	463,438	100.0	430,703	100.0	200,279	100.1

Age Group	E Number	%	F Number	%	G Number	%	H Number	%
0–13	152,726	24.4	74,141	28.1	300,355	28.7	532,363	29.5
14–19	52,839	8.4	24,530	9.3	91,334	8.7	154,645	8.6
20–24	29,876	4.8	14,218	5.4	59,849	5.7	112,668	6.2
25–44	160,810	25.7	65,234	24.8	278,398	26.6	513,160	28.4
45–64	157,847	25.2	56,718	21.5	214,048	20.4	354,569	19.7
65+	72,455	11.6	28,685	10.9	102,997	9.8	136,340	7.6
Total	626,553	100.1	263,526	100.0	1,046,981	99.9	1,803,745	100.0

income level in the subregion was among the lowest for the study area at about $1,500. The population of the area declined very slightly during the 1950–1960 decade from about 265,000 in 1950 to 264,000 in 1960.

The Juniata River is found in this subregion.

Subregion G—Harrisburg. This subregion consists of 8 Pennsylvania counties. The cities of Harrisburg, York, and Lancaster are located here. The region not only has a diversified manufacturing base but also includes some fine agricultural areas. The population in the subregion grew significantly during the 1950–1960 decade from an original level of about 896,000 to 1,047,000 in 1960.

The unemployment rate of 3.2 percent in 1960 was the lowest in the study area. Per capita 1960 income was the highest in the drainage basin at about $2,000 and was exceeded in the study area only by Baltimore.

The main stem of the river flows through this subregion, where it is joined by the Juniata. The main stem in this area is wide and meandering and of generally good quality. Codorus and Conestoga Creeks are taxed heavily by the cities of York and Lancaster, however.

Subregion H—Baltimore. Subregion H, the Baltimore metropolitan area, consists of 6 Maryland counties including the City of Baltimore. This is one of the largest urban areas in the United States.

The subregion grew rapidly during the 1950–1960 decade. Growth from a 1950 population level of 1,457,000 was aided by substantial in-migration.

The per capita income level was the highest in the study area in 1960, approximately $2,100. The unemployment rate was approximately 5.1 percent.

TABLE 6.3
Subregional Employment by Employment Category

Employment Category	Subregions A Number	A % of Total	B Number	B %	C Number	C %	D Number	D %
Agriculture	11,587	8.4	15,675	8.9	6,599	4.4	4,528	6.3
Export Mining	271	0.2	—	.0	3,968	2.7	2,315	3.2
Durable Fabricating	28,182	20.4	40,387	23.0	27,308	18.6	6,957	9.6
Nondurable Fabricating	3,602	2.6	15,697	8.9	8,925	6.1	13,872	19.2
Labor-Intensive Processing	11,906	8.6	2,761	1.6	11,030	7.5	1,829	2.6
Capital-Intensive Processing	2,167	1.6	3,196	1.8	2,566	1.7	3,334	4.6
Business-Serving	13,304	9.6	18,157	10.3	17,800	12.1	7,932	11.0
Household-Serving	64,203	46.5	77,123	43.9	63,896	43.4	31,372	43.5

Employment Category	E Number	E % of Total	F Number	F %	G Number	G %	H Number	H %
Agriculture	5,453	2.5	5,048	5.7	24,981	6.0	10,365	1.5
Export Mining	8,303	3.8	130	.0	847	.0	—	.0
Durable Fabricating	26,954	12.2	15,099	17.2	58,928	14.1	92,191	13.3
Nondurable Fabricating	40,234	18.2	6,111	6.9	40,293	9.6	18,447	2.7
Labour-Intensive Processing	2,522	1.1	6,041	6.8	22,908	5.5	48,947	7.1
Capital-Intensive Processing	3,893	1.8	3,821	4.3	15,596	3.7	28,096	4.1
Business-Serving	24,382	11.0	11,558	13.0	52,204	12.5	95,777	13.8
Household-Serving	109,193	49.4	40,684	45.8	178,666	42.7	345,996	49.9

Comparison of Subregions

It is interesting to compare the subregions in the study area in relation to population by age class, employment categories, and similar variables. Chapter 8, The Demographic Sector, spells out the need to divide the population into age groups and the rationale behind the groups selected. Table 6.2 lists the population by these age groups for each subregion. Note how the out-migration that occurred during the 1950's from Subregions D and E has tended to change the age structure of the population in these regions in relation to the remainder of the subregions in the basin. With out-migration mainly affecting the young, Subregions D and E have tended to develop a population profile weighted in favor of the older age groups. For instance, the 45–64 and the 65+ groups in these two subregions contain higher-than-average proportions of the population.

Similarly, the 0–13 group contains fewer children and the 20–24 group is smaller than normal.

The major cause of out-migration in these two subregions, unemployment, has also affected the distribution of employment among employment categories. Specifically, the "nondurable fabricating" group, which includes the garment industry, is represented at about double the level characteristic of the other subregions in Subregions D and E.[5] The surplus of labor in these two subregions apparently has attracted this labor-intensive industry. Table 6.3 shows the employment in each category in each of the subregions.

The preceding sections establish the diverse character of the subregional economies in the basin and accentuate the need for subregionalization. The chapters that follow describe the model structure that was evolved to simulate the economies of these subregions and their interrelationship with the river.

[5] The definition of employment categories used in the model is given in Chapters 9 and 10 concerning the employment sector of the model.

The purpose of this chapter is to give the reader a brief overview of the entire Susquehanna model before the details of the individual model sectors are presented in Chapters 8, 9, 10, and 11.

Each of the economic subregions in the basin specified in Chapter 6 is modeled separately but in a similar fashion. These subregional models are composed of three major sectors (Figure 7.1) representing the most important categories of variables in the model: demographic, employment, and water. The demographic and employment sectors are tied together by an important feedback loop including population, labor-force, unemployment, and migration variables.

The water sector is viewed as a "technical sector"; it could be replaced or augmented in a model of this type by other technical factors that might be of particular importance to a given region, for instance, a forest resource sector, a minerals sector, or a transportation sector. In fact, the modular construction of the model, with its groups of interrelated equations combined into sectors and subsectors and united by simple connecting relationships, allows expansion of many parts of the model without disturbing the remainder in a major way.

As explained in the preceding chapter, the subregions in the basin were selected in a manner designed to minimize their economic interdependence. Thus, while the demographic and employment sectors are tied together within each of the subregional models, they are separate from one subregion to the next. The water sectors of the subregional models are not independent, however. Such independence is impossible because upstream water use can affect both downstream water flows and downstream water quality. Therefore, each region's water sector reflects economic activity upstream as well as in its own subregion and, in turn, alters the quality and quantity of water available in all downstream subregions.

The Demographic Sector

The simplest of the model's major sectors in a conceptual sense is the demographic sector because only three factors—births, deaths, and migration—are involved

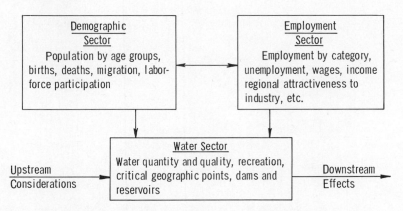

FIGURE 7.1. The three major sectors of a subregional model.

directly in population change.[1] Each of these direct determinants of population change has a related causal structure, and each of these structures requires treatment in the detail and the depth warranted by the sensitivity of population change to it.[2]

One important element common to all three of these determinants is the age structure of the population. For instance, regional populations with disproportionately large numbers of young people tend to have higher per capita birth rates, lower death rates, and a greater-than-average response to the factors causing migration. Because of the importance of age structure, the total population of each region is disaggregated into six age classes. These age classes are selected in a manner such that the age groups they encompass will have relatively homogeneous birth, death, and migration characteristics.

Figure 7.2 illustrates how flows into and out of a given age class occur over time. People enter an age class either by aging from the previous age category or by in-migrating.[3] People leave the age class by aging, dying, or out-migrating.

The demographic sector can be viewed as the "supply of labor" sector. In a similar vein, the employment sector provides the "demand for labor." Viewing these sectors in this fashion brings into clear focus why there must be an explicit tie between them. Obviously, labor supply and demand cannot each go its own way in a region indefinitely—imbalance between the two will set in motion forces tending to restore equilibrium.

The major equilibrating mechanism tying supply and demand is migration.

[1] This is not equivalent to saying that the demographic sector contains the fewest equations. In fact, it contains the most. However, the number of equations in a model or submodel is only one measure of its complexity. It is perhaps less relevant than the number of feedback loops or the form of the equations involved.

[2] Maintaining the proper balance in relation to the level of detail and depth involved in various model sectors and subsectors is a major problem and is discussed in Appendix A under the section Producing a Balanced Model.

[3] Of course, entry to the youngest age class is gained by birth, not aging.

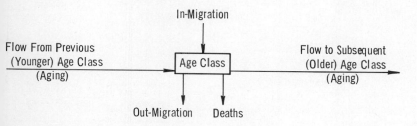

FIGURE 7.2. Flow of people into and out of an age class.

In the Susquehanna model, the rate of migration is related to the difference between the subregional unemployment rate and an assumed, long-run national rate. The subregional unemployment rate is computed endogenously, as is the differential between it and the exogenous national rate. As the subregional unemployment rate increases beyond the national rate, out-migration increases as well, and vice versa.

Migration, inward and outward, occurs continuously throughout the simulation as a function of the gap between the local and national unemployment rate. Because each age class responds differently to the unemployment situation, migration will alter the age-class structure of the population in a region. This is a very important consideration. This changed structure will, in turn, alter over-all per capita birth and death rates. Because migration is so volatile and because of its feedback on births and deaths, it is potentially the most dynamic element causing population change in a region.

The importance of the way in which the migration function is introduced as a tie between the demographic and employment sectors is stressed here because most regional analysis techniques tie the two sectors quite differently. Many techniques project population and employment separately and reconcile these projections at convenient intervals, often each 10 years. This "reconciliation approach" has the weakness that it *treats what is potentially the most dynamic element in population change as a residual.* Further, it poses the difficult question as to whether it is the population projection, the employment projection, or both, that should be changed to make unemployment rates "reasonable." Often the mechanism for reconciliation is not explicitly stated when this method is used, and it is suspected that population "adjustments" are frequently made in an "across the board" fashion as opposed to being allocated differentially among age classes as they should be.

The Employment Sector

As presently constructed, the model might be called an "employment model" because economic activity is specified in terms of employment rather than variables such as income, value added, or output. This focus on employment is not

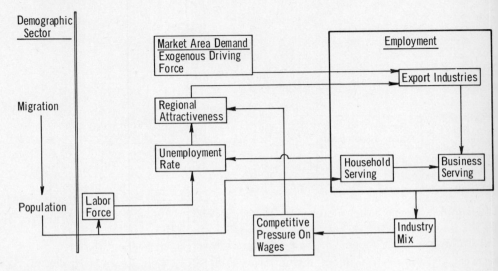

FIGURE 7.3. The employment sector.

an essential ingredient of a regional simulation model, but it is a useful and convenient simplification in light of the tie between the population and employmen sectors and because nonemployment variables such as water use and income can be derived, in part at least, from employment through the use of conversion factors that take into account such considerations as trends in productivity.

The Susquehanna model incorporates the so-called "export base theory" of employment. That is, certain of the industries are viewed as selling the majority of their output outside the subregion in which they are located. Such businesses, through these "exports," supply the volume of funds necessary for purchases of goods produced elsewhere. Because small regions are seldom self-sufficient in the United States, an "export base" is necessary to supply many of the region's needs. Declining export base employment normally implies declining over-all regional employment, and vice versa. The export industries are the first major category of employment in the model. This category is further divided into several groups.

A second major category of employment is termed "business serving." The firms classified as falling in this category supply the goods and services needed by other businesses in the subregion and grow in proportion to their growth.

The third major employment category used is "household serving." These businesses supply the needs of the ultimate consumer and encompass such employment subcategories as retail trade, doctors, local government, and so on. The employment in this group varies with subregional population.

Figure 7.3 illustrates the main features of the employment sector. The principal "driving force" of the model is Market Area Demand operating through export industry employment. The growth of these export industries is determined by (1) the relative attractiveness of the subregion to industry in relation to other areas where it might locate and (2) the demand for goods in relevant market area

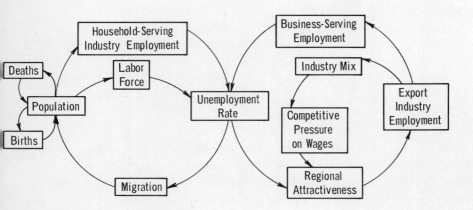

FIGURE 7.4. Selected feedback loops.

that can be supplied economically from the subregion. Attractiveness is treated explicitly through a relative cost concept embodying transportation and labor costs. Market Area Demand is specified exogenously.

Figure 7.4 shows a few of the feedback loops involved in both the demographic and employment sectors. The system depicted is easily understandable in a conceptual sense when these loops are considered one, or even several, at a time. However, because of the large number of variables and interactions involved in the total system, intuitive prediction of the precise path that will be traced in time by any one variable is impossible. Thus, the "complexity" of the model is not necessarily conceptual in nature but more in terms of computational difficulty. This problem of keeping track of the levels of a large number of variables and of changing them from one time period to the next is delegated to the computer and solved by simulation.

The Water Sector

The purpose of the water sector of the model is to simulate conditions in the river relating to both water quality and quantity.

To accomplish this goal in relation to many river basins might require an elaborate hydrological model. Such a model might define river flows during all seasons of the year at many, if not all, points along the river. Water quality might be described in even greater detail, particularly in relation to its variation over time. This variation can be significant even within the span of one day.

During the early phases of the Susquehanna research study, it became clear that such detail would not be required in order to model the Susquehanna. The reasoning behind this conclusion was largely based upon the fact that water is abundant in the basin and that there is no general, basin-wide water problem that is evident. Further, potential feedback on economic growth caused by investments in flood control, irrigation, power, or navigation were considered to be minimal or nonexistent. The problem then became one of seeking those specific locations in the basin that at that time were having problems or that might become trouble spots in the future.

Based upon analysis of field data, a number of what were termed "critical points" were selected. A simple hydrological model was constructed that treated low flows only. The level of water demand and river flow at these critical points was then compared within the model. Water quality was also examined. Thus, the most likely trouble spots were analyzed under the least favorable conditions from a water quality and quantity standpoint, namely, low-flow conditions. If, under these conditions, potential problems were shown as likely, other points in the subregion were examined until it appeared that all potential problems were uncovered.

In river basins where water problems are critical at many locations, it might be necessary to "close the loop" between the water sector and the demographic and employment sectors. That is, in these basins it might be desirable to have the water resources affect the growth of the region in addition to having growth affect water quality or quantity. In the Susquehanna River Basin, it did not appear that water quality or quantity would change sufficiently in enough places over the study period to cause significant feedback effects. Therefore feedbacks from the water sector to the demographic sector are not included, and the only feedbacks from water to employment are through river works construction and the recreation subsector.

Unlike the Susquehanna River Basin, many other basins exist where direct and marked effects of water policy on the economy are likely. Changes in supply/demand relationships at locations within such basins might increase the effective prices of water, or the costs of pollution control, sufficiently to alter industrial growth patterns. Or, in arid regions where water is scarce, political decisions regarding water are apt to change water use patterns or, possibly, perpetuate established ones. In some regions a fairly elaborate treatment of "water sector feedbacks" might be necessary and might require the inclusion of political as well as economic and technical variables.

As previously mentioned, the water sector in the model ties together all the subregions. For instance, when economic growth in an upstream subregion results in additional water consumption, this consumption is subtracted from river flow at all downstream points. Thus, at any point along the river the effect of all upstream consumption is felt.

Water quality considerations must also relate the effects of pollutants added upstream to water qualities downstream. The consideration is modeled in relation to organic pollution and its effects on the dissolved oxygen levels in the river.

One other essential feature of the water sector involves its facility to test the potential effects of constructing dams and reservoirs. The model does this in three ways. First, the feedback of dam construction activities on the economy of the subregion in which they are being built is simulated by the model. Second, the effect of flow augmentation resulting from expected reservoir releases during low river flow periods is calculated. Finally, feedback from recreation activity at the reservoirs to the local economy is simulated.

Model Output

Before exploring the three model sectors in more detail in the following chapters, a brief discussion concerning model output is desirable. As previously discussed, the DYNAMO compiler allows the listing and/or automatic plotting of any variable in the model at any time interval selected, year-by-year, decade-by-decade, etc. At first blush, problems relating to model output might seem nonexistent. However, it must be remembered that the Susquehanna model has hundreds of variables that might be selected for printing and plotting. The problem is, therefore, one of selection—selection of output designed to yield insight into the behavior of the model and to avoid overwhelming and confusing the research team with a maze of numbers.

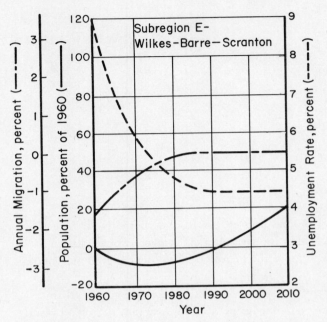

FIGURE 7.5. Plot of typical simulation of Subregion E model showing unemployment rates, migration, and total population.

Generally, the highly volatile variables with a high degree of dynamic interaction should be plotted on the same chart. For instance, Figure 7.5 shows unemployment rate and migration resulting from a typical simulation as they are plotted for Subregion E in the basin.

In addition, one may wish to plot one or more variables that may be regarded as indicative of the result of the many interactions occurring in the model. Such variables may be viewed as criteria for judging the impact of policy. Total subregional population is one such variable in the Susquehanna model. Total labor force and per capita income are others.

Some variables in the model, although of great interest, do not fluctuate sufficiently to require plotting, but merely need to be listed at intervals of from 5 to 10 years. Water quality and quantity variables are examples in the Susquehanna model. With regard to these variables, one is usually interested in whether or not they reach predefined critical levels during the simulation.

This chapter has given the reader an insight into the structure of the over-all model. The four following chapters describe the model sectors in more detail and spell out the manner in which many of the specific formulations were derived.

Chapter 8
The
Demographic
Sector

The previous chapter stressed the interrelationships among the various parts of the model. However, for purposes of exposition, this chapter will discuss the demographic sector of the model as a system in itself, stressing the interrelationships within the sector, and making only minimum reference to its ties to other sectors.

The dynamics of regional demographic factors play a major role in shaping the future of an area. However, regional analysts have tended to focus their attention on the complex problems of regional income and employment. Further, demographers do not appear to have taken a strong role in regional economic analysis. As a result, regional demographic analysis as related to regional economic factors has suffered relative neglect. Exceptions to this generalization exist, but the realm of the interrelationship between regional economic analysis and regional demography is not as well plowed as many fields and appears to be a fertile one for rewarding research activity.[1]

Regional demographic systems incorporate both positive and negative feedback loops. Some of these loops respond quickly to disturbances and have rather immediate feedback effects; the responses of others are of a longer term nature. Some of these feedbacks are direct and obvious in their action; others are indirect and often subtle.

For example, assume an exogenous force causes a fall in the employment level of a region. As a result, unemployment rises and our model assumes that out-migration begins to occur. This latter effect will begin to take place almost immediately. Soon births will begin to fall among the younger age groups in response to the unfavorable economic climate. Then, many job seekers will

[1] One exception is the recent work by Ira S. Lowry, *Migration and Metropolitan Growth: Two Analytical Models* (San Francisco, Calif.: Chandler Publishing Co., 1966). Lowry calls for research that supports the position taken in this chapter:

> The agenda of urban and regional research should give a high priority to the development of a better specified model of the dynamic interaction between migration and changes in employment—that is, to a model which specifically indicates the migration-response to a change in employment opportunities, and also the change in employment opportunities resulting from a given quantity of in- or out-migration (pp. 78–79).

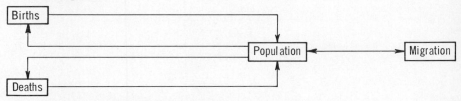

FIGURE 8.1. A simple population sector.
Mathematically,

$$L \quad POP.K = POP.J + (DT)(BRTH.J + NIM.J - DTHS.J)$$

where

POP.K	POPulation at time K,
POP.J	POPulation at time J,
BRTH.J	BiRTHs during interval JK,
DTHS.J	DeaTHS during interval JK,
NIM.J	Net InMigration during interval JK.

become discouraged and withdraw from the labor force. Such reactions to rising unemployment have direct, indirect, long-term, and short-term effects upon regional growth.

The direct effects are relatively straightforward and obvious. For example, out-migration lowers the labor force and tends to reduce unemployment. However, migration also has longer term effects that are more subtle and indirect. Because the younger age groups migrate at a higher rate than do the older groups in response to high unemployment, out-migration tends to create a population age structure composed of an abnormal number of older people. In the longer term, this restructuring of the age mix results in slower growth in population because the older groups are less fertile and have higher death rates.

The example cited mentions some of the demographic factors that interact in a complex, dynamic fashion to influence a region's development. The analysis of these factors is ideally suited to computer simulation techniques. The following sections describe how the demographic systems in the subregions of the Susquehanna River Basin were modeled and simulated.

Specification of a Generalized Model Structure

Figure 8.1 illustrates one of the simplest kinds of population sectors that might be incorporated into a regional simulation model. It shows births, deaths, and migration as functions of the total population. However, because birth, death, and migration rates are different for various age groups, the problem with such a simple demographic sector is obvious—the age structure of the population and its effects are ignored.[2] Thus, if the age structure changed significantly over time, the effects of such restructuring would be lost.[3]

[2] It is recognized that age, while an extremely important criterion relative to population classification, is not the only criterion. Income level, race, sex, education, and other criteria may be useful for subclassification and, in relation to some problems, may become the dominant classifying variables, altering the population model radically from that presented.

[3] It might be possible to take into account the restructuring of the age mix indirectly, rather than by including age groups explicitly in the model. This might be done by including feedbacks that lower births after a period of continuing out-migration, etc. Such indirect methods have not been tried to date and have the problem of not illustrating in a direct fashion the causal mechanisms that are operating.

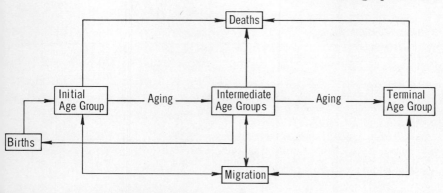

FIGURE 8.2. A generalized population sector.

Mathematically,

$$\text{POPIG.K} = \text{POPIG.J} + \text{BIRTH.J} - \text{DTHTIG.J} + \text{NMGIG.JK} - \text{NAGIG.JK}$$

$$\text{POPMG.K} = \text{POPMG.J} + \text{NAGIG.J} = \text{DTHTMG.J} - \text{NAGMG.JK} + \text{NMGMG.JK}$$

$$\text{POPTG.K} = \text{POPTG.J} + \text{NAGMG.J} - \text{DTHTTG.JK} + \text{NMGTG.JK}$$

where

POPIG	POPulation in Initial Group,
POPMG	POPulation in interMediate Groups,
POPTG	POPulation in Terminal Group,
BIRTH	Births,
DTHTIG, DTHTMG, DTHTTG	DeaTHs in Initial, interMediate, and Terminal Groups, respectively,
NAGIG, NAGMG	Number AGing from Initial and interMediate Groups,
NIMGIG, NIMGMG, NIMGTG	Net InMigration from Initial, interMediate, and Terminal Groups, respectively,

and where

J, K represent sequential points of time and *JK* the time interval between them.

While such a simple model may be useful in relation to some problems, a more elaborate model incorporating an explicit age structure will be needed in most situations. The problem, of course, is to select a level of detail for this age structure that is appropriate in relation to the goals of the modeling study.

A problem is created because of practical difficulties caused by model size. Larger models naturally require longer computer running times and are to be avoided for this reason. Perhaps of a more serious nature is the fear that the computer capacity will be reached before a model is complete. This practical limitation dictates the selection of a reasonably small number of age groups that have relatively homogeneous reactions to factors causing change.

In retrospect it appears that there may have been a degree of overconcern for this grouping problem in the Susquehanna study. The demographic sector was formulated first and appeared to be very large in terms of numbers of equations. As a matter of fact, the other sectors subsequently required fewer equations than were originally anticipated, and the potential problem became somewhat of a straw man. Nevertheless, it would be an easy matter to conceive of a demographic sector requiring so many equations as to press computer limitations.

Figure 8.2 illustrates the concept of a population sector divided into age

TABLE 8.1
Live-Birth Rates (Births/1,000 Females)

Year	Age of Mother							
	10–14	15–19	20–24	25–29	30–34	35–39	40–44	45–49
1940	0.7	54.1	135.6	122.8	83.4	46.3	15.6	1.9
1950	1.0	81.6	196.6	166.1	103.7	52.9	15.1	1.2
1960	0.8	89.1	258.1	197.4	112.7	56.2	15.5	0.9

Source: U.S. Bureau of the Census, *Statistical Abstract of the United States: 1962* (83rd ed.), Table 54, p. 55, U.S. Government Printing Office, Washington, D.C.

TABLE 8.2
Death Rates (Deaths/1000 Population)

Age	1940	1950	1960	Age	1940	1950	1960
Under 1	54.9	33.0	27.0				
1–4	2.9	1.4	1.1	45–54	10.6	8.5	7.6
5–14	1.0	0.6	0.5	55–64	22.2	19.0	17.4
15–24	2.0	1.3	1.1	65–74	48.4	41.0	38.2
25–34	3.1	1.8	1.5	75–84	112.0	93.3	87.5
35–44	5.2	3.6	3.0	85 and	235.7	202.0	198.6
over				over			

Source: U.S. Bureau of the Census, *Statistical Abstract of the United States: 1963* (84th ed.), Table 67, p. 62.

groupings. Three kinds of age groups are visualized. There are (1) an *initial group* into which births occur, (2) a series of *intermediate groups* into and out of which individuals age, and (3) a *terminal group* containing all ages above a given level. Migration occurs into, and out of, all three kinds of age groups and deaths diminish each of them. The intermediate groups account for nearly all births. The number of age groups will depend on two factors: first, the relative emphasis to be placed upon demography in the problem being studied, and, second, the degree of homogeneity that is exhibited by various age classes with respect to variables such as fertility, death rates, migration, and labor-force participation. Ages with similar characteristics in relation to these variables can be grouped because people of all ages in the group respond to a changing environment in a similar fashion.

For example, children from one year of age through the early teens are a homogeneous group in many ways. Death rates are low, fertility is virtually nonexistent in our society, they migrate with their parents, and there is virtually no labor-force participation. In a like fashion, other ages may be assembled into groups with similar characteristics, although few will exhibit as much homogeneity as do children.

The main problems in grouping seem to be related to what might be called the transitional ages, that is, those ages when the roles of individuals in society tend to change. A good example is the late teens, when young people have the alternatives of continuing their education, participating in the labor force, and

TABLE 8.3
Labor-Force-Participation Rates by Age and Sex (percent participating)

1960			1975		
Age	Male	Age	Female	Male	Female
14–17	34.4	14–17	20.8	32.1	20.2
18–19	73.1	18–19	51.0	70.0	49.7
20–24	88.9	20–44*	44.6	85.7	47.2
25–54	95.0	25–34	35.8	95.0	38.0
45–64	85.2	45–54	49.3	80.8	56.0
65+	32.2	55–64	36.7	25.4	42.5
		65+	10.5		10.5

Source: U.S. Bureau of the Census, *Statistical Abstract of the United States: 1963*, (84th ed.),
Table 288, p. 220, U.S. Government Printing Office, Washington, D.C.
* Except 25–34.

marrying. The manner in which the teenage population responds to the
environment changes rapidly with age in the late teens, requiring in the model
small age groupings of 5 years or less to assure sufficient homogeneity. Further,
the choices made by those in these age groups with regard to entering the labor
force, etc., are not static and often shift in relation to expectations, a factor not
as important to the older age groups who, in fact, often have fewer real alternatives
open to them.

The following section describes how the age groups for the Susquehanna model
were selected. Age grouping is considered relative to fertility, death, migration,
and labor-force participation. The sex and race aspects of demography have been
treated implicitly. Because only women have children, in relation to some problems
it may be necessary to tie births to a female population that is explicitly defined.
However, in most situations average birth rates by age classes that combine the
male and female population are probably sufficient. When abnormal male/female
ratios do develop and affect marriages and births, these may be treated implicitly,
for instance, by tying the cause for the uneven ratio directly to birth rates. The
race question may also be treated implicitly, for instance, by adjusting variables
such as birth rates to reflect expected changes in racial mix. However, in the
Susquehanna study area all the subregions except one had a population exceeding
95 percent Caucasians.[4]

Selecting the Age Groups for the Susquehanna Model

The initial selection of age groups must be judgmental. The judgment can be
based upon reliable data, however, and need not be made in a vacuum. Once a
model is assembled, sensitivity experiments can be performed to aid in the decision
as to whether, and to what degree, model refinement is needed.

Tables 8.1, 8.2, 8.3, and 8.4 present data that are relevant to an initial grouping

[4] Differences that may appear to be racial in some regions of the country may just as well
be socioeconomic in character. This raises the question as to whether a socioeconomic
breakout may be in order in models of such areas, say by income classes.

138   Chapter 8

TABLE 8.4
Migrants Between States, March 1959–March 1960

Percent of Civilian Population	
Age	
1–4	4.8
5–6	3.5
7–17	2.3
18–19	4.8
20–24	9.0
25–29	6.1
30–34	3.6
35–44	2.8
45+ *slowly* decreases with age from	1.3

Source: U.S. Bureau of the Census, *Current Population Reports*, Series P-20, No. 113, "Mobility of the Population of the United States, March 1959 to March 1960," Table 4, p. 15, U.S. Government Printing Office, Washington, D.C.

of ages. Some of the more obvious groupings are marked on the tables. The data are certainly suggestive of other groups, and these are discussed in the text.

In deriving such age groups, two factors were considered: first, the percentage change in relevant variables between groups on which data were available; and second, the importance of the absolute magnitudes of the variables themselves. For instance, if a rate doubles from one age category to the next, such a marked shift will be important unless the numbers themselves are so small as to be insignificant.

In relation to live births, at least three obvious groupings are apparent in Table 8.1; those 14 or less, those in the fertile ages, 15–44, and those over 44 in age. Or, several others might appear warranted, like the late teens alone.

Death rates as expressed in Table 8.2 also are strongly suggestive of at least three age groups. Those under one year of age are clearly a segregatable group because of high infant mortality. In order to avoid adding a separate age class to the model to account for infant mortality, these deaths are merely subtracted from the birth rate.

The increase in deaths subsequent to age 44 is suggestive of a grouping or several groupings in subsequent age classes.

Labor-force-participation rates are suggestive of four age groupings; 0–13, a period of virtual nonparticipation; 14–17, a transition period; 18–64, the dominant employment period; and 65+, the years of retirement. As can be seen in Table 8.3, participation rates vary greatly between men and women; not only are their current values different but the projected trends in participation for males and females often differ. This difference in levels and trends was handled implicitly in the Susquehanna model by averaging the male and female rates. An explicit treatment of the male and female population may well be necessary for some problems.

The migration characteristics of several potential age groups were also

TABLE 8.5
Preliminary and Final Age Groupings

Births	Deaths	Labor-Force Participation	Migration	Final Selection
	0–1			
0–14		0–13		0–13
			0–17	
		14–17		
	2–44			14–19
15–44			18–19	
			20–24	20–24
		18–64		25–44
			25+	
45+	45+			44–64
		65+		65+

considered and are shown in Table 8.4. These data are not particularly suggestive of any clear-cut groups. However, it may be assumed that the majority of those under 17 will migrate with their parents. Furthermore, the migration of those in the 20–24 age group is significantly higher than that of any of the other groups and perhaps deserves separate treatment.

Table 8.5 shows the more obvious groups suggested by the first four tables, and those actually selected. At least four age groups seem to be needed.

Six age groups were selected for the Susquehanna model. These were 0–13, 14–19, 20–24, 25–44, 45–64, and 65+.

The 0–13 group is quite homogeneous. Most of the few births falling in the 0–14 age category shown in Table 8.1 are probably those of 14-year-olds. A finer breakout of migration data within the 7–17 category in Table 8.4 would probably show the 0–13 group as a good choice, particularly in light of the fact that this group surely migrates with its parents. With regard to deaths, the 0–13 breakout is finer than required but not harmful. As far as labor-force participation is concerned, it is an obvious grouping.

Groupings beyond the 0–13 category were not as clear cut. Birth-rate data suggested a break somewhere prior to age 20, as did labor-force-participation data; age 19 was selected for the break.

Migration data suggested the 20–24 age grouping, though surely not in a clear-cut fashion. Birth data also suggested this as a relevant age group, again not clearly, however. Nevertheless, 20–24 was selected. The short age span of the 14–19 and 20–24 age groups reflects their transitional character.

No clear reason was readily apparent for not selecting the entire 25–44 age category as a useful grouping. Birth rates dictated that 44 be about the upper limit of this next group.[5] Also, death rates begin to increase at this point.

[5] Admittedly, birth rates are suggestive of groupings within the 25–44 span.

In a similar fashion, the 45–64 age group seemed viable. Labor-force participation dictates that those over 65 years of age be treated separately.

Several problems related to the set of age groups that were selected are readily apparent. For instance, the data used to derive them are also suggestive of other groupings, and these may be just as valid. However, validity is a difficult concept to define in this situation because not even one-year breakouts will be absolutely perfect. Usefulness is a better criterion. As this grouping was not altered during the Susquehanna program, it was obviously judged useful by the research team. This is not to say that the team would use exactly the same breakout again. But the payout from changes that might have been made always appeared lower than that which seemed available from research devoted to other parts of the model. It is, after all, a sizable task to assemble the data and make parameter estimates for new age classes for eight subregions.

If one were especially interested in the population dynamics of a particular regional economy, a more detailed breakout of age groups might be of value in relation to two kinds of age categories. First, the transition groups such as the middle and late teens, as well as the younger segments of the 24–44 group, are prime targets for further disaggregation. Second, the groups with the longer age spans, such as the 25–44, 45–65 groups, and, possibly, the 0–13 group may extend over time periods that are sufficient to mask the effects of certain population dynamics. To illustrate the latter problem, suppose a region experienced a 10-year period of heavy out-migration caused by adverse economic conditions. This migration would affect the age groups differentially, with the younger age groups experiencing the impact to the greatest degree. As a simplified example, suppose that out-migration resulted in a trough in the age structure similar to that shown in the left graph in Figure 8.3. A model with a very disaggregated age structure would move this trough as shown by the solid line on the right-hand graph in Figure 8.3. That is, over time the trough would move through the population structure virtually intact

However, the particular aging mechanism used by the model causes the trough to spread out as it moves through the population age groups (dotted line

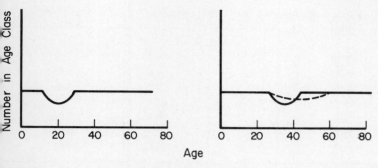

FIGURE 8.3. The movement of a trough in the age structure through the population over time.

Figure 8.3). The model views a given age grouping as being homogeneous, with an equal number of people in each age subsegment of the grouping. Further, the model ages a definite portion of each age group each time period; for example, if the age span of a group is 20 years, $\frac{1}{20}$ are aged each year. Therefore the model does not wait for the beginning dip of the trough to reach the final year in the group to decrease the number aged into the next age class. Rather, it acts as if the trough reduced the number of people in each age subsegment of the group and the number aged is reduced proportionately. Further, the next age grouping reacts immediately to the reduced inflow of people, also slowing its flow of aged people to the next group. Thus the effect of a "trough" in a particular age group spreads more quickly than desirable through the model.

Recognizing the problem caused by age groups covering long time spans, a limited number of sensitivity experiments were performed to judge the severity of the difficulties created. The dynamic effects were much less than might be expected intuitively, and the problem was not judged of sufficient magnitude to warrant further effort in relation to the Susquehanna research.

The Dynamics of Birth Rates. The preceding sections have described how the age structure of the model was selected. This and subsequent sections describe how data were assembled concerning birth, death, migration, and labor-force-participation rates. Also described are the endogenous mechanisms used by the model to vary these rates over time.

It would be an error to assume a priori that national birth data applied to an over-all study area. Not only might the area's birth rates differ from those of the nation but birth rates might differ subregion to subregion. They might also change over time in a manner divergent from national trends.

In order to examine local birth rates, data were collected on a county-by-county basis from the Departments of Health in Pennsylvania and Maryland. With the exception of the Baltimore Subregion H, birth rates in the study area are well below national average rates. And the county-by-county rates within subregions differ greatly.

TABLE 8.6
Live Births in the Susquehanna Region in 1960 (per 1,000 population)

Subregion*	Age Group			
	14–19	20–24	25–44	45–64
C	31.4	108.5	44.6	0.07
D	29.5	114.5	39.2	0.12
E	15.4	108.5	43.8	0.05
F	32.5	131.5	42.8	0.08
G	38.2	130.9	43.1	0.07
H	46.7	131.0	46.5	0.05

* Departments of Health, Pennsylvania and Maryland. No data were available for Subregions A and B at the time of the study.

The county-by-county variation was assumed, in large measure, to be due to where births were recorded, with mothers often going to hospitals outside their county of residence to give birth. However, it was assumed that most mothers would give birth within their subregion. Therefore birth rates were computed on a subregional basis by averaging individual county rates within the subregion. Nevertheless, as Table 8.6 shows, the actual rates still varied considerably among the younger age groups.

Although a number of factors might affect regional birth rates during any specific time period, economic opportunity was expected to play a major role. It was hypothesized that there was a correlation between births and the economic health of an area as reflected in the subregional unemployment rate.[6] However, it was clear that such a relationship might be difficult to detect. First, measures of unemployment rates are notoriously inaccurate. Second, the relationship would undoubtedly be a lagged one, if it existed, but the relevant lag structure was not evident. Third, the relationship might well be nonlinear, possibly appearing only in regions with extremely low and high unemployment. Of course, other problems existed, such as the likelihood that other causal mechanisms were operative.

In the light of these problems, it is doubtful that even highly sophisticated parameter estimation techniques would provide good estimates of the parameters involved. A simpler strategy was therefore employed to seek a relationship and then to measure it. The essence of this strategy was to determine if the birth-rate effect seemed to be operative on a national basis, and, if it was, to use local (Susquehanna basin) data to derive parameter estimates.

To implement this strategy and in an attempt to avoid these problems, it was decided to test for significant differences in birth rates in areas that had experienced very high and very low unemployment rates for an extended period. All major SMSA's were ranked according to their 1957, 1958, 1959, and 1960 unemployment rates. Then, those that fell in the 15 percent with the highest

[6] The substantial body of data and literature on national economic conditions in relation to birth rates was found of little use in establishing a relationship concerning subeconomies with economic conditions varying from the national conditions.

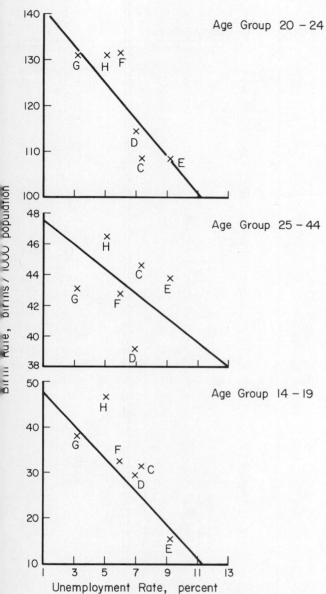

FIGURE 8.4. Unemployment rate versus birth rate for three age groups.

nemployment rates in *each* of the four years were selected as representing a group ith consistently high unemployment. Similarly, the 15 percent with the lowest ates were selected for comparison. It was hoped that the consistency of the samples a relation to unemployment over time would avoid the lag problem. Table 8.7 sts the areas identified together with other pertinent data. Census data were used or the statistical test, but the groups were identified by use of Bureau of Labor tatistics data. It was felt that the census data were more useful because of their

144   Chapter 8

TABLE 8.7
High and Low Unemployment SMSAs*

Area	1960 Unemployment Rate Census	BLS	BLS Rank in 1960	BLS Rank in 1959	BLS Rank in 1958	BLS Rank in 1957
Low Unemployment Rate Areas						
Washington, D.C.	2.8	2.6	1	4.5	4.5	9
Cedar Rapids, Iowa	2.4	2.7	2	1	1	3.5
Honolulu, Hawaii	3.8	2.8	3.5	6.5	4.5	17
Madison, Wis.	2.1	2.8	3.5	3	7.5	3.5
Des Moines, Iowa	2.9	3.0	6	4.5	2	8
Denver, Colo.	3.3	3.2	7.5	6.5	7.5	‡
Omaha, Neb.	3.0	3.2	7.5	9.5	10.5	23
Jacksonville, Fl.	4.4	3.3	9.5	8	6	5
Salt Lake City, Utah	3.4	3.3	9.5	9.5	10.5	7
Charlotte, N.C.	3.2	3.5	11	21	23	39
Oklahoma City, Okla.	3.1	3.7	12.5	12.5	14	‡
Macon, Ga.	3.4	3.8	14	16	9	31.5
Greensboro, N.C.	2.7	3.9	16.5	12.5	30.5	51
Jackson, Miss.	3.7	4.0	20	18.5	17	42
Lancaster, Pa.	2.9	4.0	20	18.5	30.5	34.5
Norfolk, Va.	5.1	4.1	23.5	36	21	13
Atlanta, Ga.	3.5	4.2	27.5	30	24	34.5
Chicago, Ill.	4.3	4.2	27.5	45	23	23
Austin, Tex.	3.3	4.2	27.5	14	14	31.5
Charlotte, S.C.	5.1	4.4	34	30.5	24	17
Dallas, Tex.	3.2	4.4	34	30.5	24	39
High Unemployment Rate Areas						
Evansville, Ind.	5.7	6.7	108	105	99	92
Detroit, Mich.	7.8	6.9	114	107	116	90
Terre Haute, Ind.	5.1	7.2	120.5	97.5	82	97
Jersey City, N.J.	5.6	7.2	120.5	97.5	88	86
Charleston, W.Va.	6.1	7.4	125	102	93	‡
Beaumont, Tex.	5.9	8.0	129	109	92	68.5
Duluth-Superior, Minn.	9.9	8.2	130.5	111.5	104	60
Atlantic City, N.J.	6.9	9.1	135	111.5	108	103
Pittsburgh, Pa.	7.1	9.3	136	108	100	68.5
Erie, Pa.	8.5	9.5	137	114.5	111	90
Altoona, Pa.	5.6	10.3	138	114.5	119	106
Huntington-Ashland, W.Va.	7.8	12.0	141	116	114	‡
Scranton, Pa.	8.2	12.6	142	118	117	107
Wilkes-Barre, Pa.	10.4	12.9	143	119	110	‡
Johnstown, Pa.	10.4	13.0	144	120	118	94
Wheeling, W.Va.	9.3	13.9	145	117	113	‡

Source: Manpower Report of the President, March 1965, U.S. Government Printing Office, Washington, D.C.; and calculations.

* New England areas are not included because birth-rate data were not readily available.

† Wilkes-Barre was included because it is in one of the subregions in the Susquehanna Basin, even though the unemployment rate was extremely low in 1957.

‡ Data not available.

nore comprehensive coverage of the labor force, but these data were available
n only 1960.

The nonparametric sum-of-ranks test (Mann-Whitney) was applied.[7] Statistically
gnificant results were obtained in relation to the 14–19, 20–24, and 25–44
ge groups. Thus, it can be inferred that there is an inverse relationship between
nemployment rates and birth rates in these age groups.

The problem then remained of making the judgment as to the degree to which
his effect was operative in the study area. For the three age groups, plots were
nade of 1960 unemployment data versus 1960 birth rates. These are shown in
igure 8.4. Because of the problems of making good parameter estimates previously
iscussed, these data were fitted by free-hand plots rather than by statistical
echniques. Further, an attempt was made to try to account for factors in addition
) unemployment when these were felt to be operative and seemed evident in the
ata. For instance, it was felt that the high birth rate of the 14–19 age group in
ubregion H (as shown in Figure 8.4) was caused by the relatively high percentage
f nonwhites in this area as compared to the other subregions. Therefore, the
ee-hand fit was drawn somewhat farther below this point than otherwise would
ave been the case.

The equations computed from these lines and the differences between the
redicted and actual birth rates (residuals) are shown in Table 8.8. The residuals
ere conceived as representing real, though unexplained, differences in births
aused by local factors. Thus, while the residuals might have been decayed to
ero over time during the simulations, they were not.

National birth-rate trends were also considered. While there appears to be a
reat deal of controversy about birth trends, a decline in rates relative to 1960
vels seems most likely in light of recent trends and the hypothesis of many
ndividuals that the availability of better contraceptives will cause further declines.
able 8.9 shows the relative birth rates used in the model for all age classes.

Sensitivity experiments in relation to birth variables were performed with the

[7] S. Seigel, *Nonparametric Statistics* (New York: McGraw-Hill, Inc., 1956), pp. 116–126.

TABLE 8.8
Birth-Rate Equations and Residuals

Age Group	Equation		Residual ($= B - \hat{B}$)					
		Subregion	C	D	E	F	G	H
14–19	$\hat{B}* = 3.6U\dagger + 45$		7.1	1.5	−5.0	1.5	−3.5	11.5
20–24	$\hat{B} = -3.6U + 141$		−6.5	−2.4	−0.5	10.1	−4.0	−3.9
25–44	$\hat{B} = -0.8U + 47.1$		2.3	−3.6	2.7	0.8	−3.2	−2.0

* B is births/1,000 population/year.   † U is unemployment rate (percent).

TABLE 8.9
Relative Birth Rates

Year	Relative Rate	Source
1960	1.00	
1962	0.95*	Vital Statistics of the United States, Vol. 1
1964	0.88*	
1965	0.82†	Monthly Vital Statistics Report
1970	0.81	
1975	0.83	Current Population Reports, P-25, #329
1980	0.85	
1990	0.86	
1995	0.85	
2000	0.85	Current Population Reports, Series B, p. 25, #286
2005	0.85	
2010	0.85	

* Derived from actual data.   † Estimated from partial data.

model during various stages of its development. Although the results of these experiments are not strictly comparable because of the different versions of the evolving model used to conduct them, all the experiments seem to indicate that long-run population levels are somewhat sensitive to birth rates and the endogenous mechanisms used to generate such rates within the model. Changes on the order of 15 percent in the population levels of the 50-year simulations can be produced by reasonable alternative assumptions about birth trends and birth-rate–unemployment relationships. The 20-year simulations show 5–6 percent shifts in population in response to the same alternative assumptions.

Death Rates. Death-rate data for the Susquehanna River Basin (Table 8.10) were obtained on a county-by-county basis from the Departments of Health in the relevant states. Generally, these were of the same order and character as the national rates shown in Table 8.2. Again, as with birth data, county-by-county data showed variation within age groupings, but when the average rates for the majority of the subregions were derived, there seemed little reason to believe that these subregions should be treated differently from one another. Subregion H was an exception, and deaths were treated separately in relation to that region so as to reflect the higher percentage of nonwhite population there.

TABLE 8.10
Death Rates, Susquehanna River Basin (per 1,000 population/year)

Year	Subregion	First Year	1–13	14–19	20–24	25–44	45–64	65+
1960*	A–G	24.0	0.56	0.7	1.0	1.9	12.0	95.0
	H	27.0	0.56	0.9	0.9	2.3	13.0	95.0
2010†	A–G	19.2	0.49	0.6	0.8	1.0	11.0	86.4
	H	21.6	0.49	0.8	0.8	1.9	12.0	86.4

* Source: State Departments of Health, Pennsylvania, New York, Maryland.
† Estimates by project staff.

Sensitivity experiments with the model confirmed what intuition indicates in light of death-rate data; namely, that long- and short-run population levels are very insensitive to likely changes in death rates. This insensitivity occurs for two reasons. First, death rates, except for the 65-and-older age group, are very low. Even driving them to zero would not really have much effect. Second, given that the only real potential impact might be among the oldest age group, the feedback effect of such a change is nil. Such groups are infertile and, by their continued life, would not produce children who would produce children, etc., raising longer-term population levels. Also, they are not labor-force participants, and therefore lack short-term and long-term effects on unemployment, migration, etc. The lack of sensitivity to death rates should be contrasted to changes in birth rates where, in a 50-year simulation, second- and third-generation effects definitely do occur.

Migration. An area's population might grow 1 to 2 percent per year given only changes due to births and deaths. Migration, however, can cause much more dramatic effects and as such is potentially the most dynamic element in regional population change. During the 1950–1960 decade, migration was an active force in most subregions in the Susquehanna study area. It both accelerated natural population growth, for instance in Subregion H, and caused declines in population, as in Subregion E.

Early in the study, it was apparent that net migration was largely a product of relative economic opportunity between a subregion and the "rest of the world." However, it was also clear that other factors were operative, that a good measure of relative opportunity would be difficult to find, and that certain areas of the "rest of the world" could have more influence on the subregion than others.

Despite its obvious limitations, the regional unemployment rate was the measure selected to gauge the relative employment opportunities in the region versus the nation as a whole. As mentioned in relation to the analysis of the effects of economic opportunity on births, one is haunted by the knowledge that unemployment rate measurements are subject to large errors, that the effect of

TABLE 8.11

Net Migration Rate as a Function of Population Size and Unemployment Rate

Functional Form: Net Migration Rate (5 Years) = a + b (Unemployment Rate) + c(1/Population)

Age Group	a	b (s)	Students T	c (s)	Students T	Standard Error of Estimate	R^2	Total F
15–19	.1313	−.02538		93			.37	
		(.0038)	−6.72†	(175)	0.53	(.068)		22†
20–24	.3262	−.06487		−93			.59	
		(.0065)	−9.93†	(227)	−0.41	(.1159)		55†
25–44	.068	−.01539		854			.38	
		(.0023)	−6.81†	(345)	2.48*	(.04)		23†
45–64	.0228	−.00668		498			.40	
		(.001)	−6.30†	(125)	3.98†	(.019)		25†
65+	.007	−.004		185			.20	9.5†
		(.0012)	−3.40†	(62)	2.99†	(.022)		

* Significant at 5 percent level.
† Significant at 1 percent level.

Note:
   (s) = the standard error of the regression coefficient estimate immediately above.
   T = the appropriate ratio of variances for testing the hypothesis that the corresponding
      regression coefficient equals zero.
Total F = the appropriate ratio of variances for testing the hypothesis that all the regression
      coefficients simultaneously equal zero.
   R = the multiple correlation coefficient.
0–14 population group migrate with parents.
Source: U.S. Bureau of the Census, *U.S. Census of Population: 1960, Mobility for States and State
Economic Areas*, Final Report PC(2)-2B, U.S. Government Printing Office, Washington, D.C.

unemployment is undoubtedly a lagged effect, and that the relationship may be nonlinear.

A major problem exists in obtaining good data regarding migration with respect to unemployment. At the time of the study, the best information seemed to be cross-section data from the Bureau of Census on State Economic Areas for the period 1955–1960.[8] A variety of regression analyses were made using these data. The regression results finally used in the model are shown in Table 8.11. These show migration as a function of local unemployment rates and of regional population size. The significance of the latter variable is discussed below. In the model, migration is specified as a function of the difference between subregional and national unemployment and national unemployment is specified exogenously at 5 percent.

As can be seen, the proportion of the variance explained is not impressive but the level of statistical significance in relation to the two independent variables is high. In addition, a relationship between unemployment and migration has been found by others.[9] These statistical results plus the confirming studies found in the

[8] U.S. Bureau of the Census, *U.S. Census of Population: 1960, Mobility for States and State Economic Areas*, Final Report PC(2)-2B, U.S. Government Printing Office, Washington, D.C

[9] J. B. Lansing, E. Mueller, W. Ladd, and N. Barth, "The Geographic Mobility of Labor: A First Report," Survey Research Center, Institute for Social Science, Ann Arbor, Michigan, p. 19. Blanco Cicely, "The Determinants of Interstate Population Movements," *Journal of Regional Science*, Vol. 5, No. 1 (1963).

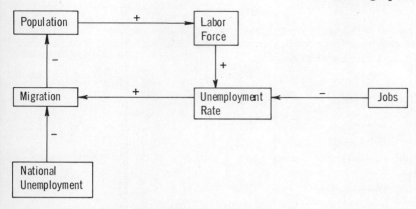

FIGURE 8.5. The unemployment feedback loop.

literature support the argument that relative employment opportunity plays an important, perhaps the most important, role in determining net regional migration. How much of the unexplained variance may be attributable to noise in the data or to lags, nonlinearity, and the effect of other causal mechanisms is as yet undetermined. In addition, the geographical location of a region is felt to be important, but this relationship was never quantified. For instance, if a region with good employment opportunity is adjacent to Appalachia, it might be expected to draw more migrants than a similar area surrounded by booming economies.

The differing effect of the average unemployment rate on migration by age group is important. As Table 8.11 illustrates, the younger age groups tend to respond most vigorously to relative employment opportunities. Thus, in an area of high unemployment, the younger groups tend to move at a relatively greater rate than their elders. Continued high unemployment, therefore, will tend to produce a population age structure that is disproportionately older in terms of national norms. Such an older population will have lower over-all birth rates and consequently a lower growth rate. Therefore migration has important feedback effects through the mechanism of altering the age structure of the population.

The results shown in Table 8.11 relative to regional population size may be surprising to many. These results seem to indicate that the more populous areas must have lower unemployment rates to draw people (or prevent out-migration) than those with less people. The interpretation given here is that the areas with higher levels of population are urban and those with fewer people are more rural. This is a reasonable assumption because the areas used in the analysis were roughly the same size and high population levels were correlated with the existence of large cities. It seems the cities or urban areas must have better employment opportunities than the rural areas to attract migrants. In light of known rural-to-urban movement in the 1950's, the conclusion seems faulty. However, cities have, in fact, presented better opportunities, and the regression result can be interpreted to mean that the rural-urban trend in migration would have been even more

TABLE 8.12
A Hypothetical Example of Migration at Two Levels of Response*

Magnitude of Assumed Unemployment Effect							
	Variable	Time 1	Time 2	Time 3	Time 4	Time 5	Time 6
1% unemployment differential moves	Population	1000	985	978	974	972	971
½ of 1% of population	Unemployment differential	+3%	+1½%	$+\frac{8}{10}\%$	$+\frac{4}{10}\%$	$\frac{2}{10}\%$	$\frac{1}{10}\%$
1% unemployment differential moves	Population	1000	978	972	971	970	970
¾ of 1% of population	Unemployment differential	+3%	$\frac{8}{10}\%$	$\frac{2}{10}\%$	$\frac{1}{10}\%$	0%	0%

* This table illustrates the effect of two levels of migration response to unemployment rates, one 50 percent more than the other. The effect of both, given that other things are equal, is for both populations, equal to 1,000 originally, to approach 970, or a zero unemployment differential, but with somewhat different timing.

TABLE 8.13
Civilian Labor-Force-Participation Rates in the Subregions of the Susquehanna River Basin. 1960*

	Age Group				
Subregion	14–19	20–24	25–44	45–64	65+
A	0.332	0.502	0.684	0.692	0.204
B	0.318	0.622	0.692	0.713	0.195
C	0.321	0.483	0.645	0.656	0.166
D	0.303	0.683	0.684	0.640	0.160
E	0.277	0.691	0.659	0.597	0.150
F	0.278	0.612	0.643	0.599	0.141
G	0.333	0.689	0.701	0.702	0.209
H	0.278	0.659	0.673	0.665	0.208

Source: U.S. Bureau of the Census, *U.S. Census of Population: 1960, State, General, Social and Economic Characteristics*, Table 83, *U.S. Summary, Detailed Characteristics*, Table 194, *Inmates of Institutions*, Table 3, *State, General Population Characteristics*, Table 27, *State, Detailed Characteristics*, Table 115, U.S. Government Printing Office, Washington, D.C.

* Several adjustments were made to the census data to arrive at these figures. Inmates and armed forces were distributed by age according to the age pattern in the United States. The census provides data on labor force for 14–17 and 18–24 groups. These were adjusted to yield the 14–19 and 20–24 age groups in the model by estimating the labor force in the 18–19 group. These latter estimates were made by applying the state participation rates, for males and females separately, to the county population.

pronounced had the cities had greater attractiveness to the population. In any case, the magnitudes of the coefficients illustrate that the bias in favor of the rural areas is not strong. Sensitivity experiments confirm this, but the variable is retained because of its statistical significance. The possibility of a spurious correlation is certainly recognized.

A number of sensitivity experiments were conducted upon the model to explore the impact of the migration functions.[10] Generally, these seemed to show that the

[10] See Chapter 12, Simulation of the Model.

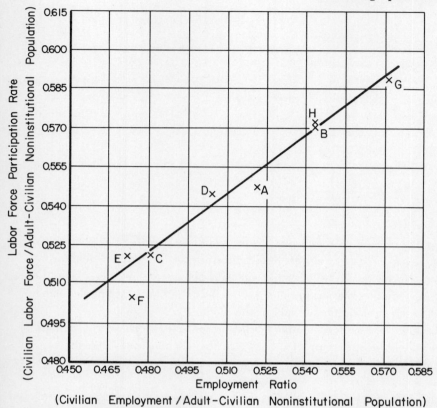

FIGURE 8.6. Relationship of labor-force-participation rates to employment ratio for Susquehanna subregions, 1960.

magnitude of the coefficient relating migration to unemployment was not of great importance. While this conclusion may at first be surprising, reference to the feedback loop tying the unemployment rate to the employment sector (Figure 8.5, p. 149) reveals that the result is reasonable. What occurs is that larger coefficients will induce higher rate of migration, tending to lower the unemployment rate relatively quickly. But, given time, a lower coefficient will accomplish the same task. Thus, the path to the end result is somewhat different—although not impressively so— but the result is the same. Table 8.12 illustrates the effect through a hypothetical example.

Interpretation of the constants in the equations shown in Table 8.11 reveals that a zero unemployment differential will produce out-migration. As the areas analyzed were in the eastern United States, and therefore are not a representative national sample, a functional relationship not passing through the origin is possible. However, the long-term population levels are reasonably sensitive to shifting the function to zero. Such a change produced approximately a 15 percent change in the 50-year population level in one version of the model.

While the foregoing discussion reveals that much more research is needed in the field of regional migration, the results of the parameter sensitivity experiments are not alarming. Yet the results are sufficiently suspect to cast a shadow on the functional forms used. As the section on skills illustrates, however, the addition of new causal variables may have much more effect than any reasonable change in the parameters of variables already in the model.

Labor-Force-Participation Rates. Table 8.3 illustrates that labor-force-participation rates differ widely by age group. Table 8.13 further demonstrates that these age-group differences show further variations among the subregions in the Susquehanna study area.

While the differences in Table 8.13 may not seem large, it should be remembered that slight shifts in labor-force participation can have dramatic impact on unemployment rates and, hence, migration. For instance, suppose an age group has an age-specific unemployment rate of 5 percent and a participation rate of 50 percent. A rather small increase of participation rate, bringing it up to 51 percent, a 2 percent change, would increase unemployment to 6 percent, a 20 percent shift.

A preliminary analysis of subregional data for the Susquehanna basin indicated that labor-force participation seemed to be tied to the unemployment rate. Figure 8.6 shows a plot of over-all labor-force-participation rates versus the employment ratio for the subregions. The employment ratio was used instead of the unemployment rate in the labor-force-participation analyses in an attempt to avoid the previously mentioned problems in measuring the latter variable.

A study of available literature uncovered three very relevant studies that reinforced the unemployment or economic opportunity hypotheses. Two of these studies found basis for what might be termed the "discouraged worker hypothesis."[11] That is, as employment opportunities decline, workers withdraw from the labor

[11] W. G. Bowen and T. A. Finegan, "Labor Force Participation and Unemployment," in *Employment Policy and Labor Market*, edited by Arthur M. Ross (Berkeley, Calif.: University of California Press, 1965), pp. 115–161; Alfred Tella, "The Relation of Labor Force to Employment," *Industrial and Labor Relations Review*, April 1964; and "Labor Force Sensitivity to Employment by Age and Sex," *Industrial Relations*, February 1965.

TABLE 8.14

Regression Results: Labor-Force-Participation Rate as a Function of Employment and Population Ratio for Susquehanna Subregions, 1960

Functional Form: $L_i/P_i = a + b(E/P) + c(P/P_i)$

Age Group	a	b (s)	F	c (s)	F	Standard Error of Estimate	R^2	Total F
14–19	0.23	0.46		−0.02				
		(0.129)	12.7*	(0.008)	6.1	(0.01)	0.83	9.7*
20–24	−0.47	1.09		0.04				
		(0.43)	6.4*	(0.008)	22.2†	(0.04)	0.83	12.1*
25–44	0.11	0.71		0.07				
		(0.10)	46.5†	(0.02)	8.9*	(0.008)	0.91	25.1†
45–64	−0.02	0.86		0.07				
		(0.24)	13.1*	(0.04)	3.2	(0.02)	0.83	12.2*
65+	−0.18	0.65		0.004				
		(0.15)	19.3†	(0.006)	0.47	(0.01)	0.84	13.3†

  * Significant at the 5 percent level.
  † Significant at the 1 percent level.

Note:
  (s) = the standard error of the regression coefficient immediately above.
  F = the appropriate ratio of variances for testing the hypothesis that the corresponding regression coefficient is significantly different from zero.
  Total F = the appropriate ratio of variances for testing the hypothesis that all the regression coefficients simultaneously equal zero.
  R = the multiple correlation coefficient.

force and cease hunting for employment. One of the studies also found evidence of the "additional worker" effect.[12] This hypothesis states that if the prime worker in the family becomes unemployed, a second family member joins the labor force. This additional-worker effect was determined to be secondary in nature, correlating well with the exhaustion of unemployment benefits. The discouraged-worker effect definitely outweighed the secondary-worker effect.

The model is quite sensitive to the inclusion of the discouraged-worker effect. This is particularly true in those subregions where unemployment is expected to fall during the 1960's. In these areas, as the unemployment rate starts to fall, people begin to return to the labor force. This holds unemployment at higher levels than otherwise would occur and causes increased net outmigration.

Thus, it can be seen that the labor force adjusts in size to employment opportunity. While this may ease the shock in an area entering hard times, it also may, in part at least, explain why it is so hard to decrease the unemployment rate in areas that have experienced chronic depression. Adding jobs in such areas also adds job seekers.

To determine the effect of the employment ratio on labor-force participation by age group a series of regressions was run. The results are shown in Table 8.14.

[12] Kenneth Strand and Thomas Dernburg, "Cyclical Variation in Civilian Labor Force Participation," *Review of Economics Statistics*, November 1964; and "Hidden Unemployment 1953 to 1962: A Quantitative Analysis by Age and Sex," *American Economic Review*, March 1966.

TABLE 8.15

Measured Skill Level, Pennsylvania State Economic Areas 1–7 and A–M

Pennsylvania State Economic Area	Education Index*	Occupation Index†	Industry Index‡
1	0.99	1.00	1.26
2	0.99	0.86	1.07
3	0.99	0.96	1.34
4	0.84	0.91	0.92
5	0.91	0.93	1.11
6	0.88	0.84	1.21
7	0.87	0.87	1.20
A	1.05	1.05	1.25
B	0.99	1.01	1.15
C	0.93	0.87	1.15
D	1.00	1.08	1.20
E	0.84	0.96	1.11
F	0.94	1.05	0.88
G	0.90	0.81	1.13
H	1.05	1.01	0.90
J	0.85	0.95	1.28
K	0.90	0.92	1.25
L	0.86	0.91	1.34
M	0.92	0.96	1.43

* Education Index equals median education in the State Economic Areas divided by the median education in the United States (10.6 years).

† Professional workers, managers, and craftsmen as a percent of the total labor force was computed for the State Economic Areas and the United States (U.S. percent = 33.1). The Occupation Index equals the State Economic Areas percentage divided by the U.S. average percentage.

‡ Employment in the construction, manufacturing, professional, and related-services industries was calculated as percent of total employment in the State Economic Areas and the United States (U.S. percent = 44.7). The Industry Index equals the percentage in the State Economic Areas divided by the percentage in the United States.

Preliminary Consideration of Skills Influences

Figure 8.2 and the discussion that follows it present a generalized demographic sector as reflecting age differences in the population and the various behavioral differences attributable to age. Sex and race aspects of demography have been treated implicitly. However, increasingly in our society the educational and skills characteristics of the population have been recognized as critical influences on regional growth.

It is easy to demonstrate that all of the population behaviors included in the model (i.e., birth rate, death rate, labor-force participation, and migration) are not only dependent upon age but also upon education and skills. Birth rate and even death rate can be shown to be declining functions of educational level. Labor-force-participation rate increases noticeably as education and skills rise. Migratory habits shift drastically as educational level exceeds high school completion. These facts suggest that the demographic sector might have been organized along education and skills lines instead of on age basis. More appropriately, they indicate that education and skills considerations demand inclusion in a regional demographic model, along with age and perhaps other distinguishing characteristics.

Unfortunately, any attempt to treat the skills dimension rigorously runs into major measurement difficulties. First is the fact that the concept of skill level is itself a relative one; it is culturally determined. Work held to be skilled in one society or at one point in time may be regarded as semiskilled in another. Second is that no one measure of acquired training can be used as a standard for describing the relative skills of different worker groups. Work proficiency is acquired through formal instruction, more or less informal training, and work experience. Moreover, formal instruction may be of the public-schooling variety (including trade school) or of the sort provided in in-plant courses. Mixtures of several of these training systems may be required to produce a particular skilled worker, and various training times of one type may be traded off against different training times of another type to produce equivalent capabilities. In view of this measurement problem, the U.S. Census does not even use the designation "skilled workers." The most closely related group is "craftsmen, foremen, and kindred workers."

To assess the possibility of including skills influences in the Susquehanna River Basin model, three indices were examined:

1. Median level of education of the population 25 years and older;
2. Ratio of professional, technical, managerial, craftsmen, foremen, and kindred workers to the total labor force;
3. Ratio of construction industry, durable goods industry, nondurable goods industry, professional and related-services industry to total employment.

These indices were used to reflect education, occupation, and industry of employment as possible skills characterizations of the work force. Unfortunately, as Table 8.15 shows, the different indices produce somewhat different results,

TABLE 8.16
Index of Educational Attainment in the Susquehanna River Basin (1960)

Subregion	A	B	C	D	E	F	G	H	U.S.
Index	105.9	103.2	100.3	93.9	92.4	96.5	98.9	94.9	100.0

Derived from: U.S. Bureau of the Census, *U.S. Census of Population: 1960, General, Social and Economic Characteristics*, U.S. Summary, Table 76, p. 207, Maryland, Table 83, pp. 22–149, 22–150, New York, Table 83, pp. 34–359, 34–365, Pennsylvania, Table 83, pp. 40–480, 40–486, U.S. Government Printing Office, Washington, D.C.

TABLE 8.17
Relation Between Educational Level and Migration Rate by Age

	Migration Rate (%/Year)	
Years of School Completed	25–44 Age Group	45–64 Age Group
0–7	5.2	2.9
8	5.7	2.3
9–11	5.8	2.6
12	5.2	3.0
13+	10.7	3.5

Source: U.S. Bureau of the Census, *Current Population Reports*, Series P-20, No. 127, "Mobility of the Population of the United States, April 1961 to April 1962," Table B, p. 4, U.S. Government Printing Office, Washington, D.C.

indicating that skill level is at least a composite of several variables and is not readily measured by a single index.

The inconsistent results obtained in the Table 8.15 analyses indicated that inclusion of a skills variable in the demographic sector, on a basis comparable to the simpler characteristic of age, would be fraught with the dangers of producing misleading results. To do a sufficiently adequate and rigorous job for all the subregions also appeared to be an expensive research undertaking. It was therefore decided to omit the skills factor from the basic comparative model simulations. Yet surely so important a variable could not be ignored.

Here the strength of the dynamic simulation approach proved useful. It was decided to develop an experimental version of a skills sector and to use it to test the model's sensitivity of response to various skills-related assumptions. The experiments could be conducted during several simulation runs, leaving the basic model unaffected for the remainder of the desired regional simulations.

In these experiments it was decided, despite the recognized limitations, to use educational attainment as the proxy for skill level. In this choice we were supported by a number of studies, including the Bureau of Labor Statistics' research on worker training. "It is clear that among all workers, exclusive of those with 3 or more years of college, educational attainment is the key to the extent of vocational training: the more education, the more formal vocational training."[13] Data on current educational attainment of the population in the various subregions of the Susquehanna basin as illustrated in Table 8.16 show a wide spread around the national average. If educational attainment affects subregional performance (as

[13] Bureau of Labor Statistics, *Training of American Workers*, April 1963, quoted in *Manpower Report of the President*, March 1964, p. 66.

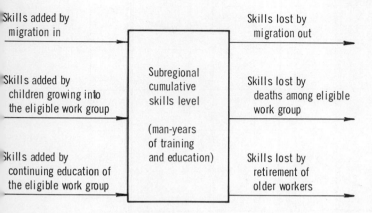

FIGURE 8.7. Influences on cumulative skills level.

TABLE 8.18

Out-Migration (25 Years and Older) by Level of Education, Harrisburg SMSA, 1955–1960

Level of Education	Resident Population	Out-Movers	Out-Migration, % of 1955 Resident Population
5–8 years	70,567	4,142	5.9
9–12	98,017	9,669	9.9
13 plus	26,703	5,984	22.4

Source: U.S. Bureau of the Census, *Population Characteristics, Mobility for Metropolitan Areas, 1960,* U.S. Government Printing Office, Washington, D.C.

we shall soon demonstrate), this variation will help produce diverse patterns of subregional growth in the Susquehanna area.

For initial experimental modeling purposes it was decided to focus on the effect of skills level on migration. As shown in Table 8.17 for the United States as a whole, those with some college education migrate more frequently, particularly in the age group under 45 years old. Table 8.18, showing data for the Harrisburg SMSA, also illustrates these findings on migratory behavior. The high school group is far more mobile than less educated groups, while the college group is still more active as a source of out-migration.

To model the influence of skill level on a subregion's migration, a variable was defined to represent the cumulative man-years of education and training of all people in the subregion encompassing ages 14–64, in effect the age range of the labor force. Added to the cumulative man-years of education existing at the beginning of the simulation are those brought in by children aging into the labor force age group, by migrants into the subregion, and by the continuing education and training of those over 14 years of age. Lost from the subregion's cumulative skills are those withdrawn due to deaths and outward migration among the eligible work group (age 14–64) and those due to the retirement of older people from the work force. The factors modifying over-all cumulative skills level are shown in Figure 8.7.

The average skills level in a subregion (man-years of education and training

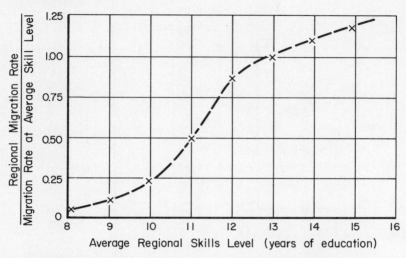

FIGURE 8.8. Migration related to average regional skills level.

per man) is determined by dividing this cumulative skills level by the subregion's population regarded as being in the eligible work group (age 14–64).

In modeling the skills added by entry of the young into the eligible work group, the character of compulsory education was noted in that all youths becoming 14 years old are regarded as having completed 8 years of education. Further education beyond the age of 14 is represented initially (1960) as providing approximately 3.6 years of education and training to every growing child and teenager, trending upward during the course of the simulation run. The model recognizes the fact shown previously that people who migrate tend to be more highly educated than those who do not migrate. This was accounted for in the model by assuming that skills carried into (or out of) a subregion by a migrant are greater than the average subregional skills level. Furthermore, it was assumed that skills lost through retirement are less per man than the subregion's skill level.

Using the data of Tables 8.17 and 8.18 a curve for the effect of average skill on migration was developed as shown in Figure 8.8.

In addition to this migration effect, it was postulated that education and training affect labor productivity in such a way that the wage costs in the particular subregion relative to the nation are modified in proportion to the relative skills levels. For example, if local skills average 125 percent of national average, then it was assumed that effective local wages will be only 80 percent of comparable national wages. With this assumption, and a rising trend in the subregion's relative education level, the simulation results indicated an employment growth over 50 years to be 40 percent greater than in the base run. This ever-increasing impact from a skills buildup indicated one of the most sensitive areas of the Susquehanna model. Clearly the possible important contribution to improved understanding of regional development strategies suggests expanded treatment of skills consideration in future regional research efforts.

Chapter 9
The
Employment
Sector

This chapter describes those aspects of the model concerned with determining the level of industrial activity in a local economy. The following chapter continues the discussion and concentrates on export industry considerations. The model measures industrial activity in terms of employment rather than variables such as income, value added, or output. This focus on employment is a useful and convenient simplification in view of (1) the relative availability of employment data and (2) the ease with which employment variables may be related to demographic ones. Further, values for other variables can be derived from employment through the use of conversion factors that take into account such considerations as trends in productivity. This is done, for example, to project wage income.

Figure 9.1 illustrates the basic model structure. Employment is classified into two types: one aimed at provision of goods and services within the region and the other at production for export out of the region. In projecting the growth of local service industries, the model incorporates the so-called "export base theory" of employment. The increased demand for local service industries occurs for two reasons. First, there is the direct requirement of the export industries for business services. Second, growth in population generates demand for household services.

It is assumed, in accordance with export base theory, that investment in subregional export industries is not restrained by the lack of capital. Capital is viewed as flowing freely into and out of areas in response to profitable opportunities. An industry will, therefore, grow in the area where it has access to the inputs for its production and a market for its output at competitive costs.

The model adopts a relatively simple concept of industrial location theory. Location theory, as formulated by Isard for example, embodies the concepts of access to market, access to raw materials, and production costs including wages.[1] The model also embodies these concepts. The model, in line with location theory,

[1] See Walter Isard, *Location and Space-Economy* (New York: The Technology Press of Massachusetts Institute of Technology and John Wiley & Sons, Inc., 1956).

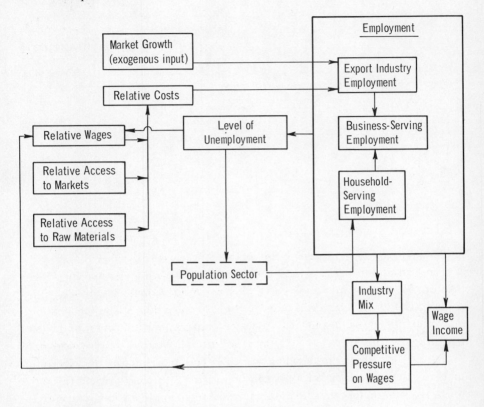

FIGURE 9.1. Overview of employment sector.

assumes that industries will grow faster in regions with relatively low costs of production and distribution.

The "market-demand growth rate" is used as a starting point for the computation of the subregional growth rate of a given industry or groups of industries. The demand is specified exogenously, based on national and other considerations, as mentioned in the next chapter.

The growth of a particular industry within a subregion, as contrasted with the growth of the market for its product, is determined by its relative advantage with respect to costs incurred in manufacturing and distributing the product. A cost index is formulated that compares the total cost of manufacturing and distribution from the subregion with the total costs of industry in other regions serving the same market. For instance, an index of 0.95 would indicate costs 5 percent below average. The model incorporates measures of regional cost differentials related to labor, to delivery of output to market, and in the case of processing industries, to obtaining needed raw material inputs. The cost measures incorporate information on the relative importance of different kinds of costs to different industries and are thus determined separately for each industry group. Furthermore, these cost measures are modeled to change over time to represent changing conditions in the subregion. A subregion's wage structure, for example,

Industries / location / influences	Local Serving		Export Industries			
	Household Serving	Business Serving	Manufacturing		Mining and Agriculture	Government, Education, and Military Services
			Fabricating	Processing		
Access to markets	X	X	X	X		
Access to labor			X	X		Noneconomic Influences
Access to natural resources				X	X	

FIGURE 9.2. Industry groups matched with locational influences.

changes in response to the amount and kind of industrial growth that takes place in the subregion. The wage structure, in turn, as shown in Figure 9.1, has a feedback effect on the future pattern of industrial growth. As will be illustrated in the discussion of model experiments in Chapter 12, this feedback loop plays a very important role in relation to the model's dynamic behavior.

The remainder of this chapter as well as Chapter 10 discusses both the implementation of, and the support for, the employment sector of the model. The discussion conveniently falls into three major parts: (1) method of classifying employment, (2) growth of local service employment, and, in Chapter 10, (3) growth of export industry employment. In order to save the reader from excessive detail in these two chapters, certain aspects of the model construction are relegated to technical appendixes.

Classifying Employment[2]

The first problem in connection with modeling employment is arriving at suitable employment categories. In arriving at employment categories, an attempt was made to group industries that have similar cost characteristics and therefore are under similar locational influences. Figure 9.2 shows a breakdown of various industry groups matched with their locational influences. For instance, local serving industries are viewed, as their name implies, as locating primarily in relation to the market, with access to labor and natural resources playing no significant role in the location decision. In contrast, agriculture and mining are viewed as primarily resource oriented.

Local Serving Versus Export Industries. As a first step in the classification procedure, industries were separated into local serving and export industry categories.

[2] This section describes the procedures used to classify and group economic activities at a general level. The detailed results of this breakdown as well as a more detailed description of the procedures used are presented in Appendix B.

Industries classified at the Standard Industrial Classification Manual[3] 3- or 4-digit levels are allocated to export or local serving categories on an all-or-nothing basis.[4] Those industries judged to be mainly, but not necessarily entirely, oriented to nonlocal markets are classified in the export category. The remainder are placed in the local serving category. These classification decisions are based both on the knowledge of the shipment patterns of the industry in general and, in some cases, on information on the activities of particular firms in the subregion in question. In many cases, the judgment of industry specialists was used to augment other available knowledge on particular industries.

This procedure results in all SIC agriculture, mining, and manufacturing industries (Standard Industrial Classification Numbers 1 through 14 and 19 through 39) being classed as export, with several important exceptions. The exceptions are those mining and manufacturing industries whose products are produced largely for local consumption, such as sand and gravel, dairy products, newspapers, bakery products, commercial printing, public utilities, and construction. These industries were removed from the export classification and designated as local serving employment. All other industries, including SIC Numbers 15 through 17 and 40 through 89, are classified as local serving.

The local serving group of industries is further subdivided into household serving and business serving by the same procedures. It should be noted that the business-serving group as defined here does not, as the name might seem to imply, include all industries that sell to other industries. It includes such industries as transportation, communication, commercial printing, and other industries that serve a wide variety of different kinds of businesses and thus are not dependent on any one kind of industrial customer for their growth. On the other hand, the business-serving group excludes electronic-component manufacturers who sell to

[3] *Standard Industrial Classification Manual*, Executive Office of the President, Bureau of the Budget, 1957.

[4] In a few instances involving the railroad industry, government and education, and recreation, the 1960 employment is split between export and local industries. In these cases a modified minimum-requirements approach is used and details are described in Appendix B.

electronic-device manufacturers; it excludes the forgings and casting industry, which sells to fabricated steel producers; and in general it excludes industries, commonly called suppliers, that sell primarily to one particular segment of industry. Such industries are often integrated into one complex, and, in general, are difficult to separate from each other. Employment in these "supplier" categories was, therefore, counted as export employment. Similarly those industries such as dental supply and food wholesalers that sell primarily to household-serving industries are counted as household-serving employment.

Export Industry Breakdown. The export industries as seen in Figure 9.2 are broken down in somewhat more detail than the local serving industries. In the case of the export manufacturing industries, an attempt was made to group industries that were relatively homogeneous with respect to the importance of the three locational influences—costs of transportation to markets, or market access, costs of procuring raw materials, or access to raw materials, and the costs of labor. As a first step, the export manufacturing SIC 2-digit industries were classified as "processing" or "fabricating" owing to the added importance of transportation costs of raw materials in influencing the location of the former. Next, indices of the importance of (1) labor costs, (2) transportation costs of product to the market, and, in the case of the processing industries, (3) transportation costs of raw materials were developed. The ratio of total payroll to value of shipments was used to indicate the importance of labor costs, while the value of shipments per ton of product (and materials) was used to indicate the importance of transportation costs. An analysis of this data led to dividing the export manufacturing industries into four relatively homogeneous groups: capital-intensive processors, labor-intensive processors, durable fabricators, and nondurable fabricators. The detailed procedures used for arriving at these groups are described in Appendix B.

In addition to these four export manufacturing industry groups, the model treated the following as separate activities: agriculture, mining, government and education, and military services.

Estimating Employment. Once industry groups had been specified, an estimate was made of the amount of employment in each group for each subregion in 1960.

TABLE 9.1

Estimated Employment in Each Industry Group in Susquehanna Subregions, 1960

Industry Groups	Subregions							
	A	B	C	D	E	F	G	H
Agriculture	11,587	15,675	6,599	4,528	5,453	5,048	24,981	10,365
Export mining	271	—	3,968	2,315	8,303	130	847	—
Durable fabricating	28,182	40,387	27,308	6,957	26,954	15,099	58,928	92,191
Nondurable fabricating	3,602	15,697	8,925	13,872	40,234	6,111	40,293	18,447
Labor-intensive processing	11,906	2,761	11,030	1,829	2,522	6,041	22,908	48,947
Capital-intensive processing	2,167	3,196	2,566	3,334	3,893	3,821	15,596	28,096
Business serving	13,304	18,157	17,800	7,932	24,382	11,558	52,204	95,777
Household serving	64,203	77,123	63,896	31,372	109,193	40,684	178,666	345,996
Export, government and education	3,545	2,475	4,507	—	—	—	21,707	27,860
Military services	181	85	310	47	270	181	2,298	25,081
Water-based recreation	51	62	152	15	48	65	170	42
Subregional total employment	138,999	175,618	147,061	72,201	221,252	88,738	418,598	692,802

The procedures used to make these estimates, which are shown in Table 9.1, are described in Appendix B.

Growth of Local Service Employment

Modeling the growth of local serving employment has been simplified by an appropriate geographic breakdown of the Susquehanna River Basin. Subregions have been specified so that they are approximately equal to the market area served by the local industries. This means that the amount of competition from service industries outside the subregion is minimized. There is, of course, competition from different sites within the subregions, for example, a suburban shopping center and a downtown center. However, in the model the major interest is in the total level of employment in the subregion, not in its spatial distribution. Differences in costs or access characteristics of alternative sites within a subregion were therefore neglected.

The main determinant of growth in the local serving industries is the size of the local market. Because the household- and business-serving industries serve different local markets, their growth is specified differently.

Growth of Household-Serving Employment. Household-serving employment is modeled to respond to growth in the size of the local population. The parameters for the relationship between household service employment and population were estimated by a cross-section analysis of data from the Susquehanna subregions. Figure 9.3 shows a plot of these data along with the statistically estimated linear

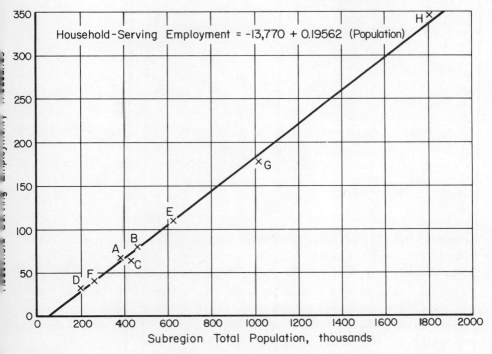

IGURE 9.3. Subregion household-serving employment against subregion total population, 960.

quation. The line in this plot, it will be noted, crosses the horizontal axis to the ght of the origin. This means that the ratio of household-serving workers to opulation increases as the population grows; this coincides with findings in ther studies.[5] It may be explained by import substitution. According to Tiebout,

> ... with more consumers a market develops for specialty items: a legitimate heater, a local baseball team, a Japanese curio shop and other such activities. n added impact comes at the indirect consumer level. With more food stores in he community, a local bottling plant becomes profitable and soda pop need not e imported. Added local dentists make a local dental-supply house feasible. s economists put it, the size of the market is now sufficient in terms of economies f scale to support these new activities.[6]

It also may be explained to some extent by the tendency for a larger area to xport a higher proportion of its services. Recall that all employment in industries hat were not *mainly* oriented towards nonlocal markets was classified in the ocal serving category. Some of this employment will serve nonlocal people. Large ities, because they have special services not available in smaller cities, are more kely to attract nonlocal clientele.

INCOME EFFECTS. In view of its importance in economic theory, some thought vas given to the inclusion of income into the formulation. According to the theory

[5] See, for example, a summary of empirical findings of economic base studies in "The asic-Non-Basic Concept of Urban Economic Functions," by John W. Alexander in H. M. layer's *Reading in Urban Geography* (Chicago, Ill.: University of Chicago Press, 1959).

[6] Charles M. Tiebout, *The Community Economic Base Study*, Supplementary Paper No. 16, ommittee for Economic Development, December, 1962, p. 66.

of consumption, all other things constant, people tend to spend more as their incomes increase. In addition, there is some indication that as incomes grow, proportionally more is spent on services. These two considerations lead one to suspect that household-serving employment will be higher in areas with higher per capita incomes. To test this quickly, data on per capita income were checked against the unexplained residuals in Figure 9.3 and found to have no apparent relationship to these residuals.

This may be explained by several factors.

1. Per capita income reflects the general wage level of the regions. Household-serving workers in areas with high per capita incomes would probably be paid higher wages than those in areas with lower per capita incomes. Therefore, although higher per capita incomes might result in more dollars being spent in these service industries, there is reason to believe that this increased spending may not produce proportionately more employment because of the wage differentials involved.

2. A good portion of the increased spending may be used to buy more expensive products and services that do not require more workers. It might be spent for fancier waiters in fancier restaurants, doctors who charge higher fees, higher paid mechanics who service Cadillacs instead of Chevrolets, and so on.

3. Part of the increased spending may be used to buy specialized services that are not available in smaller towns. People in small towns, especially richer people, may go to larger cities outside their home areas for specialized legal services, medical services, financial services, etc.[7] A significant amount of the increased purchase of services stemming from increased incomes may thus take place in the larger cities. This phenomenon is consistent with existing

[7] See Charles M. Tiebout, "Community Income Multipliers," *Journal of Regional Science* Vol. 2, Spring 1960. Tiebout found in his study of Ann Arbor, Michigan, Evanston, Illinois, and Lake Forest, Illinois, that higher-income spending units had increased tende to buy durable goods and clothing outside of the community.

formulation because, as noted, allowance is made for the tendency of larger areas to sell a greater share of their services to nonlocal clientele.

In view of these considerations, and because the equation with population alone ovided such a good fit, income was not included in the model as a determinant growth in household-serving employment.[8]

TREND IN HOUSEHOLD-SERVING EMPLOYMENT. There is a belief among economists t employment in the service industries will increase relative to other industries er time. Colin Clark writes, "A wide, simple and far-reaching generalization in s field is to the effect that, as time goes on and communities become more onomically advanced, the numbers engaged in agriculture tend to decline ative to the numbers in manufacture, which in turn decline relative to the mbers engaged in services."[9] This belief is based on several underlying ;uments as follows:

This formulation is viewed as being consistent with conventional labor market analysis. nsider, for example, the household-serving industries' demand for labor:

Demand: $L^d = \alpha_0 + \alpha_1(w/p) + \alpha_2 Y + \alpha_3 P$

ere total income Y, total population P, and wage price ratio w/p affect the demand for products of these industries and hence the derived demand for inputs including labor L. e supply of labor is

Supply: $L^s = \beta_0 + \beta_1(w/p) + \beta_3 P$.

equilibrium

$L^d = L^s = L$

m (1) we have

$w/p = (1/\alpha_1)(\alpha_0 + \alpha_2 Y + \alpha_3 P - L)$.

ostituting for w/p in (2) we have

$L = \beta_0 + (\beta_1/\alpha_1)(\alpha_0 + \alpha_2 Y + \alpha_3 P) + \beta_3 P$.

w if $\beta_1 \alpha_2/\alpha_1$ is small, income will not appear in Equation 5, and we have

$L = \gamma_0 + \gamma P$.

e that β_1 in the labor supply function may very well be small. Further, since we may ect that $0 < \alpha_2 < 1$, $(\beta_1)(\alpha_2)$ will be even smaller, thereby providing some support Equation 6.

Colin Clark, *The Conditions of Economic Progress*, Third Edition (London: Macmillan & Ltd., 1960), p. 492.

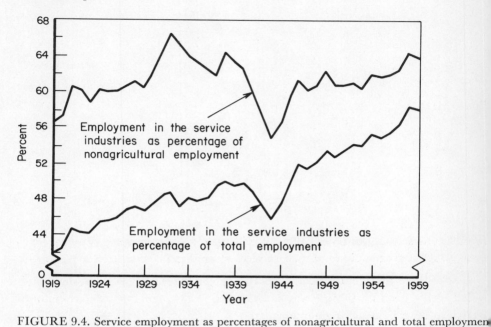

FIGURE 9.4. Service employment as percentages of nonagricultural and total employment 1919–1959. (From J. P. Henderson, *op. cit.*, p. 22.)

1. "Many of the refinements and economies of civilization only become possible under conditions of much higher population density."[10]
2. As per capita income increases, relative demand for agriculture falls and relative demand for manufacture first rises and then falls in favor of services.
3. In addition to changes in relative demand, there are changes in relative productivity with which different industries satisfy demand. In particular, it is argued that output per man-hour will increase faster in manufacturing than in service industries.

In considering the question of whether or not to include a trend factor in the model, one must consider both (1) the validity of these arguments and (2) the extent to which the formulation as it exists without a trend factor takes those arguments that are valid into account.

As a first check on the validity of these ideas, we may look at the actual behavior of employment in the United States. Some data compiled by Henderson,[11] shown in Figure 9.4, summarize this experience between 1919 and 1959. The upward trend in percentage of service employment is most marked when it is compared with total employment. This primarily reflects the declining employment in agriculture. When service-industry employment is compared with nonagricultural employment, the recent postwar experience shows a slight upward trend, but no long-term trend is clearly evident.

[10] Clark, *op. cit.*, p. 493.

[11] J. P. Henderson, *Changes in the Industrial Distribution of Employment 1919–1959*, Bureau of Economic and Business Research, Bulletin Number 87, University of Illinois, 1961.

The argument that productivity increases in service industries are significantly
ss than those experienced in manufacturing, in particular, seems to have drawn
iticisms. Critics have "drawn attention to the very great improvement in
ficiency which these service industries can show in an advancing economy."[12]
Both the other two reasons, (1) increased population density, and (2) increased
er capita income, given to support an upward trend are, as just discussed,
onsidered in the existing formulation.[13] They help explain why the line plotted
Figure 9.3 crosses the horizontal axis to the right of the origin. According to
is formulation, the upward trend in service industry employment is caused by
creased urbanization and the special services that this makes economically
asible.
The failure to find a systematic relation between per capita income and the
nexplained variation after population size is considered does not negate the idea
at increasing per capita income increases the relative importance of services.
suggests rather that the main effect of increases in per capita income in a
articular area may be to increase that area's tendency to import services from
her, more densely populated areas that have the specialized services. This
nding does not, however, mean that the growth in per capita incomes over time
ill not cause an upward shift in the line plotted in Figure 9.3. In particular,
might be expected that as incomes grow, the larger cities will export a greater
are of services. The ratio of household-serving workers to population in these
ties may tend to go above that which the current formulation leads one to expect
e., above the line in Figure 9.3).
To test whether this phenomenon was occurring, we estimated the amount of

---

[12] Clark, op. cit., p. 494. Estimates made by economists at Battelle tend to support this.
ttelle economists estimate that, for the recent past, productivity increases in manufacturing
2½ percent per year have not been much greater than the 2 percent per year experienced
the service industries.

[13] Certain sectors of the service industry that are expected to grow particularly fast are
ucation and government. To an important extent, these services will tend to be exported
om one area to another.

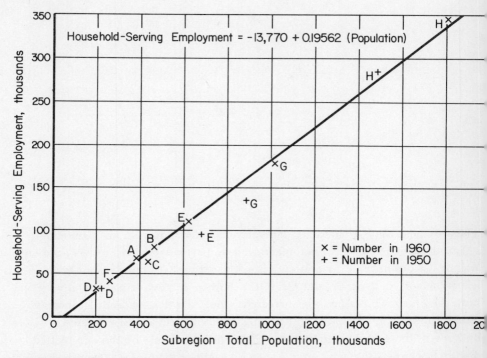

FIGURE 9.5. Subregion household-serving employment against subregion total population, 1950. Data for Subregions D, E, G, and H superimposed on 1960 data.

household-serving employment and population in 1950 for four of the subregions in the study area. These data are superimposed on the 1960 data in Figure 9.5. The results are somewhat mixed. If per capita income were causing an upward shift, the effects would have been expected to be greatest in the two more highly populated subregions, G and H. But the experience in these two subregions indicates no noticeable upward shift. Instead it is the less populated subregions, E and to a minor extent D, that show upward shifts. Furthermore, it is difficult to explain these upward shifts by increases in per capita incomes because both of these subregions, especially E, were experiencing the effects of a traumatic decline in the anthracite coal industry during this decade. It seems that the explanation for the behavior of these two subregions during 1950 to 1960 must be sought elsewhere.

Both these subregions, along with the anthracite area in general, experienced (1) a net decline and aging of population and (2) some degree of transition from mining to manufacturing employment. Both these changes could conceivably have contributed to higher ratios of service employment to population. Perhaps an older population demands relatively more service than a younger population. Also it is noted that the transition to manufacturing was brought about significantly by increased employment in the textile and apparel industries. The presence of these industries created increased job opportunities for females, which resulted in

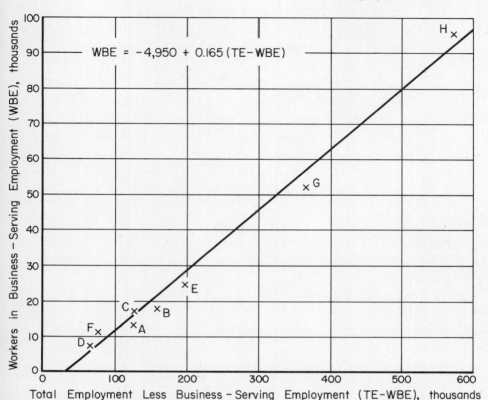

FIGURE 9.6. Subregion business-serving employment against total subregion employment less business-serving employment, 1960.

their increased participation in the labor force.[14] This in turn may increase the relative demand for services if working wives decide to use more outside help to do their household work. In view of these considerations, further research may be indicated to confirm the existence of these or other factors affecting the amount of service employment.

No explicit trend factor was introduced into the basic model. In view of the somewhat mixed results discussed in the preceding paragraph, however, the sensitivity of the final projections to such a trend factor was tested. This test showed that when household-serving employment is trended upwards by 15 percent over the 50-year period, the total population projection goes up a little less than 9 percent.

Growth in Business-Serving Employment. Business-serving employment is modeled to respond to the growth in all other industrial activity in the area. As in the

[14] See W. G. Bowen and T. W. Finegan, "Labor Force Participation and Unemployment," in *Employment Policy and Labor Market*, edited by Arthur M. Ross (Berkeley, Calif.: University of California Press, 1965), p. 135. This study demonstrates that industry mixes that offer increased opportunity to females significantly increase female labor-force-participation rates.

case of household service employment, the parameters of this relationship were estimated by a cross-section analysis of subregional data. Figure 9.6 illustrates the resulting model equation.

This chapter has explained the over-all method used to divide employment into the export and local serving categories. The formulation then used to specify growth in the two categories of local serving industry, business-serving and household-serving, is then spelled out. The following chapter describes the mechanisms used to specify the growth of the export industries.

The purpose of this chapter is to describe the mechanisms by which the model provides for growth of the export industries.[1] The reader will recall that the export industries are defined as those industries producing goods for sale primarily to nonlocal markets. Export producers include both final goods producers and intermediate goods producers selling to firms that produce for sales outside the region.

While an important feature of the model is the attempt to treat export industry locational influences endogenously, employment projections in a few export industries were prepared by conventional methods outside the model and entered as direct inputs to the model. This procedure was adopted for export governmental, educational, and military employment because these activities locate and grow as a result of noneconomic influences that are beyond the scope of the model. Mining and agriculture are handled this way for a similar reason. The location of these latter economic activities is tied to access to natural resources. Access to these resources is not significantly changed during the time period of interest by forces operating within the regional economy. The growth and decline of these two activities, therefore, hinge on changes in demand and technology that are independent of the regions.

Here, in order to concentrate attention on the model, the remaining discussion is limited to those industries, the export manufacturers, whose employment is determined by the model formulation.[2]

The basic hypothesis implemented in the model is that the growth of a region's employment in an industry depends primarily on factors affecting the relative

[1] Much of the work in connection with grouping procedures and measurement of access and market growth factors described in this section and in Appendices B and C is due largely to the effort of David Boyce, currently assistant professor of regional science at the University of Pennsylvania.

[2] Two special employment categories not treated in this chapter are water works construction and water-based recreation. These are both very small employment categories, and because they are directly related to water resource development, they are more appropriately discussed in Chapter 11.

cost of serving markets from the region as opposed to serving them from other regions. As discussed previously, a simple adaptation of this hypothesis was developed for the model. This adaptation involved a fairly high degree of aggregation. The manufacturing industries were divided into four industry groups: capital-intensive processors, labor-intensive processors, durable fabricators, and nondurable fabricators. For each of these industry groups, an index was developed that measured the relative cost of that industry group conducting operations in the region. These cost indices incorporated measures of the weighted importance of the different factors of production—labor, transportation, and capital—to each industry group. The cost indices, which are described later in some detail, were completed by combining these weights with measures of the relative cost of obtaining these factors in the region.

This approach can perhaps best be put into perspective by contrasting it with the more conventional trend-share analyses. Under this more conventional approach, information on national employment growth projections and past regional share by industry is extrapolated to arrive at future employment in the region. This latter procedure is not inconsistent with industrial location theory if we can assume that the comparative costs or trends in comparative costs experienced by a region will tend to persist through time. It is this assumption of unchanging regional cost characteristics with which the approach used in this study is most at odds. In attempting to preserve the feedback nature of the real world, we have been led into the question, "How do a region's comparative costs change over time in response to its own pattern of growth?" This, of course, is an extremely complicated question, and the model described here represents only a small beginning toward implementing the concepts derived. This beginning has been made largely in connection with labor costs, which represent one of the more significant sources of regional cost differences. A region's relative wage (i.e., labor costs) is modeled to respond both to the changing industry mix and to the degree of local labor market tightness. An extension of this approach would necessarily require investigation of other potential feedbacks from a region's

ndustrial growth pattern to its comparative costs, for example, the feedback of
growth onto transportation or land costs.

The remainder of this chapter discusses the implementation of this concept and
related empirical work. The discussion conveniently falls into two parts: (1) the
employment growth equation and (2) the relative cost equation.

The Employment Growth Equation

The basic equation that determines a subregion's employment growth rate as a
function of market growth and relative costs is as follows:

$$PI \cdot K = GDI \cdot K - (CEI)(1.0 - RCI \cdot K) \tag{10.1}$$

where

$PI \cdot K$ Percent change in employment in the Ith industry group at time K
(1/year),

$GDI \cdot K$ percent market Growth in labor Demand in the Ith industry group at
time K (1/year),

CEI percent Cost Elasticity of Ith industry group,

$RCI \cdot K$ Relative Cost of Ith industry group at time K.

f a subregion offers costs lower than subregions competing for the same market
because of lower labor costs or better access to market and raw materials, the
cost index $RCI \cdot K$ is less than 1.0. However, if the access characteristics of the
subregion and its labor costs are higher than in competing subregions, a cost
index greater than 1.0 results. A cost index equal to 1.0 indicates that the
industry growth rate for the market $GDI \cdot K$ also applies to the subregion. This
growth rate is adjusted up or down in relation to a low- or high-cost region by an
amount proportional to the cost elasticity CEI. Implementation of this equation
requires specification of the market growth rate, which is an exogenous input to
the model, and the cost elasticity parameter. The specification of these two factors
described following a brief discussion of some relevant empirical findings.

Some Empirical Findings. It was hoped that empirical analyses would permit direct support for the cost elasticity concept as well as an estimate of its numerical value. Attempts to measure this parameter, however, have been unsuccessful largely owing to the difficulty of obtaining suitable data on costs at alternative locations. In view of these difficulties, empirical analysis was aimed at the less ambitious goal of developing some indirect support for the employment growth formulation. For this purpose, available data on gross profits and new capital expenditures was used. Gross profits by industry and state are assumed to reflect some combination of favorable relative costs and market conditions. New capital expenditures are used as a measure of the rate of growth. According to the model formulation we expect states experiencing higher profits in a given industry to experience faster growth in that industry, leading to the following regression equation:

$$(I_{ij})_t = a(P_{ij})^b_{t-1}$$

where

$\quad (I_{ij})_t$ new capital Investment of ith industry in jth state,

$\quad (P_{ij})_{t-1}$ gross Profit of ith industry in jth state.

The data used in the analysis are a series drawn from the *1958 Census of Manufactures* and the 1959 to 1962 *Annual Survey of Manufactures*.[3] For this 5-year period, the following variables for SIC 2-digit industries for states having a significant amount of the industry were compiled: payroll, value added by manufacture, and capital investments (new). Value added is the total value of output minus the cost of inputs purchased outside the firms. Payroll is the cost of production and nonproduction employees. Gross profits are measured by taking

[3] U.S. Department of Commerce, Bureau of the Census, *1958 Census of Manufactures* and *Annual Survey of Manufactures, 1959–1962*, U.S. Government Printing Office, Washington, D.C.

TABLE 10.1
Correlation and Regression Coefficients for New Capital Expenditures as Function of Gross Profits
in Preceding Year

Industry	1959	1960	1961	1962
Primary metals				
a	0.02	0.01	0.02	0.01
b	1.19	1.28	1.16	1.18
Percent of variation explained (r^2)	0.89	0.89	0.89	0.89
Fabricated metal products				
a	0.08	0.09	0.06	0.03
b	1.03	1.01	1.04	1.10
Percent of variation explained (r^2)	0.95	0.97	0.97	0.93
Machinery, nonelectrical				
a	0.23	0.06	0.08	0.07
b	0.95	1.05	1.02	1.05
Percent of variation explained (r^2)	0.94	0.95	0.91	0.95
Transportation equipment				
a	0.51	0.11	0.16	2.23
b	0.86	0.98	0.94	0.72
Percent of variation explained (r^2)	0.89	0.88	0.78	0.72

value added minus payroll. These series were compiled for the following four
-digit industries:

3—Primary metals industries,
4—Fabricated metal products,
5—Machinery, except electrical,
7—Transportation equipment.

The analysis was carried out by year for each of the four industries. Table 10.1
shows the results. The results, as indicated by the high r^2, provide encouraging
support for the hypothesized regional growth mechanism. They suggest, in
particular, that there is some promise for the use of an aggregated and relatively
simple growth-rate approach, such as in the model, toward the forecasting of
regional export industry growth.

Parameter Estimates

COST ELASTICITY. According to the employment growth equation, if a subregion's
costs are equal to national costs, then the subregion's employment growth rate is
taken to be the market-demand growth rate. The cost elasticity parameter determines
how much faster or slower an industry will grow given a certain cost advantage or
disadvantage. Although the empirical results discussed in the preceding paragraphs
provide some support for this concept, these results cannot be used to obtain
numerical estimates of the parameter. Consequently, it was necessary in estimating

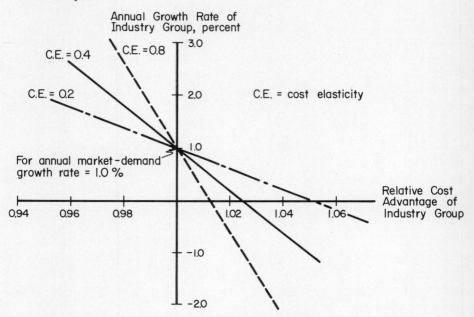

FIGURE 10.1. Annual growth rate versus relative-cost advantage.

the parameter to rely on more subjective analysis. On this basis, several values, as shown in Figure 10.1, were selected and tested in sensitivity runs. The value of the cost-elasticity parameter that led to the most reasonable results in terms of stability of the model output was 0.4 percent.[4] A value twice as large, 0.8 percent, resulted in nearly 10 percent higher employment in 20 years and 14 percent higher employment in 50 years. A value one-half as large, 0.2 percent, resulted in nearly 6 percent less employment in 20 years and 10 percent less employment in 50 years. Compared with many other sensitivity results, these changes are regarded as relatively large, although not unduly so. They do, however, indicate the need for further empirical effort.

INDUSTRY MARKET-DEMAND GROWTH RATES. The market-demand growth rates used in the model are not market area growth rates in the usual sense of an area's rate of change of demand for a particular product. Rather, they are the rate of change of a weighted function of projected industry employment in the U.S. census regions. The weights assigned to census region employment are proportional to the importance of markets in each region to the Susquehanna basin. Therefore, the market-demand growth rate refers neither to the demand growth rate for the products of a given industry nor to a market as a specific area within the United States. Rather, it is the growth rate of employment in all regions in the United States combined in proportion to the importance of these regions as markets for the Susquehanna basin. As defined in this manner, the market-demand growth rate

[4] Higher values produced fluctuations in the local unemployment rate that were believed to be implausible.

of employment for a given industry is taken as an estimate of the growth rate of that industry in a Susquehanna subregion, given that the costs of production and distribution for that subregion are equal to the average costs nationally.

The steps in computing the market-demand growth rate for a given SIC 2-digit industry are as follows:

1. Compile 1960 and 1975 employment totals for each U.S. census region from "State Projections to 1975." [5]
2. Compile the percentage distribution of destination of shipments from the Middle Atlantic census region to each census region for the industry from the *1963 Census of Transportation*.[6]
3. Compute the market-demand employment for 1960 and 1975 by weighting the employment in each census region by the percentage of shipments to that census region from the Middle Atlantic region.
4. Compute the market-demand growth rate by dividing 1975 market-demand employment by 1960 market-demand employment.

The National Planning Association's 1960 estimates and 1975 forecasts of state employment in SIC 2-digit industries are the basis for the 1960 and 1975 census-region employment totals.[7] Because the *1963 Census of Transportation* was not available for all SIC 2-digit industries, it was necessary to aggregate certain industries at this stage of the analysis. Census-region employment was therefore compiled for the following SIC 2-digit industry groups: 20, 21, 22-23-31, 24, 25-39, 25, 27, 28, 29, 30, 32, 33, 34-19, 35, 36, 37, and 38.

The percentage distribution of the destination of products shipped from the Middle Atlantic census region (New York, Pennsylvania, and New Jersey) was the best data available on the location of the markets of the Susquehanna basin.

[5] National Planning Association, "State Projections to 1975," Report No. 65-II, Table 11, Washington, D.C., 1965.

[6] U.S. Bureau of the Census, *Census of Transportation, 1963*, Shipper Series Reports, TC63(P)C1, Table 7, U.S. Government Printing Office, Washington, D.C.

[7] National Planning Association, *op. cit.*

TABLE 10.2
Examples of Market-Demand Growth-Rate Computations

Census Region	Distribution by Destination from Middle Atlantic,* (percent)	1960 Employment,† (1,000)	1975 Employment,† (1,000)	1960–1975 percent change
	Paper and Allied Products (SIC 26)			
New England	8.4	79.5	77.8	−2.1
Middle Atlantic	62.6	148.8	157.6	+5.9
East North Central	8.4	167.2	189.1	+13.1
West North Central	2.4	34.5	65.9	+91.0
South Atlantic	15.4	83.3	121.3	+45.6
East South Central	1.3	34.6	54.3	+56.9
West South Central	0.8	37.8	42.6	+12.7
Mountain	—	2.2	5.3	+140.9
Pacific	0.7	59.3	88.2	+48.7
Market Demand	100.0	128.7	143.0	+11.1
	Electrical Machinery (SIC 36)			
New England	7.7	155.9	226.3	+45.2
Middle Atlantic	33.3	420.4	525.2	+24.9
East North Central	19.6	476.0	564.6	+18.6
West North Central	5.4	72.1	111.5	+54.6
South Atlantic	13.5	71.7	167.2	+133.2
East South Central	3.8	44.4	93.2	+109.9
West South Central	4.2	26.9	82.6	+207.1
Mountain	2.4	9.0	29.3	+225.6
Pacific	10.1	181.1	500.7	+176.5
Market Demand	100.0	280.3	389.9	+39.1

$$\text{Paper Market-Demand Growth Rate, } 1960\text{–}1975 = \frac{(143.0 - 128.7)}{128.7} = +11.1 \text{ percent}$$

$$\text{Electrical-Machinery Market-Demand Growth Rate, } 1960\text{–}1975 = \frac{(389.9 - 280.3)}{280.3} = 39.1 \text{ percent}$$

* U.S. Bureau of the Census, *Census of Transportation, 1963*, Shipper Series Reports, TC63(P)C1, Table 7, U.S. Government Printing Office, Washington, D.C.

† National Planning Association, "State Projections to 1975," Report 65-II, Table 11, Washington, D.C., 1965.

Therefore these distributions were compiled for the seventeen 2-digit industries indicated and were used to determine the importance of each census region as a market for the Susquehanna basin.[8] The 1963 distribution of products shipped was used for both 1960 and 1975 market-demand employment computations in lieu of any means of forecasting any shifts in the shipment pattern.

Table 10.2 illustrates the reason for the low growth rate of the Middle Atlantic region compared with that of other regions of the country. Within the framework

[8] SIC Industries 21 and 27 for which no *Census of Transportation* data are available are assumed to have the same shipping distribution as industries 22-23-31, and 25-39, respectively.

TABLE 10.3
Market-Demand Growth Rates for Industries in the Susquehanna River Basin

SIC Industry	1960 Market-Demand Employment (1,000)	1975 Market-Demand Employment (1,000)	Market-Demand Growth Rates 1960–1975, percent
20	259.7	283.8	+9.3
21	21.5	16.0	−25.6
22-23-31	576.1	523.7	−9.1
24	41.5	36.6	−11.8
25-39	157.4	167.6	+6.5
26	128.7	143.0	+11.1
27	208.4	236.9	+13.7
28	185.9	217.1	+16.8
29	42.1	26.8	−36.3
30	77.3	95.2	+23.2
32	126.1	120.9	−4.1
33	332.0	318.6	−4.0
34-19	262.6	291.7	+11.1
35	293.8	331.6	+12.9
36	280.3	389.9	+39.1
37	257.7	323.7	+25.6
38	70.2	99.2	+41.3

of the industry-growth mechanism just described, the Susquehanna basin's growth rate is a function of the growth rate of a census region weighted by the importance of that region as a Middle Atlantic market. Table 10.2 shows that the major markets for the Middle Atlantic region are the slower growing census regions. For instance, in the case of the paper industry (Industry 26), 71 percent of the Middle Atlantic region's products are destined to the two slowest growing census regions, Middle Atlantic and New England. Furthermore, because the Middle Atlantic region is the second largest employer in both 1960 and 1975, its low 5.9 percent growth for the 15-year period is a major factor in determining the market-demand growth rate of 11.1 percent. Similarly, in the nationally fast-growing electrical-machinery industry, over one-half of the Middle Atlantic region's products are destined to the two slowest growing regions of the country. Table 10.3 shows the market-demand growth rates for all 17 industries.

AGGREGATION TO INDUSTRY GROUP MARKET-DEMAND GROWTH RATES. In order to use these growth rates in the model, they must be aggregated to the four export industry groups. The growth rates are combined in proportion to the 1960 industry employment distribution in each subregion. Therefore the industry-group growth rates reflect the mix of 1960 subregional employment and, in general, are different for each subregion. Finally, the 1960–1975 industry-group growth rates are converted to an annual rate that is assumed to hold over the 50-year forecast period. Table 10.4 shows the market-demand growth rates for the four industry groups and eight subregions for the 1960–1975 period. The difference in growth

TABLE 10.4
Market-Demand Growth Rates 1960–1975 for the Susquehanna Subregions and Industry Groups

Industry-Group Growth Rate (percent)

Subregion	Durable Fabrication	Nondurable Fabrication	Capital-Intensive Processing	Labor-Intensive Processing
A	+17.6	−10.8	+11.5	−4.1
B	+22.6	−10.6	+13.0	−6.0
C	+25.6	−10.2	+12.1	−0.7
D	+20.7	−16.2	+11.1	−3.2
E	+19.8	−10.5	+10.9	−1.7
F	+18.2	−10.4	+14.7	+1.8
G	+17.1	−10.2	+9.3	−1.3
H	+23.8	−9.1	+10.7	−2.7

rates among subregions are an indication of a fast- or slow-growing mix of industries. For example, the relative concentration of employment in subregion F in the paper industry (Industry 26) accounts for the positive rate of growth in the labor-intensive processing group in that subregion.

The Relative-Cost Equation

For a particular industry, a subregion's growth rate, as contrasted with that of its market, is determined by its relative advantage with respect to costs. The model at present incorporates measures of regional cost differentials related to labor and transportation. These two cost components were included because they represent the most significant sources of variation in costs between regions. Other kinds of regional cost differentials such as those related to electric power, water, site availability, plant construction, or local tax structure were excluded because they were not thought to be significant location influences either (1) in the studied regions or (2) in relation to the fairly aggregated industry groups that were chosen for modeling. The inclusion of additional kinds of costs and cost-related factors is, however, viewed as an important area for further model refinement. Such refinement would be particularly important if the model were to be applied to other areas where different cost factors, for example, exceptionally low taxes, were expected to play an important role in attracting industrial growth.

Figure 10.2 shows how the relative-cost index is constructed. Information on cost conditions in the subregion is combined with information on industry cost characteristics to arrive at the relative cost for each industry group. In the current formulation the industry cost weights are assumed to remain constant. In the cases of both transportation and labor costs, an attempt is made to represent their dynamic behavior over time in the model. Transportation costs are varied to incorporate major changes in the transportation system that are expected to occur, such as the construction of interstate highways. Wage costs are determined

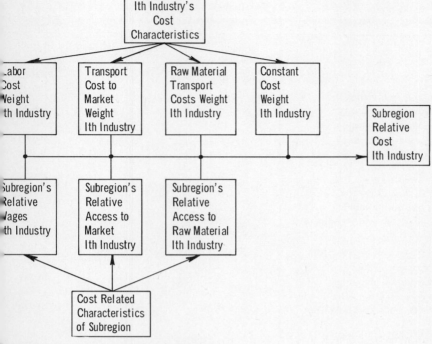

FIGURE 10.2. The relative-cost equation.

Mathematically,

$$\text{RCI} . \text{K} = (\text{WLI})(\text{RWI} . \text{K}) + (\text{WTI})(\text{AMI} . \text{K}) + (\text{WRI})(\text{ARI}) + \text{WCI}$$

where

RCI . K	Relative Cost of Ith industry group at time K,
WLI	Weight, Labor costs in Ith industry group,
RWI . K	Relative Wages of Ith industry group in subregion at time K,
WTI	Weight, Transport costs to market in Ith industry group,
AMI . K	relative Access to Market of Ith industry group from subregion at time K,
WRI	Weight, Raw material transport costs in Ith industry group,
ARI	relative Access to Raw materials in Ith industry group from subregion,
WCI	Weight, constant Cost in Ith industry group.

endogenously and, as shown in Figure 9.1, are part of the major feedback loop in the employment sector of the model.

The remainder of this chapter discusses the work done in relation to the relative cost equation. The discussion is conveniently divided into two parts, one dealing with industry and the other with regional cost characteristics.

Industry Cost Characteristics. The extent to which different locations offer cost advantages to industries depends not only on cost characteristics of the different locations but also on cost characteristics of industries. Industries with a higher proportion of labor costs, for example, will find more advantage, other things being equal, in low wage locations. This industry effect is represented in the relative cost equation by a set of cost weights that reflect the relative importance of different kinds of costs in the industry group. To estimate the numerical value

TABLE 10.5

Ratios of Payroll and Transportation Costs on Output and Input to Producer's Value of Product fc

SIC Code	Industry	Producer's Value of Product, (millions of dollars)	Payroll,† (millions of dollars)	Payroll/ Value of Product
(1) Nondurable Fabricating				
21	Tobacco manufacturers	5,918	295	0.050
22	Textile mill products	12,811	2,288	0.179
23	Apparel and related products	16,544	4,252	0.257
31	Leather and leather products	3,985	1,146	0.288
(2) Durable Fabricating				
25	Furniture and fixtures	4,795	1,389	0.290
27	Printing and publishing	12,613	4,480	0.355
30	Rubber and plastics products	6,842	1,723	0.252
34	Fabricated metal products	18,161	5,056	0.278
35	Machinery, except electrical	24,738	7,304	0.295
36	Electrical machinery	21,174	5,606	0.265
37	Transportation equipment	39,252	9,165	0.234
38	Instruments and related products	5,040	1,578	0.313
39	Miscellaneous manufacturing	5,306	1,461	0.275
(3) Labor-Intensive Processing				
24	Lumber and wood	8,373	1,986	0.237
26	Paper and allied	13,167	2,780	0.211
32	Stone, clay, and glass	9,652	2,595	0.269
33	Primary metals	28,296	6,854	0.242
(4) Capital-Intensive Processing				
20	Food and kindred	63,925	7,553	0.118
28	Chemicals and allied	24,469	3,397	0.139
29	Petroleum and coal	17,343	1,117	0.064

* National Economics Division, Office of Business Economics, U.S. Department of Commerce, Washington, D.C.

of these cost weights, actual costs as percentage of producer's value of product for each of the four industry groups were used.

Data on total producer's value of product, transport costs on inputs, and transport cost on outputs were obtained for each input-output industry from tabulations made by the Department of Commerce in connection with the 1958 input-output study. Total payroll for each of these input-output industries was obtained from the *1958 Census of Manufactures*. These input-output industries are then aggregated, first to the SIC 2-digit industries and then into the final export industry groups themselves. In aggregating the input-output industries, the data for each industry are accumulated, so that the resulting cost component reflect the relative size of each industry in 1958 as measured by its producer's value of product. Therefore, for example, in the Capital-Intensive Processing industry group, the food and kindred products industry's cost characteristics xport Manufacturing Industries (1958 Input-Output Study)*

Transport Cost on Output (millions of dollars)	Transportation Cost (Output)/ Value of Product	Transport Cost on Input (millions of dollars)	Transportation Cost (Input)/ Value of Product
122	0.021	68	0.012
336	0.026	301	0.024
383	0.023	138	0.008
92	0.023	56	0.014
144	0.030	97	0.020
256	0.020	178	0.014
190	0.028	146	0.021
434	0.024	281	0.016
548	0.022	293	0.012
468	0.022	257	0.012
733	0.019	592	0.015
146	0.029	54	0.011
144	0.027	80	0.015
830	0.099	268	0.032
819	0.062	483	0.037
675	0.070	493	0.051
1,144	0.040	1,170	0.041
2,406	0.038	2,521	0.039
1,290	0.053	650	0.027
1,249	0.072	837	0.048

† U.S. Bureau of the Census, *1958 Census of Manufactures*, Vol. 1, Summary Statistics, 'ashington, D.C.

:ceive about $1\frac{1}{2}$ times as much weight as the chemicals and petroleum industries)mbined. Table 10.5 shows the data and calculations for each 2-digit industry. able 10.6 shows the finally estimated cost weights for each industry group. We e from this table that substantial differences exist between the different groups. or example, the processing groups have much higher transportation costs than 1e fabricating groups. Also of interest is the comparatively high labor cost weight r the Nondurable Fabricating Group.

In contrast to the regional cost factors that are modeled to vary, these industry)st weights are assumed constant over time. The major objection to this sumption is that technological innovations during the projection period are likely lead to changes in industrial cost characteristics. Economic theory leads us to :pect, for example, that labor-saving innovations will result in proportionately ss use of labor and hence in labor costs that are a smaller percentage of total

TABLE 10.6
Industry Cost Weights as Percent of Producer's Value of Product

Industry Group	Labor Cost Weight	Transport Costs of Output to Market Weight	Transport Cost on Raw Material Input Weight	Constant Cost Weight	Sum of Weights
Nondurable fabricating	20.33	2.37	—	77.30	100.0
Durable fabricating	27.38	2.20	—	70.42	100.0
Labor-intensive processing	23.90	5.83	4.06	66.21	100.0
Capital-intensive processing	11.41	4.68	3.79	80.12	100.0

costs. There is, however, evidence that this does not happen. Bela Gold in a recent study deals directly with this question.[9] Gold selects six industries, blast furnaces, steel mills, coke ovens, cement, petroleum refining, and canned fruits and vegetables, that have experienced major technological innovations. Despite these innovations, it is shown that the proportion of costs attributable to materials wages, salaries, and other costs plus profits remained relatively constant over a considerable period of time. Gold suggests several possible explanations for this. One explanation is if costs in a certain category get out of "normal" proportion management will respond by (1) intensifying engineering efforts to reduce use of more costly factors and (2) substituting less costly factors. This, in addition to other considerations, leads Gold to conclude that

. . . the variety of influences tending to maintain stable cost proportions and their conformity both with managerial cost reduction objectives and with organization pressures suggests that the tendency toward stable cost proportions is less likely to prove a happenstance outcome in the few industries studied than one of the most pervasive sectors of economic stability yet uncovered in industrial operations

Gold's findings were used to support the assumption of constant cost weights as useful first approximation. It is believed, however, that this assumption should be relaxed in future more refined versions of the model. In general, weighting the importance of different kinds of costs by their current percentage of total costs is an expedient. It reflects past decisions that have probably attempted to minimize these costs. For instance, the importance of labor to the garment industry may be understated because the industry has located in low labor cost areas. In terms of Gold's analysis location or relocation is, in fact, one of the means by which management may keep cost proportions under control. To avoid this problem, a somewhat different cost formulation might be developed in which total cost is computed by multiplying unit input requirements by the unit costs of these inpu

[9] B. Gold, "Economic Effects of Technological Innovations," *Management Science, 11* (September 1964).

[10] *Ibid*, p. 127.

TABLE 10.7
Access to Markets Factors for Subregions by Industry Groups

Subregion	Access Factor 1960	1975	Change of Access* 1960–1975 percent	Subregion	Access Factor 1960	1975	Change of Access* 1960–1975 percent
Durable Fabricating Industries				Nondurable Fabricating Industries			
A	0.95	0.92	−4	A	0.98	0.95	−3
B	0.99	0.95	−4	B	1.01	0.96	−4
C	0.89	0.83	−6	C	0.94	0.86	−8
D	0.76	0.72	−4	D	0.92	0.88	−5
E	0.93	0.87	−7	E	0.98	0.90	−8
F	0.87	0.86	−2	F	0.92	0.90	−2
G	0.89	0.87	−2	G	0.89	0.87	−3
H	0.85	0.82	−3	H	0.91	0.88	−4
Labor-Intensive Processing Industries				Capital-Intensive Processing Industries			
A	1.14	1.09	−4	A	0.85	0.83	−3
B	0.69	0.66	−4	A	0.96	0.92	−4
C	0.74	0.69	−6	C	0.81	0.77	−5
D	0.66	0.63	−5	D	0.78	0.73	−6
E	0.75	0.69	−7	E	0.78	0.72	−8
F	0.77	0.76	−1	F	0.67	0.66	−2
G	0.75	0.74	−1	G	0.72	0.71	−2
H	0.83	0.87	−2	H	0.77	0.74	−4

* Change-of-access percentages are not strictly comparable because of rounding.

or example, as follows:

$$\text{Total Cost/unit} = (\text{hours of labor/input})(\text{hourly wage})$$
$$+ (\text{average miles shipped/unit})(\text{transport cost/mile})$$

It is expected that future research efforts will include an investigation of this kind of formulation.

Regional Cost Characteristics. To complete the relative cost equation, information about regional cost characteristics must be added to the industrial cost weights. These regional cost characteristics are represented in the model by three measures: 1) relative access to markets, (2) relative access to raw materials, and (3) relative wages.

ACCESS FACTORS. Relative access to market was measured essentially by taking the ratio of subregional transportation costs to national average transportation costs for the products of a given industry group. A rather straightforward, but computationally involved, procedure was developed to estimate these access factors on the basis of *1963 Census of Transportation* data. These factors were estimated for the years 1960 and 1975, the latter estimates reflecting the changes in access due to the construction of the interstate highway system. Table 10.7 shows the final estimates. A detailed description of the estimating procedures for these as well as the raw material access factors is provided in Appendix C.

TABLE 10.8
Access Factors for Raw Materials for Subregions of the Susquehanna River Basin

Access to Resources for Processing Industries

Subregion	A	B	C	D	E	F	G	H
Labor-Intensive	1.22	1.22	1.17	1.41	1.45	1.49	1.37	1.01
Capital-Intensive	1.29	1.29	1.09	1.25	1.29	1.24	1.21	1.04

Relative access to raw materials was viewed conceptually in the same way as access to markets. Due to the lack of comparable data in this case, however, access factors for raw materials were developed in a highly subjective fashion, described in Appendix C. Table 10.8 shows the resulting estimates for each of the two processing industry groups.

RELATIVE WAGES. To complete specification of the relative cost equation, we need a procedure for determining the relative cost of labor in different subregions. In the case of labor costs particularly, it was felt that a subregion's relative position could change considerably over time in response to changing conditions in the local labor market. Effort was thus devoted to implementing this feedback in the model. In developing a measure of relative labor costs, it was assumed, for the sake of simplification, that differences in wage rates between areas for a particular (2-digit) industry were not caused by differences in labor productivity.[11] Under this assumption, relative wage was used as a measure of a subregion's relative labor costs. The relative wage is defined as the ratio of actual average hourly manufacturing earnings to the hypothetical average that would be paid if all industries in the area paid at their national average rates. Its value for 1960 was computed for each subregion as follows:

$$RW_k = \frac{PY_k}{\sum_j (E_{jk})(NW_j)}$$

where

RW_k Relative Wage of kth subregion, 1960,

PY_k total PaYroll for all manufacturing industries in kth subregion, 1960,

E_{jk} Employment in jth 2-digit manufacturing industry of kth subregion, 1960,

NW_j average National Wage of jth 2-digit manufacturing industry, 1960.

[11] Some model experiments were conducted in which this assumption was relaxed by the introduction of labor skills into the model. This preliminary skills sector, described in Chapter 8, has not as yet been empirically implemented.

TABLE 10.9
Relative Wage by Subregion, 1960

Subregions	A	B	C	D	E	F	G	H
Relative Wage	0.94	0.99	0.90	0.90	0.89	0.89	0.92	1.00

Sources: *Employment and Earnings Statistics for State and Areas 1939–1962*, Bulletin No. 1370, U.S. Department of Labor, 1963; *Employment and Earnings Statistics for the United States 1909–1962*, Bulletin No. 1312-1, U.S. Department of Labor, 1963; U.S. Department of Commerce, Bureau of the Census, *Annual Survey of Manufactures, 1960*, U.S. Government Printing Office, Washington, D.C.

The results of these computations, shown in Table 10.9, reveal that, with the exception of subregion H (Baltimore), the study area had relatively low labor costs in 1960.

At first it was believed that a single relative wage measure would provide an adequate representation of a subregion's relative labor cost position. The empirical findings in relation to the effects of local labor market conditions on wages led, however, to the introduction of two relative wage measures—one for high-skill-using and another for low-skill-using industry groups. The final formulation used in the model is described following a discussion of the empirical findings.

EMPIRICAL FINDINGS. It was hypothesized that wage rates, and hence relative wage rates, would vary over time in response to changing local labor market tightness. This hypothesis is supported by several studies that show that as the unemployment rate decreases, the percentage change in the money wage increases.[12] The findings in these studies were based on analysis of national time series data. As a first step in this study, a quick check was made to see if a similar relationship would hold up across metropolitan areas. Data on unemployment rate in 1960 and 1962 and changes in earnings are plotted for 30 SMSA's in Figure 10.3. As can be seen, the plot is not entirely convincing.

Several possible explanations for the unsatisfactory fit shown in this plot are as follows:

. The method used for calculating average wage change between 1960 and 1962 incorporated the change in industry mix as well as the change in relative wage. Some areas, for example, may have experienced an increase in over-all average wage due to expansion of high-paying industries at the same time that no change was occurring in their relative wage. Related to this is the possibility that different industries may respond differently to labor market tightness. In this case, areas with the same

[12] See, for example, A. W. Phillips, "The Relation Between Unemployment and the Rate of Change of Money Wage Rates in the United Kingdom, 1862–1957," *Economica* November 1958).

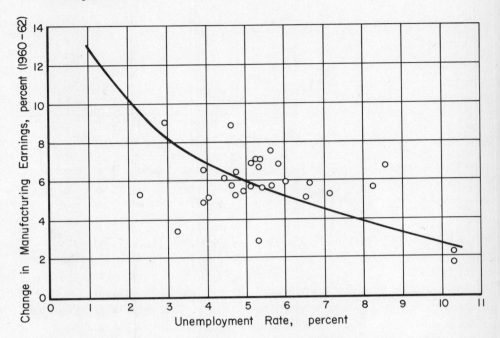

FIGURE 10.3. Percent change in manufacturing earnings (1960–1962) and 1960 unemployment rate for 30 standard metropolitan statistics areas in the northeastern states. (Department of Labor figures used for both unemployment rate and earnings.)

unemployment rate but different industry mixes would have different changes in over-all average wage.

3. Industry mix may be important for still another reason. In a particular area, one industry may be forced to bid labor away from other industries. If high-paying industries tend to predominate in an area, this may in itself lead to a high relative wage as competitive bidding forces wages up.

4. The accuracy with which local unemployment rates are measured is open to serious question. In particular, the Department of Labor's figures appear to be in wide disagreement with census estimates for the same areas.[13]

5. Assuming that local unemployment rate has been measured accurately, there is still some question as to whether it adequately reflects the tightness of labor markets within the SMSA's. One reason for this is that a metropolitan area may differ with respect to availability of labor in nearby rural areas. With differences in availability of rural labor, two metropolitan areas with the same unemployment rate may have quite different labor market conditions.[14]

[13] See, for example, Joseph C. Ullman, "How Accurate Are Estimates of State and Local Unemployment?" *Industrial and Labor Relations Review*, Vol. 16, April 1963, and John Lindauer, "The Accuracy of Area Unemployed Estimates Used to Identify Depressed Areas," *Industrial and Labor Relations Review*, Vol. 19, April 1966.

[14] See George Borts and Jerome Stein, *Economic Growth In A Free Market* (New York and London: Columbia University Press, 1964). This consideration was motivated by the findings of Borts and Stein that the proportion of region's workers outside manufacturing has an important influence on its labor supply to the manufacturing industries. See p. 82.

These considerations led to a reformulation of the regional wage adjustment hypothesis as follows:

Local relative manufacturing wages will increase faster where (1) local markets are tight, (2) there are fewer workers available from nearby rural farm areas, and (3) high-paying industries tend to predominate.

To test this hypothesis, regression analysis was applied to an equation of the following form for each of four selected industries:

$$\Delta W_{ij} = a_i + b_i \frac{(RP)_j}{(TP)_j} + c_i W_j + d_i \frac{E_j}{(TP)_j - (RP)_j}$$

where

ΔW_{ij} change in average Wage for production workers from 1958 to 1963 for the ith industry in the jth state. (Source: *Census of Manufactures, 1958*, Table 4, and *1963* Table 5.)

E_j total nonagricultural Employment in the jth state in 1960. (Source: *Manpower Report of the President, 1965*, Table D-1)

$TP)_j$ Total Population in jth state in 1960. (Source: *Statistical Abstracts of the United States, 1964*.)

$RP)_j$ Rural farm Population in jth state in 1960 (Source: *Statistical Abstracts of the United States, 1964*.)

W_j average Wage for *all* manufacturing production workers in the jth state in 1958. (Source: *Census of Manufactures, 1958*, Table 4.)

In order to avoid problems of industry mix, wage changes within a particular -digit SIC industry were used. Of course, for a given 2-digit category, the 3- and -digit mix may vary so this problem is not avoided completely. Four 2-digit industries (textiles, food, fabricated metals, and primary metals) were selected for purposes of making a preliminary exploration. These particular industries were selected with an eye to getting one from each of the four export manufacturing groups and to cover the full spectrum from low- to high-wage industries. The national average wages in 1958 were $1.54 for textiles, $1.97 for food, $2.32 for fabricated metals, and $2.81 for primary metals.

To facilitate the measurement of farm worker availability, the analysis was conducted on state rather than metropolitan area data. This led to the use of the ratio of rural farm population to total population in each state as an index of the availability of workers from rural areas. 1960 data were used as a proxy for the regional values of this index during the 1958–1963 period.

In view of the problems associated with measuring unemployment rate, it was decided to use the ratio of urban employment to urban population as an alternative measure of local labor market tightness within a state. This decision was motivated by the fact that a major problem in getting reliable measures of unemployment is distinguishing the people who are unemployed from those who are not in the labor force. The use of the employment ratio avoids this particular measurement problem because it requires that only employed and nonemployed be distinguished. As in the case of the rural farm population ratio, 1960 data were used as a proxy for the values of the urban employment ratio during the 1958–196 period.

The average wage for all production workers in the state is used to reflect the extent to which higher paying industries predominate in the area. Average wage data for 1958 were used as a proxy for the 1958–1963 period. The correlation with the same variable in 1963 is 0.98, confirming that the 1958 average wage is in fact good measure of regional differentials in average wage during the whole period.

Finally, wage change over the 1958 to 1963 period was used as the dependent variable to take advantage of the *Census of Manufactures* publications in those years

The results of the regression runs are shown in Table 10.10. The only variable that is consistently significant is the average wage for all manufacturing productio workers. The textile industry, the lowest paying of the four industries, is the only one with no variables entering significantly. Possibly this can be explained by the impact of the Federal Minimum Wage Law that went into effect toward the latte

TABLE 10.10

Regression Results: Change in Average Hourly Wages of Production Workers by Industry by State (1958–1963) as a Function of the Ratio of Rural Farm Population to Total Population by State (1960), the Average Hourly Wages of Production Workers (All Manufacturing Industries in State, 1958), and the Ratio of Nonagricultural Employment to Nonrural Population by State (1960)

Functional Form $\Delta W_{ij} = a_i + b_i \dfrac{(RP)_j}{(TP)_j} + c_i W_j + d_i \dfrac{E_j}{(TP)_j - (RP)_j}$

Industry	a	b (s)	F	c (s)	F	d (s)	F	Standard Error of Estimate	R^2	Total F
Textiles	.283	−.322		−.0057		−.05			.05	
		(.30)	1.16	(.053)	.012	(.513)	.009	.086		.516
Food	−.565	.352		.208		1.327			.46	
		(.194)	3.28*	(.05)	17.6†	(.435)	9.29†	.097		12.3
Fabricated Metals	−.128	−.309		.166		.182			.34	
		(.193)	2.58	(.050)	11.0†	(.436)	.174	.0955		7.05
Primary Metals	.181	.0015		.245		.077			.32	
		(.32)	.00	(.068)	13.0†	(.569)	.018	.12		5.50

* Significant at the 5 percent level.

† Significant at the 1 percent level.

Note:

Due to unavailability of data, the sample sizes for each industry differ. The sample sizes used for each industry are as follows: Textiles, 31 states; Fabricated Metals, 46 states; Food, 48 states; Primary Metals, 39 states.

It is of interest to note that essentially the same results were obtained when percentage change in wage (percent ΔW_{ij}) was used as the dependent variable. This is to be expected because of the high correlation (.93 for textiles, .95 for food, .93 for fabricated metals, and .88 for primary metals) between ΔW_{ij} and percent ΔW_{ij}.

(s) is the standard error of the regression coefficient estimate immediately above. F is the appropriate ratio of variances for testing the hypothesis that the above regression coefficient equals zero. Total F is the appropriate ratio of variances for testing the hypothesis that all the regression coefficients simultaneously equal zero. R is the multiple correlation coefficient.

part of the period in September 1961. This law would have had the greatest effect in those areas where wage levels were lowest and hence operated to cancel the effects that we were attempting to analyze.[15]

The food industry, the next lowest paying of the four, is the only industry in which the labor-market tightness hypothesis is supported. This gives a preliminary indication that the mechanism applies only to low-paying industries that use predominantly unskilled workers. A further indication of this is that, if we exclude the textile industry, the coefficient of employment ratio gets progressively smaller as the wage level of the industry goes up—food industry with 1.3, fabricated metals

[15] See, for example, "Newest Problem: Mill Costs," *Textile World*, June 1961. This article points out that the minimums brought into effect by this act would tend to hit different regions in which the textile industry is located differently. For example, only 10 percent of the textile workers in the Northeast earned less than $1.25 in 1961 as compared with 23 percent in the South.

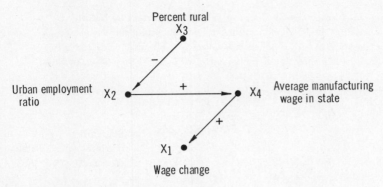

FIGURE 10.4. Model I, primary-metals industry.

with .18, and primary metals with .077. These findings suggest that variations in labor-market tightness primarily reflect variations in the availability of unskilled workers and that the effect of labor-market tightness on wage changes will be operative in an industry only to the extent that the industry uses unskilled workers.

The significance of the fraction of people on farms in the food-industry equation gives no support to the farm-worker-availability hypothesis because it has a positive coefficient. According to the hypothesis, the coefficient should be negative. That is, states with a high fraction of people on farms, because they have more farm workers available, should have smaller wage increases. The positive coefficient in this case no doubt reflects the role that the agricultural sector of the economy plays as a supplier to the food industry.

Summing up these regression results, strong support is obtained for the hypothesis that wages in a particular industry tend to increase faster when there are other high-wage industries in the vicinity. There is no support for the hypothesis that farm worker availability directly affects the rate of wage change. Labor market tightness does appear to have some effect but primarily on the low-wage, and presumably low-skill-using industries.

The fact that no *direct* causal link exists does not necessarily imply that *indirect* links do not exist. Possibly the average level of wages in a state is an intervening variable through which these other factors, availability of farm workers and labor market tightness, have their effects. In order to explore this question, the Simon-Blalock method of causal analysis was applied to the data. This technique allows us "to make causal inferences concerning the adequacy of causal models, at least in the sense that we can proceed by eliminating inadequate models that make predictions that are inconsistent with the data."[16] The technique involves the consideration of alternative causal models. The adequacy of a particular model

[16] Hubert M. Blalock, *Causal Inferences in Nonexperimental Research* (Chapel Hill, N. C.: The University of North Carolina Press, 1964); also see Herbert A. Simon, "Spurious Correlations: A Causal Interpretation," *Journal of the American Statistical Association, 49,* 467–479 (1954).

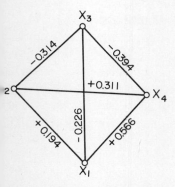

IGURE 10.5. Correlation coefficients network: primary-metals industry (39 observations).

tested by using the empirical correlation coefficients.[17] If predictions implied by
model are not in reasonable agreement with the actual correlations among the
ariables in the model, then it is rejected.

The results obtained in connection with the primary-metals industry are
escribed here in detail. Similar results, with a few minor exceptions, were obtained
>r both the fabricated-metals and food industries.

The first test was conducted on Model I, shown graphically in Figure 10.4.
he arrows in this figure indicate the direction of causal influence. For example,
ıe arrow going from X_3 to X_2 represents the hypothesis that X_3 causes X_2.
ı Figure 10.4:

X_1 change in average wage by state for production workers from 1958 to
1963 in the primary-metals industry, i.e., ΔW_{ij},

X_2 ratio of nonagricultural employment to urban plus rural nonfarm
population by state, 1960, i.e., $E_j/[(TP)_j - (RP)_j]$,

X_3 fraction of state population that is rural farm, 1960, i.e., $(RP)_j/(TP)_j$,

X_4 average wage for all production workers in state, 1958, i.e., W_j.

The hypothesized negative effect of X_3 on X_2 is explained by migration from
ıral areas in response to job opportunities that will tend to keep down the
ıployment ratio in the cities. The positive effect of X_2 on X_4 is due to the tight
bor market effect.

To test the adequacy of Model I it is necessary to see whether or not the
edictions it implies are consistent with the data. The relevant data for the test
e summarized in the network of correlation coefficients shown in Figure 10.5.
sing these correlation coefficients, a set of predictions, implied by Model I, can
made. In particular, predictions can be made about the value of the correlation
efficients between each pair of variables that could possibly be connected but are

[17] Assumptions underlying use of this method are (1) variables conform to multivariate
rmal distribution, (2) relationships are additive and linear, (3) other causes of each
riable are not correlated with other variables in the system of relationships, and (4)
ısation is unidirectional.

TABLE 10.11
Predictions and Degrees of Fit for Models I, II, and III of Regional Differences in
Wage Changes in the Primary-Metals Industry

Predictions	Degrees of Fit Expected	Actual	Differenc
	Model I		
$r_{34} = r_{32}r_{24} = (-.314)(.311) =$	−.098	−.394	.296
$r_{31} = r_{32}r_{24}r_{41} = (-.314)(.311)(.566) =$	−.055	−.226	.171
$r_{21} = r_{24}r_{41} = (.311)(.566) =$	.176	.194	.018
	Model II		
$r_{31} = r_{34}r_{41} = (-.394)(.566) =$	−.223	−.226	.003
$r_{21} = r_{24}r_{41} = (.311)(.566) =$	.176	.194	.018
	Model III		
$r_{32} = r_{35}r_{52} = (.731)(-.575) =$	−.420	−.314	.106
$r_{34} = r_{35}r_{54} = (.731)(-.592) =$	−.433	−.394	.039
$r_{24} = r_{25}r_{54} = (-.575)(-.592) =$	.340	.311	.029
$r_{51} = r_{54}r_{41} = (-.592)(.566) =$	−.335	−.410	.074
$r_{31} = r_{35}r_{54}r_{41} = (.731)(-.592)(.566) =$	−.245	−.226	.019
$r_{21} = r_{25}r_{54}r_{41} = (-.575)(-.592)(.566) =$	.193	.194	.001

not. Thus for Model I we may predict expected values of the correlation
coefficients r_{34}, r_{31}, and r_{21}, corresponding respectively to the three unconnected pai
of variables X_3X_4, X_3X_1, and X_2X_1,. To illustrate, we take the pair X_3X_4. Accor
ing to Model I, no *direct* relation exists between X_3 and X_4, but we should expect
some nonzero correlation between them because of the indirect effect of X_3 on
X_4 through the intervening variable X_2. It turns out that the amount of correlatic
expected is simply equal to the product of the correlation between X_3 and X_2
(i.e., r_{32}) and the correlation between X_2 and X_4 (i.e., r_{24}). That is, Model I
predicts that r_{34} will equal the product $r_{32}r_{24}$, which we see from Figure 10.5 is
equal to $(-.314)(.311) = -.098$. To test the model's adequacy, we compare
this expected value to the actual value of r_{34}, which we see from Figure 10.5 is
equal to − 394 We see that the actual relation between percent rural X_3 and
average manufacturing wage X_4 is significantly more negative than predicted by
this model.

The remaining predictions implied by Model I are made in a similar fashion.
Table 10.11 summarizes the results and shows that the fit between Model I and
the data is not very good. In addition to the discrepancy just mentioned, we see
that the actual relation between percent rural and wage change is more negative
than predicted by this model.

Both these findings suggest adding a direct causal link, from percent rural to
average manufacturing wage (see Figure 10.6). Such a link could be interpreted
as follows: In high rural areas there is a readily available supply of workers to th
manufacturing sector. The workers coming off the farms, however, are relatively
unskilled in relation to manufacturing. They, therefore, result in a pool of unskill

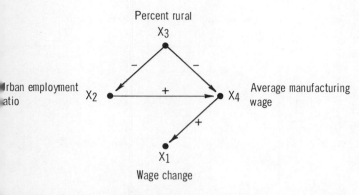

Wage change

'IGURE 10.6. Model II, primary-metals industry.

abor which in turn attracts low-skill and hence low-wage industries. It is the
»redominance of low-wage industries that results in the low average wage. The
ddition of this link, as shown in Table 10.11, results in an extremely good fit
»etween the model and the data. Model II thus represents an adequate model of
he situation.

The fact that Model II fits the data does not mean, of course, that it is the
nly model that is consistent with the data. In fact, as part of this exploration
third model was considered. In both the first two models, the percentage of rural
opulation was used to represent the availability of a pool of labor for urban jobs.
)ne might readily argue, however, that just because people live and work in the
ural or agricultural sector does not necessarily mean that they are available for
actory work in the city. A worker's availability will depend on how well he is
oing on the farm. Areas with proportionately more low-income farms should
nerefore have more farm workers available for other employment. Possibly the
elationships between percent rural and urban employment ratio, and percent
ural and average wage, are spurious in that, if we controlled for the effect of
)w-income farms, the correlations would vanish. To test this, Model II was
xpanded to include the low-income farm variable.[18] The direct links between
X_3 and X_2 and X_3 and X_4 were replaced by indirect links going through this
ew variable. In addition, the link between X_2 and X_4 was dropped. This latter
eletion was made to see if adding the low-income farm variable would make this
onnection unnecessary. The resulting model is shown in Figure 10.7.

Figure 10.8 shows the expanded network of correlations.

Table 10.11 shows that this expanded model also fits the data remarkably well.
he correlations between X_3 and X_1 and X_2 and X_1 are explained just as well,
not a little better, with Model III than they were with Model II. In addition

[18] This variable was measured by taking the number of Class VI farms (i.e., those having
a annual income of $3,000 or less) per capita. Data were obtained from the U.S. Bureau
the Census, *U.S. Census of Agriculture: 1959*, Vol. II, General Report, Statistics by Subject,
hapter XI, Economic Class of Farm, U.S. Government Printing Office, Washington,
.C.

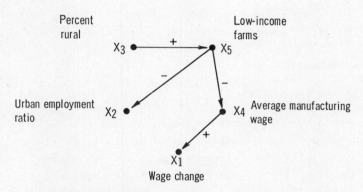

FIGURE 10.7. Model III, primary-metals industry.

to this, Model III provides new insight into the causal structure. When we control
for the number of low-income farms per capita, as suspected, the relation between
percent rural and average manufacturing wage disappears. The same seems to be
true for the relation between percent rural and urban employment. The hypothesis
that low farm income causes rural migration to the cities is therefore confirmed.
Furthermore, we see from Table 10.11 that the relation, previously existing in
Model II, between urban employment ratio and average state wage turns out
to be a spurious one when viewed in light of the expanded model. That is, when
we control for low-income farms, the relation vanishes. This has the important
implication that the tight labor market in the cities has *no* causal influence, either
direct or indirect, on the rate of wage change (at least for the primary-metals
industry).

   The picture of regional relative wage change that now emerges is considerably
different from the one that was originally postulated. The preliminary formulation
was based on a conception of regional labor supply as being primarily urban and
homogeneous. The empirical evidence shows that if we are to capture the true
dynamics of regional wage adjustment, we must revise this conception and
recognize (1) the importance of rural labor supply[19] and (2) the importance of
distinguishing between skilled and unskilled labor. Indeed, it is the presence of the
pool of unskilled, underemployed (or low-income), agricultural workers that
appears to be the key. The presence of agricultural underemployment results in
a pool of unskilled workers being available. This attracts low-wage industry to
the area. The prevalence of low-wage industries not only keeps average wage down
but also keeps the rate of change, and hence relative wage, down.

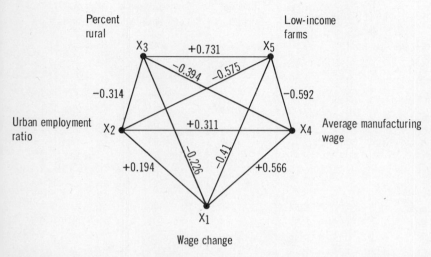

FIGURE 10.8. Expanded correlation coefficient network, primary-metals industry (39 observations).

A major implication of these findings is that local relative wage is directly determined by local industry mix. That is, we should expect, if this interpretation is correct, that those areas that have low- (high-)wage industry mixes also have low (high) relative wages. The Federal Reserve Bank of Boston conducted a study of wage differences among a set of metropolitan areas that bears on this question. They determined the extent to which the difference between local and national average wage was due to different industry mix and to what extent it was due to an area effect or what we have called relative wage. Their results are shown in Table 10.12. A strong positive relation between the two effects is clearly evident. This agrees with our interpretation of the regional wage adjustment mechanism.

In addition to the primary-metals industry, Model III was applied to both the food and the fabricated-metals industries. The basic causal structure found in the primary-metals industry continues to hold for these two industries. In each case, however, additional links, shown by the dotted lines in Figure 10.9, were indicated in order to achieve a better fit with the data. The X_3 to X_1 and X_5 to X_1 links in the case of the food industry again reflect the special relation of that industry to the agricultural sector (although it is somewhat difficult to interpret the link from low-income farms to wage changes). The most interesting result is that the tight urban labor market X_2 now does tend to have some causal effect on wage

[19] This finding is consistent with the findings of Borts and Stein, *op. cit.*

TABLE 10.12

Industry and Area Influences on Manufacturing Earnings

	Average Earnings June 1960	Differential from U.S. Average ($2.29)	Effect of Industrial Structure on Differential*	Effect of Area on Differential†
Greensboro-High Point, N.C.	$1.58	−$.71	−$.42	−$.29
Manchester, N.H.	1.63	−.61	−.32	−.29
Providence, R.I.	1.86	−.43	−.20	−.23
Dallas, Tex.	1.96	−.33	+.06	−.39
Atlanta, Ga.	2.05	−.24	−.04	−.20
Worcester, Mass.	2.19	−.10	+.06	−.16
Springfield-Holyoke, Mass.	2.20	−.09	+.03	−.12
New York, N.Y.	2.24	−.05	−.21	+.16
Boston, Mass.	2.25	−.04	−.02	−.02
New Haven, Conn.	2.28	−.01	+.02	−.03
Waterbury, Conn.	2.32	+.03	+.06	−.03
Philadelphia, Pa.	2.37	+.03	+.01	+.07
Hartford, Conn.	2.39	+.10	+.16	−.06
Bridgeport, Conn.	2.40	+.11	+.17	−.06
Kansas City, Mo.	2.42	+.13	+.12	+.01
Minneapolis-St. Paul, Minn.	2.42	+.13	+.10	+.03
Cleveland, Ohio	2.69	+.40	+.23	+.17
Pittsburgh, Pa.	2.78	+.49	+.39	+.10
San Francisco-Oakland, Calif.	2.79	+.50	+.13	+.37
Detroit, Mich.	2.92	+.63	+.35	+.28

* National average earnings ($2.29) subtracted from hypothetical area earnings if all local industries paid the national industry average.

† Actual earnings minus the hypothetical earnings.

Source: Data from U.S. Bureau of Labor Statistics, *Census of Manufactures*, in *New England Business Review*, February 1962, published by Federal Reserve Bank of Boston.

change. Both of these industries have national average wages somewhat lower than those for the primary-metals industry, indicating the use of a somewhat lower labor-skill mix. This supports the hypothesis that the variations in labor-market tightness primarily reflect variations in the availability of unskilled workers. Therefore the effect of labor-market tightness on wage changes will be operative in an industry only to the extent that the industry uses unskilled workers.

MODEL IMPLEMENTATION. The major findings (1) that regional differences in industry wage change are due primarily to differences in the over-all regional wage level and (2) that the level of labor-market tightness primarily affects only

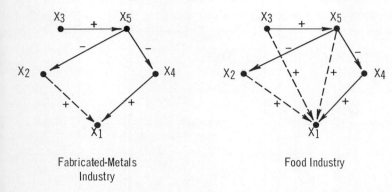

Fabricated-Metals
Industry

Food Industry

FIGURE 10.9. Models IV and V, fabricated-metals and food industries.

the low-wage, low-skill-using industries were implemented in the model.[20] To
implement these findings in the model, two relative wages, one for high-skill-using
and the other for low-skill-using industries, were used. In each case, the subregion's
relative wage was modeled to move toward a target relative wage specified as
follows:

$$TRWH . K = .4 + .3(AWG . K) \qquad (10.2)$$

$$TRWL . K = .525 + .3(AWG . K) - 2.5(LUR . K) \qquad (10.3)$$

where

$TRWH$ Target Relative Wage for High-skill-using industries,

$TRWL$ Target Relative Wage for Low-skill-using industries,

AWG local Average WaGe (dollars/hour),

LUR Local Unemployment Rate (%).

According to these equations, the subregion's average wage affects the relative
wage in all industries, while labor-market tightness, as indicated by the local
unemployment rate, affects only the low-skill-using industries.

Because this formulation was not anticipated at the time when industry groups

[20] A complete implementation of the empirical findings would, of course, involve the
explicit incorporation of the "availability of low-income farm workers" variable. A quick
examination revealed, however, that the probable payoff, in the context of the Susquehanna
region, could not justify the probable cost of undertaking this task. First of all, introducing
the farm-worker-availability effect would entail somewhat elaborate changes in other parts
of the model, for example, with respect to agriculture and migration. Most important,
however, in comparison to other areas of the country there are virtually no significant
pools of low-income farm workers in the study area. Whereas the national average number
of Class VI farms per capita in 1960 was .0026 (with a standard deviation of .003), of all
the states only New Jersey, Massachusetts, and Rhode Island, each with .0001, had less
than New York, which had .0002. Besides these, only Nevada, with .0003, had less than
Pennsylvania and Maryland, each of which had .0004. We must conclude, in view of the
relatively healthy status of agriculture in this region, that the availability of underemployed
(or low-income) farm workers will not have a significant effect on its relative wage.

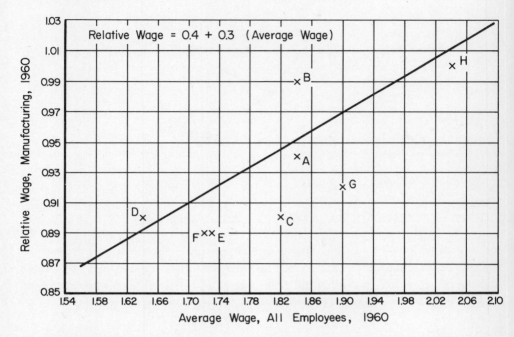

FIGURE 10.10. Relative wage versus average wage, Susquehanna subregions, 1960.

were determined, skill-using characteristics of industries were not considered in the grouping procedures. Fortunately, however, the existing groups did permit a rough breakdown into high- and low-skill categories. In particular, all of the 2-digit industries included in the nondurable group fell into the low-skill-using group. Recall that this group is made up of the tobacco, textile, apparel, and leather industries. The remaining three export industry groups, being made up predominantly of higher wage and skill industries, were modeled, for purposes of the relative wage formulation, in the high-skill-using category.

Estimating the parameters for Equations 10.2 and 10.3 was complicated by the fact that industry-specific wage data were not readily available for most of the subregions in the study area. Budget constraints at this point in the study further dictated against elaborate data gathering. It was, therefore, decided to make rough parameter estimates on the basis of available data and judgment which could then be subjected to sensitivity analysis.

The regression results shown in Table 10.10 indicate that the coefficients of average wage are approximately the same for different industries. The model coefficient was, therefore, assumed to be the same for both relative wage equations. Its value was estimated by plotting the average wage versus relative wage for each of the subregions. A line fitted to this plot, shown in Figure 10.10, yielded parameter estimates of .4 and .3. These estimates were used in Equation 10.2 and applied to the high-skill-using industry groups.

The coefficient of local unemployment rate was kept the same as it was in the

TABLE 10.13
Estimated Relative Wages by Subregion and Industry Group, 1960

Subregion	A	B.	C	D	E	F	G	H
Low-Skill-Using Industry Group	0.953	0.998	0.852	0.878	0.843	0.870	0.952	1.025
High-Skill-Using Industry Group	0.939	0.987	0.910	0.926	0.948	0.895	0.907	0.998

earlier formulation, at −2.5.[21] Sensitivity analysis showed that doubling and reducing this coefficient to zero resulted in only very minor changes in the simulation results.

Finally, the intercept of Equation 10.3 was set by assuming a value that was consistent both with the other coefficients and a steady-state condition. According to Equation 10.2, an average wage of $2.00 would result in a target relative wage for the high-skill-using industries equal to the national average (i.e., 1.0). For the low-skill-using industries, it was correspondingly assumed that this average wage combined with a national average local unemployment rate (assumed equal to .05) would result in a national average target relative wage.

Next, initial values of relative wages for both the high- and low-skill-using industries were estimated. These estimates were made using the available data on relative wages shown in Table 10.9 together with the assumption that the initial residuals between the actual and target relative wages were the same for both industry groups.

The resulting estimates in Table 10.13 show that the over-all pattern of relatively low labor costs, shown previously in Table 10.9, is maintained. In addition, the table reveals two other patterns, both of which are consistent with general knowledge of local labor-market behavior. First, we see that the amount of variation in relative wages between subregions is much greater for the low- than the high-skill-using industries. This is consistent with the higher degree of variability among areas that we should expect in the supply of less mobile, unskilled workers. Second, we see that the subregions with the larger excess labor pools (i.e., Subregions C, D, E, and F) all have comparative labor cost advantages in the low-skill industries.

[21] This coefficient was estimated for the earlier formulation from data on relative wages and local unemployment rates for the Susquehanna subregions. The data are plotted in Figure 12.2. Lack of data on relative wage for low-skill-using industries precluded the possibility of re-estimating this coefficient directly for the revised formulation. Because the coefficient was so insensitive, no special effort was directed at obtaining a more reliable estimate.

Finally, to complete implementation of the relative wage formulation, it is necessary to specify average wage. Essentially average wage is modeled as the product of an industry mix and a regional effect. The industry mix effect is represented by weighting the national average wage of each industry group according to its proportion of total employment in the subregion. To determine the *local* average wage at any point in time for each manufacturing industry, each manufacturing wage is multiplied by the appropriate relative wage. This procedure it should be noted, treats the national average wage for each industry group as a constant. This is tantamount to the assumption that the trend in the national average wage due to such factors as productivity change and inflationary pressure will tend to cancel out from one region and industry to another and hence not to affect relative wage. That is, if the trend effects result in an across-the-board increase of 3 percent in all industries and regions, then there should be no effect on the *relative* position of one region to another. There is some evidence to justify this simplification. "In a study of manufacturing wages Cullen found a 'definite secular stability over the 1899–1950 period' in percentage wage differentials, although several subperiods were characterized by a slight widening or narrowing of the same."[22]

The local average wage of three industry groups, namely, agriculture, export mining, and government and education, are modeled as constants. The relative wage multiplier is not used because it is felt that these industries are much less affected by local competitive bidding forces because of spatial and, in the case of government and education, "institutional" distance from the local urban labor market.

Finally, in modeling the wages of the household-serving group, its relation to total population, as shown in Figure 10.11, is taken into account. This relationshi may be interpreted as reflecting the increased introduction of specialized,

[22] Quoted from L. Chimerine, "An Econometric Analysis of Regional Wage Differentials unpublished dissertation prepared at Brown University, 1965, p. 165, who quoted Cullen, "The Inter-Industry Wage Structure, 1899–1950," *American Economic Review*, XLVI, 356–369 (June 1956).

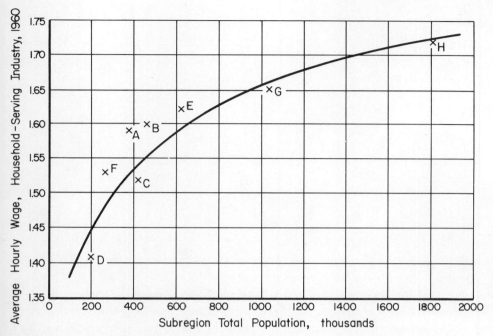

FIGURE 10.11 Relationship between average hourly wage in household-serving industry and subregion population.

high-wage-paying services as the population in a region grows. The decreasing rate of increase in wages, as indicated by the decreasing slope of the relationship, is also consistent with this interpretation. As the population grows, especially as it gets well past the one and a half million mark in a given subregion, as in Baltimore, most of these special services will already have been introduced. At this point, additional employment growth will take place more and more through growth of existing services at similar wages rather than by introduction of new services at higher wages.

Previous chapters have analyzed the demographic and employment sectors of the Susquehanna model in relation to the general problem of model-building for regional economic analysis. These two sectors are clearly the basic ingredients of a model designed to study regional economic growth. Such sectors, therefore, should appear in all regional growth models, though perhaps in modified form. The Susquehanna model also has a water sector, primarily because the sponsors of the original project were interested in defining the role of water in the development of the Susquehanna basin. It was desired to see the effect of the economy upon the river, to judge the adequacy of water resources to support economic growth, and to gauge the impact of alternative systems of river works construction upon the economy.

Because of its special character, the water sector may be viewed as a "technical sector" that is tied to a more general regional simulation model. The function of the water sector of the model is to interrelate the general economic forces in the basin with water resource demands and supplies. As we suggest in the final section of this chapter, there can be many sorts of technical sectors that might be constructed for integration into a model of regional growth, depending upon the goals and nature of the study. For example, a transportation sector might be developed to show the important feedbacks between regional growth and development and alternative sets of transportation systems. Our purpose in this chapter is to discuss the methodology and a few of the modeling problems in use of a river system as a technical sector and thereby to illustrate the nature of a technical sector within the context of regional development. We will refer to the Susquehanna study as a source of illustrative material and not attempt a detailed description of the water problems in the Susquehanna basin. This chapter will be of primary interest to readers interested in the developmental aspects of water resources; other readers may elect not to read it.

Methodology

Our approach to the water sector, with its emphasis on regional growth, may be contrasted with other models that view water resource management as the major source of concern. For example, in Chapter 4 we discussed the Lehigh Basin Simulation Model[1] that was developed specifically to optimize water resource management and to design an optimal system of river works given *prior* assumptions about economic development patterns in the region. That is to say that water demands were developed *outside* the model. Moreover, there are no feedbacks from the water model back on the economy as a whole. The Lehigh simulation model is, therefore, a computer simulation of engineering options and hydrologic variables, not a model designed to see the role of water within the context of regional development.

However, we do not wish to claim too much. Because of our focus on the needs of the Susquehanna River Basin, the water sector that was developed is not what might be termed "general purpose" in nature. As we shall note, some aspects of water resource development not important in this basin, e.g., navigation and irrigation, were not included. In addition, other basic outputs of river development, such as flood control and hydropower, were omitted for other reasons. Therefore considerable modification or expansion of the water sector might be necessary before adaptation to other basins could be made. The size and completeness of the water sector would also be a function of the nature and goals of the study undertaken. Nevertheless, the way in which the sector in the Susquehanna model is formulated and results obtained are interesting and provide some methodological generalizations.

Study Procedure. For purposes of study and explanation, the water problem was separated into two parts: water-quantity and water-quality considerations. These two factors are interrelated. Limited quantities of water can affect quality, and on the other hand, poor-quality water may be useless for certain purposes even

[1] Maynard M. Hufschmidt and Myron B. Fiering, *Simulation Techniques for Design of Water-Resource Systems* (Cambridge, Mass.: Harvard University Press, 1966).

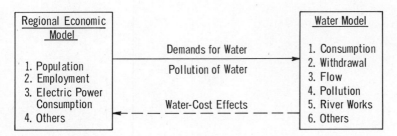

FIGURE 11.1 Two submodels forming the regional model

when available in abundant quantities. Despite these obvious limitations, the separation is a useful one.

At the outset of the research program, it was hypothesized that water quality and quantity might now be or might become a constraint on the growth of the economy of the Susquehanna River Basin. As the problem was originally conceived, two submodels were to be constructed. One model was to be concerned with the economy of the region and the other with water. The two submodels were then to be combined into an over-all regional and water-resource model by the interrelationships (feedbacks) between them. This scheme is shown conceptually in Figure 11.1.

As the research progressed, it became evident that the feedback loop from water to the economy was in all likelihood "inoperative" with regard to economic growth in the Susquehanna basin. Within the bounds in which water-supply and water-quality variables now exist and will probably exist in the future, the water-related factors are unlikely to have major effects on economic growth. That is, water costs are unlikely to rise or fall significantly and thereby influence growth. This conclusion stems principally from the large size of the Susquehanna River and its tributaries in relation to the size of the economy in the area.

The Critical Point Concept. A complete audit of "all" present water uses and an attempt to predict "all" future uses in a major river basin would be an enormous task. Such a comprehensive survey would clearly be very costly and time consuming. There is also the important consideration of whether such comprehensiveness is actually needed in designing a water sector as part of a regional growth model. Yet, this is the procedure often suggested when river basins are to be studied. As an alternative point of departure we adopted what we call the "critical point concept" as a way to identify and pinpoint critical water problems and critical points in a river system. Simply stated, this approach concentrates initially on finding points that appear to be most likely to create water problems in a subregion: separate critical points concepts are often needed in relation to quantity and quality considerations. If water quality and quantity do not appear to be problems at these critical points now or in the future, then we assume that problems will not develop at less critical points.

As applied to water-quantity considerations, the critical point concept is simple. Enough water must be available at various points along the river to supply present and future needs, otherwise water costs may rise and reduce economic growth. The basic premise of the critical point concept is that if the largest city or cities or large water-using industries in a region have sufficient flow for their present and projected needs, then the smaller cities or industries will also have sufficient flow. The critical point concept was focused primarily on the Susquehanna River's main stem and major tributaries. The cities and industries investigated were using the river as a source of supply, or conceivably could develop this source of water supply during the next 50 years (see Figure 11.2). The model projects demand for water supply at the critical point by adjusting withdrawal in relation to growth or decline of economic activity in the region (population and employment). Consumption of water upstream from each critical point is deleted from available stream flow at the critical point throughout the projection period.

For water-quality considerations, the critical point concept was used to identify points of pollution in the river system. If pollution problems were general or widespread instead of being the exception, such a procedure might not be warranted. Generally, critical points in relation to pollution were found to be associated with outfalls from municipal and industrial disposal systems. We therefore concentrated primarily on the problem of low dissolved oxygen levels (DO). The computational process involved locating the critical points that existed in each of the subregions and then computing how DO would change in the future with changes in population, economic activity, river flow, and levels of treatment.

The model developed is capable of accepting inclusion of hypothetical or predicted outfalls. It is therefore possible to insert an outfall at a proposed site along the river to show how the proposed development may affect DO. Further,

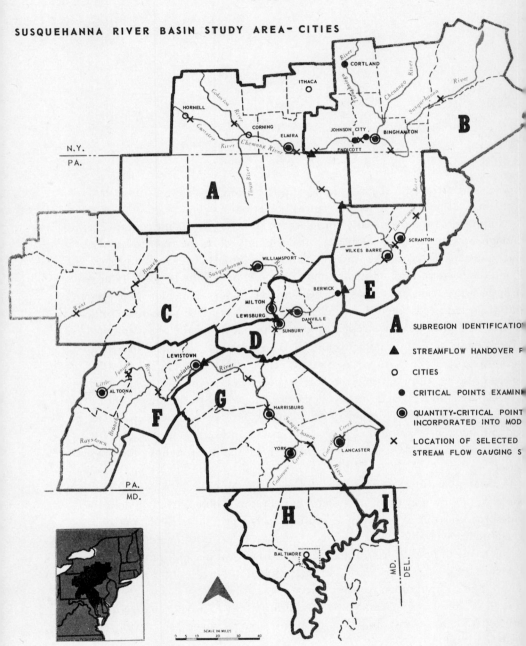

FIGURE 11.2. Critical points and gauging stations in the basin.

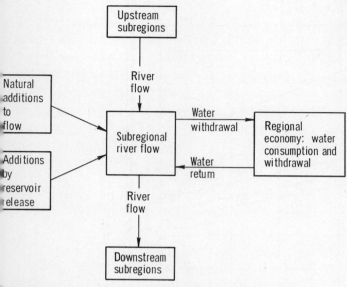

FIGURE 11.3. Diagram of the water-flow submodel.

is possible to change treatment levels at specified points in time or to trend
them over time.

River Simulation. In order to simulate the river, taking into account changes in
flow values that may be caused by economic activity and other factors, it is
necessary to incorporate a mechanism into the model that will specify additions
to and deletions from flow. For planning purposes, flows will have to be computed
at least on a subregional basis, and often they will be needed at specific
geographical points. In order to accomplish this, the model follows a scheme
outlined in Figure 11.3. The water flow from upstream regions is discharged into
a given subregion of interest (center box, Figure 11.3). The flow then may be
augmented from two principal sources: (1) natural additions, such as those from
tributaries, and (2) man-made additions, for instance, from reservoirs.

A third source also appears possible. Withdrawals from ground-water resources
may be discharged into the river with a resulting increase in flow. However, one
must be careful that so-called "ground water" sources are not, in fact, actually
derived from the river indirectly and that they do not have immediate or lagged
effects on river flow. Nevertheless, ground water is abundant in the Susquehanna
basin and is a significant source of supply.

Before the river flows into the next subregion downstream, it is necessary to
subtract the water consumed by the economy of the subregion under consideration.
Figure 11.3 shows that water is withdrawn by the economy and that a certain
percentage of this withdrawal is then consumed. The remainder is returned to
the stream to be discharged into the next subregion.

It is important to distinguish between water withdrawal and water consumption.
Withdrawal is important only at the point where it occurs. Consumption has

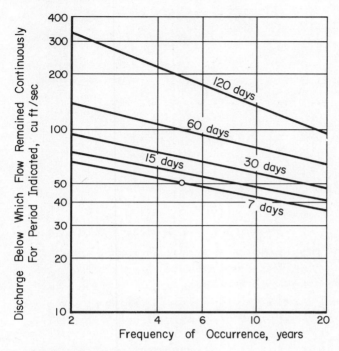

FIGURE 11.4. Low-flow interval curves.

downstream effects. An economy may withdraw a tremendous amount of water from the river but return nearly all of it. While it is true that at any given point on the river it is the relationship between river flow and withdrawal that is important, withdrawal by itself has no downstream significance except as it affects consumption. If the economy of an area withdrew water and returned all of it to the river in the exact quality and quantity as withdrawn, the only problem would be to ensure sufficient flows or impoundments at each point on the river to supply potential withdrawals. There would be no downstream effects. However consumption must be considered because water consumed upstream means that less water will be available downstream.

The graphic model described here and shown in Figure 11.3 was translated into equation form and served to provide estimates of water use and flow in the basin.

In line with the critical point philosophy, it was decided to concentrate on low-flow periods in the river basin when presumably most of the problems of water quantity and quality would be most serious. The low-flow period selected was the 7-day, 5-year flows calculated from data provided by the district offices of the U.S. Geological Survey. It was found that the flow level was generally insensitive to changes in duration and frequency of low flow occurrences.

Figure 11.4 shows a typical set of curves from which flow data can be derived. The value of 50 cubic feet per second (cfs) for the 7-day, 5-year flow is found by reading on the right horizontal axis to the 5-year point (frequency of occurrence).

rojecting this point vertically onto the 7-day curve, and reading the point on
ie vertical axis opposite this point. Note that increasing the recurrence interval
) 20 years, a 400 percent increase, decreases the flow only by about 30 percent.
imilarly, note that the curves come closer and closer together each time the
iterval of low flow is halved, that is, 120 days to 60 days to 30 days, etc. Thus,
:ducing the flow interval to $3\frac{1}{2}$ days or even less would produce a negligible
ffect on the critical-flow value.

Water Variables Excluded. For various reasons, it was decided to exclude from the
ater sector a number of water-related variables that are often part of
)mprehensive studies of water resources. Water variables excluded are flood
)ntrol, acid mine drainage, hydropower production, navigation, and irrigation.
'he major variables included in the model are water quantities and qualities
)r various kinds of uses. The water sector is also seen as having feedbacks on the
:onomy stemming from the construction of river works and from activity
:nerated by new recreation facilities. The remaining part of this section provides
ir reasoning for the exclusions. In most cases, the variables were studied at
ngth before the decision was made not to treat them in the actual model.

Flood Control. Flood abatement will undoubtedly represent a major justification
)r the construction of river works in the Susquehanna River Basin. Therefore,
is important to note that a flood-control sector has not been included in the
irrent model. There are three major reasons for excluding such a sector. First,
ie research necessary to compute direct benefits from flood-abatement projects
ight well have exceeded the total effort of the research reported here. In the
jht of this high cost, and because the Corps of Engineers was studying flood-control
ternatives in the Susquehanna basin at the time of our study, research on the
iture and magnitude of the direct benefits involved was not recommended or
>nducted. Further, it is difficult for other than a public agency to assemble much
˙ the requisite data.

A second major reason for not including flood control is the lack of impact of
ater consumption by the economy on river-flow values at flood stages. While

at low flows an expanding economy could have measurable (though perhaps not significant) influence on river flows and water-quality levels, such impacts at flood levels are unlikely. Thus, the model simulates the river at low-flow levels but not at flood levels.

A third reason for not including a flood-control sector concerns the dearth of general information and theory concerning how flood-abatement benefits, or a lack of them, affect a local economy. For instance, under what kind and degree of conditions are the needs for flood abatement a constraint upon a regional economy? What are the alternative patterns of regional expenditures with and without flood protection and what alternative patterns of employment do they create? Because of the lack of information with regard to the feedbacks created by flood control, it was necessary to assume that any constraints to economic growth that may exist in the Susquehanna basin will be removed by federal, state, or local government, or by private investment. It should be noted that this question of regional impact is not equivalent to the measurement of the impact of floods on a given site, a reach of the river, or even a city. Although flood danger may indeed prevent the development of certain sites in an area, the effect could be that of merely displacing economic activity to another site in the same region. The degree of impact, from a regional point of view, may be negligible. This depends also on how the region itself is defined.

Because of the lack of knowledge and theory concerning the interrelationship of flood abatement and regional economic growth, research on this topic, independent of the present effort, seems warranted. In addition, once the results of the research conducted by the Corps of Engineers in the basin are available, it may be desirable to incorporate the more conventional flood-related benefit/cost calculations within the model for the sake of completeness. This latter inclusion would also allow sensitivity experiments to be conducted in relation to flood-abatement benefits.

Acid Mine Drainage. Water pumped or seeping from operating and abandoned coal mines is often highly acid and contains high concentrations of inorganic materials held in solution. Such pollution is often severe enough to kill all life in a stream. In addition, the banks of the stream may be stained a characteristic yellow. The acid attacks engineering structures such as bridges. Acid mine drainage does not prevent all forms of recreation, however. For instance, the research team noted swimming, boating, and water skiing under surprisingly high-acid conditions. In addition, acid-polluted streams are often crystal clear and are generally pleasing in appearance to many people.

Acid mine drainage is prevalent along the West Branch of the Susquehanna as far east as Lock Haven (Subregion C, Williamsport).[2] It is also present to varying degrees on the North Branch.[3] Many fish-kills have been attributed to "slugs" of acid moving down the stream and killing fish in areas that are not normally acidic.

In order to specify how acid mine drainage was to be treated in the model, it was necessary to answer the question, "What regional economic impact would occur if the problem were lessened or eliminated?" In answering this question it was essential to remember that the over-all research study focused on the growth of subregions, not the distribution of activity within such subregions.

Perhaps the main indicator of economic growth is employment. Therefore, for acid pollution to have a significant impact on economic growth, it would have to affect employment growth in some way. Such an impact is unlikely on a subregional basis. True, certain industries might avoid acid-polluted reaches of the river, and specific recreational activities might be impaired. But even in Subregion C where acid pollution is common, there are many nonpolluted sources of water either from ground water or unpolluted reaches of the river. In addition, the region does not lack in the outdoor recreation amenities. Fishing could be enhanced by eliminating the acid pollution problem, but the amount of employment created

[2] The chemical quality of water in the West Branch of the Susquehanna is discussed in E. F. McCarren, "Chemical Quality of Surface Water in the West Branch of the Susquehanna River Basin," U.S. Geological Survey Water Supply Paper 1779-c (1964).

[3] "North Branch of the Susquehanna River Mine Drainage Study," Pennsylvania Department of Health, Publication No. 5 (April 1963).

by fishing is certainly small and might merely be displaced from other parts of the subregions in question. It should be kept in mind that fishing will not add to local employment unless the participants are drawn from other regions or more local fishermen stay in their own region to fish.

In addition to the doubtful benefits to be achieved in terms of regional growth, it appears that the costs of preventing, or even significantly reducing, acid mine pollution are truly enormous. A good deal of research is under way to identify and test methods to attack the problem, but a significant technological breakthrough appears to be needed before a logical and economic method or combination of methods can be put into force.

Because of the doubtful benefits in terms of subregional growth to be achieved and because of the high costs of prevention or treatment, it appeared that modeling the acid pollution problem would be no more than an expensive exercise, and for these reasons the problem is not treated in the model.

Other Exclusions. Other exclusions from the water sector are hydropower production, navigation, and irrigation. Most authorities are agreed that navigation and irrigation possibilities in the Susquehanna area are minimal. Limited opportunities for the development of hydropower production do exist. However, a study of the costs involved indicates that the threshold of power costs is not likely to be changed by the additional hydropower. Moreover, upon examination, the possible feedbacks upon economic growth in the basin from all three of these variables seems to be negligible. It is possible, however, that some construction might be justified on an individual project basis. The potential feedback on the economies of the basin from projects of this type is judged to be minimal.

General Water Quality and Water Quantity Considerations

Organic Pollution. Water has the capability of absorbing small quantities of oxygen. This oxygen performs some very important functions in a watercourse. Among the most important are the support of fish life and the assimilation of organic waste materials. Fish need oxygen to various degrees depending upon the

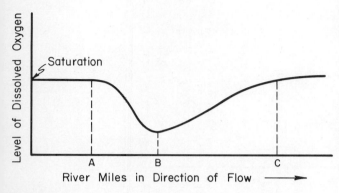

FIGURE 11.5. An oxygen sag curve.

species. At low levels of dissolved oxygen, fish will not spawn, and, of course, very low levels bring about death.

Organic pollutants are often called degradable because they are subject to aerobic degradation when stream biota break these wastes down into their inorganic compounds. Nondegradable pollutants include such inorganic substances as inorganic colloidal particles, sodium chloride, and the salts of numerous heavy metals. Of recent origin is a third group of pollutants, sometimes called "persistent" pollutants. Some degradation takes place but so slowly that these pollutants remain in virtually unchanged form for long stream distances. Detergents and phenols are perhaps the most common of the persistents.

In many ways, the assimilation of organic wastes can be viewed as an economic use of a watercourse. Streams are often used to carry away these organics from our cities, factories, and agricultural operations. The stream not only transports these wastes, but its oxygen reacts with them in a time-dependent, organic chemical reaction. If the demands of the organic materials for oxygen are not too great, the resultant depletion of oxygen does not interfere with other beneficial uses of the water. However, the pressure on the water resource is often such that conflicts of water use appear and must be resolved.

A stream is able to capture oxygen from the air. In fact, it can lose oxygen to organic matter in the water and reabsorb it from the air simultaneously. The differential rates at which this absorption and the organic chemical reaction proceed determines whether the dissolved oxygen content of the stream is decreasing or increasing at any given point in time at a specific location on the river. The mathematical and graphic descriptions of this phenomena have been termed the "oxygen sag curve." Such a curve is shown in Figure 11.5.

Figure 11.5 depicts the very simple case of a stream saturated with oxygen receiving a discharge or "outfall" of organic matter at Point A. At this point, the organic matter proceeds to absorb oxygen from the stream at a faster rate than it can be reabsorbed from the air. A lowering of the oxygen or an "oxygen sag" thus occurs. At Point B the organic reaction has proceeded to the point that much

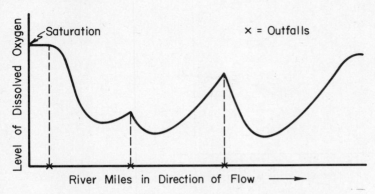

FIGURE 11.6. A "dissolved oxygen profile" of a reach of a river.

of the organic material has been assimilated. The remainder of the organic waste material continues to consume oxygen, but at a slower rate than oxygen is reabsorbed from the air. The oxygen level then begins to recover at B. It reaches saturation again at C.

Figure 11.5 presents a very simple situation. In the real world, organic discharges may occur at frequent intervals, cascading sag curve on sag curve and creating multiple curves such as are shown in Figure 11.6. In addition, river flows, levels of treatment, temperature, the nature of the river channel, and other factors affect the oxygen levels that occur. These factors seldom are constant from reach to reach along the river.

The complexities of multiple outfalls, the time-variant nature of the chemical reaction involved, and the potential for significant changes in amount of organic wastes being discharged at various points make the "dissolved oxygen problem" one that is difficult to treat intuitively. Further, flows at any point on the river will be affected by upstream consumption, which will, in turn, be affected by upstream economic activity. Levels of treatment will affect the actual amount of oxygen-consuming material discharged as will economic growth. Reservoirs built for the purpose of providing augmentation could provide dilution water. All of these factors, combined with the problem that low levels of oxygen were known to occur at a number of places on the river, dictated that the problem be treated in the model.

A series of equations was written that enabled the model to specify the level of dissolved oxygen at various critical points in each of the subregions during low flow periods.[4] Those points that were felt to represent the worst existing or potential future conditions were selected. This was, of course, "an analysis of extremes" as previously mentioned. The philosophy of approach was that if the

[4] The equations for dissolved oxygen levels used were adapted from G. M. Fair and J. C. Geyer, *Elements of Water Supply and Waste Disposal* (New York: John Wiley & Sons, Inc., 1958), pp. 511, 518–519. The section "How the Water Sector Functions and Some Specific Details of Use" describes how these equations were incorporated into the model as well as the nature of the hydrologic simulation used.

oints selected did not produce dissolved oxygen problems in simulations of the future, less critical points would not. If serious problems were evident among the critical points first selected, then additional critical points would be added to the model until all potential trouble spots were located.

The economic activity of the various subregions was apportioned to the critical points selected on the basis of their present share of the subregional economy. This economic activity was then converted to pounds of oxygen-demanding organic materials through a technical coefficient.[5] Any of the variables involved can be varied with time, including the percentage of subregional activity associated with a given city or other geographical point.

Two features of the water model are important to note at this stage. First, because of the impact of upstream economic activity on downstream river conditions, it was necessary that the water model tie all of the subregions together.[6] Second, the model derived showed the impact of the economy on the river but not the impact of organic pollution on the economy.

The latter issue is not a well-understood phenomenon, and because field work and associated analysis revealed that the economic impact on growth was presently nonexistent, it was decided to determine if the model predicted a significant worsening of the problem over time before a large research effort was devoted to it. The reasoning and analysis leading to this decision are presented in the following section.

Organic Pollution in the Basin. The Susquehanna River is generally free of excessive

[5] The total oxygen-demanding waste was assumed to arise from residences and industry. Residential discharges were derived from "Tabulation and Summary—Community Waste Data—Susquehanna River Basin," April 1964, U.S. Public Health Service. Industrial waste figures were derived from a wide variety of sources including unpublished data.

[6] This is an important practical consideration in terms of simulation of the model on the computer. While the economic portions of the model can be simulated on a subregion-by-subregion basis, the tying of the water sectors together requires that all subregions be simulated simultaneously. Thus, potential model size problems are created in terms of compiler size limitations and computer running times. Such problems never assumed significant proportions during the Susquehanna study.

organic pollution. There is good fishing on long reaches of the river, and sections of the North Branch have been considered a candidate for the "Wild Rivers Program." However, field trips and a limited amount of stream data collected by various governmental groups revealed that low levels of dissolved oxygen occurred at several places on the river and its tributaries during low-flow periods. In a number of cases where low "sag curves" were suspected (and later confirmed through model use) local opinion varied about the severity of the problem.

Analysis revealed that the large majority of cases in which low levels of dissolved oxygen occur were related to one or more of the following circumstances:

1. A relatively large city on a relatively small tributary—the cities of York and Lancaster, Pennsylvania, on Codorus and Conestoga Creeks, respectively, are examples.
2. The discharge of raw, untreated sewage—the city of Scranton was an example at the time of the study.

However, none of the problems uncovered seemed to threaten economic growth. All of the subregions involved have access to abundant supplies of water suitable for industrial purposes at many locations, and water for municipal use can usually be provided from several alternative sources for most cities. It was therefore judged that the organic pollution problem would have to become much worse before economic growth was threatened. And it was decided to allow the model to specify whether such a deteriorating situation would occur.

The model revealed that a serious deterioration of the current, generally good, situation was unlikely. A few trouble spots of the "large city, small tributary type" will persist, but treatment plants under construction or being planned seem likely to solve a number of other problems. A number of the specific technical details of this analysis are described in the section on How the Water Sector Submodel Functions.

Water Shortages. The dissolved-oxygen problem described in the previous two sections required the use of a simple, low-flow river-simulation model. The

existence of this model for use in determining dissolved oxygen plus repeated
references to "water shortages" in the basin brought about the modeling of the
water supply problem.

Again, the "critical point concept" was used. The places in each subregion that
appeared to be the most critical were selected. To these places, a portion of
subregional economic activity was allotted. This activity was then converted to
water withdrawal by technical coefficients.[7] The model then compared the flow
in the river with the demand at the critical point. As the economy grows, the
demand rises. Further, economic growth reduces downstream water availability
because of increased upstream consumption.

Only one critical point showed a flow-to-demand ratio less than 3.0 at low
flow at any time during the 50-year simulation. This was true even under
assumptions designed to lower the ratio below that which seemed most likely.

This result seemed in conflict with reported "water shortages" in the basin
during recent drought years. Field work was therefore undertaken to look into
the specific nature of these shortages.

The evidence uncovered during the field work reconciled the apparent
inconsistency. The water shortages reported were in terms of the inabilities of
current water treatment, storage, and distribution systems, rather than the
scarcity of the water resource itself. Many cities and towns in the basin were
reluctant to invest in water systems designed to provide water to meet all water
demands at all times, and many municipal systems had proved inadequate to
meet these demands under severe drought conditions. However, the river and often
other alternative sources of supply were able to provide sufficient water once the
decision to invest in an expanded water system was made.

How the Water Sector Submodel Functions: Some Specific Details of Its Use. The
preceding sections have provided a general overview of how the water-quality and
quantity sections of the water sector function but have not specified many of the

---

[7] These coefficients are described in How the Water Sector Submodel Functions: Some
Specific Details of Its Use.

details of how the hydrologic and dissolved-oxygen portions of the model function. This section presents a few of the more salient details.

The hydrologic section or equations provide the basis for both the water-quantity and water-quality analysis. The hydrologic simulation used is very simple First, the amount of water entering a subregion during the low-flow period is determined from one of the numerous river gauging stations maintained by the U.S. Geological Survey. If a gauge is not located at or near a subregional boundary, interpolations of flow can be made by examining the flow of the closest gauges on either side of this boundary.

In keeping with the analysis-of-extremes concept, the 7-day, 5-year flow was used. This flow is the lowest mean discharge expected for seven consecutive days occurring with a frequency of every five years.

The amount of water received from upstream is then acted upon by the subregion. Additions to flow occur from tributaries or from reservoir releases. Hypothetical reservoirs can be inserted in the model and low-flow values altered to account for flow augmentation from such reservoirs. Deletions from flow arise from economic activity. As this activity increases, water is withdrawn, a percentage is consumed, and the remainder is returned to the stream.

The following estimates of water withdrawal and consumption were employed:

1. Urban withdrawal   —160 gal/capita/day
    Urban consumption in relation to withdrawal—9 percent
2. Rural withdrawal   —140 gal/capita/day
    Rural consumption in relation to withdrawal —20 percent
3. Processing industries[8]
        withdrawal   —5,700 gals/employee/day
    Processing industries
    Consumption in relation to withdrawal   —8 percent

[8] See Chapter 10 on Employment Sector for definition of these industry groups.

4. Fabricating industries[9]
   withdrawal   —250 gal/employee/day
   Fabricating industries
   Consumption in relation to withdrawal   —4 percent

These values seemed the highest likely in light of national and Pennsylvania data.[10]

In keeping with testing extremes, all the water withdrawn and consumed above that used in 1960 was assumed to come from the river. This was done despite the fact that much of this water would undoubtedly be drawn from other sources such as ground water. The assumption eliminated the need to explore potentially complex river–ground-water interactions.

The urban withdrawal was increased at a rate of 1.4 percent per capita per year during the simulations. Per capita rural withdrawal was held constant as was per employee industrial withdrawal. The later assumption about withdrawal was the result of two counteracting forces: (1) technological developments, resulting in

---

[9] *Ibid.*

[10] J. W. Mangan and J. B. Graham, *The Use of Water in Pennsylvania, 1951*, U.S. Geological Survey Circular 257, 1953.

K. A. MacKichan, *Estimated Use of Water in the United States, 1950*, U.S. Geological Survey Circular 115 (1950) and same for 1960, Circular 456 (1961).

W. L. Ricton, *Water Use in the United States 1900–1980*, U.S. Department of Commerce (1960).

D. R. Woodward, *Availability of Water in the United States with Special Reference to Industrial Needs by 1980*, Thesis No. 143, Industrial College of the Armed Forces, Washington, D.C., 1957.

O. Wilhelmy, Jr., and D. E. Debeau, *Development of Procedures for Forecasting Water Demand*, Battelle Memorial Institute, 1959.

R. K. Linsley and J. B. Franzini, *Water Resource Engineering* (New York: McGraw-Hill, Inc., 1964).

U.S. Senate Committee on National Water Resources, *Water Supply and Demand, Water Resource Activities in the United States*, U.S. Government Printing Office, Washington, D.C., 1960.

U.S. Department of Commerce, Bureau of the Census, *Census of Manufactures, 1958*, Vol. 1, Summary Statistics (1961), U.S. Government Printing Office, Washington, D.C.

TABLE 11.1
Flow-to-Demand Ratios at Typical Critical Points

Subregion	Typical Critical Point*	Flow-to-Demand Ratios	
		1960	2010
A	Elmira	8	5
B	Binghamton	14	7
C	Williamsport	33	16
D	Danville	25	13
E	Sunbury	†	100
F	Lewistown	50	33
G	Harrisburg	33	20

* City nearest or at critical point. See Figure 11.2 for location.

† Demand is an insignificant percentage of flow.

greater water reuse, and (2) automation, resulting in fewer employees (recall that water use is tied to employment in the model).

Table 11.1 presents the results of a model simulation designed to examine the availability of river water at various critical points. The simulation presents flow-to-demand ratios under the water-use factors and economic projections that seem most likely. Other simulations that altered these factors had insignificant impact on these ratios.

The model formulation used to derive the levels of dissolved oxygen at critical quality points is somewhat more complex than that used for the water-quantity considerations. Actually, the equations used to compute the basic nature of the existing dissolved oxygen situation in the basin are solved in a submodel. This model computes coefficients that are then inserted into the main model. The sag curves are adjusted by the main model to account for economic growth, changing levels of treatment given to organic materials prior to their discharge to the river, and for flow augmentation.

Table 11.2 presents the results of two simulations in relation to a number of typical critical points and their water quality as measured by dissolved oxygen levels. Since the exact numerical results of these simulations are obviously subject to question because of the many assumptions required and the time period involved, the output values have been divided into three categories:

Category A. Model results in this category show present or predicted DO values above 8 ppm. The conclusion with regard to this category is that pollution problems in relation to DO at these critical points are deemed unlikely, although they cannot be ruled out completely through this type of analysis.

Category B. Model results in this category show DO values between 8 ppm and 4 ppm. Such critical points should be monitored as potential trouble spots.

TABLE 11.2
Dissolved Oxygen at Critical Points—Susquehanna River Basin

Subregion	Location* Below	River	Treatment: Year:	Current Level 1960	1980	2010	Higher Level 1980	2010
A	Hornell	Canisteo		A	A	A	A	A
A	Elmira	Chemung		B	B	C	B	B
B	Cortland	Tioughnioga		B	B	C	A	B
B	Binghamton	North Branch		C	C	C	A	A
C	Lock Haven	West Branch		B	C	C	A	A
D	Bloomsburg	North Branch		B	B	C	A	A
D	Danville	North Branch		B	B	C	A	A
D	Sunbury	Main Stem		A	A	A	A	A
E	Mouth of the Lackawanna			C†	C†	C†	A†	A†
F	Newton-Hamilton	Juniata		B	B	B	A	A
F	Tyrone	Juniata		B	C	C	C	C
G	Harrisburg	Main Stem		A	A	A	A	A
G	York	Codorus Creek		C†	C†	C†	C†	C†
G	Lancaster	Conestoga Creek		C†	C†	C†	C†	C†

Note: Values selected are at low flows (7-day, 5-year) for points in various subregions where problems are likely to exist. Because field work did not include river sampling, some problems may have been missed. Symbols are used rather than actual DO values to stress the tenuous nature of the values; however, they do appear reasonable and are consistent with existing information uncovered during the study.

Key

Dissolved-Oxygen Level	Symbol
≥8 ppm	A
<8 ppm but ≥4 ppm	B
<4 ppm	C

* See Figure 11.2.

† Problem might be solved by transporting wastes to main branch instead of or in combination with treatment.

Category C. Model results in this category show DO values less than 4 ppm. Critical points in this category will probably experience, or are experiencing, DO pollution problems.

The results are shown by (1) subregion; (2) at three time periods, 1960, 1980, and 2010; and (3) at two levels of treatment, (*a*) the present level, and (*b*) increase in treatment to the secondary level (removal of 80–85 percent of oxygen demand) at all points. As can be seen, increased levels of treatment will alleviate the problem at many, but not all, of these points. These conclusions are not sensitive to reasonable alternative assumptions about regional growth or water consumption.

At those places where serious pollution is threatened, special engineering and economic studies are required to select least-cost alternative actions. The model has been used to identify places where such detailed and costly investigations appear worth while.

TABLE 11.3
Projections for Subregion C in Relation to Two Systems of River Works

| | Population | | Unemployment | | Visitor Days | | Migrants | | Per Capita Income | |
| | Present | Elaborate | Present | Elaborate | Present | Elaborate | Present | Elaborate | Present | Elaborate |
Year	System	System	System	System	System	System	System	System	System	System
1960	430,700	430,700	7.37	7.37	2,029	2,029	−5,019	−5,019	1,332	1,332
1965	424,500	424,500	6.51	6.51	2,100	2,100	−3,570	−3,570	1,616	1,616
1970	423,900	423,900	5.62	5.62	2,197	2,197	−2,165	−2,165	1,906	1,906
1975	432,600	434,700	4.98	4.74	2,344	3,441	−1,151	−752	2,265	2,292
1980	449,800	452,600	4.51	5.53	3,623	8,453	−393	−419	2,608	2,603
1985	474,100	477,500	4.17	4.15	3,978	9,290	206	246	3,031	3,032
1990	505,000	508,600	3.94	3.96	4,406	11,687	667	646	3,433	3,427
1995	541,600	545,400	3.80	3.81	4,907	13,015	1,006	989	3,950	3,944
2000	583,500	587,600	3.74	3.75	5,483	14,541	1,209	1,201	4,446	4,440
2005	630,400	634,900	3.73	3.73	6,136	16,272	1,310	1,315	5,101	5,094
2010	682,300	687,200	3.74	3.74	6,869	18,220	1,367	1,380	5,728	5,721

Water-Sector Feedback on the Economy. While the results presented to this point do not indicate that the construction of systems of works on the Susquehanna River will have significant feedback effects on the economy of the subregions, two factors seemed certain to produce such feedbacks. First, the construction activities seemed certain to result in at least a short-run impact on regional employment and income. Second, the recreational activities associated with specific reservoirs might well create measurable employment and related effects.

Impact of River-Works Construction. The economic impact of works construction is incorporated into the model by converting the expenditures involved in building any given set of works to be tested in the model into employment. All employment is regarded as export industry employment because the funds for works construction are generally conceived as arising from nonlocal sources.[10] Certain kinds of labor are regarded as moving to the region during the construction period; for instance, engineering, technical, and supervisory personnel. Other personnel are drawn from the subregional labor pool.

When a test of the impact of works construction on a subregion's economy is desired, it is necessary to describe the kind of works involved—earth fill, etc. The nature of the structure determines the allocation of the costs of the construction to labor, materials, etc.[11]

Table 11.3 and Figure 11.7 illustrate the typical kind of impact the model predicts. In this example, a fairly elaborate system of works is hypothesized for construction during the 1970's and early 1980's in subregion C.[12] A total of about $350,000,000 would be spent, with the majority of the funds expended in the early 1970's. The projections relating population, unemployment, visitor days, migrants,

[10] Export industry employment is defined and described in Chapter 9, The Employment Sector.

[11] Bureau of Labor Statistics, "Labor and Materials Requirements for Civil Works Construction by the Corps of Engineers," U.S. Department of Labor, Bul. No. 1390, March 1964, 82 pp.

[12] This system involved every dam and reservoir ever seriously suggested for the region.

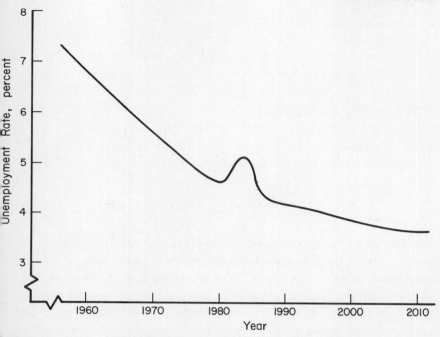

FIGURE 11.7. Unemployment projections for elaborate and present systems of works—
Subregion C.

and per capita income[13] are shown for this elaborate system and the present
system (existing or under construction during the time the study was conducted).
As can be seen, the results are not dramatic but are interesting. In regard to
population, a 2,800-person increase is specified for 1980, and a 4,900 increase by
the year 2010. These increases represent about 0.6% and 0.7% changes
respectively. The impact on unemployment rates is dynamic in that these rates
seem to oscillate, falling below the current system rates during the period of
works construction and increasing above these rates thereafter, and finally
returning to identical levels. The impact on visitor days at reservoirs in the
systems of works considered is large. Income effects appear desirable during the
construction period and are not truly discernible subsequently. Over all, it is not
easy to say whether or not the impact on regional development is beneficial, and
this points up the problem of selecting goals for regional planning as discussed
in Chapter 3.

Impacts of elaborate systems in other subregions were much less discernible;
most of the other areas were either larger in terms of population and the impacts
had less relative effect or a logical large system of works could not be defined.[14]

[13] Defined here as wages plus transfer payments as discussed in Chapter 10.

[14] The reader should keep in mind that these works, or others, may be desirable because
their direct benefits (water supply, flood control, recreation, etc.). It is the feedback on
the economic growth of the region that is evaluated here.

Recreation. The long-term effects of the elaborate set of works are caused by the recreational activity on the reservoirs. Further, any set of works constructed in the Susquehanna River Basin will undoubtedly be appealing from the point of view of recreation—the basin does lack an abundance of lakes. Reservoirs constructed with recreation in mind can be expected to draw many thousands of visitors each year. Therefore, it was necessary to determine if such recreational activity would have a significant impact on the local economy. Because it was obvious that some measurable employment impact would occur, it was decided to include recreation variables in the model. The problem was as follows: to devise a way for predicting attendance at a reservoir and then to convert this attendance to employment.

Predicting attendance at a reservoir is not an easy task. A host of variables must be considered and weighed for importance. The research program classified such variables as falling into four basic categories:

1. *Accessibility*—the time required to travel from population centers to the reservoir.
2. *Attractiveness*—the "drawing power" of the facility because of its features or setting.
3. *Competition*—the impact of competing opportunities.
4. *Capacity*—the ability of the reservoir and its associated facilities to accommodate visitors without overcrowding.

An attempt was made to develop measures of each of these factors so that the model could be used to estimate recreational attendance for reservoirs that might be built in the basin. Multiple regression analysis was employed by correlating visitor attendance with a large number of variables related to the four categories specified. Data originating in several states were analyzed. Different results were obtained in different states, but the following equation was judged as the most applicable for the Susquehanna region:

$$V_j = .99 + 2.9I_j + .09C_j - 2.0M_j + 11.9W_j,$$

V_j total Visitors expected at park j per year (thousands),

TABLE 11.4
Weights Used to Derive
the Activities Index

Activity	Weight
Swimming	29.5
Picnicking	26.2
Camping	18.4
Fishing	14.5
Boating	11.4
	100.0

I_j a weighted activities Index derived from published data,

C_j an estimate of the Capacity of the park as measured by the capacity of parking facilities,

M_j Miles from park j to nearest interstate highway,

W_j square root of Water acreage at park j.

The multiple correlation coefficient was 0.78, indicating that the regression equation explained 78 percent of the variance. The F-ratio (38.5) is significant at the 1 percent level (3.76). All the signs of the coefficients are intuitively correct. The weighted activities index I_j is regarded as a measure of attractiveness. Table 11.4 illustrates the weights assigned to the attractiveness of various recreational activities as derived from data about preferences for outdoor recreational activities reported in the literature.[15] For any given park, the index ranges from 0.0 to 1.0, depending on the range of recreational opportunities offered by the park. No attempt was made to assess the quality of the specific facilities presented.

Park capacity was measured in terms of the capacity of parking facilities C_j of the parks in absence of a better measure.

Access seemed measured best as the distance to the nearest interstate highway M. Interestingly, no measure of population entered the results in a statistically significant fashion although a number of such relationships were tested.

The square root of water acreage W_j can be regarded as a measure both of capacity and attractiveness.

While these results are far from perfect, they did allow the attendance benefits at a hypothetical reservoir to be estimated by (1) specifying what kinds of facilities were to be provided (I_j), (2) indicating the "planned" capacity of the facility (C_j), (3) specifying the location (M_j), as well as (4) specifying the planned

[15] Outdoor Recreation Resources Review Commission Study Report 19, "Travel and Use Survey," Division of Parks, Ohio Department of Natural Resources, Columbus, Ohio, 1958 and 1963; Leslie M. Reid, *Outdoor Recreation Preferences*, thesis, Michigan State University, 1963.

water acreage (W_j). Attendance was then converted to employment by multiplying each 1,000 visitors by 0.142.[16] This employment was then divided into two portions that needed to support "export" recreation and that which supported the recreational activities of the local inhabitants. This was done on the basis of a judgment concerning the percentage of visitors that a given reservoir would attract from outside of its subregion. Under the assumption that "local serving" recreation employment represented a diversion of funds from other local serving activities, economic growth in the model was related to only the "export" portion of the employment.

As was shown in Table 11.3, recreation, given sufficient investment, may have a measurable regional impact. Given this preliminary finding, further research on the subject is recommended.

Summary of the Sector. The water sector allows the assessment of important aspects of works construction in the basin in relation to water quality (namely, dissolved oxygen levels), water quantity, the economic impact of recreation, and the economic impact of the construction of the works themselves. The water sector ties the subregions together in a manner designed to show the impact of upstream economic and river works development on downstream water flows and water quality. The sector has been developed within the context of the problems of the Susquehanna basin and the potential interaction between the economy and the river in that area.

The approach used has been termed the "critical point" concept. That is, extreme situations are examined and if they do not appear to present significant problems, problems are assumed not to exist at places where less extreme situations are found. While such an approach will yield a different model under a variety of different situations, it is deemed a practical approach when the focus is on a given basin rather than upon building a general model. It is also a device for guiding the use of scarce research funds and personnel.

[16] Basic data used to derive this estimate are to be found in *Outdoor Recreation for America*, Outdoor Recreation Resources Review Commission, Study Report 24, ORRRC, Washington, D.C., 1962.

The major conclusion reached is that the construction of works on the river will
ot significantly accelerate the economic development of the basin. This conclusion
ɔes not infer that constructing river works is obviously unwise. Indeed, in a
umber of instances, the direct costs of works construction may be exceeded by the
irect benefits. Certain flood control projects may well fall in this category. But
ıe region should not pin its economic development hopes on river works.

ther Kinds of Technical Sectors

The water sector may be viewed as merely one kind of a "technical sector"
ıat can be tied to a regional simulation model. It is not difficult to imagine how
milar sectors could be constructed for regions where attention is focused on other
ıtural resources. Forestry, land, and minerals are obvious examples. On the
her hand, the technical sector might deal with policy, investment, or other
ctors relating to other than natural resource variables. Transportation and
lucation and training are obvious examples.[16]
While many suggestions for such technical sectors can be made, this section
ınits itself to the brief examination of only one such idea for the purposes of
ustration.
It is well recognized that resource management can affect economic development.
ɔr instance, the economic health and development of many economic areas in
ᴇ western United States are tied to the forest resource of the region and its
anagement. Many western areas are heavily forested and dependent on timber
owing, timber harvesting, and forest product manufacturing for their income.
. these areas much of the forest is owned by government—federal and state.
ften the federal ownership is not controlled by one agency but by two or more;
: example, the Forest Service and the Bureau of Land Management. The
ɔlicies of forest management of these governmental bodies can have short- and
ng-run effects on the economies of the regions where they manage timber
ources.

[16] Chapter 8, Demographic Sector, discusses some preliminary work in the education
skills area.

The problem faced by these agencies is very complex. They must consider the nation's present and future supply and demand for timber, the regional economic impact of their policies, as well as the alternative uses of the land they manage; for instance, recreation, forage, wildlife maintenance, etc. The problems involved are intertwined in a complex economic system where feedbacks, lags, and trends combine to form a system ideally suited to dynamic analysis by computer simulation.

In such a system, forest management in its broadest sense can be viewed as the technical sector of the model. The forest is a unique dynamic system in itself. Trees are both a factory and an inventory of wood. A policy of heavy cutting provides wood for the economic system now but destroys the factory and lowers the inventory. On the other hand, a very conservative cutting policy results in making more wood available for the future but reduces regional income. Of course, the future is not without its uncertainties, and conservative cutting practices may conserve wood that will not be in demand in the future.[17]

Figure 11.8 illustrates the dynamic system involved. A number of the relevant variables involved in "multiple use" forest land management are shown on the upper left of this figure. Some of these uses of the forest or land that can be employed for forestry conflict to various degrees. For instance, some aspects of recreation conflict with maximum timber production. In any case, the policy-mak has the choice of a wide variety of management policies involving various mixes of timber production, watershed yield, recreation, etc. The policy selected will ha two kinds of feedback effects. First, current policies begin to alter the nature of the forest itself; cutting more timber than is being produced will eventually reduc the timber inventory and growth to the point that a new policy will be needed.

The second feedback involves the impact on the region and how the feedback from the region may affect policy. Sharp cutbacks in the allowable cut of timber may have direct impacts on employment. In some areas, county taxes and/or

[17] Some interesting comments on this subject are made by R. W. Trestrail, "Whither Stumpage Values," Battelle Memorial Institute (staff paper), Columbus, Ohio.

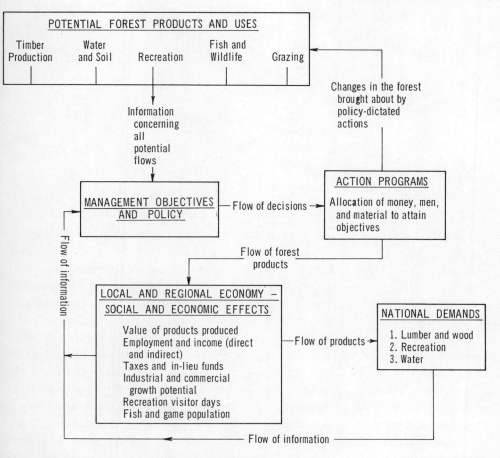

FIGURE 11.8. The environment of forest land management.

expenditures will be affected because a portion of the revenue from the sale of timber is allocated to these local governmental units. Political pressures are certain to be generated within such a system at all times.

If the region is large enough, the policies enacted can affect the national scene. For instance, a wholesale shift in the forest management policies of the Bureau of Land Management, the Forest Service, or both could easily affect timber prices.

The complexities and dynamic nature of this problem dictate the use of computer simulation as a tool for analysis. The objective of such an analysis would be to show explicitly the effects of a wide variety of policy choices. Again, the concept of optimality probably does not apply because in such a system few would profess to be so wise as to select the criterion by which optimum answers can be selected.

The preceding chapter described some of the model simulation results in connection with the water sector. This chapter describes some of the simulations made in connection with the employment and demographic sectors of the model. Altogether more than 200 major simulations of the model were made.[1]

In keeping with our iterative research strategy, the simulations were made at different stages in the model's development in order to increase understanding of its dynamic behavior and determine which were its more sensitive parts.[2] The results of these simulation experiments were then used for directing model improvement effort. In addition, the results of these simulations are relevant in answering the question of to what extent our integrated dynamic approach represents a potential advantage over more conventional approaches for analyzing regional performance.

Our approach has stressed taking explicit account of the dynamic interaction between demographic and employment variables. There is still the question, however, of whether or not the interdependence between regional population and employment is actually so important that failure to take it into account is likely to be misleading. To shed light on this question, we describe model simulation experiments in which changes are introduced one at a time, first in the employment sector and then in the demographic sector of the model. If significant changes in one sector of the model produce significant changes in the other, then this will lend support to the argument that the dynamic interaction between the two sectors should be an important consideration in regional analysis.

Similarly, within the employment sector itself, our approach, in contrast to more conventional trend-extrapolation approaches, has stressed the importance of

[1] A "major simulation" is one whose results the research team felt were worthy of recording in detail. Many less significant but useful simulations often led to one where the results were preserved. These "minor" simulations taught the team much about the model's properties.

[2] The iterative strategy is explained in Chapter 13 and elsewhere.

preserving the feedback effects of employment growth on regional costs. In particular, the feedback of labor costs on future growth and structure of the region's employment has been stressed. Again the question is raised as to whether or not these feedback effects are so important that failure to take them into account may be misleading. To shed light on this question we describe several experiments on the wage feedback loop to see whether or not changes in the formulation produce significant effects on regional performance.

In addition to these experiments, two other sets of experiments of interest are described. The first involves the preliminary skills sector mentioned in Chapter 3, and the second involves an attempt to see how well the demographic sector of the model, initialized in 1950, can predict 1960 population. These latter experiments were designed as a partial "test" of the model's validity; i.e., to see if the model is a "reasonable" representation of the complex processes of the real world.

A Typical Model Run

Before discussing the model experiments in detail, it is helpful to have an over-all view of the dynamic behavior of the model. An appreciation of these dynamics can best be obtained through use of a concrete example. A typical 50-year simulation of the Wilkes-Barre–Scranton subregion turns out to be a particularly good example for this purpose because it shows a turnaround situation as it unfolds. Figure 12.1 is a plot of several selected variables resulting from such a simulation. We see from this figure that the economy starts out in a very unhealthy state, with unemployment well above the national average. As the simulation unfolds, however, this condition is dramatically reversed until, toward the end of the period, the rate of unemployment levels off below the national average (assumed to be 5 percent).

Inspection of the plotted variables reveals that two effects are operating to produce this result. First, the high level of unemployment at the beginning of the period is accompanied by a low relative wage for the low-paying, low-skill-using

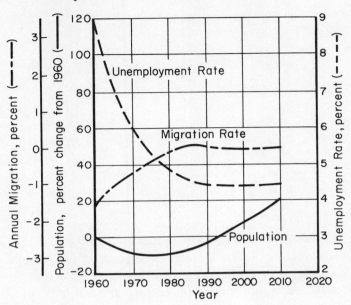

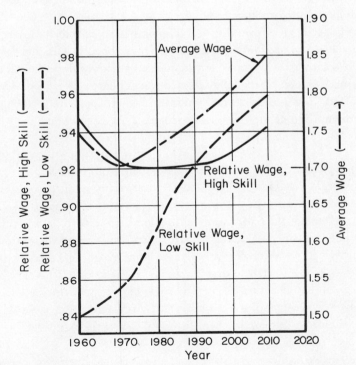

FIGURE 12.1. 50-year simulations, Wilkes-Barre–Scranton, Subregion E.

industries.[3] This low relative wage attracts new industry that helps absorb the unemployed labor. Second, because of the relative lack of job opportunity, we see that a high rate of outmigration occurs. This leads to a reduction of the labor force, which also contributes to the drop in the rate of unemployment.

In addition to the decline in unemployment rate, we see from Figure 12.1 that, as the simulation unfolds, population at first falls and then increases so that by the end of the period it is growing at a modest rate. The population decline in the early part of the period is produced by a combination of direct and indirect effects all stemming from the high level of unemployment. Following directly from the high unemployment rate is a lowering of age-specific birth rates and, as mentioned, a net out-movement of people. In addition to its direct effect, out-migration also produces indirect effects that contribute to the population decline. The indirect effects occur because younger people account for a disporportionate share of the out-migration. Following a period of heavy out-migration, the subregion is therefore left with a relatively older population. This produces an additional decrease in the net reproduction rate by lowering the average birth rate and raising the average death rate. As the unemployment rate falls, all the effects that produced a decline in population are reversed or moderated so that, as we see in Figure 12.1, population eventually starts growing.

[3] Recall from Chapter 10 that relative wage is defined as the ratio of actual average hourly manufacturing earnings to the hypothetical average that would be paid if all industries in the area paid at their national average rates. Its value for 1960 was computed for each subregion as follows:

$$RW_k = \frac{PY_k}{\sum_j (E_{jk})(NW_j)}$$

where

RW_k Relative Wage of kth subregion, 1960,

PY_k total PaYroll for all manufacturing industries in kth subregion, 1960,

E_{jk} Employment in jth 2-digit manufacturing industry of kth subregion, 1960,

NW_j average National Wage of jth 2-digit manufacturing industry, 1960.

As described in Chapter 10, this basic relative wage is then broken down into two parts— relative wage for low- and relative wage for high-skill-using industries.

The lower part of Figure 12.1 shows a plot of the relative and average wage variables from this simulation.[4] This plot illustrates some of the dynamics of regional income behavior. Both average and relative wages start out comparatively low. Because the high rate of unemployment is associated mainly with an excess of unskilled, as opposed to skilled, workers, the relative wage of the low-skill-using, low-paying industries is considerably lower than the relative wage of the higher-paying industries. This leads to faster growth in employment in the low-paying industries so that average wage, which reflects industry mix, declines during the first decade. The increasing presence of low-wage industry in the area makes it easier for high-paying firms to acquire all the labor they need without significant wage increases so that the relative wage for high-paying industry declines. Meanwhile, as unemployment falls, and excess unskilled labor is absorbed, the relative wage of low-paying industries rises until eventually it goes above the relative wage of the high-paying industries.[5] This change in local labor market conditions favors the growth of higher-, as opposed to lower-paying industries. The increasing presence of high-paying industry together with the rising wages of the low-paying industries combine to produce a turnaround in the subregion's average wage. As the average wage grows, it becomes increasingly difficult for even the high-paying industries to acquire labor at existing wage levels. Consequently, during the latter part of the period, the relative wage of the high-paying industries begins to grow along with the relative wage of the low-paying industries.

The simulation results shown in Figure 12.1 have been discussed in relation to the dynamic properties of the model. These plots and the printouts for all

[4] Average wage as defined here is not the same as average wage in the usual sense of the term. As described in Chapter 10, average wage as used here primarily reflects the effects of industry mix and relative wage. It differs from the usual meaning by excluding productivity, inflationary, and other trend effects.

[5] The reader should note that the discussion is about relative, not absolute, wages; therefore it is possible for the relative wage for low-skill workers to exceed the relative wage for high-skill workers.

the subregions presented in Appendix D can also be viewed as subregional projections of population, employment, income, water use, etc. We prefer to discuss the differences between simulations (projections) rather than their absolute levels for the following reasons:

1. The study was aimed at determining the impact of systems of river works and the interrelationship between water and the economy as well as the dynamics of regional growth. With this kind of emphasis, the impact of changes in assumptions, data, and policies was of major interest and the absolute levels of values generated by the model were of secondary interest.
2. Differentials between runs are felt to be more meaningful and reliable than their absolute levels.
3. We believed most readers would not have specific interest in the subregional economies except as they are illustrative of findings and general principles.

Selected Model Experiments

The dynamic characteristics of the model can further be understood by means of sensitivity experiments. These experiments consist of making changes in the model, usually in the value of a particular parameter, and comparing the path of the economy simulated *with* the change to the path simulated *without* the change. This procedure is helpful in identifying those parameters or aspects of the model that could make significant differences in the projections. To the extent that the model validly represents the real world, these same parameters also represent prime targets for policy measures aimed at affecting the future course of subregional economies.

Some Experiments Relating to the Employment Sector. Here we describe some experiments on the important wage-adjustment, employment feedback loop. During the course of the research, the wage adjustment formulation underwent several changes. Before describing the experiments on the final version, we describe briefly experiments on an earlier version in order to provide the reader with some idea of our iterative strategy.

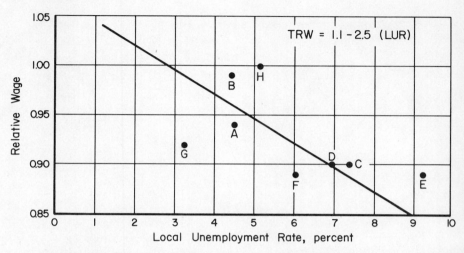

FIGURE 12.2. Manufacturing relative wage versus local unemployment rate, Susquehanna subregions, 1960.

EXPERIMENTS ON PRELIMINARY VERSION OF WAGE FORMULATION. Recall from Chapter 10 that local wages were first hypothesized to respond to the tightness of the local labor market as measured by the local unemployment rate. Using subregional data on relative wage and unemployment rate, a relationship was estimated, shown in Figure 12.2, as follows:

$$TRW = 1.1 - 2.5(LUR)$$

where

    TRW Target Relative Wage,

    LUR Local Unemployment Rate.

This preliminary formulation, in addition to not providing a very satisfactory fit with the data, also has the problem of making it virtually impossible for the relative wage to reach the national average level of 1.0.[6] From Figure 12.2, we see that a subregion's unemployment rate would have to fall below the extremely low level of 3 percent before its relative wage would be driven up to the national average. In Run 59, an experiment was therefore tried in which the relationship between the unemployment rate and target relative wage was shifted upward to a more plausible position. In this position, shown in Figure 12.3, a subregion approaches the national average relative wage when it experiences a national average unemployment rate assumed to be 5 percent.

Table 12.1 shows how several model outputs were affected by this change. We see first of all that the results vary somewhat from subregion to subregion. This is to be expected because the projections, in addition to depending on the particular change introduced, also, of course, depend on the model's initial

[6] Recall that the lack of support for this formulation was further established by a larger sample of data shown in Figure 10.3.

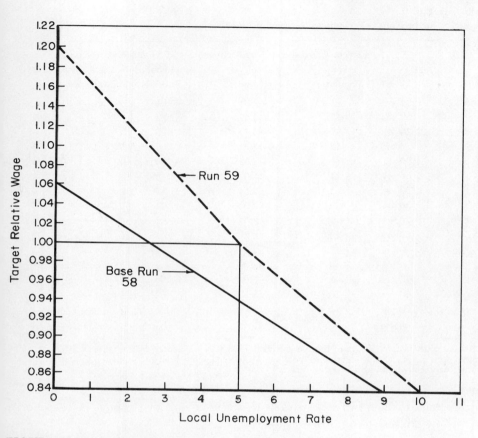

FIGURE 12.3. Relative wage functions assumed in sensitivity analysis.

conditions. And each of the subregions starts out in a somewhat different initial situation. In general, we see that although in the short run the effect on both employment and population projections is minor, in the long run the impact on these variables is over 10 percent. This, in comparison to other sensitivity experiments, is a fairly substantial change.[7]

Because these experiments were conducted on an early version of the model, the dynamics underlying these results are somewhat different from those in the typical run described. The main point of these results can be made, however, without going into a description of these dynamics. That is, taken together with the unsatisfactory nature of the preliminary formulation, these sensitivity results served to motivate further research on the wage adjustment process.

EXPERIMENTS ON THE FINAL VERSION OF THE WAGE FORMULATION. Recall from Chapter 10 that the empirical investigation resulted in a wage adjustment

---

[7] In judging whether or not the simulation results were sensitive to a particular change in a parameter value, its effect was compared with the effect produced by a given change in other parameters or formulations. Most of the sensitivity experiments produced changes well under 10 percent in the 50-year projections. Any change producing a change in projections over 10 percent was therefore considered *relatively* significant.

TABLE 12.1

Sensitivity Analysis of the Preliminary Version of Wage-Adjustment Formulation

| | | Percent Comparison of Projections in Run 59 versus Base Run 58 | | | |
| | | Total Population | Total Employment | Unemployment Rate | Per Capita Income* |
Subregion					
A	20 yrs	−1.6	−2.8	+8.1	—
	50 yrs	−10.7	−12.1	+15.2	—
B	20 yrs	−1.9	−3.3	+10.9	—
	50 yrs	−12.4	−13.5	+15.5	—
C	20 yrs	−1.6	−2.6	+8.5	—
	50 yrs	−11.1	−12.6	+18.5	—
D	20 yrs	−1.4	−2.5	+6.3	—
	50 yrs	−9.3	−10.9	+12.4	—
E	20 yrs	−1.4	−2.5	+8.1	—
	50 yrs	−10.6	−12.2	+15.1	—
F	20 yrs	−1.6	−2.7	+8.5	—
	50 yrs	−10.4	−11.9	+12.7	—
G	20 yrs	−1.8	−3.0	+10.6	—
	50 yrs	−10.7	−12.0	+13.2	—
H	20 yrs	−1.4	−2.0	+8.6	—
	50 yrs	−9.7	−10.5	+14.7	—

* Because this early version of the model did not contain an income sector, no comparisons on per capita income are possible. However in the experiments that follow this variable will also be examined.

formulation in which two relative wages were used, one for the high-skill- and one for the low-skill-using industries, as follows:

$$TRWH = .4 + .30(AWG)$$
$$TRWL = .525 + .30(AWG) - 2.5(LUR)$$

where

TRWH   Target Relative Wage for High-skill-using industries,

TRWL   Target Relative Wage for Low-skill-using industries,

AWG   Average WaGe,

LUR   Local Unemployment Rate.

Four experiments were conducted on this formulation in which the coefficients of average wage and unemployment rate were each increased and decreased. The experiments in this case, as well as most of the ones that follow, were conducted on the Wilkes-Barre–Scranton subregion.[8] Table 12.2 summarizes the

[8] Only one subregion was used in most of the model experiments in order to allow for maximum computer experimentation within the research budget. The results, of course, may be expected to vary somewhat depending on initial conditions, as shown in Table 12.1. The Scranton–Wilkes-Barre subregion was, in fact, selected for experimentation primarily because it started out in 1960 as a depressed area and therefore represents a regional problem of general interest.

TABLE 12.2

Sensitivity Analyses of Changing Parameters in Relative Wage Equations

$TRWH = .4 + .3(AWG)$

$TRWL = .525 + .3(AWG) - 2.5(LUR)$

Simulation Run*	Parameter Change†	Percent Comparison of Changes with Base Run			
		Total Population	Total Employment	Unemployment Rate	Per Capita‡ Income
170	Base Run	0	0	0	0
172	Coefficients of average wage increased to .50				
	20 yrs	+2.3	+4.1	−0.60	−2.3
	50 yrs	+20.8	+24.7	−1.17	−0.9
173	Coefficients of average wage decreased to 0.15				
	20 yrs	−1.5	−2.6	+0.37	+1.1
	50 yrs	−9.9	−11.3	+0.56	+0.1
174	Coefficient of unemployment rate increased to 5.0				
	20 yrs	+1.2	+1.6	−0.18	−0.10
	50 yrs	+2.3	+2.2	+0.05	+0.09
175	Coefficient of unemployment rate decreased to 0.0				
	20 yrs	−1.1	−1.6	+0.19	+0.2
	50 yrs	−2.7	−2.7	−0.03	−0.07

* Numbers correspond to computer simulation identification system used by the Battelle research group.

† In each experiment the intercept terms were changed so that the equations would be consistent with a steady-state condition. Under this condition, an average wage of 2.00 and a local unemployment rate equal to the national average (assumed to be 5 percent) would produce relative wages equal to the national average (i.e., 1.0).

‡ Per capita income as used here refers to only wages and salaries and selected transfer payments. It is computed essentially as follows: [(Average wage)(Number employed) + (Average unemployment insurance)(Number of unemployed) + (Average old-age and survivors insurance)(Number of people over 65)]/total population.

results and reveals that, whereas changing the coefficient of unemployment has very little impact, changing the coefficient of average wage has considerable impact on the long-run projections.

Figure 12.4, a plot of Run 172, superimposed on its base run 170, illustrates what is happening. The subregion starts out with a comparatively low average wage. Increasing the value of the coefficient of average wage thus results in lowering both of the relative wages significantly below their base run values. The lower labor costs attract more industrial growth and produce a faster drop in the rate of unemployment. The lower rate of unemployment in turn slows

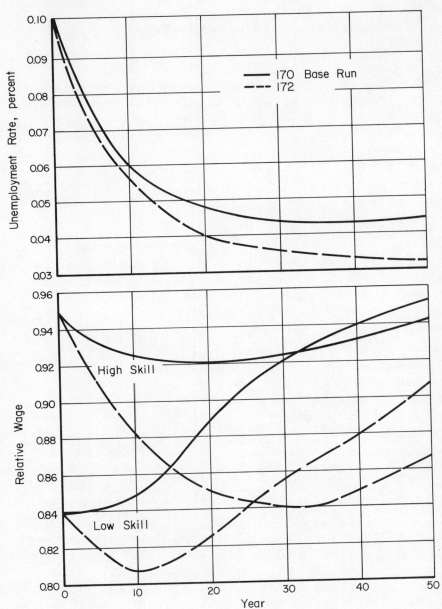

FIGURE 12.4. Run 172 superimposed on base run.

out-migration and increases birth rates, both of which contribute to significantly higher population projections.

These experiments illustrate the important role that the employment wage feedback can play in determining regional performance. They suggest that it may be reasonable to use conventional extrapolation methods, which ignore these effects, for short-run analyses; but it is important, if we are interested in long-run implications of alternative regional programs, to attempt to improve our understanding and ability to estimate this kind of feedback.

Finally, we see (Table 12.2) that the effect on the population projections were almost equal to the effect on employment projections. This illustrates that changes in the employment sector are transmitted to the population sector and implies that regional population projections should not be made independently of employment considerations. In the next section, in which we describe several experiments on the demographic sector of the model, we examine whether or not the reverse of this proposition, i.e., that employment projections should not be made independently of population considerations, is also true.

Some Experiments Relating to the Demographic Sector. Here we describe three sets of experiments relating to the demographic sector of the model. The first set explores the effects of changing parameter values in the migration functions. The second describes an attempt to see how well the demographic sector of the model, initialized with 1950 conditions, can predict the 1960 conditions experienced in two of the subregions. The third set explores the preliminary formulation showing the relation of skills and education to regional growth patterns.

SOME EXPERIMENTS RELATING TO MIGRATION. In the case of small, open regions, like the kind represented in the Susquehanna model, migration is typically the most volatile and least predictable component of population change. Moreover, the variables currently used in the model to generate migration rates explain, according to the regression analyses reported in Chapter 8, less than 50 percent of their variation. It is, therefore, of interest to see how sensitive the model behavior is to changes in the current parameter estimates. Recall from Chapter 8 that, for each age group, a migration function was estimated of the following form:

$$NM = A + B(DUR) + C(1/POP)$$

where

NM Net in-Migration rate,

DUR Difference between local and national Unemployment Rates (national unemployment assumed constant at .05 for model runs),

POP Total POPulation.

TABLE 12.3

Sensitivity Analyses of Changing Parameters in Migration Equations

$NM = A + B(DUR) + C(1/POP)$

Simulation Run Number*	Parameter Change†	Percent Comparison of Projections with Base Run			
		Total Population	Total Employment	Unemployment Rate	Per Capita‡ Income
170	Base Run	0	0	0	0
191	A increased				
	20 yrs	+11.3	+6.0	+34.3	−4.7
	50 yrs	+16.2	+11.7	+34.2	−3.9
192	A decreased				
	20 yrs	−10.5	−5.8	−35.4	+5.2
	50 yrs	−15.1	−11.2	−36.5	+5.0
193	B increased				
	20 yrs	+0.6	+0.5	+1.7	−0.2
	50 yrs	−0.2	−0.01	−1.4	+0.2
194	B decreased				
	20 yrs	−0.5	−0.4	−1.3	+0.1
	50 yrs	+0.2	+0.03	+1.4	−0.1
195	C increased				
	20 yrs	+0.2	+0.2	+1.1	−0.1
	50 yrs	+0.3	+0.2	+0.7	−0.03
196	C decreased				
	20 yrs	−0.2	−0.2	−1.1	+0.1
	50 yrs	−0.3	−0.2	−0.5	+0.03

* Numbers correspond to computer simulation identification system used by the Battelle research group.

† All parameter changes were equal to one standard error of estimate of the parameter involved.

‡ Per capita income as used here refers to only wages and salaries and selected transfer payments. It is computed essentially as follows: [(Average wage)(Number employed) + (Average unemployment insurance)(Number of unemployed) + (Average old age and survivors insurance)(Number of people over 65)]/total population.

Altogether a series of six experiments was made in which each of the three parameters was increased and decreased by an amount equal to one standard error (see Table 8.11). Table 12.3, which summarizes the results, reveals that the projections are very insensitive to changes in either the B or C coefficients. Changes in the intercepts (i.e., the A terms) made in Runs 191 and 192, however, produce a considerable impact on the projections.

Figure 12.5, a graph of Run 191 superimposed on the base run, 170, illustrates what is happening here. Increasing the migration intercept, first of all, significantly reduces the rate of out-migration. This causes a direct increase in the population. We might have further expected an indirect effect on population due to the age selectivity of migration. Other things being equal, the slowdown in out-migration should result in a younger average age mix in Run 191 and hence a higher natural rate of population increase. Somewhat surprisingly, however, we see that the natural rate of population increase (births less deaths divided by population)

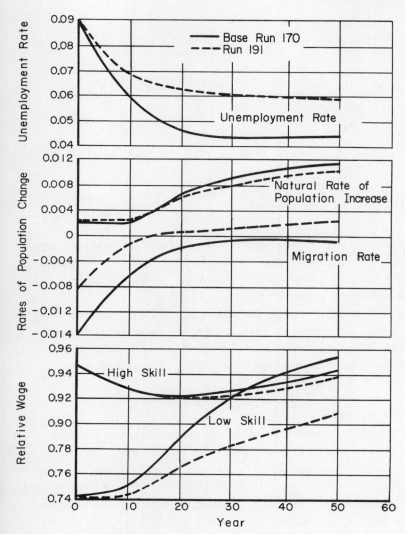

FIGURE 12.5. Run 191 superimposed on run 170.

is actually slightly less in Run 191 than in the base run. This is because the slowdown in out-migration, in addition to the age-mix effect, also produces a higher level of unemployment. The higher unemployment in turn results in lowering the age-specific birth rates, thereby offsetting the age-mix effect on the natural rate of population growth.

Most importantly, we see by looking at the results of Run 191 that this change in the migration formulation not only affected the total population values but also had considerable impact on employment levels. This is caused first of all, of course, by the direct effect of increased population on the household-serving industries. Second, it results from the indirect effect that increased population, and hence the labor force, has on keeping the relative wages down. Recall from the description of the relative wage experiments that the higher unemployment rate represents an increased availability of unskilled workers. This allows the relative wage for low-skill workers to decline, thereby increasing the relative attraction of the area to low-skill-using, low-wage industries. As employment in these industries increases, the average wage in the area is reduced and the competitive bidding pressure for labor is reduced so that, toward the end of the period, the relative wage of high-skill-using industries is also reduced slightly from its base run value. This reduction in labor costs accounts for additional increased growth in employment.

Interestingly, we see that, while population and employment are increased, per capita income is actually decreased. Two factors account for this: (1) the higher percentage of low-wage industry and (2) the higher unemployment rates that mean a smaller percentage of the population is gainfully employed.

We conclude from these experiments on migration that whereas the projections are amazingly insensitive to the coefficients of the variables currently incorporated in the migration equations, they are very sensitive to changes in the intercepts of these equations. Clearly, the amount of unexplained variation in the treatment of migration is a matter of concern for future research. Another finding of some interest is that changing the migration function does not have as dramatic an effect on per capita income as it does on population. This shows up in both Runs 191 and 192.

At first glance, this finding might seem to suggest that policies for depressed areas that emphasize increasing out-migration might not be effective in increasing per capita incomes. However, a study of Table 12.3 shows that per capita income does increase when out-migration is increased. Moreover, the results of many of our experiments seem to suggest that large changes in per capita incomes are difficult to produce. In this light, the increase in per capita incomes when out-migration is increased may be viewed as important and substantial.[9]

[9] These simulation results concerning the relation between out-migration and per capita incomes are consistent with empirical findings for per capita income changes by states, 1870–1954, presented by Harvey S. Perloff et al., *Regions, Resources, and Economic Growth* (Baltimore, Maryland: The Johns Hopkins Press, 1960), Chapters 27 and 28.

TABLE 12.4

Comparison of Sensitivity Experiments on Relative Wage and Migration Parameters

Simulation Run*	Parameter Change	Percent Comparison of Changes with Base Run			
		Total Population	Total Employment	Unemployment Rate	Per Capita Income
191	Intercepts in Migration Equations Increased				
	20 yrs	+11.3	+6.0	+34.3	−4.7
	50 yrs	+16.2	+1.7	+34.2	−3.9
	(Outmigration decreased)				
172	Coefficients of Average Wage Increased in Relative Wage Equations				
	20 yrs	+2.3	+4.1	−0.60	−2.3
	50 yrs	+20.8	+24.7	−1.17	−0.9
	(Relative Wages decreased)				

* Numbers correspond to computer simulation identification system used by the Battelle research group.

Finally, we see from these experiments that significant changes in the demographic sector have important ramifications for employment projections. And, just as the preceding experiments indicate that population projections are not independent of what happens to employment, these experiments show that employment projections are not independent of what happens to population. We conclude from this that treating these two aspects of regional performance in an interdependent fashion does have strong justification.

COMPARISON OF MIGRATION WITH WAGE EXPERIMENTS. Before proceeding to the next experiment, it is informative to compare the migration experiment with the experiment on the wage formulation (see Table 12.4). Both experiments produce about the same increase in the 50-year population projections. Aside from this similarity, however, the two experiments have relatively little in common. First of all, we see that reducing wages, in Run 172, has virtually no impact on the short-run population projections, whereas reducing out-migration does. This is because reducing out-migration has immediate and direct impact on population growth. Reducing wages, on the other hand, has an impact on population only after the creation of new employment opportunities that in turn induce a slowdown in out-migration. Interestingly, the wage reduction experiment, although it is much slower to produce increases in population, eventually at the 50-year mark surpasses the increases produced by the out-migration reduction experiment. Furthermore, we see that Run 191 generates significantly more unemployment, while Run 172 despite its rapid population growth produces less unemployment. The lower unemployment rate in Run 172 has two other implications that help explain why the impact on per capita income is more favorable (or at least less unfavorable) for this run. Both runs, we see, produce lower per capita incomes than the base run. We might, however, have expected Run 172, because it involved a direct lowering of wages, to have produced the larger loss in per capita incomes. This does not occur, however, for two reasons. First, the mere fact that the unemployment rate is lower in Run 172 means higher average incomes because a higher fraction of the working-age people are gainfully employed. Second, and more indirect, is the effect that the lower unemployment rate has on the comparative attractiveness of the subregion to high- and low-wage industries. By examining Figure 12.4, we see that the lower unemployment rate, which is maintained throughout Run 172, results in a relatively greater advantage for high-wage industries than in the base run. This industry-mix effect together with the lower unemployment rate tends to offset the initial tendency, due to lower wages, toward lower per capita income. Indeed, by the end of the simulation period, we see that per capita income is virtually back to its base run level.

We conclude from this comparison that for long-run projections the wage formulation shows as much sensitivity as the migration formulation, although for short-run projections it is substantially less sensitive. Future model refinement aimed at improving the short run as opposed to long-run projections should thus be more heavily focused on improving the migration formulation. Finally, even though we might at first expect that altering the wage behavior would have significant effects on regional per capita income, this does not appear to be the case. In either case, whether the alteration produces decreased wages, as in Run 172, or increased wages, as in Run 173, canceling forces are set into motion. Although minor changes occur in per capita incomes in the short run, these are virtually eliminated in the long run.

A VALIDATION EXPERIMENT. In the course of the research program, we stressed the use of sensitivity experiments as a means of identifying those parts of the model that are most sensitive and therefore most promising candidates for further research. The results of these sensitivity experiments depend, however, on the structure of the model, and the conclusions drawn from these experiments are therefore based on the assumption that the model structure is a valid representation of the real world. The model's validity can be tested only by comparing its output

TABLE 12.5
Average Annual Rate of Unemployment for Labor Market Areas of Subregions E and G

Year	Local Unemployment Rates Subregion E	Subregion G	National Unemployment Rates	Difference Between Local and National Unemployment Rates Subregion E	Subregion G
1950	9.3	3.3	5.3	4.0	−2.0
1951	8.9	2.2	3.3	5.6	−1.1
1952	9.2	2.2	3.1	6.1	−0.9
1953	9.4	1.9	2.9	6.5	−1.0
1954	14.5	5.0	5.6	8.9	−0.6
1955	13.1	3.8	4.4	8.7	−0.6
1956	11.3	3.3	4.2	7.1	−0.9
1957	11.0	4.1	4.3	6.7	−0.2
1958	16.3	6.2	6.8	9.5	−0.6
1959	15.2	4.5	5.5	9.7	−1.0
1960	12.7	4.7	5.6	7.1	−0.9

Sources: Subregions E and G data from Bureau of Employment Security, U.S. Department of Labor, Pennsylvania Office.

National data from *Labor Force, Employment, and Unemployment Statistics*, 1947–1961 by the U.S. Bureau of Labor Statistics, October 1962.

to real world data. This may be done for example, by seeing how well the model can reproduce past regional performance.[10] Unfortunately, in attempting to conduct validation runs of this kind, our experience has been that obtaining reliable and comparable data for past years takes a great deal of effort and is extremely difficult. Although several runs of this type were made, because of these difficulties with the data, our original plans for conducting more extensive validation tests were abandoned.

Because producing the required past data inputs was particularly difficult in relation to the employment sector, it was further decided to limit the validation test to the demographic sector only, or at least to an early version of that sector of the model.[11] This was done by separating the demographic sector from the rest of the model and providing estimated values of the local-national unemployment rate differentials as input. The experiments were still further limited by applying the tests to two subregions only, namely, Subregion E (Wilkes-Barre–Scranton) and Subregion G (Harrisburg). These particular subregions were selected because, in addition to having the necessary data more readily available than some of the other subregions, they represent opposite ends of the spectrum with respect to economic health during the period. Table 12.5 shows that Subregion G had

[10] As time goes on, the model can also be "tested" with 1970 and 1975 data. Partial data assembled to date seem to indicate the model is behaving well during the 1960's. In particular, the turnaround situation predicted for subregion E seems to have occurred.

[11] In particular, the simulations were conducted before the empirical work on birth rates was undertaken. In contrast to the final model, in which birth rates are inversely related to the level of unemployment, age-specific birth rates were assumed constant at the same value for the two tested subregions.

TABLE 12.6
Comparison of Model Versus Census
Cumulative 1950 to 1960 Net Migration, Births, and Deaths, Subregions
E and G

	Subregion E		Subregion G	
	Model	Census	Model	Census
Cumulative Net Migration				
1950–1960	−162,730	−111,948	+10,899	+22,181
Cumulative Births				
1950–1960	144,660	123,967	225,390	225,293
Cumulative Deaths				
1950–1960	82,883	80,347	112,350	96,093
Total Population 1960	593,977	626,600	1,019,539	1,046,981

unemployment rates consistently below, while Subregion E had unemployment rates considerably above, the national average during the 1950–1960 decade.[12] To conduct the tests, these estimates of unemployment rates were fed into the demographic model that was initiated using 1950 census data. The main purpose was to see how well the model would predict the 1960 census data.

Table 12.6 showing the cumulative 1950 to 1960 totals of net in-migration, births, and deaths projected by the model compared to the corresponding census estimates, summarizes the results of these experiments. We see that the model was much closer to Subregion G's population totals (missing by only 2.6 percent) than to Subregion E's, which it missed by 5.2 percent. We note first that, whereas the births are estimated almost exactly for Subregion G, they are significantly overestimated for E. This may well be accounted for by the fact that the early version of the model used in these experiments did not incorporate the effect of the depressed economic conditions in Subregion E on birth rates. If this effect were included (and subsequent research as described in Chapter 8 confirmed that this effect does in fact exist), then the predicted births for Subregion E would have been much lower.

In addition to this discrepancy in the predicted births, we see there is another discrepancy (to some extent canceling the first) in the amount of predicted migration. The amount of out-migration is significantly overestimated for Subregion E and apparently to some extent for Subregion G also. Some light is shed on the problem by analyzing the population projections on an age-specific basis. Looking at Table 12.7, we see that the discrepancy in total population is much less than some of the discrepancies for individual age groups. Unusually large model overestimates occur in both subregions for the 15–19 and 20–24 age groups. This could be accounting for the errors in the cumulative migration because

[12] The only annual unemployment-rate data available were the data based on Bureau of Employment Security estimates. This may not be entirely reliable as indicated in the previous discussion on data. And, because the BES areas do not exactly coincide with our subregion boundaries, an additional source of error is introduced.

TABLE 12.7
Comparison of Model Versus Census
Population by Age Group, Subregions E and G

Age Group	Percent Difference Between Census and Model Subregion E, 1960*	Percent Difference Between Census and Model Subregion G, 1960*
0–14	−10.0	−13.2
15–19	6.9	18.7
20–24	11.3	36.5
25–44	−2.0	−1.1
45–64	−11.2	−7.4
65+	−7.3	−9.5
Total Population	−5.2	−2.6

* Computed by taking [(100)(Model 1960 − Census 1960)]/Census 1960.

these younger groups tend to move out much more rapidly than the older groups, and they tend to move out even when the local unemployment conditions are slightly better than the national average, as they are in Subregion G.

The fact that the 0–14 group is being underestimated by a considerable amount despite the fact that the number of births is not being underestimated indicates that some problem could exist in the model's "aging" mechanism. It appears that the model may be aging children into teenagers and young adults too quickly. Recall that for purposes of simplification the model ages a constant fraction of the people in each age group, each year, to the next age group. For example, every year it ages $\frac{1}{13}$ of children (i.e., 0–14 age group) into teenagers. This procedure could lead to difficulty if there were a sharp skewing of the number of children toward the younger part of the 0 to 14 group.[13] In this case, less than $\frac{1}{13}$ of the group would grow into teenagers per year in the real world and the model would overestimate the fraction of children growing into teenagers. Because a postwar baby boom started in 1945, we might suspect that this in fact could be a source of trouble. Table 12.8 confirms this, showing a skewing toward the 0 to 4 group within the 0–14 interval for both subregions.

We concluded from this validation experiment that the model was behaving fairly well in relation to aggregate population projections. This success in relation to the aggregates is somewhat misleading, however, because in part it was due to a cancellation of errors. In particular, in Subregion E, an overestimate of births was offset by an underestimate of net in-migration.[14] The birth overestimate was traced to a failure of this version of the model to take the relationship between an area's economic conditions and its birth rate into account. This finding in

[13] This aging problem is discussed in Chapter 8.

[14] Of course, it should be remembered that Subregion E, with its high unemployment rates (as high as 16 percent) and high out-migration, represents about as severe a test of the model as could be selected.

TABLE 12.8
Distribution of Population Within 0 to 14
Age Interval, Subregions E and G, 1950

Age	Subregion E	Subregion G
0–4	62,877	92,340
5–9	53,482	75,453
10–14	50,171	64,148

Source: U.S. Bureau of the Census,
U.S. Census of Population: 1950, Vol. II,
Characteristics of the Population,
Part 38, Pennsylvania, U.S. Government
Printing Office, Washington, D.C.

relation to the validation experiments plus the additional finding that the long-run
projections were highly sensitive to the birth-rate specification subsequently led
to research aimed at incorporating the unemployment-rate, birth-rate loop into
the model. The migration discrepancy was traced to problems with the model's
simplified aging mechanism. This aging mechanism in particular does not provide
a good representation of the actual aging pattern that occurred during the 1950
to 1960 decade. Of course, it must be remembered that the problem of that decade
was due importantly to peculiar initial conditions of 1950 brought about by
the postwar baby boom. When the model is initialized in 1960, as it is for all the
other simulations, the baby boom had lasted 15 years and the problem of the
skewed distribution within the 0–14 age class had significantly diminished. For
this reason, although it is felt that future work should be directed at improving the
model's aging mechanism, this task was given lower priority than the other tasks
that found support within the program's budget.

SOME EXPERIMENTS RELATING TO SKILLS. To conclude the section on demographic
experiments, we describe several experiments relating to skills. There is a growing
awareness and concern about the effects of education and skill level of labor on
regional growth and vitality. Unfortunately, as pointed out in Chapter 8, in
treating a variable such as skill level, the investigator is confronted with conceptual
and measurement difficulties. Despite this lack of measurable cause and effect,
it was decided to take advantage of the simulation approach and explore several
speculative hypotheses involving skill factors. Because of the lack of empirical
support for the parameters used in this sector of the model, the skills sector was
not employed for the other simulation runs. Several experiments were made,
however, in order to determine the potential significance of the modeled skill
effects on a local economy. Three of these experiments, summarized in Table 12.9,
are reported here.

In Run 186 a relationship between migration and skill level was hypothesized.

TABLE 12.9

Sensitivity Analyses of Skills Effects on Relative Wage Costs and Migration

Simulation Run*	Model Change		Percent Comparison of Projection with Base Run†		
			Total Population	Total Employment	Unemployment Rate
170	Base run		0	0	0
186	Migration directly	20 yrs	+7.3	+4.8	+22.7
	related to skill level	50 yrs	+2.6	+2.9	−1.6
187	Relative skills	20 yrs	−0.1	−0.1	0.0
	inversely related	50 yrs	+2.5	+3.7	−9.1
	to relative wage costs				
	(both high- and low-skill				
	relative wages)				
189	Same as Run 187, except	20 yrs	+0.8	+2.0	−7.4
	trend in national skills	50 yrs	+28.0	+39.5	−65.1
	is retarded relative to				
	region				

* Numbers correspond to computer simulation identification system used by the Battelle research group.

† Per capita income comparisons are not provided for these experiments because, in order to implement the hypothesis relating skills inversely to relative labor costs, the value of relative wages generated in the model was no longer appropriate for measuring wage income.

According to this hypothesis, as the average skill level in an area increases, the migration rate is modified by an effect of the skill index (Figure 12.6). Of interest, we see in Table 12.9 that the effect on the short-run population projections is much greater than it is on the long-run projections. This occurs because the region starts out with a relatively low average skill level of 10 years per person, which results in a lower rate of out-migration. As the simulation unfolds, however, average skills increase, approaching the 13-year per person level, so that this effect (see Figure 12.6) is reversed, thereby accounting for the smaller long-run impact.

In addition to the influence of skills on migration, some experiments were made in which labor productivity was assumed to vary with skills. It was hypothesized that a region with higher average skill level has more productive labor and hence can supply more labor output per dollar of wage, thereby cutting total labor costs. In order to experiment with this productivity influence, a number of changes were introduced to the initial model of skills factors. An equation representing an national average skills level per person was added as an exogenous consideration, with the average skills growing 25 percent over the 50-year period of the simulation. Wages in the subregion (relative to national wages) were then formulated as partially dependent upon the ratio of the subregion's average skills level to that of he nation, as shown in Figure 12.7. This effect, in runs described here, applied equally to the relative wages of both high- and low-skill-using industries.

Two runs made to test the effect of skills on relative wage costs are summarized

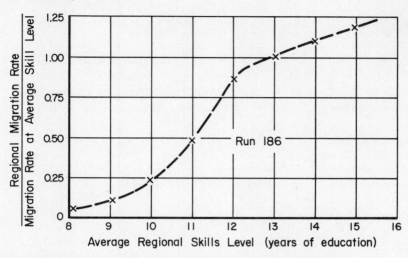

FIGURE 12.6. Migration related to average regional skills level.

in Table 12.9. For Run 187, a positive but small effect occurred on population and employment in the long run due to a subregional skills growth that was slightly faster than the national average. But Run 189 shows some of the real potential for regional development contained in the underlying assumptions regarding skills effects. In this run the subregion was allowed to outstrip the national average in the education and training of its population. The subregion's higher quality of labor, as reflected in its low relative wage, resulted in such rapid employment growth that the rate of unemployment was lowered by the end of the period to 65 percent below its base run value, or slightly less than 2 percent. This lower unemployment rate in turn generated a much larger amount of in-migration. The result was an extremely large increase, in fact the largest of any of the other sensitivity runs, in the projected population of 28 percent. This brief experiment suggests that if an area can significantly outstrip the nation's averages in the education and training of its population, then significant growth is possible. Moreover, the effects of such skills buildup are cumulative and ever increasing.

Summary and Conclusions

The major finding and conclusions derived from the model simulation experiment can be stated briefly. The experiments have reinforced our original feeling that regional models and regional projection methodologies should explicitly take into account the mutual interdependence between demographic and industrial aspects of regional performance. This conclusion has been supported most strongly by the experiments on migration and wage adjustment formulations that demonstrate that significant changes produced in either the demographic or the employment sectors of the model have quantitatively important ramifications for the other sector. The experiments on the wage-employment feedback loop have, in addition, reconfirmed our belief in the importance, especially for questions of long-run

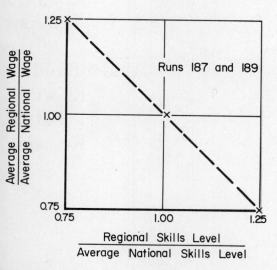

FIGURE 12.7. Relative skills level related to relative wage costs.

impact, of considering the effects on regional cost characteristics that occur in the regional industrial growth process and in turn affect the amount and makeup of future regional growth. Finally, we believe, on the basis of the evidence provided by the preliminary skills exploration, that educational and skills factors may well have, through their effects on migration and labor costs, extremely important consequences for regional growth and vitality. We suggest the agenda of regional research should therefore give high priority to developing increased understanding and ability to quantify these heretofore elusive skills factors.

Chapter 13
Implications
of the
Model-Building
Effort for
Future
Research

In this chapter an effort will be made to present some of the lessons and principles relating to the model-building process which emerged from the Susquehanna regional model-building effort. Because the art of building large-scale simulation models of combined social and physical systems is a relatively young one, it seems important to consider the model-building process explicitly. After doing this and comparing alternative approaches to model-building, attention will be devoted to cataloguing some salient features of the present model and presenting suggestions for further research. Finally, the chapter will be concluded with a résumé of possible uses and applications of the present model and/or others similar to it.

Lessons Learned From This Model-Building Experience

Planning a Model-Building Effort. The first thing to be realized, which is perhaps obvious, is that a model-building effort requires much thought and planning. Further, it is usually the case that a serious model-building effort will take a fair amount of time, perhaps several years, and that crash model-building programs are not likely to be very successful.[1] As has been remarked, a crash program in research to a large extent resembles an effort to have a baby born in one month by getting nine women pregnant. What does make for rapid progress, however, is a well-thought-out approach combined with energetic, competent, and resourceful model-builders.

To begin with, a well-thought-out approach will entail setting forth the objective of the research effort as clearly as possible. In the present instance, these included production of a set of consistent and well-understood generalizations of value in (*a*) enhancing understanding of a set of regional phenomena, (*b*) gaining insight about the probable future course of important regional variables, and (*c*) analyzing the consequences of specific alternative policies affecting a region. The statement of objectives is of great importance because it focuses the research effort. If the

[1] The hastily constructed economic models that produced the well-known poor predictions of economic conditions following World War II constitute a good example of the failure of a crash program in economic research.

objectives are too broad or poorly defined, then it is difficult to decide on an appropriate methodological approach. That is, if the objectives are too broadly defined, it is usually the case that no methodological approach is capable of realizing them. In the Susquehanna research effort, the decision to use a large-scale simulation modeling approach was made only after alternative approaches had been considered in relation to the objectives of the research.

With the objectives mentioned, it was almost immediately apparent that any reasonable approach would have to be multidisciplinary[2] both because of the nature of the objectives and because of the techniques required for achieving these objectives. In the Susquehanna model the areas of knowledge required included

a. Economics: regional economics, economic demography, water resources, econometrics, location theory, and mathematical economics.

b. Computer techniques: programming simulations.

c. Systems analysis: formulation and analysis of models representing complex social and physical systems.

d. Data collection, evaluation and analysis.

e. Hydrology: water flow, pollution, and water uses.

Given the objectives and a recognized need for a multidisciplinary approach, it was found that the next requirement of an appropriate approach is a *research strategy*. Having a good research strategy is important because considerable resources, human and nonhuman, are to be allocated in a serious model-building effort. In fact, such an effort can fruitfully be viewed as an investment-production process characterized by considerable uncertainty and stochastic elements (e.g., surprises, disappointments, and errors). Naturally, in this investment-production process we want as high a rate of return as possible. To attain a high rate of return it will of course be necessary to ensure that the many and varied tasks involved

[2] This term was suggested to the author by David D. Moore as being better than "interdisciplinary."

in building a model are carried out in an efficient and coordinated manner.[3] Managerial skills and talents must be present to allocate responsibility for the completion of tasks to appropriate individuals, to supervise and plan temporal dovetailing of subprojects, and to deal with inevitable research and personnel problems that arise in large-scale projects involving a number of individuals with varied backgrounds and interests. Tough decisions must be made with respect to the amounts of time and resources to be devoted to specific subprojects.

While research and managerial skills and talents of a high order are necessary for success in a model-building effort, they are not sufficient. What was found to be needed in addition is a good research strategy. In general, our experience has indicated that it is inadvisable to pursue inflexible "once-and-for-all" or "all-or-nothing-at-all" strategies. Rather, we have reached the belief that a *balanced, flexible, iterative* strategy is much more likely to lead to a high payoff. Such a strategy, which resembles that used in the Susquehanna model-building effort, can be described as follows.

Description of Iterative Research Strategy. After agreeing on the objectives of the research effort, there should be an initial exploratory study to determine the feasibility of the research effort and the methodological approach that seems most appropriate. This study should provide estimates of the scope and magnitude of the required research effort for alternative methodological approaches along with an assessment of the degree to which objectives will be realized for each alternative methodology. This will provide a basis for selecting a particular approach. Once a particular methodological approach, say a simulation model approach, has been selected, then the exploratory study should determine the nature and availability of needed inputs including financing, personnel, computer facilities, data, previous research findings and studies, etc. If this study shows that the undertaking is feasible and likely to be successful, then the second phase or iteration, model construction, can be entered.

In the second phase, model construction, a key point is the formulation of an

[3] See Appendix A where this important topic is discussed.

initial model. As far as we know, no one completely understands how a model is born.[4] However, involved in the birth process are usually (1) *hard work, accompanied by labor pains, to understand and relate results and findings in the literature,* (2) several hard looks at the data, (3) synthesis of previous and current ideas into an initial model, (4) consistency check of the initial model, and (5) use of available data, insights, and whatever other information is available to determine appropriate functional forms for relationships, forms of time responses, and approximate parameter values.

Regarding the form of the initial model, it is useful to recognize that models can be roughly classified as follows: small and simple, large and simple, small and complicated, and large and complicated. Along with Jeffreys[5] and others, we feel that it is desirable to emphasize sophisticated simplicity in model construction because simple models are usually more easily understood, more esthetically pleasing, and are easier to implement than are complicated models. However, the goal of simplicity obviously does not necessarily imply that a model will be both simple and small. In the present instance, a small model could not possibly yield the detail required to realize the objectives of the research program. Further, limiting the size of a model to too great a degree may mean that an undesirable level of aggregation is employed. For example, in the present research, results were required for subregions, for particular kinds of industries, for specific points on the river, etc. This detail could not be given by a model with only a few equations. However, even though the objectives implied a large-scale model, this does not necessarily mean that its structure has to be unduly complicated. In fact, effort was expended to ensure that this would not be the case. One particularly important point here is to have a "modular" model, that is, one that consists of simple components that can be isolated for study.

[4] An interesting work dealing with related issues is J. Hadamard, *The Psychology of Invention in the Mathematical Field* (New York: Dover Publications, Inc., 1945).

[5] H. Jeffreys, *Theory of Probability* (2nd ed.; Oxford: Clarendon Press, 1961) and *Scientific Inference* (Cambridge, England: University Press, 1957).

With the initial model formulated, the next iterations are quite analogous to what an engineer does in checking out an airplane design by subjecting a model to wind-tunnel experiments. With the aid of computer simulation techniques, experiments with the initial model should be performed to appraise and understand its structure and dynamic properties and its sensitivity to changes in various specifying assumptions and parameter values.

On learning about and studying the results of these experiments, it will usually be necessary to reformulate the initial model to incorporate changes revealed desirable by the "wind-tunnel" experiments and new ideas generated in the course of experimentation. For example, it may be found that a particular functional form for a migration relationship leads to absurd decade changes in population for a region. Or the form of a dynamic response may produce oscillations that are deemed unreasonable on the basis of past data and experience. Further, modifications may also be suggested by analyses of additional data, particularly data relevant for study of parts of the model whose formulation sensitivity affects the model's outputs.

When changes of this kind have been made, more wind-tunnel experiments accompanied by checks of the model's outputs against outside data should be performed. Again, it is to be expected that improvements will have to be made and further data and thought will have to be brought to bear on insecure parts of the model.

Then again, further experimentation and reformulation will probably be required, and so on. This iterative procedure, accompanied by validation checks of the model using as much new data as possible, appears to us to constitute a fruitful, if not necessary, approach to model-building. Of course, validation checks are extremely difficult to perform given that limited outside data are available or if the outside data are of poor quality or are measurements on variables whose definitions do not stand in a one-to-one correspondence with those employed in model construction. With these obstacles, appraisal of the model will involve many informal judgmental checks. For example, it may be found that a particular

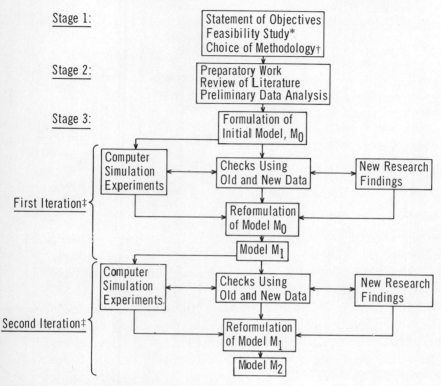

FIGURE 13.1. Schematic of research strategy.

  * It is assumed that this study shows the project to be feasible.

  † It is assumed that a "modeling" approach is selected.

  ‡ The iterative procedure may disclose problems in the original formulation of goals, feasibility, and methodology so that refining and reformulation of the effort may not be confined solely to the model itself. That is to say, goals.

formulation produces wildly oscillating outputs. From qualitative and quantitative knowledge regarding the behavior of regional economies, this formulation would be judged quite doubtful and another would be sought that yields more reasonable results.

Figure 13.1 presents a graphic representation of this research approach. This representation may be useful as a reference point in the comparison of the approach described with others that have been employed in other model-building efforts.

Comparison With Other Model-Building Approaches. While what has been said about the process of obtaining a good model may seem reasonable and perhaps even obvious, it is a fact that quite a few previous model-building efforts have not incorporated even the general features of this iterative research strategy. For example, many models, which have been reported in the literature, were built with no or very little wind-tunnel experimentation, that is, computer simulation experiments. In some cases, models consisting of many stochastic difference equations, sometimes linear but often nonlinear, have been presented to the profession and to other groups with their structural and dynamic properties not fully—or even partly—understood by anyone including the model-builders themselves. This seems to be a particularly bothersome feature of the Brookings-SSRC model[6] to date.

In some instances, it is not hard to understand why this has occurred. Perhaps budgetary and staff limitations precluded experimentation using simulation techniques. In other cases, simulation techniques as a tool in exploring models' features have been overlooked or could not be readily applied either because of the complexity and size of certain models and/or the lack of good computer programs for model simulation. While these and other reasons can be advanced to explain past limited experimentation with previous models, it seems obvious that models whose properties are not well understood are probably unsatisfactory for most serious uses because they are nothing more than mysterious black boxes. Understanding properties of models is in our view a key requirement of good model-building.

Next we note that some model-building efforts have departed from the iterative research strategy by being linked too closely and inflexibly to one given set of data. That is, at times models are warped just to permit them to be implemented with available but inadequate data.[7] In principle, if data are inadequate, efforts should be exerted to get better and more adequate data. If this is not possible, the problem then often becomes one of a choice between a model design constrained by the given data versus one incorporating the information in the available data and whatever other qualitative, theoretical, and judgmental information is available. To be specific, suppose that interest centers on a short-run model but that short-run data are lacking. If just annual data are available, it is usually the case that workers formulate a model with the fundamental unit of time

[6] J. S. Duesenberry et al. (eds.), *The Brookings Quarterly Econometric Model of the United States* (Chicago: Rand McNally & Co., 1965).

[7] This was a characteristic of many, if not all, early econometric business-cycle models that were constructed on an "annual basis" because the available data were annual data.

taken to be a year *because that is the unit of time in the available data* and this results in a warped data-oriented model relative to the objective of having a useful short-run model.

In such circumstances, it appears more useful to formulate models involving the time period that is deemed most relevant on theoretical and practical grounds, say a month, and then to study the properties of such models. Among other things, their ability to explain the variation in the annual data could be assessed. Needless to say, with annual data it will be difficult, though not impossible, to estimate parameters of a short-run model. It is here that good intuition and judgment play a role. In addition, the technique of computer simulation can be a powerful tool. Of course, getting the needed short-run data, if this is possible, would be most desirable. While this is recognized, in their absence there seems to be little justification for working with a data-oriented "annual" model if interest centers on short-run phenomena. That is, it is not obvious that a warped "data-oriented" model is to be preferred to one that goes beyond the available data to use more informal kinds of information.

While inadequate data may be responsible for some model warping, it appears that some mathematically inclined model-builders have the habit of distorting their models to make them mathematically tractable.[8] That is, some introduce specifying assumptions just for the sake of getting systems that can be solved analytically. At times this practice may be harmless. However, on other occasions it may lead to elegant, correct solutions to wrong problems. It cannot be denied that the generality of mathematical solutions is much to be desired, but this desire should not unduly influence model construction, particularly when computer techniques are available for model solution and study.

Last, in many model-building efforts heavy emphasis is placed on purely statistical criteria, for example, goodness of fit, properties of estimation techniques,

---

[8] For example, in many economic growth models, population is assumed to grow exogenously at some given rate. This assumption simplifies the mathematics but may distort the model.

standard test procedures, etc.[9] In this connection, it appears important to emphasize that model-building usually involves *finding good relationships*, often with very limited data. Unfortunately, good statistical techniques for finding relationships are not too well developed, especially when data are limited.[10] In such circumstances, there is a great danger that standard statistical procedures can produce misleading results. For example, use of a goodness of fit criterion when data are limited and variation not too pronounced can lead to acceptance of relations whose economic and other implications may be absurd. Or it may be that a given body of data has been used over and over again to test a range of hypotheses. This in itself is not necessarily a bad practice. However, it should be realized that usual significance levels of standard tests and properties of usual estimators are vitally affected by this practice. What must be emphasized is that statistical tools have to be used in a sophisticated manner in the model-building process.

Instead of assuming that we have a true relationship, it is probably safer to assume that a relationship may be in error and seek to discover the nature of the error or errors. For example, a thorough study of residuals is helpful to check on the appropriateness of choice of functional form, to determine whether variables may have been omitted, and to give some information regarding possible aggregation and measurement-error problems. Usually an analysis is not regarded as complete until these items, and possibly others, have been considered and checked.

In the Susquehanna research, it was found in some simulation experiments that outputs were not very sensitive to substantial variation in many of the parameter values included in the model. However, outputs were often very sensitive to changes in the functional forms of relationships. Further, omitting an important variable often produced substantial effects on outputs in the

[9] This is true of many econometric model-building efforts.

[10] G. E. P. Box and W. J. Hill, "Discrimination among Mechanistic Models," *Technometrics*, 9 (1967), 57–71, present some interesting results which appear useful in certain situations.

simulation experiments. This implies that, rather than considering statistical analysis to be simply the estimation of parameters in given models, model-builders must use statistical techniques designed to check the adequacy of formulations in conjunction with simulation experimentation. This whole area of model formulation and variable identification deserves much additional attention.

Further, as mentioned, in the process of model-building, the forms and properties of relationships are often not very precisely known. The implications of this state of affairs for choice of an estimation technique are important. In this connection, it seems incorrect to place sole or major emphasis on the criterion of efficiency in selecting an estimator. The properties of estimators have been derived under the assumption that we are estimating a "true" relation and, therefore, are not entirely relevant when we are uncertain about the nature of the relation under study.

It might be thought that robust estimation procedures, that is, procedures that are relatively insensitive to errors in the assumptions incorporated in a model, should be used. In some contexts this is appropriate. A difficulty here is that the "robustness" of various estimation procedures has not been fully or even partially investigated. In addition, to the extent that robust methods "work well" in the face of specification errors, that is, errors in the assumptions, it may be difficult to find such errors. It is not inconceivable that "good" estimation procedures that are sensitive to the presence of specification errors could be useful in the search for specification errors. Also, this discussion has relevance for choice of testing procedures.

This brief discussion of statistical methodology, in the context of model-building, should alert us to the danger of applying standard statistical techniques in a mechanical and thoughtless manner. Then too, much more work on statistical methods to implement procedures for finding good models would be welcomed. Until these appear, judgment, theory, informal information, simulation experiments, etc., and statistical analyses, rather than the latter alone, are required in the model-building process.

Salient Features of the Susquehanna Model

In this section some salient features of the Susquehanna model are summarized. Then some areas in which additional research appears useful will be mentioned.

First, the model reported herein is a mathematical model. That this is the case means that assumptions about behavior, technology, and institutions are translated into the universal language of mathematics, a language noted for its rigorous logical precision. With a mathematically formulated model, such assumptions are relatively explicit and open for examination. This contrasts with what is the usual case for "implicit" or "nonmathematical" models. Still, it must be noted that additional work on better ways of characterizing the properties of large mathematical models would be welcomed. With respect to *linear* models, many valuable mathematical concepts and results are available that characterize their dynamic properties.[11] To do this with current mathematical techniques requires much tedious and lengthy computation.[12] Thus, even with linear systems, computer simulation solutions may be the only practical approach. When large systems that are nonlinear in both parameters and variables are the subject of study, computer simulation solution appears to be the only workable approach in almost all cases.

[11] That is, if we represent an m-equation linear model as

$$B_0 y_t + B_1 y_{t-1} + \cdots + B_\theta y_{t-\theta} + \Gamma z_t = 0$$

where the B's and Γ are $m \times m$ and $m \times k$ coefficient matrices, respectively, with B_0 assumed nonsingular; $y_t' = (y_{1t}, y_{2t}, \ldots, y_{mt})$ is a vector of variables whose variation is to be explained by the model, $z_t' = (z_{1t}, z_{2t}, \ldots, z_{kt})$ is a vector of exogeneous variables whose properties are determined outside the system, and the subscript "t" denotes the value of a variable in time period t. Then, given initial conditions, it is possible to solve the system to obtain a mathematical expression showing the paths of the m components of y_t for given values of z_t. Also, other quantities can be derived that characterize the response of the model to given changes in an element or elements of z_t. These results for linear systems are indeed useful in characterizing properties of a model. Further study of linear systems to provide convenient and simple methods for appraising how changing particular elements in the B or Γ matrices affects dynamic properties would be of value.

[12] See, for example, A. S. Goldberger, *Impact Multipliers and Dynamic Properties of the Klein-Goldberger Model* (Amsterdam: North-Holland Publishing Co., 1959).

Further, in using a computer simulation approach to study the properties of models, it is the case that the investigator is planning and designing experiments to yield output. This is to a large extent analogous to what experimentalists do in general, and thus "design of experiments" considerations should play a role in the design of computer simulation experiments just as they do in other experimental situations. The object should be to use an experimental design that yields as much information as possible, given cost constraints. For example, if ten simulation experiments are planned, good design will result in a good deal of information being obtained, whereas poor design may produce little more information than could be obtained from two or three well-designed experiments. Unfortunately, not very much work has been done on this problem of the design of experiments as it relates to computer simulation experimentation.

Second, the model is an operational model. That is, it is a model that is on the computer and that can be operated without much difficulty and at very low cost. Having an operational model in existence is a major step forward in the task of modeling river basin and/or regional economies in that experiments can be run off and new improvements introduced if needed. It should be recognized that while the current model incorporates the results of much current and past research, future research will undoubtedly produce refinements and new results. Research on the determinants of birth rates, locational choice, labor-market operation, etc., is being carried forward by a number of researchers. As results appear in these specific areas, and possibly in others, they can be incorporated into the model. By doing this, we can understand how changing our views with respect to behavior in specific areas affects our views with respect to how the model, and the economy it represents, works. Also, over-all model performance should be improved. Without an operational model, it would be difficult, if not impossible, to accomplish these ends.

Third, the model to a large extent is data based. That is, many of its relationships have been formulated and tested using actual data. The model's outputs can be checked against actual data. Clearly, these points are important because the degree of confidence we have in a model depends to a great degree on the extent to which it is able to explain past variation of variables and to predict future variation. It is no small task to formulate and implement a model with measurable quantities, a task that is particularly difficult when regional data are as poor in quality and quantity as they currently are. And because additional data cannot be generated by controlled experiments, tests of the model's predictive ability are not currently as extensive as could be desired.

In the future, it is possible to increase the extent and quality of the data base, an effort that would be extremely beneficial in terms of assisting basic research and model development. Having good and extensive data relating to numerous regional economies is one important way of expanding the data base. With such data available, it will be possible to subject parts of the model to more strenuous testing than is currently possible. More good data will also mean that parameters and other features of the model can be determined more precisely. The importance of these data problems cannot be overemphasized. It appears that a large-scale effort to improve the quantity and quality of regional data would yield extremely high returns in terms of a better understanding of regional phenomena and superior models.

Fourth, relative to many economic models in use, the present model is noteworthy for the extent of its disaggregation. It treats subregions separately. Water problems are treated with reference to different parts of the river. Demographic and certain economic relations are age specific. Employment growth is considered industry by industry. With this detail, it is possible to trace out developments for specific subregions, specific industry groups, specific parts of the river, and for specific age groups. This detail provided by disaggregation is invaluable and essential for achieving the objectives involved in the present work. Not only is information required in such detail but also it is questionable that a model formulated at a high level of aggregation would provide meaningful and reliable results. For example, suppose that the demographic sector had been formulated in aggregate terms involving such aggregate variables as total net out-migration, total births derived using an average birth rate, total deaths derived using an average death rate, and total population. It is apparent that such a framework does not accommodate the effects of changes in age distribution on births, migration, population, and labor force. Because behavior with respect to many of these items differs systematically with age, an aggregate formulation would at best provide a blurred picture. Finally, because conditions are different in the subregions, aggregation over them would indeed present another source of difficulty.[13]

These are just some of the problems that would arise if the demographic sector were formulated in aggregate terms. Many other problems of a similar nature would appear if other sectors were dealt with at the aggregate level. Taken together, the problems associated with a model formulated in aggregate terms are probably so serious as to make such a model practically useless for the analysis of the kinds of problems investigated with the present model. While it is difficult to define sharply what is an "optimal" level of disaggregation, it is the case that the present model is distinguished by its attempt to disaggregate in dimensions considered to be necessary to represent behavior meaningfully and to produce a wide range of specific outputs rather than a narrow range of aggregate outputs. Further experimentation with alternative levels of disaggregation would be interesting and valuable even though further disaggregation might entail collection and/or generation of new data.

Fifth, the model incorporates significant steps forward in the formulation of the demographic sector. Age-specific birth rates, death rates, migration rates, and labor-force-participation rates have been employed, which make the model's outputs change in extremely significant ways in response to changes in the age distribution of the population. Such change feeds back on the demographic sector through time delays and induced economic effects to influence the pattern of

[13] For analysis and discussion of aggregation problems, see, for example, H. Theil, *Linear Aggregation of Economic Relations* (Amsterdam: North-Holland Publishing Co., 1954), and G. H. Orcutt, "Micro-analytic Models of the United States Economy: Need and Development," *American Economic Review, 52* (1962), 229–240.

demographic development that produces further change, and so on. These endogenous interactions between the demographic and economic sectors appear to be vital elements in the process of regional economic growth. Further study of them would be extremely valuable.

Sixth, another striking feature of the model is that it generates outputs relating to water quantity and quality for various points on the river and affords an opportunity to appraise the importance of feedbacks from the water sector on other sectors of the model. This appears to be an important methodological breakthrough in the analysis of water problems. Often such problems are investigated taking economic and demographic change as determined independently of the problems of water quantity and quality. That the present model has the capability to investigate possible dependencies of the economic and demographic sectors' growth pattern on water quantity and quality is valuable. Further work to study further possible linkages between water quantity and quality and regional growth in other river basin economies would be intriguing and informative.

Seventh, and last, this model affords a good example of how the computer has affected research in the social sciences. In this model-building effort the computer was used to perform calculations in statistical analyses of data and for simulation runs. Many modern multivariate statistical analyses would be impractical without the aid of electronic computers. Simulating a model with more than a thousand equations would be impossible without an electronic computer and highly developed simulation programs. Further research on the methodology of computer use in the social sciences will enable social scientists to use computers more effectively in future research.

Future Uses of Regional Simulation Models

The present model has been designed and used to analyze various features of a particular river-basin economy. While the characteristics of this economy and the problems considered conditioned the design of the model, this conditioning was not so severe as to prevent the model from being useful in studying other problems. Of course, in applying the model to problems other than those for which it was designed, it may be necessary to introduce modifications, append additional sectors, and elaborate some sectors already in the model. We now review briefly a range of problems for which this model, perhaps suitably modified, or others like it, will be useful.

Public Policy Uses of Regional Simulation Models. The present work represents an example of the use of a simulation model to throw light on a question of public policy concerning river works construction. It is clearly the case that models like the present one, or the present one with suitable modification, can be of value in helping to appraise the possible effects of various kinds of public investment or disinvestment programs on regional economic growth. Such public programs may involve investment in transportation facilities, say highway construction or airport construction, subsidies to develop new forms of rail transport, or development of new waterways and harbors. With an expanded transportation sector, the present model or others like it may be helpful in providing estimates of the extent to which different forms of transportation investment affect economic growth. Such information could be of great value in reaching decisions with respect to the nature of transportation investment for a region.

Another area of public investment that could be studied using regional simulation models is that of investment or disinvestment in military installations. How do increased or decreased levels of expenditures on military installations affect regional economic growth? The answers to these questions may indeed be useful both in planning such changes and in coping with the effects of such changes.

Another very important area of public investment is that of education. The present model may be found to be useful in planning investment in educational facilities because it generates population by age group for specific subregions. Thus the model gives some information on the numbers of those of school age through time. Also, although preliminary, some work has been done on the effects of skill levels and education on regional economic growth. Elaboration of this work and perhaps finer detail with respect to educational systems would be helpful in attempts to appraise the effects of regional investment programs in education on regional economic growth.

An expansion of the labor market sector of the model might permit it to be a tool in analyzing how money spent to improve or change the operation of labor markets might affect regional employment and growth. Included here might be worker retraining programs, programs to affect worker mobility, and improvement in labor market informational flows.

Resource problems relating not only to water but to forests, land, fish, minerals, etc., can be approached with the aid of models like the present one augmented with specialized resource sectors. For example, conservation programs in the areas of forestry or fisheries could be modeled in an effort to get better programs than we now have. Such models could also serve as testing grounds for trying out alternative proposals.

The economic effects of state and local fiscal and tax policies might be considered within the context of regional simulation models. Of course, this presupposes the existence of a model that adequately incorporates governmental units and their instruments for affecting economic activity. The nature and strength of possible feedbacks from the economic sector on the government sector would also have to be considered.

Finally, a regional simulation model linked to a national model or to a set of other regional models might be quite useful in determining how national policies and policies affecting other regions will affect a particular region. Much work must be done, however, before this goal can be realized.

Private Uses of Regional Simulation Models. Naturally, many private parties are interested in economic trends. To the extent that models like the present one enable us to understand regional trends better, they may be found of assistance in such diverse uses as selecting plant locations, planning firms' investment programs, aiding real estate developers in selecting sites, guiding sales promotional campaigns and projecting demands for various goods and services. The outputs of the model including total population, population by age group, income per capita, and relative labor cost, as well as others, are variables appearing in many decisions made by firms. For example, many of them would be relevant for assessing the future demand for electricity, telephone service, and transportation services. Of course, particular applications will generally involve special studies leading to the addition of specialized submodels that can be grafted to the over-all model. These special studies would provide additional valuable information about regional economies to private parties and would improve their ability to plan for the future.

In certain cases, large firms or industries are dominant factors in regional economies. How developments within such firms or industries affect the regional economy is of great concern to management and stockholders. The case of the effects of a large firm's plans for expansion or contraction on a regional economy is of importance in many instances. By understanding such firm-region interactions, management is better able to choose appropriate rates of expansion or contraction.

In publicly regulated industries, it is important that private firms have information regarding future demand and cost conditions in order to deal with the problem of rate regulation in an informed manner. Simulation models appear capable of playing a useful role in this connection.

Concluding Remarks

In summary, then, regional simulation models appear to have many and varied important uses. The present work is an explicit example of one such use. The experience and lessons learned in this effort and others like it will be valuable in future modeling efforts. Couple this with the facts that (*a*) more and more researchers are acquiring the skills required in model-building, (*b*) more and better data are becoming available, (*c*) our knowledge and techniques are improving rapidly, and (*d*) computers are generally available, and the conclusion that emerges is that many of the suggested uses of regional simulation models will soon be explored further than they already have been. It is our belief that the results of these activities will be of immense value to society.

Appendix A
The Management
of a
Multidisciplinary
Research Project

This appendix discusses problems and ideas concerning the management of multidisciplinary research projects. Although many of the problems discussed are presented within the context of the Susquehanna program, the authors have encountered similar problems in relation to other studies. Some of the management techniques employed in the Susquehanna study in an attempt to avoid these problems are a result of this prior experience.

The discussion focuses upon project management. This particular focus is needed because the research management literature is surprisingly sparse in relation to how relatively small, multidisciplinary efforts should be managed.[1] The literature is probably thin in this area because the interests of those who usually coordinate small projects normally lie in specific subject areas rather than in project management. That is, most small projects are coordinated by individuals whose interests are largely associated with doing parts of the research and who have much less interest in managing the work of others.

Too often there seems to be an implicit assumption that assembling a group of individually competent personnel will automatically lead to an efficient and competent research team. However, the truth of the matter is that many highly competent individuals cannot be integrated into effective research teams; many more have neither the interest nor the ability to coordinate the work of others. This is especially true once the constraints of time and budgets are superimposed above and beyond those involving the research problem, per se.

It is becoming clear that the nature of modern problems dictates the need for an increasing amount of multidisciplinary research. We must learn to manage such research. The comments offered present a few guidelines and point out some

[1] There can be no hard and fast definition of what constitutes a "small" study. Small studies in the aerospace industry are often viewed as enormous studies when performed at the same level of effort in the social sciences. A small study, as referred to here, is one that does not reach the proportions where formal management techniques are obviously required in the eyes of most researchers. Efforts requiring inputs from three to fifteen people often fall in this class.

pitfalls in relation to multidisciplinary research, or for that matter, any multiperson study, particularly those in the modeling field.

The Nature of the Problem and Some Suggestions

Research programs may involve a number of individuals for a variety of reasons. First, there is often a desire to condense the time period encompassed by the study, and this can be accomplished by bringing more manpower to bear over a shorter time span. Of course, the study may require inputs from a variety of disciplines. It is often the case that individuals with different points of view within the same discipline may make valuable contributions. Perhaps more often, a combination of these and other reasons generates the need for a team effort.

Because efficient use of personnel on a research project dictates that all those assigned to the project not work on the same tasks, subdivision of effort is required. It is this subdivision of effort that brings about the need for coordination and management.

The research manager or project coordinator encounters a number of problems in directing a research team. These often involve the personal characteristics of the individual team members as much as any other one factor. For instance, some individuals will wish to be kept completely abreast of developments on all phases of the program at all times, often to the point that the work on their subtask suffers. Others will attempt to proceed with their work without regard to the over-all program, viewing their subtask as an end in itself. Both these extremes must be curbed. In the former case too much time is wasted through curiosity about the over-all. In the latter case work on subtasks, once completed, may not fit the over-all study objectives.

In relation to the Susquehanna study, both formal and informal exchanges were encouraged among the project staff developing various portions of the model.[2] Such meetings were very necessary because at times this project team was composed

---

[2] The reader may wish to refer to the Preface, which outlines the various major phases of the Susquehanna study and the nature of the project team.

of as many as fifteen individuals—professional Battelle staff members from a variety of disciplines, consultants, and research aids. Some of these individuals were geographically separated from the Battelle facilities in Columbus, Ohio. To ensure that at least a minimum of such interaction took place, formal project meetings were held in which progress and problems on each of the program's major tasks were discussed. The frequency of the meetings was varied in relation to the then current pace of the project and the amount of informal exchange known to be taking place. In addition, the project manager encouraged meetings between selected individuals to discuss how the sectors they were developing were to eventually mesh.

It is much more difficult to control "idle curiosity" than lack of communication because the former is so difficult to define. However, idle curiosity often takes the form of too much interest by one team member in the incidental details of the work being done by others. Such curiosity is often regarded as meddling by team members. During the Susquehanna program such idle curiosity did not appear to be a major problem.

Modeling programs have desirable attributes from a communications point of view. This is because the model can be used as a communications tool by the research team. Because models are explicit, everyone on the team can use the model to define how his subtask meshes with the over-all program. Thus, the risk of a mismatch between the output of a subtask and input needed by the over-all program (model) is lessened in relation to the risks that exist in more qualitative research undertakings.

On the other hand, a model can be a terrible taskmaster. Models demand precision, and each little odd and end must be accounted for before a sector is inserted into the over-all model. For example, all linkages to the main model from the sector must be specified. The model is not "sympathetic" when the researcher finds time to study only three of four mechanisms generally agreed to be important or if the main model demands an input not provided. In such cases, the modeler may be forced to omit the link, admitting it could be important, or he must quantify his best judgment on the nature of the link without the benefit of extensive research. In any case, what he has done will be evident. Thus, the modeler is not allowed the luxury often enjoyed by those involved in more descriptive and nonquantitative studies in which it is usually possible to make a few last-minute comments about how a variable might affect other variables but leave rather unclear just how the variable was actually blended into the over-all analysis.

Modeling studies demand more rigorous scheduling than more qualitative efforts. The development of one model sector often requires definitive information concerning the nature of the input requirements and outputs of other sectors. Therefore, problems encountered attempting to define and complete one sector can delay the research on other sectors. Of course, qualitative research can be delayed by incomplete tasks also, but the problem seems more serious in modeling studies. Perhaps the reason for this is that in qualitative studies so often only the general nature of the output from one task is needed in order to begin the next, while quantitative programs often require very specific tasks results, e.g., equations, before succeeding steps can get under way.

In order to keep the Susquehanna project on schedule, several kinds of rather elaborate flow charts of the project were constructed. The charting technique employed in the earlier phases of the study embodied many of the concepts of critical path programming, although the problem was never programmed for computer analysis. These charts defined the sequence in which tasks had to be completed and identified those tasks which seemed to be the most critical from the point of view of their potential for delaying the over-all program.[3]

Figure A.1 illustrates a simple flow chart concerning the construction of one of the model's sectors, the demographic sector.

Such a chart is useful for identifying the various sequences that are involved in reaching a given goal, in this case a first operative model of the demographic

[3] A relatively complex but useful technique used during the early part of the study is recommended by J. J. Moder in *Engineering News-Record*, March 14, 1963, p. 31.

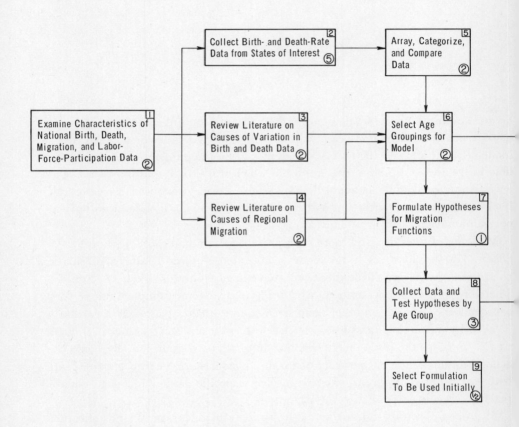

FIGURE A.1. A simple flow chart for planning purposes and for scheduling control.

sector. By inserting (in circles inside boxes) estimates of elapsed time needed to complete these tasks, some idea of where bottlenecks lie may be achieved. Such bottlenecks may delay the entire program. For example, suppose the birth- and death-rate data (Task 2) cannot be procured from the states within the five weeks that have been allotted, or suppose the subregionalization process is not completed by the time the team is ready to process the data by subregion (Task 10). The usefulness of such charts is that once such dangers are identified, they can be monitored and often avoided. For instance, if the data procurement from the states cannot be accomplished by mail within the time allotted, a staff member

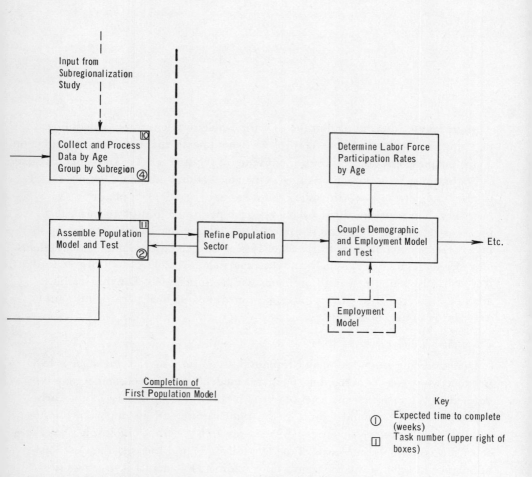

Input from
Subregionalization
Study

Collect and Process
Data by Age
Group by Subregion ④

Determine Labor Force
Participation Rates
by Age

Assemble Population
Model and Test ②

Refine Population
Sector

Couple Demographic
and Employment Model
and Test

Etc.

Employment
Model

Completion of
First Population Model

Key

① Expected time to complete
(weeks)

▢ Task number (upper right of
boxes)

might be sent to visit the state government agencies involved in an attempt to
speed up this portion of the study.

While simple charts of the type shown are useful, they will often fall far short
of the mark in terms of yielding an understanding of the complexity of the
problem being faced. In particular, such simple tools do not shed much light on
the range of uncertainty surrounding the completion of a given sequence of events
on a given date. Further, more complex charts that specify the assignment of
manpower to the identified tasks must be used in order to ensure that intolerable
peaks and valleys of effort among individual team members is avoided.

Many in the research field argue that the whole problem of the scheduling, planning, and control of research projects is not one amenable to detailed direction. These people point out that even if estimates of required effort can be made, these estimates must be continually revised. Our belief is that the effort required to plan and control is worth while even if constant revisions in planning are necessary. The alternative is to allow research programs to drift and to face problems as they arise instead of anticipating these problems and attempting to take corrective action at an early date. However, the skeptics about the usefulness of positive and aggressive small study management are correct to a degree in that it is certainly doubtful that all problems will be anticipated. For this reason, adequate reserves of resources, including time, must be incorporated into any program plan and budget.

Producing a Balanced Model

In a modeling study, the major responsibility of the program manager is to produce what may be termed a "balanced model." A balanced model may be defined as one in which the level of research effort devoted to developing each of the model's sectors and subsectors is commensurate with its importance to the over-all problem being investigated.[4] As a research program unfolds, it is necessary to review continually the goals of the over-all study and to assess the question of balance in light of the program's prior findings. Further, it is necessary to remember that the goals of the work may be modified with time. In light of prior findings and redefinition of research goals, the view of what constituted a balanced model changed a number of times during the evolution of the Susquehanna study.

The creation of a balanced model requires that the program manager have flexibility in assigning talent to various subtasks. Such flexibility can be lost at the

[4] The level of effort devoted to a model sector is not always correlated with the size of that sector that finally evolves when size is measured in terms of number of equations. Often, a rather large sector is fairly easy to assemble; just as often, much research is required merely to define the functional form of one important equation.

initiation of a project when the initial research team is selected unless the manager realizes the program management implications of this team selection process.[5] This selection process normally involves a very critical element, namely, a commitment to the individuals concerned in terms of some range of effort for a given period of time.

As the study evolves, the need for the capabilities of a given individual may change radically from that originally anticipated. For instance, a problem element originally conceived as important may be found to be noncritical. Thus, the demand for the inputs of the individual(s) originally assigned to this problem may be lessened or eliminated. Depending upon the institutional environment, the flexibility of the individual, and the nature of the original commitment, attempting to alter the nature of a commitment may present various kinds and degrees of problems. Certainly, no individuals or organizations are infinitely flexible in terms of assignments. Therefore reorientation of effort is usually accompanied by some kind of difficulty. The problem is minimized when the individual concerned has a variety of alternative tasks that he can undertake, either related to the same over-all program or to other programs. However, change of assignment is a particularly traumatic event when there are no alternative assignments readily available for the individual. For instance, the latter situation might involve the case of a person conducting research in connection with the pursuit of an academic degree in which the original subtask assigned to the individual also forms the basis of his financial support and the basic elements of a dissertation or thesis. When a study is staffed by a number of such individuals, program management may not include the option of reallocation of effort except within very narrow boundaries. In instances where program direction and flexibility are restrained by commitments such as those cited, the research sponsor should recognize that

[5] It is recognized that a good team is seldom selected by a completely authoritative procedure. In some research settings it may be necessary to spend much time convincing people that they should join the team. In any setting, some degree of "selling" the team on the study is usually necessary.

the financial commitment made is often in terms of training men rather than the solution of a problem.[6]

Perhaps a good way to minimize the team selection problems is to begin multidisciplinary and other multiperson programs with a small staff of flexible individuals and to proceed initially at a low rate of effort. Once preliminary results point toward the critical elements in the over-all problem, specialists can be brought to bear on these elements and firmer commitments established. Still, the problem of assignment flexibility always exists, and any time the allocation of effort to study becomes completely "frozen" the research is apt to suffer.

In regard to the Susquehanna study, a feasibility or planning study was conducted first. This study resulted in several revisions in thought concerning the nature of the problem. Prior to and in the early phases of this "initial cut," a 2-sector model was generally conceived; one with an economic sector and a water sector. However, initial study revealed that (1) water of useful quality seemed in general abundance in the region, and (2) regional economic studies often neglected the role of the region's population in the development of an area. In light of these findings, it was decided to build a model (1) containing an explicit and detailed population sector and (2) suitable for testing the criticality of water in the development of the region.[7] Subsequent study was then planned to refine and expand problem areas where water appeared important. This decision led to much less emphasis on water than was anticipated originally. As can be seen, an original commitment to construct a detailed hydrological model would have had to be reversed because the research problem was the major criterion for defining the research program. Personnel commitments would have had to be adjusted correspondingly.

[6] When training is a goal, or *the* goal, commitments to people primarily, and problems secondarily, are certainly proper.

[7] Chapter 11, The Water Sector, describes the "critical-point" concept that was used to pinpoint sensitive water variables and water areas at a complete audit. A complete audit of all water aspects was found unnecessary and research costs were thereby reduced considerably.

Throughout the Susquehanna program, the nature of the research inputs to the study shifted. To a degree, some of these shifts were foreseen. In assembling the first workable model, much data assembly effort was involved. However, after the assembly of the first model, data collection was de-emphasized for two reasons. First, much more attention was devoted to analysis, and second, the data assembly was routinized by exploiting the experience gained in the assembly of the first model. This change in emphasis resulted in a change in the complexion of the research group, with nonprofessional and clerical assistants taking a large role in data assembly because much less judgment was required in the subsequent phases of this activity. This particular change in the nature of the research and of staff needs was foreseen.

Sensitivity experiments with the original model gave substantial guidance to the remainder of the research program. Critical elements in the system were defined through model simulation, and work to investigate these elements was organized and planned. At this point in the program, it became possible to organize the studies of these critical problem areas on a semi-independent basis as the model itself provided guidance to the researcher as to where his task fitted in the scheme of things. The management problem then became one of keeping the model in balance by ensuring that the individual problems being investigated did not receive attention out of proportion to one another and to the goals of the program.

To accomplish this coordination and guidance, constant effort was maintained to keep the staff members aware of the over-all problem so that they themselves could aid in deciding how far to carry their work. But the nature of a good researcher is to immerse himself in his assignment. Thus, a reluctance to "let go of the problem" is only natural. However, when the researcher takes on the attributes of what might be termed a "research alcoholic," always wanting to use "one more" hour of computer time, to investigate "one more" variable, to spend "one more" day on a problem, he has often gone too far and must be redirected.

Nevertheless, discontinuance of the research effort in a particular problem area against the advice of the team member directly involved is not an easy decision for a program manager to make. Disregarding problems of team morale as a consideration (which is usually impossible), contentions that a little more effort will bear large returns may be correct. Of course, it may also drain resources from more important problems and lead to no concrete results.

The preceding paragraphs have largely stressed the role the problem should play in the guidance of a research program. Of course, there are other pressures that shape the scope and direction of research, and these must be recognized and dealt with. One of the most interesting of these involves the acceptance of the research by the lay and professional worlds. It is often necessary to do things as part of a research program basically for the purpose of making the work convincing to others. In terms of modeling research, one must face the fact that many people will judge a model by the sophistication of the model sector relating to the subject matter with which they are most familiar. Taking the Susquehanna model as a case in point, a demographer will usually study the demographic sector of the model first. If he finds it "uninteresting," perhaps only in the respect that he feels it does not make a contribution to his field, he is apt to judge the whole model on this basis. Therefore those interested in gaining a measure of acceptance for a model often feel pressure to develop certain sectors far enough to please experts in the subjects treated by those sectors regardless of whether such sophistication is needed from the point of view of the main research problem. Depending upon the importance of widespread model acceptance, the research manager will or will not yield to this latter pressure as a practical expedient. However, the program manager should avoid the trap of carrying the work too far from the point of view of the over-all problem faced, and yet not far enough to satisfy the "expert" whose acceptance is sought. This middle area of no man's land is often quite broad, and the jump from the problem-oriented level of development to that which the expert regards as "interesting" is often a big one.

Aids to Research Management

Unlike his modern counterparts in the production and sales functions, the research manager is not blessed with an abundance of management tools. Perhaps the only such aid commonly found is an accounting system whereby research costs are reported. If such a system is not available to the program director, he will be wise to devise one of his own, even if it is designed and maintained on only an informal basis. Even within organizations providing cost accounting services, the project director may find it desirable to augment this system with some bookkeeping of his own in order to fill in for obvious deficiencies in report timing and the formats provided by the system.

Although a properly designed accounting system is obviously useful in terms of project management, it is a fact that many research organizations and research laboratories make little use of such systems. For instance, many laboratories have only a general R & D budget and do not attempt budgeting and costing at the individual project level. While many argue that research cannot and should not be controlled with precision, perhaps a more likely reason for this low level of application of accounting systems to project management is that so many research personnel strongly resist the discipline imposed by an accounting system.

Despite the apparent lack of intensive application of accounting systems, a good accounting system is often about the only formal aid to project management that is ever given to the project director. Project managers must normally devise their own systems for judging the research progress that is being made in relation to costs. Of course, flow charts such as those mentioned earlier may be used to plan the project and to monitor progress, but such aids are not services normally provided to the manager. Instead, he must usually devise his own procedures. In some organizations, critical path programming services may be available, but these are often too expensive to use on small projects.

It would appear that considerable research is warranted for useful management services that can be provided to the coordinators of small research efforts in order to raise research efficiency.

Summary

This appendix has stressed the fact that management is an important ingredient in multidisciplinary studies. It has also stressed that the management role in such studies is often virtually ignored because small project coordinators often have little interest in project management per se, emphasizing instead their research specialties.

In small studies, the personal traits of the various research team members are often important. Some must be urged to communicate with other project staff, others must be constrained from overcommunicating.

In modeling studies, the major goal of the research should be to study the problem at hand by construction of a balanced model. To do so, the project manager must have the management flexibility to reassign people among tasks and to alter the make-up of the research team. Without such flexibility, the research effort will suffer.

A good accounting system is about the only management aid a manager of a small project can expect to have. He will often need to devise other aids on an ad hoc basis. Because so much research is carried out by small groups, more attention should be devoted to the management of such studies and to providing the directors of this research with better tools for achieving higher research efficiency.

For modeling purposes, employment has been classified into the following industry groups:

I. Local Serving Industries
    A. Household-Serving
    B. Business-Serving
II. Export Industries
    A. Agriculture
    B. Export Mining
    C. Export Manufacturing
        1. Durable Fabricators
        2. Nondurable Fabricators
        3. Labor-Intensive Processors
        4. Capital-Intensive Processors
    D. Export Government and Education
    E. Export Water-Based Recreation
    F. River Works Construction

This appendix supplements Chapters 9 and 10 by outlining the procedures for classifying employment in order to arrive at these groups. The description is divided into two parts: (1) separating employment into local serving and export categories, and (2) arriving at the four export manufacturing groups. Following this description, a complete listing of industry groups and a discussion of the procedures used for estimating the amount of employment in each group are provided.

Separating Employment Into Local Serving and Export Categories

In most cases industries classified at the Standard Industrial Classification Manual[1] 3- or 4-digit levels are allocated to export or local serving categories

[1] *Standard Industrial Classification Manual*, Executive Office of the President, Bureau of the Budget, 1957, p. 114.

on an all-or-nothing basis. Those industries judged to be mainly oriented to
nonlocal markets are classified in the export category.[2] The remainder are placed
in the local serving category. The all-or-nothing allocation is not used in the cases
of railroad, government and education, and recreation-related employment.
Due to the special circumstances surrounding these industries, employment in
these industries is divided between the export and local categories according to the
procedures described here.

   Subdividing Railroad Employment. Care is required in dealing with the railroad-
transportation employment data. It is an important source of employment in
several of the subregions. Part of the employment in this category belongs in the
business-serving group and part of it in the export group.

   The Standard Industrial Classification Manual, under a subcategory of Railroad
Equipment, group 3742, Railroad and Street Cars, states, "Repair shops owned
and operated by railroads or local transit companies, rebuilding or repairing cars,
or building new cars for their own account, are classified in major groups 40
and 41."[3] In this study area, there are several repair shops owned by railroad
companies that carry on this type of activity. The Pennsylvania Railroad has a
large shop in the Altoona area and a small one in Harrisburg; the Erie-Lackawanna
has one in Scranton; and the Baltimore & Ohio has one in Baltimore. By the
criterion applied in this study, the employment in these shops belongs in export
manufacturing. However, it is lumped together with other employment in Group
40, railroad transportation, which belongs in the business-serving group. To
subdivide the data into these two parts, a modified minimum-requirement
approach is used. According to an unpublished study by Dacey, the minimum
requirement for transportation and communication employment varies from 1.8

   [2] The basis of this judgment is spelled out in Chapter 9, under the section Local Serving
Versus Export Industries.

   [3] *Op. cit.*

TABLE B.1

Subdivision of Railroad-Transportation Employment into Business-Serving and Export Groups

Subregions	1 Total Manufacturing Employment*	2 Estimated Business- Serving Employment in Railroad Transportation†	3 Total Railroad- Transportation Employment (SIC 40)*	4 Estimated Export Employment in Railroad Transportation‡
A	45,947	827	3,450	2,623
B	65,509	1,179	2,209	1,030
C	51,531	928	4,100	3,172
D	28,305	509	1,103	594
E	78,325	1,410	4,532	3,122
F	24,610	443	9,254	8,811
G	146,893	2,644	7,504	4,860
H	199,613	3,593	11,370	7,777

* U.S. Bureau of the Census, *U.S. Census of Population: 1960, Detailed Characteristics,* Pennsylvania, Table 85, U.S. Government Printing Office, Washington, D.C.

† 1.8 percent of Column 1.

‡ Column 3 minus Column 2.

to 3.6 percent of total manufacturing, depending on the size of the population.[4]

Because communication is lumped together with transportation data, Dacey's results cannot be applied directly. As a rough approximation, 1.8 percent is selected as the minimum requirement for all the subregions; a portion of railroad employment equivalent to 1.8 percent of total manufacturing is therefore put into the business-serving group. Next, this estimated minimum requirement is subtracted from the total railroad-transportation reported, and the difference is put into the export-manufacturing group. In particular, this difference is treated as employment in Transportation Equipment (SIC 37). Table B.1 shows the results.

Subdividing Government and Education Employment. Most government and education employment is oriented to serving local needs. Exceptions to this occur in connection with universities attended largely by nonlocal students and higher level government activities serving nonlocal functions. Universities of major nonlocal enrollment were identified in Subregions A, B, C, and H. Furthermore, in Subregion G there is a significant amount of state level government activity in the state capital at Harrisburg. No major export government or educational activities could be found, however, in Subregions D, E, and F. All government and education activity in

[4] M. F. Dacey, "1960 Data for Minimum Requirements Method," Table 1, Wharton School of Finance and Commerce, University of Pennsylvania (mimeographed, no date). We recognize the theoretical difficulties of the minimum-requirements technique, but the rough approximations it provides here are useful.

TABLE B.2

Ratio of Employment in Government and Education to Population in Subregions D, E, and F

Subregion	Total Population*	Local Government and Education†	Local Government and Education/Total Population
D	200,279	5,075	0.02534
E	626,553	15,384	0.02455
F	263,524	5,947	0.02257
Average			0.024

Sources:

* U.S. Bureau of the Census, *U.S. Census of Population: 1960, Detailed Characteristics*, Pennsylvania, Final Report PC(1)-40B, (1961), 40-55-40-61, U.S. Government Printing Office, Washington, D.C.

† U.S. Bureau of the Census, *U.S. Census of Population: 1960, Detailed Characteristics*, Pennsylvania, Final Report PC(1)B403 (1961), 40-494-40-500, U.S. Government Printing Office, Washington, D.C.

these three subregions was, therefore, assumed to be locally oriented and information on these subregions was used as a basis for estimating local employment in the other subregions.

The ratio of employment to total population in these three subregions was determined. As shown in Table B.2, the ratios were very nearly the same for each of the three subregions, averaging to about .02415. This ratio was assumed to be a reasonable approximation of the minimum governmental and education employment per person required for serving local households. This ratio was then applied to Subregions A, B, C, G, and H in order to obtain local government and education figures. These figures were subtracted from the total reported government and education figures. Table B.3 shows the results.

Estimating and Subdividing Water-Based Recreation Employment. Water-based recreation generates employment related to (1) direct service at the recreation sites and (2) indirect service at restaurants, service stations, groceries, and other places of business in the area near the site.[5] Because recreation employment cuts across the standard industrial classification categories, it is necessary first to separate it from these categories before dividing it into export and local serving parts. To do this the number of workers needed per visitor-day is estimated. Multiplying this factor by the number of visitor-days yields the required estimate of total water-based recreation employment. This total is then divided into export and local serving parts on the basis of judgments concerning the percentage of visitors attracted from inside and outside the subregion.

ESTIMATION WORKERS NEEDED PER VISITOR-DAY. In order to estimate the number of workers needed for direct service, rough estimates were made of workers used per visitor-day at the sites for which worker data were available. Seasonal workers were weighted less than full-time workers in accordance with the time they

[5] See Chapter 11.

TABLE B.3

Subdivision of Government and Education Employment into Local and Export Parts
for Subregions A, B, C, G, and H

Subregion	Total Population*	Total Government and Education†	Local Government and Education	Export Government and Education
A	385,627	12,858	9,313	3,545
B	463,438	13,667	11,192	2,475
C	430,703	15,699	10,401	5,297
G	1,046,981	46,992	25,285	21,707
H	1,803,745	71,240	43,560	27,679

Sources:

* U.S. Bureau of the Census, *U.S. Census of Population: 1960, Detailed Characteristics*,
Pennsylvania, Final Report PC(1)-40B, (1961), 40-55-40-61, U.S. Government Printing
Office, Washington, D.C.

† U.S. Bureau of the Census, *U.S. Census of Population: 1960, Detailed
Characteristics*, Pennsylvania, Final Report PC(1)-403, (1961), 40-494-40-500. U.S.
Government Printing Office Washington D.C.

actually spent working. It was finally estimated that .00005 worker is needed for
every visitor-day.

In order to estimate the number of workers needed per visitor-day for indirect
services, data from ORRRC Study Report 24 were used.[6] Data showing average
cash outlay per person on food, lodging, transportation, and miscellaneous
services near the recreation site were combined with data on the average wages
paid in each of these kinds of service establishments. On the average, computations
showed that 0.000092 worker would be needed for indirect service per visitor-day.
This was added to the workers needed for direct service to arrive at an estimated
0.000142 worker needed per visitor-day.

DIVIDING RECREATION EMPLOYMENT INTO EXPORT AND LOCAL SERVING PARTS. The
number of local serving workers in a subregion is determined by multiplying the
total workers by the estimated percentage of visitors originating from within the
subregion.

The percentage of total visitors originating from within 50 miles of a park has
been found to range from 45 to 95 percent, depending on the attractiveness of
the site. These factors were assumed to be valid for entire subregions. Relative
attractiveness indexes were estimated, as shown in Table B.4, for each subregion,
based on judgments about each subregion's over-all scenic appeal.[7]

As this attractiveness index depends only on scenic appeal, the proportion of
visitors originating from within 50 miles is also dependent on the highways and
population in the subregion. Taking these three factors into account, as well as

[6] Outdoor Recreation Resources Review Commission, Study Report 24, "Outdoor
Recreation for America," Washington, D.C., 1962.

[7] A more refined procedure, which due to budget limitations was not attempted, would
have been to use separate estimates of attractiveness for each recreation site.

TABLE B.4

Numerical Estimates of Recreation Attractiveness of Subregions in the Susquehanna River Basin

Subregions	Local Recreational Attractiveness Index
A	0.92
B	0.68
C	1.28
D	0.72
E	0.72
F	1.45
G	0.95
H	0.22

the size of the subregions, it was estimated that the percentages of visitors coming from within the subregions (local visitors) are as given in Table B.5.

After 1975, the factors for Subregions C, D, and E became 25, 25, and 30, respectively, because the opening of the new interstate highway is expected to bring more nonlocal visitors into the regions.

Grouping Export Manufacturing Industries[8]

The procedure described for classifying industries into local and export parts results in a large number of manufacturing industries being assigned to the export sector. It is desirable, if possible, to aggregate these industries into groups that are homogeneous with respect to locational influences. To accomplish this, the SIC 2-digit industries in the export sector that had similar transportation and labor costs characteristics were grouped together.

As a first step, the export industries were classified as "processing" or "fabricating" owing to the added importance of transportation costs of raw materials in influencing the location of the former. This classification follows a scheme suggested by Perloff et al.[9] based on an analysis of the 1947 input-output table.[9] The only changes made in Perloff's classification were textiles, which were switched from processing to fabricating, and chemicals, which were shifted to processing. These changes were made on the basis of data on cost characteristics presented in the following paragraphs.

Next, indices of the importance of labor costs and transportation costs were

[8] In general, the industry groups described here were developed before data was available from the *1963 Census of Manufactures*, the *1963 Census of Transportation*, and the 1958 Input-Output Table. When these data sources became available late in the study several suggested regroupings became obvious. These revisions were not implemented because of time constraints. For a discussion of these points see H. R. Hamilton et al., "A Dynamic Model of the Economy of the Susquehanna River Basin," Battelle Memorial Institute, Aug. 1, 1966, Append. I, p. I–5.

[9] Harvey S. Perloff, Edgar S. Dunn, Jr., Eric E. Lampard, and Richard E. Muth, *Regions, Resources, and Economic Growth*, Resources for the Future, Incorporated (Baltimore, Md.: The Johns Hopkins Press, 1960), p. 75.

TABLE B.5
Estimated Percentages of Visitors Originating from Within 50 Miles and
Estimated Percentages of Visitors Originating from Each Subregion

Subregion	Estimated Percentage of Visitors from 50 Miles of Center of Subregion	Estimated Percentage of Visitors from Subregion
A	65	55
B	90	80
C	60	40
D	85	40
E	80	45
F	75	40
G	75	50
H	90	75

computed. The ratio of total payroll to total value of shipments was adopted as a useful index of the importance of labor in each manufacturing industry. For transportation costs of raw materials and products, a similar index, the ratio of transportation costs to value of shipments was considered. However, to a significant extent, the observed proportion of product value expended on transportation reflects the results of past location decisions rather than the importance of this cost in reaching new decisions. Value of shipments per ton of product, on the other hand, indicates more directly the importance of transportation cost for a given product. Consider, for example, a product with low value per ton. For this product, transportation costs are important in selecting a production location because the cost of transporting the product will be high as a percent of its value. However, if this industry is located close to its market or raw materials so as to minimize these high transport costs, the transportation costs actually observed might be relatively low. Therefore it is believed that value per ton provides a more meaningful index for grouping than does transportation cost.

For the fabricating industries, value of shipments per ton was computed as an index of the importance of transportation costs. For the processing industries, the value of input shipments per ton of raw material was computed in addition to the index on product shipments because of the importance of raw material transportation costs. Transportation costs on inputs to fabricating industries were not included in the grouping scheme because these costs are determined to a large extent by the location of the processing industries.

Grouping of Processing Industries. The seven SIC 2-digit processing industries were aggregated to form two industry groups, capital-intensive and labor-intensive processing industries. The groupings were made on the basis of three indices of the importance of labor and transportation costs for the processing industries in Table B.6.

The index of labor costs was derived from the 1962 *Annual Survey of Manufactures* and is the ratio of total payroll to value of shipments. The value of shipments per ton of shipments (product) index was derived from the Interstate

TABLE B.6

Indices of Importance of Labor and Transportation Costs for Processing Industries

SIC Code	Industry	Payroll/Value of Shipments (Outputs)*	Value of Shipments (Outputs)/Ton of Output† dollars/ton	Value of Inputs/Ton of Inputs‡ dollars/ton
20	Food and kindred products	0.128	300	75
24	Lumber and wood products	0.257	110	13
26	Paper and allied products	0.214	100	8
28	Chemicals and allied products	0.162	180	40
29	Petroleum and coal products	0.064	50	25
32	Stone, clay, and glass	0.269	40	17
33	Primary metal industries	0.222	200	23

* U.S. Department of Commerce, Bureau of the Census, *Annual Survey of Manufactures, 1962*, "General Statistics for Industry Groups and Industries," M62(AS)-1 (Revised), U.S. Government Printing Office, Washington, D.C.

† Interstate Commerce Commission, Bureau of Transport Economics and Statistics, "Freight Revenue and Wholesale Value at Destination of Commodities Transported by Class I Line-Haul Railroads, 1959," Washington, D.C., October 1961.

‡ W. D. Evans and M. Hoffenberg, "The Interindustry Relations Study for 1947," *Review of Economics and Statistics*, 34, 2 (May 1952).

Commerce Commission publication "Freight Revenue and Wholesale Value at Destination of Commodities Transported by Class 1 Line-Haul Railroads, 1959." The 1947 input-output table was used to identify inputs and their proportions for each SIC 2-digit industry. These proportions were used to weight the value of inputs per ton of inputs estimated for each industry. Plots of the indices given in Table B.6 are shown in Figures B.1 and B.2.

These indices served to identify labor-intensive and capital-intensive processing industries. For example, the chemical and allied products industry (28) and the petroleum and coal products industry (29) each have a low ratio of payroll to value of shipments. The food and kindred products industry (2) also has a low ratio of payroll to value of shipments and was therefore included with industries 28 and 29 to form a "capital-intensive processing" group. The remaining four industries have significantly higher and very similar ratios of payroll to value of shipment and were classified into the "labor-intensive processing" group.

Figure B.1 shows that the values of shipments per ton of product shipments for the seven industries are quite similar, and that it is not possible to distinguish between the two groups on this basis. However, Figure B.2 shows differences in value of input per ton of inputs for the seven industries, the labor-intensive processing industry having somewhat lower valued inputs per ton than the capital-intensive processing industry, implying a higher transportation cost component on inputs for the former.

Grouping of Fabricating Industries. Indices for labor and transportation costs for fabricating industries were developed in a similar manner to those for the processing industries. The ratio of payroll to value of shipments was estimated

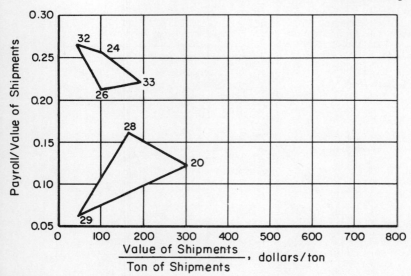

FIGURE B.1. Payroll/value of shipments versus value of shipments per ton for processing industries.

from the 1962 *Annual Survey of Manufactures*. Value of shipment per ton of output was estimated from the Interstate Commerce Commission study, as in the processing industries. For the fabricating industries, which tend to utilize highway transportation to a larger extent than do processing industries, these estimates are probably questionable. In some cases, namely, apparel and instruments, no data were available from the ICC study, and judgmental estimates were used. Table B.7 lists the values of these indices for the 13 fabricating industries. Figure B.3 is a plot of these indices. An index on the value of inputs per ton of input was not developed for the fabricating industries on the assumption that these industries are principally oriented toward the location of markets in their location decisions and that the processing industries locate with reference to the fabricating industries, which are their principal markets.

The classification developed, as shown, in Figure B.3, is primarily a value per ton classification. Those industries with a higher value of product per ton were grouped into a "nondurable fabricating" industry group. These industries are the textile, apparel, leather, and tobacco industries. The durable fabricating industries formed a second group that had lower-valued products per ton. The printing and publishing industry (27) and the rubber and plastics industry (3) were classified as durable fabricating industries because of their lower value of output per ton, although these industries are generally classified by the Bureau of the Census as nondurable goods manufacturing.

Estimating Employment in Industry Groups

Table B.8 shows the detailed makeup of each industry group used in the model in terms of SIC industries. Once these industry groups were specified, the amount

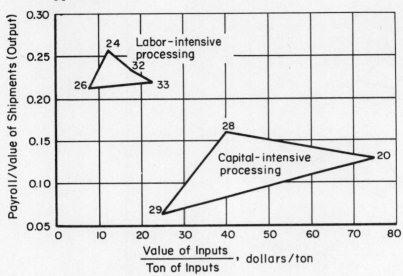

FIGURE B.2. Payroll/value of shipments versus value of inputs/ton for processing industries.

of employment in each group was estimated. Because population and labor force data were derived from the *U.S. Census of Population*, it was desirable, for the sake of consistency, to use this census for employment as well. Unfortunately, employment data in the census are mainly aggregated into 2-digit categories or groups of 2-digit categories. For purposes of estimating model groups a finer breakdown was needed, in some cases as fine as the 4-digit level.

To resolve this difficulty, other sources with finer breakdowns were consulted. These were *County Business Patterns* (*1962*) published by the Department of Commerce and *Employment by Industry Group* published by the Department of Internal Affairs of the Commonwealth of Pennsylvania. Data from these sources were not complete, in many cases because of the nondisclosure of data in counties where only one or a few firms were located. Despite this, from the combined use of these sources, estimates were made of employment by county for the finer employment categories as needed. These estimates were totaled and compared with the totals of the grosser categories provided by the U.S. Census. In most cases the two totals were very close. In all cases, the estimates of employment in the finer categories were then revised in order to make their totals equal to the corresponding U.S. Census totals.

These revisions were made through judgments based largely on information provided by the *Industrial Directories* of *Pennsylvania* (1960), *New York* (1958), and *Maryland* (1958). These directories report employment estimates by firms in each county and, as a result, were especially helpful in improving previous estimates that may have been inaccurate because of the nondisclosure problem. The revised estimates were then aggregated into estimates of employment for each industry group.

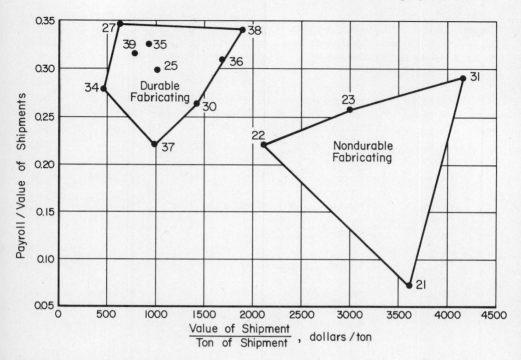

FIGURE B.3. Payroll/value of shipment versus value of shipment/ton for fabricating industries.

TABLE B.7
Indices of Importance of Labor and Transportation Costs for Fabricating Industries

SIC Code	Industry	Payroll/Value of Shipments*	Value of Shipments/Ton,† dollars/ton
21	Tobacco manufactures	0.074	3,600
22	Textile mill products	0.221	1,980
23	Apparel and related products	0.258	3,000‡
25	Furniture and fixtures	0.295	1,010
27	Printing and publishing	0.347	640
30	Rubber and plastics products	0.264	1,420
31	Leather and leather products	0.292	4,170
34	Fabricated metal products	0.280	460
35	Machinery, except electrical	0.325	930
36	Electrical machinery	0.310	1,700
37	Transportation equipment	0.220	970
38	Instruments and related products	0.341	1,900‡
39	Miscellaneous manufacturing	0.317	1,280

* U.S. Department of Commerce, Bureau of the Census, *Annual Survey of Manufactures, 1962*, "General Statistics for Industry Groups and Industries," M62(AS)-1 (Revised), U.S. Government Printing Office, Washington, D.C.

† Interstate Commerce Commission, Bureau of Transport Economics and Statistics, "Freight Revenue and Wholesale Value at Destination of Commodities Transported by Class I Line-Haul Railroads, 1959," U.S. Government Printing Office, Washington, D.C., October 1961.

‡ No data available—Battelle estimate.

TABLE B.8
Industry Groups

I. Local Serving Industries
  A. Household-Serving

50	Wholesale trade
52, 53, 54	Retail trade
55, 56	
57, 58,	
59	
60	Banking
61	Credit agencies
62	Security and commodity brokers
63, 64, 65	Insurance carriers and real estate
66, 67	
70	Hotels, rooming houses, camps, etc.
72	Personal service
73	Miscellaneous business services
75	Automobile repairs
76	Miscellaneous repairs
78	Motion picture
79	Amusement and recreation services (subtract water-based recreation)
80	Medical and other health services
81	Legal services
82, 91, 92, 93	Local serving part of government and education (as described)
84	Museum, art galleries, etc.
86	Nonprofit membership organizations
88	Private households
89	Miscellaneous services
202	Dairy products
271	Newspapers
323	Glass products of purchased glass
2051	Bread and other bakery products
2071	Candy and other confectionery products
2511	Wood household furniture, except upholstered
2519	Household furniture, n.e.c.
3732	Boat building and repair
3981, 3987,	Miscellaneous manufacturing industries
3992, 3993,	
3995, 3999	

  B. Business-Serving

40	Local serving part of railroad transportation (as described)
41	Local and suburban transit
42	Warehousing and motor freight transportation
44	Water transportation
45	Transportation by air
47	Transportation services
48	Communication
49	Electric, gas, and sanitary services
275	Commercial printing

TABLE B.8 (Continued)

I. Local Serving Industries (*contd.*)

278	Bookbinding and related industries
279	Service industries for printing
324	Hydraulic cement
325	Structural clay products
327	Concrete, gypsum, and plaster products
328	Cut stone and stone products
347	Coating, engraving, and allied services
2951	Paving mixtures and blocks
3271, 2, 3, 4	Concrete and lime
15	Building construction
16	Highway and street construction
17	Construction—special trade contractors
14	Mining and quarrying of nonmetallic minerals except fuels

II. Export Industries

A. Agriculture

01	Commercial farms
02	Noncommercial farms
07	Agricultural services and hunting and trapping
08	Forestry
09	Fisheries

B. Export Mining

10	Metal mining
11	Anthracite mining
12	Bituminous coal and lignite mining
13	Crude petroleum and natural gas

C. Export Manufacturing

1. Durable Fabricators

25—Furniture

251	Household furniture
252	Office furniture
253	Public buildings and related furniture
254	Partitions, shelving, etc.
259	Miscellaneous furniture and fixtures
2512	Wood household furniture, upholstered
2514	Metal household furniture
2515	Mattresses and bedsprings

27—Printing

272	Periodicals
273	Books
274	Miscellaneous publishing
276	Manifold business forms manufacture
277	Greeting-card manufacture

30—Rubber

301	Tires and inner tubes
302	Rubber footwear
303	Reclaimed rubber
306	Fabricated rubber products, n.e.c.
307	Miscellaneous plastic products

TABLE B.8 (Continued)

II. Export Industries (*contd.*)

34—Fabricated Metal Products

341	Metal cans
342	Cutlery, hand tools, and general hardware
343	Heating apparatus (except electric) and plumbing fixtures
344	Fabricated structural metal products
345	Screw machine products, etc.
346	Metal stampings
348	Miscellaneous fabricated wire products
349	Miscellaneous fabricated metal products

35—Machinery

351	Engines and turbines
352	Farm machinery and equipment
353	Construction, mining, and materials-handling machinery and equipment
354	Metalworking machinery and equipment
355	Special industry machinery, except metalworking machinery
356	General industrial machinery and equipment
357	Office, computing, and accounting machines
358	Service industry machines
359	Miscellaneous machinery

36—Electrical Machinery

361	Electric transmission and distribution equipment
362	Electrical industrial apparatus
363	Household appliances
364	Lighting and wiring devices
365	Radio and TV sets
366	Communication equipment
367	Electronic components
369	Miscellaneous electric machinery, equipment, and supplies
3641	Electric lamps
3642	Lighting fixtures
3643	Current-carrying wiring devices
3644	Noncurrent-carrying wiring devices
3671–2, 3, 9	Electronic components and accessories
3691–2, 9	Miscellaneous electronic machinery, equipment, and supplies

37—Transportation Equipment

371	Motor vehicles and equipment
372	Aircraft and parts
373	Ships and boats
374	Railroad equipment
375	Motorcycles, bicycles, and parts
379	Miscellaneous transportation equipment
3731	Ship building and repairing

38—Instruments

381	Scientific instruments
382	Mechanical measuring devices
386	Photographic equipment
387	Watches, clocks, and parts

TABLE B.8 (Continued)

II. Export Industries (*contd.*)

    39—Miscellaneous Manufacturing

391	Jewelry, silverware, and plated ware
393	Musical instruments and parts
394	Toys and sporting goods
395	Pens, pencils, and other office and artists' materials
396	Costume jewelry, etc.
398	Miscellaneous manufactures
3949	Toys and amusements, sporting goods, n.e.c.
3982	Linoleum, etc.
3983	Matches
3988	Morticians' goods

    40—Export part of Railroad Transportation (as described)

2. Nondurable Fabricators

    22—Textile

221	Weaving mills, cotton
222	Weaving mills, synthetics
223	Weaving, finishing mills, wool
224	Narrow fabric mills
225	Knitting mills
226	Textile finishing, except wool
227	Floor covering mills
228	Yarn and thread mills
229	Miscellaneous textile goods

    23—Apparel

231	Men's and boys' suits and coats
232	Men's and boys' furnishings
233	Women's and misses' outerwear
234	Women's undergarments
235	Hats, caps, and millinery
236	Children's outerwear
238	Miscellaneous apparel and accessories
239	Fabricated textiles, n.e.c.

    31—Leather

311	Leather tanning and finishing
313	Boot and shoe cut stock and findings
314	Footwear, except rubber
316	Luggage
317	Purses and small leather goods

    21—Tobacco

212	Cigars
214	Tobacco stemming and redrying

3. Labor-Intensive Processors

    26—Paper

261	Pulp mills
262	Paper mills except building
263	Paperboard mills
264	Converted paper and paperboard products, except containers

TABLE B.8 (Continued)

II. Export Industries (*contd.*)

	265	Paperboard containers
	266	Building paper and building board

33—Primary Metals

	331	Steel rolling and finishing
	332	Iron and steel foundries
	333	Primary nonferrous metals
	334	Secondary nonferrous metals
	335	Nonferrous metals rolling and drawing
	336	Nonferrous foundries
	339	Miscellaneous primary metals

24—Lumber

	241	Logging camps and logging contractors
	242	Sawmills and planing mills
	243	Millwork and related products
	244	Wooden containers
	249	Miscellaneous wood products
	2432	Veneer and plywood plants

32—Stone, Clay, and Glass Products

	321	Flat glass
	322	Glass and glassware
	326	Pottery and related products
	329	Abrasive, asbestos, and miscellaneous nonmetallic mineral products
	3275	Gypsum products

4. Capital-Intensive Processors

28—Chemical Products

	281	Basic chemicals
	282	Fibers, plastics, rubber
	283	Drugs
	284	Soap, detergents, cosmetics, etc.
	285	Paints, varnishes, etc.
	286	Gum and wood products
	287	Agricultural chemicals
	289	Miscellaneous chemicals

29—Petroleum and Coal Products

	291	Petroleum refining
	293	By-product coke ovens
	295	Paving and roofing materials
	299	Miscellaneous products
	2952	Asphalt felts and coatings

20—Food Products

	201	Meat products
	203	Canned and frozen foods
	204	Grain mill products
	205	Bakery products
	207	Confectionery and related products
	208	Beverage industries
	209	Miscellaneous food preparations and kindred products

TABLE B.8 (Continued)

II. Export Industries (*contd.*)

2031	Canned and cured seafoods
2032	Canned specialties
2033	Canned fruits, vegetables, preserves, jams, jellies
2034	Dried and dehydrated fruits and vegetables
2035	Pickled fruits and vegetables, vegetable sauces and seasonings, and salad dressings
2036	Fresh or frozen packaged fish
2037	Frozen fruits, juices, vegetables, and specialties
2052	Biscuits, crackers, and pretzels
2072–3	Chocolate, cocoa products, and chewing gum
2082	Malt liquors
2083	Malt
2084	Wines, brandy, and brandy spirits
2085	Distilled, rectified, and blended liquors
2086	Bottled, canned soft drinks and carbonated waters
2087	Flavoring extracts and flavoring syrups, n.e.c.

D. Export Government and Education

82
91
92   Export part of government and education (as described)
93

E. Export Part of Water-Based Recreation (as described)

F. River Works Construction

Appendix C
Computation of
Access
Factors[1]

Recall from Chapter 10 how a subregion's exports manufacturing industry is modeled to grow. For each industry group, a subregion's growth rate, as contrasted with that of its market, is determined by its relative advantage with respect to costs. Market growth is forecast and inserted exogenously into the model. Regional cost characteristics are represented in the model by three measures: (1) relative access to markets, (2) relative access to raw materials, and (3) relative wages. Chapter 10 describes the relative wage formulation. This appendix describes how we estimated the two access factors. First, the derivation of the relative access to markets is described, and then relative access to raw materials is discussed. It may be noted at this point that the description of these two access factors is very uneven, with much more detail provided on access to markets. This is because, although raw material access was viewed conceptually in the same way as market access, recent location trends indicate access to markets far more important in determining location. Furthermore, lack of comparable data in this case compelled us to use more subjective, and therefore less explicit, access to raw material estimation procedures that are difficult to describe.

Access to Market

Relative access to market may essentially be thought of as the relative cost of delivering or transporting products to market. If the relevant data on transportation costs were available, it would be measured as follows:

$$AM_{ij}{}^t = TC_{ij}{}^t / TC_{iN}{}^t \tag{C.1}$$

where

$AM_{ij}{}^t$ relative Access to Market for ith industry group from jth subregion at time t,

---

[1] The work described in this appendix is due largely to the efforts of David E. Boyce, currently assistant professor of regional science at the University of Pennsylvania. See H. R. Hamilton et al., "A Dynamic Model of the Economy of the Susquehanna River Basin," Battelle Memorial Institute, August 1, 1966.

$TC_{ij}{}^t$ average Transportation Costs to market for ith industry group from the jth subregion at time t,

$TC_{iN}{}^t$ National average Transportation Costs to market for the ith industry at time t.

Unfortunately, the relevant cost data needed to implement Equation C.1 were not available. Therefore, we decided to use shipment distance, for which data was available from preliminary reports of the 1963 *Census of Transportation*,[2] as a proxy for transportation costs. The *Census of Transportation* reports in particular provided estimates of tons shipped and ton-miles between the nine U.S. census divisions by major shipper groups. From these estimates it is possible to compute the average shipment distance from an origin census region to a destination census region, as well as the average shipment distance for the entire United States.

While shipment distance cannot be considered a perfect proxy, it is believed to be a reasonable proxy for transportation costs. This is because transportation costs tend to be proportional to distance, particularly for shipment distances greater than 100 miles. Because the *Census of Transportation* excluded all local shipments as well as those commodities that are principally consumed locally from the sampled bills of lading, the shipment distances represented in the sample should tend to be a linear function of transportation cost. In view of these considerations, relative access to market was measured essentially, with the one modification described in the next paragraph, by taking the ratio of shipment distance to market from the subregion to the national shipment distance to market.

Perhaps the most important reason why distance may fail to be a suitable proxy for costs is that the quality of transportation facilities may vary from one part of the country to another. To handle this variation in quality, at least in part, distance measures were adjusted to reflect differences and anticipated changes in the quality of highway facilities. To account completely for this variation in the

[2] U.S. Bureau of the Census, *Census of Transportation, 1963,* Commodity Transportation Survey, Shipper Series TC63(P)C1, U.S. Government Printing Office, Washington, D.C.

quality of transportation facilities, of course, other kinds of facilities besides highways, i.e., rail, water, and air, should also be considered eventually, when suitable data becomes available.

To sum up these preliminary remarks, the access-to-market measures used in the Susquehanna model, though crude, are believed to be adequate for our purposes. We believe the measures of market access could be substantially refined if data on shipment distances were available by mode of transport, and if curves for transportation costs versus shipment distance reflecting those transportation rates carrying substantial volumes of freight traffic were available. Using these curves for each mode of transportation, average shipment distances could be transformed to an average transportation cost by mode, which could then be combined across modes to obtain an average transportation cost for a given industry group and subregion. In view of the level of refinement of other aspects of the employment sector, however, the use of average shipment distances alone is probably adequate.

In accordance with these considerations the access to market factors were derived as follows:

$$AM_{ij}{}^t = AASD_{ij}{}^t / AASD_{iN}{}^t \qquad\qquad\qquad (C.2)$$

$$AASD_{ij}{}^t = ASD_{ij} + ADJH_j{}^t \qquad\qquad\qquad (C.3)$$

$$AASD_{ij}{}^t = ASD_{iN} + ADJH_N{}^t \qquad\qquad\qquad (C.4)$$

where

$AM_{ij}{}^t$ relative Access to Market for ith industry from jth subregion at time t,

$AASD_{ij}{}^t$ Adjusted Average Shipment Distance for products of ith industry to market from jth subregion at time t,

$AASD_{iN}{}^{t}$ Adjusted Average Shipment Distance for products of ith industry to market for Nation at time t,

ASD_{ij} Average Shipment Distance for products of ith industry from jth subregion,

$ADJH_{j}{}^{t}$ ADJustment of average shipment distances for quality of Highway facilities from the jth subregion to its market at time t,

ASD_{iN} Average Shipment Distance for products of ith industry to market for the Nation,

$ADJH_{N}{}^{t}$ ADJustment of average shipment distances for the quality of Highway facilities in the nation at time t.

The remainder of this discussion on access to market can conveniently be divided into three parts as follows:

1. Aggregation procedures used to transform available categories of industry and regional data into categories suitable for the Susquehanna model,
2. Measurement of average shipment distances (i.e., ASD_{ij} and ASD_{iN} in Equations C.3 and C.4), and
3. Adjustment of average shipment distances for quality of highway facilities available (i.e., $ADJH_{ij}{}^{t}$ and $ADJH_{iN}{}^{t}$ in Equations C.3 and C.4).

Aggregation Procedures

AGGREGATION OVER INDUSTRIES. Because the data used for deriving access factors were not directly available for the modeled industry groups or the modeled subregions, it was necessary to devise procedures for transforming the available data to the desired measures. One such adjustment involved aggregating data available by shipper group into the four export industry groups (nondurable fabricators, durable fabricators, capital-intensive processors, and labor-intensive processors) used in the model.[3] This was accomplished by weighting the industry access factors by the 1960 subregional employment in each industry as follows:

$$AMI_j^t = \sum_{i \in I} (AM_{ij}^t) E_{ij}^{60} \qquad (C.5)$$

where

AMI_j^t relative Access to Markets for Ith industry group from the jth subregion at time t,

AM_{ij}^t relative Access to Markets for the ith SIC 2-digit industry (or group) from the jth subregion at time t,

E_{ij}^{60} 1960 Employment in the ith SIC 2-digit industry (or group) in the jth subregion.

This procedure, it will be noted, is fairly straightforward, although it does involve the implicit assumption that the SIC 2-digit industry mix of the four model industry groups will remain the same. We cannot be entirely happy with this assumption, but short of further industry disaggregation, there appears to be little that can be done to improve on it.

AGGREGATION OVER SPACE. Besides industrial aggregation there is the question of spatial aggregation. In Equation C.3, both the variables on the right-hand side of the equation, ASD_{ij} and $ADJH_{ij}^t$, apply to shipments and routes that have several different destinations. In particular, both these variables represent

[3] In order to use the shipper series reports in conjunction with the data on SIC 2-digit subregional employment, the shipper groups were combined to form SIC 2-digit industries or groups of 2-digit industries. Fifteen industries are defined, consisting of the following SIC 2-digit industries: 20, 21-22-23-31, 24, 25-27-39, 26, 28, 29, 30, 32, 33, 34-19, 35, 36, 37, 38. SIC Industries 19 and 27, for which no *Census of Transportation* data are available, are assumed to have transportation characteristics like those of Industries 34 and 25-39, respectively. SIC Industry 21, tobacco manufacturing, is assumed to have transportation characteristics similar to the textile, apparel, and leather industries. The shipper group information on tobacco cannot be used because it is aggregated with candy and beverage shipments in shipper group 3.

weighted averages of their respective values over all destinations as follows:

$$ASD_{ij} = \sum_d (ASD_{i,j \to d}) P_{i,j \to d} \tag{C.6}$$

$$ADJH_j^t = \sum_d (ADJH_{j \to d}^t) P_{i,j \to d} \tag{C.7}$$

where

ASD_{ij} Average Shipment Distance for products of the ith industry from the jth subregion,

$ASD_{i,j \to d}$ Average Shipment Distance for products of the ith industry from the jth subregion to the dth market destination,

$P_{i,j \to d}$ estimate of the Proportion of total shipments in the ith industry from the jth subregion to the dth market destination,

$ADJH_j^t$ ADJustment of average shipment distances for the quality of Highway facilities from the jth subregion to its market at time t,

$ADJH_{j \to d}^t$ ADJustment of average shipment distances for the quality of Highway facilities from the jth subregion to the dth market destination.

Before proceeding with a detailed description of how shipment distances $ASD_{i,j \to d}$ and highway quality adjustments $ADJH_{i,j \to d}^t$ were derived, a few words on how we estimated the proportion of total shipments from each subregion to each market destination (i.e., the $P_{i,j \to d}$ in Equations C.6 and C.7) are in order. First of all, market destinations were defined by dividing the nation into a set of mutually exclusive areas. In doing this, we were for the most part constrained by the data available to us at the time to dealing with the nine U.S. census divisions. In particular, the 1963 *Census of Transportation* provided data on the proportion of tons shipped for each industry from the Middle Atlantic region to each of the eight other census regions. Because the Susquehanna subregions are nearly all in the Middle Atlantic region, it was assumed that these proportions applied to each subregion.[4] Furthermore, lacking data for other years from which perhaps a trend might have been extrapolated, these proportions were assumed constant over time.

The preceding description takes care of those destinations outside of the Middle Atlantic census region. Arriving at similar estimates of proportion of tons shipped to destinations inside the Middle Atlantic created a special problem because no direct data were available on intracensus region shipments. To solve this problem, the Middle Atlantic census region was divided into five pie-shaped sectors centered on the major metropolitan areas of New York, Philadelphia, Pittsburgh, Buffalo, and Albany. Then, lacking data on tons shipped, sector population was used as a proxy for the size of the market in each sector.

Measurement of Average Shipment Distances. Deriving average distances shipped from the Susquehanna subregions involves three steps: (1) finding average distances shipped for each industry (i.e., shipper group) from the Middle Atlantic census region to each of the other census regions outside the Middle Atlantic, (2) converting these distances so that they pertain to the Susquehanna subregions, rather than to average Middle Atlantic origins, and (3) arriving at average distances shipped from the Susquehanna subregions to other destinations inside the Middle Atlantic. These three steps are described in turn below.

[4] All of the subregions in the Susquehanna study area, with the exception of the Baltimore subregion, lie inside the Middle Atlantic census region. It should be noted that generation of access factors for the Baltimore subregion, which lies outside the Middle Atlantic census region, was undertaken exactly in the same way as the other subregions, as if Baltimore were a part of the Middle Atlantic census region. The implicit assumption in this procedure is that the shipment patterns of Baltimore are similar to and can be derived from those of the Middle Atlantic region. This assumption seems quite realistic; the alternative procedure would be to derive Baltimore's access factors from South Atlantic census region data, a procedure that would introduce problems of comparability between subregional access factors. In the final publication of the *Census of Transportation, 1963,* which was not available for this study, there may be data available on shipment patterns for the Baltimore metropolitan area alone, as well as for other groups of metropolitan areas in the Susquehanna basin and the Middle Atlantic census region. When this publication becomes available, it might be desirable to revise these access factors on the basis of this more complete tabulation of the census results. However, in lieu of these data and in light of the relative insensitivity of the model to small changes in access factors, the procedure used to generate access factors for Baltimore is considered adequate.

AVERAGE DISTANCE FROM THE MIDDLE ATLANTIC TO OTHER CENSUS REGIONS. The 1963 *Census of Transportation*, Shipper Series reports, Table 7, contains estimates of tons of shipments and ton-miles between U.S. census regions by industry (i.e., shipper group).[5] Using these data, average shipment distances from the Middle Atlantic census region to each destination census region are computed for each industry. This distance is computed by dividing the number of ton-miles shipped from the Middle Atlantic region to a given destination region by the tons shipped as follows:

$$ASD_{i, MA \to d} = \frac{TMS_{i, MA \to d}}{TS_{i, MA \to d}} \tag{C.8}$$

where

$ASD_{i, MA \to d}$ Average Shipment Distance for products of the ith industry from the Middle Atlantic census region to the dth market destination (i.e., census region outside the Middle Atlantic),

$TMS_{i, MA \to d}$ Ton-Miles Shipped from ith industry in the Middle Atlantic census region to the dth market destination,

$TS_{i, MA \to d}$ Tons Shipped from ith industry in the Middle Atlantic census region to the dth market destination.

AVERAGE SHIPMENT DISTANCES FROM SUBREGIONS TO CENSUS REGIONS OUTSIDE THE MIDDLE ATLANTIC. To arrive at average shipment distances from the Susquehanna subregions to the destination census regions (i.e., $ASD_{i, j \to d}$), it is necessary to adjust the average shipments distances from the Middle Atlantic region to the destination census regions (i.e., $ASD_{i, MA \to d}$). This adjustment is made by adding (or subtracting) what may be called a differential distance as follows:

$$ASD_{i, j \to d} = ASD_{i, MA \to d} + DD_{i, j \to d} \tag{C.9}$$

[5] U.S. Bureau of the Census, *Census of Transportation, 1963*, Shipper Series, TC63(P)C1, U.S. Government Printing Office, Washington, D.C.

where

$ASD_{i,j \to d}$ Average Shipment Distance for products of the ith industry from jth subregion to dth market destination,

$ASD_{i,MA \to d}$ Average Shipment Distance for products of the ith industry from the Middle Atlantic region to the dth market destination,

$DD_{i,j \to d}$ Differential Distance between jth subregion and the Middle Atlantic region's average origin for products of the ith industry being shipped to the dth market destination.

In order to measure the differential distance variable in Equation C.9, it is necessary to identify three locations: (1) the subregional center, (2) the average origin location, and (3) a representative destination point. Before describing how these three locations were determined, it is helpful to see how they are used to implement Equation C.9. Figure C.1 illustrates the procedure. First, a line is drawn from the MA average origin location to the destination point. Second, the average destination location is estimated by measuring the average shipment distance from the MA average origin toward the representative destination point along this line. This average destination may be nearer or farther than the region's representative destination point. Finally, the distance from the average destination to the subregional center is taken as the average shipment distance from the subregion to that census region.

Next we describe how the three locations used in Figure C.1 were determined. The subregion center was simply chosen as the major metropolitan center in each subregion. Thus, Elmira, Binghamton, Williamsport, Sunbury, Scranton, Altoona, Harrisburg, and Baltimore were the eight subregion centers used. Destination points were chosen by taking major cities believed to be representative destinations for interregional shipments to their regions. The principal criterion in selection of the destination point was that it be a large SMSA, centrally located in the census region, or at least having several of the SMSA's lying along a line from

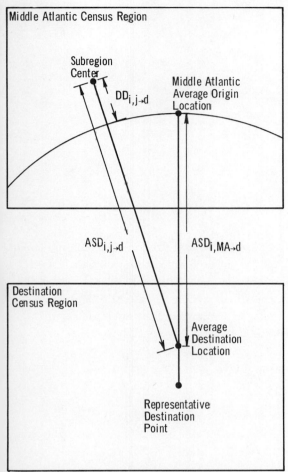

FIGURE C.1. Illustration of procedure used to implement Equation C.8.

the average origin to the destination point. Using this criterion we selected the following destination points:

New England—Boston	East South Central—Birmingham	West North Central—Omaha
Middle Atlantic—New York	West South Central—Dallas	Mountain—Denver
South Atlantic—Atlanta	East North Central—Chicago	Pacific—San Francisco

Finally, to complete the specification of the three locations used in Figure C.1, we must determine the average origin location for the Middle Atlantic region. For this purpose, the mean location of all metropolitan-area employment for a given industry in the Middle Atlantic region of New York, New Jersey, and Pennsylvania is chosen. Industry employment estimates for standard metropolitan statistical areas are drawn from the *1964 County Business Patterns*.[6] These employment estimates and the location of the central city of each metropolitan area are used to compute a mean location of employment for each industry.

To make these calculations, an x–y coordinate system for the Middle Atlantic region is constructed by overlaying a map with transparent cross-section paper and noting the coordinates of the central city of each SMSA. If X_k, $Y_k =$ arbitrary coordinates for the kth SMSA, and E_{ik} = Employment in the ith industry in the kth SMSA, then the location of the average origin $(\bar{X}_i, \bar{Y}_i)$ for the ith industry is given by

$$\bar{X}_i = \frac{\sum_k X_k E_{ik}}{\sum_k E_{ik}}, \qquad \bar{Y} = \frac{\sum_k Y_k E_{ik}}{\sum_k E_{ik}} \tag{C.10}$$

The location of this point does, of course, vary among industries. For most of the industries, the average origin location falls in northeastern Pennsylvania. For industries with heavy concentration of employment in a few cities, such as the primary metals industry, this location is shifted markedly, in the instance of primary metals to a location near Altoona, Pennsylvania.

Finally, by way of illustration, Table C.1 shows the results of the computations for the Harrisburg subregion for the Fabricated Metals Products Industry (SIC 34). For this industry, the average origin location in the Middle Atlantic region is roughly 50 miles northeast of Allentown, Pennsylvania. Therefore, as shown in Table C.1, Harrisburg has greater-than-average shipment distance than other census regions to the New England region but less-than-average shipment distance to all other regions in the United States. In a similar fashion, average shipment distances from each subregion center to each destination census region for each of the other fourteen industries are derived.

[6] U.S. Bureau of the Census, *County Business Patterns, 1964*, U.S. Government Printing Office, Washington, D.C.

TABLE C.1

Average Shipment Distance from the Harrisburg Subregion for the Fabricated Metal Products Industry (SIC 34)

Destination Region	Origin Point	
	Harrisburg $ASD_{34,H \to d}$	Middle Atlantic $ASD_{34,MA \to d}$
New England	276	205
East North Central	344	399
West North Central	816	876
South Atlantic	316	382
East South Central	570	639
West South Central	1,166	1,234
Mountain	1,788	1,848
Pacific	2,380	2,444
United States	—	298

AVERAGE SHIPMENT DISTANCES FROM SUBREGIONS TO OTHER DESTINATIONS INSIDE THE MIDDLE ATLANTIC REGION. A special problem exists in applying the procedure described to estimate average distances to destinations inside the Middle Atlantic region. Although an intra-Middle Atlantic average shipment distance (i.e., $ASD_{i,MA \to MA}$) is available from the *Census of Transportation*, there is no straightforward way of comparing a subregional origin with the average Middle Atlantic origin for the adjustment of this average shipment distance, as in the interregional shipment case.

In solving this problem, although special procedures were used, essentially the same principle developed for the interregional shipments was applied to the intraregional case. As a first step, the Middle Atlantic region was divided into five sectors centered on the major metropolitan areas of New York, Philadelphia, Pittsburgh, Buffalo, and Albany (see Figure C.2). Each of these five sectors is then treated in a fashion analogous to how census regions outside the Middle Atlantic are treated. For each destination sector, an equation analogous to Equation C.9 is used as follows:

$$ASD_{i,j \to d_{MA}} = ASD_{i,MA \to d_{MA}} + DD_{i,j \to d_{MA}}$$ (C.11)

where

$ASD_{i,j \to d_{MA}}$ Average Shipment Distance for products of the ith industry from the jth subregion to the dth market destination inside the Middle Atlantic region,

$ASD_{i,MA \to d_{MA}}$ Average Shipment Distance for products of the ith industry from the Middle Atlantic origin to the dth market destination inside the Middle Atlantic region,

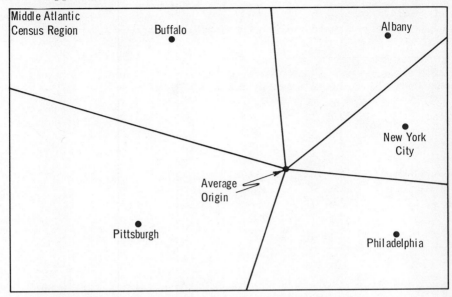

FIGURE C.2. Division of Middle Atlantic census region into sectors.

$DD_{i,j \to d_{MA}}$ Differential Distance between the jth subregion and the
Middle Atlantic Region's average origin for products of the
ith industry being shipped to the dth market destination inside
the Middle Atlantic region.

The same kinds of information used in the previous case are again required, as
Figure C.3 illustrates, to implement this equation. In short, everything done in this
case is exactly the same as in the preceding case, with one minor complication.
This complication arises because the *Census of Transportation* does not provide data
on average shipment distances from the Middle Atlantic region to each of its
five sectors. (Thus $ASD_{i,MA \to d_{MA}}$ cannot be estimated as its counterpart $ASD_{i,MA \to d}$
was in the preceding case by Equation C.8). All the census provides is data on
average shipment distances from Middle Atlantic origins to Middle Atlantic
destinations (i.e., $ASD_{i,MA \to MA}$). This value is adjusted to arrive at the desired
average shipment distance for each sector by a measure reflecting the relative
distance from the Middle Atlantic average origin to each of the respective sector
representative destination points as follows:

$$ASD_{i,MA \to d_{MA}} = (D_{MA \to d_{MA}}/\bar{D}_{MA})ASD_{i,MA \to MA} \qquad (C.12$$

$$\bar{D}_{MA} = \sum_d [(D_{MA \to d_{MA}})P_d]/P_d \qquad (C.13$$

where

$ASD_{i,MA \to d_{MA}}$ Average Shipment Distance for products of the ith industry
from the average Middle Atlantic origin to the dth market
destination inside the Middle Atlantic region,

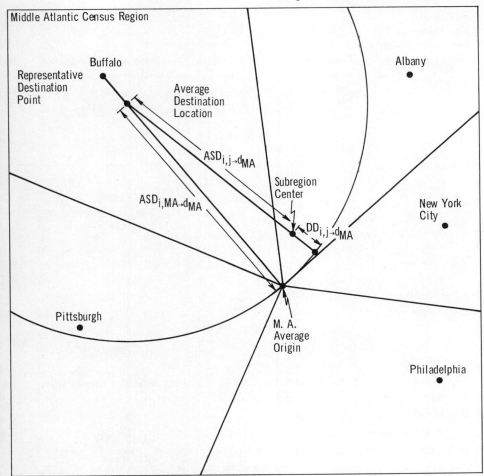

FIGURE C.3. Illustration of procedure used to implement Equation C.11.

$D_{MA \to d_{MA}}$ Distance from the average Middle Atlantic origin to the destination point of the dth sector in the Middle Atlantic region,

$\bar{D}_{MA}$ average of all $D_{MA \to d_{MA}}$ weighted by the estimated size of the market in each sector of the Middle Atlantic region,

$ASD_{i, MA \to MA}$ Average Shipment Distance from Middle Atlantic origins to Middle Atlantic destinations,

P_d Population of the standard metropolitan statistical areas of the dth sector in the Middle Atlantic region (used as an index of market size).

By way of illustration, Table C.2 shows the results for the Harrisburg subregion and SIC Industry 34. As one would expect, because the average origin of this

TABLE C.2

Average Shipment Distances from the Harrisburg Subregion to Middle Atlantic Sectors for SIC Industry 34

Sector Center	Distance from Middle Atlantic Average Origin to Sector Center $D_{MA \to d_{MA}}$	Average Shipment Distance from Middle Atlantic Average Origin to dth market destination $ASD_{34,MA \to d_{MA}}$	Harrisburg to dth market destination $ASD_{34,H \to d_{MA}}$
New York	90	80*	144
Philadelphia	66	59	77
Pittsburgh	277	202	137
Buffalo	221	197	183
Albany	162	144	211

Note: Average distance weighted by sector SMSA population—112 miles.
Intra-Middle Atlantic average shipment distance—100 miles.

* e.g. $^{90}/_{112} (100) = 80$.

industry is about 50 miles northwest of Allentown, Harrisburg has greater-than-average shipment distance to New York, Philadelphia, and Albany, but less-than-average shipment distance to Pittsburgh and Buffalo. In this manner, average shipment distances to the five sectors of the Middle Atlantic region are generated for each subregion and each of the fifteen industries.

This completes the procedure for estimating average distance shipped from Susquehanna subregions to their markets. Next we describe how information on highway quality is used to adjust these estimates.

Adjustment of Average Shipment Distances for Highway Quality. Because the estimated average shipment distances to market are to be used as proxies for transportation costs to market, an adjustment was made to reflect varying operating costs over highways of varying quality (i.e., $ADJH_N{}^t$ and $ADJH_{j \to d}^t$ in Equations C.4 and C.7).[7] To do this, all highway shipment distances are standardized by operating costs. These adjustments are implemented first for the 1960 highway system and second for the 1975 highway system, the estimated completion year of the Interstate Highway System. From the average shipment distances for these two years, a rate of change in the accessibility factor is derived for the period from 1960 to 1975.

Making adjustments for highway quality involves two steps, (1) determining the amount of adjustment for highways of different quality, and (2) using this information to arrive at the adjustment factors.

ADJUSTMENT FACTOR FOR HIGHWAY QUALITY. Basically, two types of highways are available for commodity movements—limited-access, divided highways (typical of the Interstate Highway System and toll-road facilities) and two- or four-lane,

---

[7] Of course, only a portion of the tons of shipments and ton-miles data used to derive the average shipment distance result from highway transportation. Therefore these adjustments for highway facilities are applied only to that portion of these commodity flows occurring on highways.

unlimited-access, undivided facilities. According to an Interstate Commerce Commission study for the Middle Atlantic region,[8] the average operating speed of line-haul units in 1960 was about 30 mph. The line-haul cost per vehicle mile for this average operating speed for that year was 39.4 cents per mile. On the other hand, average operating speed over limited-access freeways is generally about 45 mph. According to the same study, the line-haul cost per vehicle mile for 45-mph operation is 32.7 cents per mile. Thus the cost for the average speed, which is assumed to reflect operation over unlimited access highways, is about 20 percent higher than that for 45-mph or limited-access highway operation. Therefore, for those shipment distances for which limited-access highways are not available, the shipment distance is increased 20 percent to reflect the higher cost of operation over lower quality highways.

COMPUTATION OF HIGHWAY ADJUSTMENTS. Implementation of the 20 percent adjustment required that the number of miles of limited-access and unlimited-access highways between each subregion and each census region's representative destination be computed. For each pair of points, the 1960 low-cost route is determined, that is, the route that minimized the total line-haul operating costs is computed at the rates just cited.[9] Limited-access and unlimited-access highway route segments are then identified. These route segments are compared with the average shipment distance, and those portions of the average shipment distance over unlimited-access highway segments are increased in length by 20 percent. In accordance with this reasoning, the following equation is applied to the low-cost

---

[8] Interstate Commerce Commission, "Cost of Transporting Freight by Class I and Class II Motor Common Carriers of General Commodities," Statement No. 1-62, Washington, D.C., 1962.

[9] It was found that the simplest operational procedure for identifying the low-cost route was to compute the costs for several alternative routes. First, the estimated cost for the minimum distance route (as given in "Standard Highway Mileage Guide" published by Rand McNally & Co., 1960) was computed. Then longer alternate routes incorporating freeways not on the minimum-distance route are considered. Examination of a few obvious alternatives in this fashion leads to identification of the low-cost route.

routes to arrive at a highway quality adjustment factor:

$$ADJH^{60}_{i,j\to d} = (NFM^{60}_{i,j\to d})\left(\frac{C_{\text{avg}}}{C_{45}} - 1\right)PH_{i,MA} \tag{C.14}$$

where

$ADJH^{60}_{i,j\to d}$ ADJustment of average shipment distances for the quality of Highway facilities from the jth subregion to the dth market destination in 1960,

$NFM^{60}_{i,j\to d}$ NonFreeway Mileage included in $ASD_{i,j\to d}$ in 1960,

C_{avg} operating Cost per mile at average speed (estimated to be 39.4 cents per mile),

C_{45} operating Cost per mile at 45 mph (estimated to be 32.7 cents per mile),

$PH_{i,MA}$ Proportion of tons shipped by Highway in the ith industry from the Middle Atlantic census region (data given in Table 6, Shipper Series Reports, *1963 Census of Transportation*).

To obtain an adjusted factor for 1975, the 1960 adjustment factor was modified as follows:

$$ADJH^{75}_{i,j\to d} = (ADJH^{60}_{i,j\to d}) \frac{LCM^{75}_{j\to d}}{LCM^{60}_{j\to d}} \tag{C.15}$$

where

$LCM^{t}_{j\to d}$ Low-Cost route Mileage from jth subregion to dth destination at time t.

The low-cost route for 1975 was determined in the same manner just described for 1960, except that this time the Interstate Highway System was assumed to be completed.[10]

[10] A convenient source of information for these computations is Portland Cement Association, "Interstate Highway System Map and Mileages" (available upon request from P.C.A., 33 W. Grand Avenue, Chicago, Ill.).

TABLE C.3

Adjusted Average Shipment Distances for Harrisburg for SIC Industry 34 for 1960 and 1975

Destination	Average Shipment Distance from Tables C.1 and C.2	Adjusted Average Shipment Distances* $AASD^t_{i,j \to d}$	
		1960	1975
New York	144	144	138
Philadelphia	77	77	77
Pittsburgh	173	173	173
Buffalo	252	287	287
Albany	257	257	231
Middle Atlantic (Weighted Mean)†	—	147	142
New England	276	304	285
East North Central	344	344	344
West North Central	816	836	807
South Atlantic	316	359	327
East South Central	570	649	571
West South Central	1,166	1,299	1,179
Mountain	1,788	1,942	1,816
Pacific	2,380	2,616	2,377

* 69 percent of tons shipped of SIC Industry 34 products from Middle Atlantic region are by truck, therefore 31 percent of the shipment distance was held constant.

† The Middle Atlantic adjusted average shipment distance is computed by weighting the sector distances by the proportion of metropolitan population in each sector.

To complete estimation of highway quality adjustment factors, it is only necessary to point out that the adjustment for the national average shipment distance (i.e., $ADJH^t_{i,N}$) is estimated in a fashion completely analogous to Equations C.14 and C.15. In particular, the computation equations may be arrived at by replacing the subscript, $j \to d$, in Equations C.14 and C.15 with the subscript N, indicating that the variables represent national averages.

Again by way of illustration, the results of these computations for the Harrisburg subregion for SIC Industry 34 are shown in Table C.3. Because Harrisburg in 1960 had limited-access facilities to New York, Philadelphia, Pittsburgh, Albany, and Chicago, the adjusted distance for these destinations is the same as the average shipment distance shown in Tables C.1 and C.2. For some of these destinations, the distance is slightly shorter for 1975 due to the construction of more direct routes. For destinations south of the Middle Atlantic region and west of the East North Central region, the 1960 adjusted distance is considerably longer than the average shipment distance due to the lack of limited-access highways in these regions. By 1975, these distances are reduced somewhat due to the effect of the construction of the Interstate Highway System. However, for some destination points such as Buffalo, the 1960 and 1975 adjusted distances are equal because no major highway improvements are contemplated in this corridor during this period.

The adjustments shown in Table C.3 reflect the fact that 69 percent of tons of shipments of SIC Industry 34 products from the Middle Atlantic region in 1963 were by motor carrier or private truck. The use of this proportion for all shipments probably results in too small an adjustment for short trips and too large an adjustment for long trips because the percent of tons of shipments by truck is generally not constant with length of shipment. However, in lieu of any interregional-shipment data by mode, the constant percentage is used. Because these adjusted average shipment distances are combined to form an average shipment distance to the United States (as in Equation C.6), these differences tend to cancel out in the final computation.

Access to Raw Materials

Conceptually, access to raw materials is viewed in the same way as access to markets, that is, as the ratio of subregional to national transportation costs for each processing group. Due to lack of comparable data in this case, however, access factors for raw materials were developed in a much more subjective fashion. For the two processing industry groups, the capital-intensive processors and the labor-intensive processors, raw materials were identified using the 1958 Input-Output Tables.[11] For each raw material, a judgment was made regarding the accessibility of a subregion to the raw material relative to the accessibility of nearby competitors.[12] For example, the access of each subregion to iron ore was compared with the access of Morristown, Pennsylvania, Sparrows Point, Maryland, and Pittsburgh, Pennsylvania, to iron ore. Only the Baltimore subregion has as good an access to iron ore as these other viable competitors, and therefore it was

[11] See M. R. Goldman, et al., "The Interindustry Structure of the U.S.," *Survey of Current Business*, November 1964, pp. 10–29.

[12] The primary source of information on each subregion's access to resources was the *1962 Minerals Yearbook*, Volume III, Area Reports, U.S. Department of Interior, Bureau of Mines, U.S.G.P.O., 1963.

given a value of 1.0. The other subregions had less favorable access and were assigned values greater than 1. Had a region had better access than its principal competitors, it would have received a value less than 1. These judgment indices are then weighted by the input-output coefficients to obtain a subregion index for that Input-Output industry. These Input-Output industry accessibility indices are then weighted by the ratio of subregional employment in that industry to the subregional employment in the processing industry group in question. This procedure yields a raw material accessibility index weighted according to subregional employment patterns. The estimated market and raw material access factors are shown in Tables 10.7 and 10.8.

Appendix D
Technical
Description
of the Model

The "model of the Susquehanna River Basin" may or may not be viewed as single model; what actually constitutes a model depends upon one's point of view. If one were to count each major computer simulation carried out during the research program as representing an individual model, he would discover 200 models. If he were to count only changes in equation formulation and ignore simple parameter changes, he would find 50 models. By contrast, from the standpoint of regional analysis, it might be maintained that only two models exist—a model of the entire Susquehanna basin divided into eight subregions and a model of one subregion in the basin. During the study, the single subregion model was used to test new formulations in order to save computer time and programming expense. Only after the new equations were showed to be an improvement were they introduced in the larger basin-wide model.

This appendix gives the equations of the one subregion model as it existed at the end of Phase III.[1]

The names of variables and constants that are associated with a particular subregion end with the letter Z in the model presented here. Z is replaced with the letters A, B, C, D, E, F, G, and H to form the multiregion model in order to designate specific subregions. The letter immediately preceding the Z designates the functional subsector with which the quantity is associated, for instance, the letter P refers to the population subsector. If the quantity is common to all areas of the basin, there is no Z, and the final letter designates the subsector.

The constants and initial values that were required in order to simulate this model were taken from Subregion E.

Demographic Subsector[2]

The demographic subsector describes the growth (or decline) of the population in an area. The population is divided into six age classifications. Each age

[1] See the Preface for a description of the three research phases.
[2] See Chapter 8.

classification grows by people reaching the entering age and by people migrating into the area. The classifications decline because people grow out of the age-class and because people emigrate or die.

Population. The total population in an area is the sum of the number of people in each of the six age classifications in that area:

```
POPDZ.K=CHLDZ.K+TNDZ.K+YADZ.K+PMDZ.K+MADZ.K+      1, A
  OLDZ.K
```

```
     PUPDZ - POPULATION (MEN)
     CHLDZ - CHILDREN, AGES 0 TO 13 (MEN)
     TNDZ  - TEENAGERS, AGES 14 TO 19 (MEN)
     YADZ  - YOUNG ADULTS, AGES 20 TO 24 (MEN)
     PMDZ  - PRIME AGED, AGES 25 TO 44 (MEN)
     MADZ  - MIDDLE AGED, AGES 45 TO 64 (MEN)
     OLDZ  - OLDSTERS, OVER 65(MEN)
```

The number of children, ages 0 through 13, is a level formed by the rates of children born and children migrating into the area less the rates of children growing out of this age group and those dying:

```
CHLDZ.K=CHLDZ.J+(DT)(BCHDZ.J+MCHDZ.J-GCHDZ.J-      2, L
  DCHDZ.J)
```

```
CHLDZ=152726                                       2A, N
```

```
     CHLDZ - CHILDREN, AGES 0 TO 13 (MEN)
     BCHDZ - BIRTHS OF CHILDREN (MEN/YR)
     MCHDZ - MIGRATING CHILDREN(MEN/YR)
     GCHDZ - GROWN CHILDREN (MEN/YR)
     DCHDZ - DEATHS OF CHILDREN (MEN/YR)
```

The number of teenagers, ages 14 through 19, is a level formed by the rates of children growing into the teenager class and teenagers migrating into this area less

[3] 1, *A* is the equation number followed by the variable type. The variable types are
A—auxiliary or rate
C—constant
L—level
N—initial value or initially computed constant
S—supplementary (only necessary for printing or plotting results).
For further details on equation writing see Chapter 5.

teenagers growing out of this age class and teenagers dying:

```
TNDZ.K=TNDZ.J+(DT)(GCHDZ.J+MTNDZ.J-GTNDZ.J-        3, L
    DTNDZ.J)

TNDZ=52839                                         3A, N

    TNDZ  - TEENAGERS, AGES 14 TO 19 (MEN)
    GCHDZ - GROWN CHILDREN (MEN/YR)
    MTNDZ - MIGRATING TEENAGERS(MEN/YR)
    GTNDZ - GROWN TEENAGERS (MEN/YR)
    DTNDZ - DEATHS OF TEENAGERS (MEN/YR)
```

Similarly, young adults, aged 20 through 24, prime aged, 25 through 44, and middle-aged, 45 through 64, are levels:

```
YADZ.K=YADZ.J+(DT)(GTNDZ.J+MYADZ.J-GYADZ.J-        4, L
    DYADZ.J)

YADZ=29876                                         4A, N

    YADZ  - YOUNG ADULTS, AGES 20 TO 24 (MEN)
    GTNDZ - GROWN TEENAGERS (MEN/YR)
    MYADZ - MIGRATING YOUNG ADULTS(MEN/YR)
    GYADZ - GROWN YOUNG ADULTS (MEN/YR)
    DYADZ - DEATHS OF YOUNG ADULTS (MEN/YR

PMDZ.K=PMDZ.J+(DT)(GYADZ.J+MPMDZ.J-GPMDZ.J-        5, L
    DPMDZ.J)

PMDZ=160810                                        5A, N

    PMDZ  - PRIME AGED, AGES 25 TO 44 (MEN)
    GYADZ - GROWN YOUNG ADULTS (MEN/YR)
    MPMDZ - MIGRATING PRIME AGED(MEN/YR)
    GPMDZ - GROWN PRIME AGED (MEN/YR)
    DPMDZ - DEATHS OF PRIME AGED (MEN/YR)

MADZ.K=MADZ.J+(DT)(GPMDZ.J+MMADZ.J-GMADZ.J-        6, L
    DMADZ.J)

MADZ=157847                                        6A, N

    MADZ  - MIDDLE AGED, AGES 45 TO 64 (MEN)
    GPMDZ - GROWN PRIME AGED (MEN/YR)
    MMADZ - MIGRATING MIDDLE AGED(MEN/YR)
    GMADZ - GROWN MIDDLE AGED (MEN/YR)
    DMADZ - DEATHS OF MIDDLE AGED(MEN/YR)
```

The number of oldsters, over 65, is also a level formed by the rates of people growing out of the middle-aged class and oldsters migrating into the area less oldsters dying:

```
OLDZ.K=OLDZ.J+(DT)(GMADZ.J+MOLDZ.J-DOLDZ.J+0)    7, L

OLDZ=72455                                        7A, N

    OLDZ  - OLDSTERS, OVER 65(MEN)
    GMADZ - GROWN MIDDLE AGED (MEN/YR)
    MOLDZ - MIGRATING OLDSTERS(MEN/YR)
    DOLDZ - DEATHS OF OLDSTERS (MEN/YR)
```

Birth Rates. The birth rate is defined here to be the live birth rate less the death rate of children under 1 year:

```
BCHDZ.K=LBCDZ.K-DNCDZ.K                           8, A

    BCHDZ - BIRTHS OF CHILDREN (MEN/YR)
    LBCDZ - LIVE BIRTHS OF CHILDREN (MEN/YR)
    DNCDZ - DEATHS OF NEW CHILDREN (MEN/YR)
```

The live-birth rate is the sum of the birth rates to individuals in each of the four fertile age classifications. The birth rate in any age classification is the product of the birth rate per person of that class times the number of people in the class:

```
LBCDZ.K=(BRTDZ.K)(TNDZ.K)+(BRYDZ.K)(YADZ.K)+      9, A
 (BRPDZ.K)(PMDZ.K)+(BRMDZ.K)(MADZ.K)

    LBCDZ - LIVE BIRTHS OF CHILDREN (MEN/YR)
    BRTDZ - BIRTH RATE TO TEENAGERS(1/YR
    TNDZ  - TEENAGERS, AGES 14 TO 19 (MEN)
    BRYDZ - BIRTH RATE TO YOUNG ADL(1/YR
    YADZ  - YOUNG ADULTS, AGES 20 TO 24 (MEN)
    BRPDZ - BIRTH RATE TO PRIME AGD(1/YR
    PMDZ  - PRIME AGED, AGES 25 TO 44 (MEN)
    BRMDZ - BIRTH RATE TO MIDDL AGD(1/YR
    MADZ  - MIDDLE AGED, AGES 45 TO 64 (MEN)
```

The birth rate per person in each of the fertile age classifications depends on the local unemployment rate and a trend over time. Before the trend adjustment, the birth rate is computed as the sum of a basic birth rate, depending on unemployment and a residual that forces the birth rate to equal the known birth rate at time equal to 0.

```
BRTDZ.K=(TRBRD.K)(BBTDZ.K+RBTDZ)                      10, A

      BRTDZ - BIRTH RATE TO TEENAGERS(1/YR
      TRBRD - TREND IN BIRTH RATES (D)
      BBTDZ - BASIC BIRTH RATE-TEENAGR (1/YR)
      RBTDZ - RESIDUAL IN BIRTH RT-TEENAGR (1/YR)
```

The trend over time is provided in a table:

```
TRBRD.K=TABLE(TTBRD,TIME.K,0,50,5)                    11, A

TTBRD*=1/.8195/.8087/.8306/.8471/.8565/.8556/         11A, C
   .8507/.849/.849/.849

      TRBRD - TREND IN BIRTH RATES (D)
      TTBRD - TABLE FOR TREND IN BIRTH RATES (D)
      TIME  - TIME
```

The basic birth rate is related to the smoothed local unemployment rate by another table:

```
BBTDZ.K=TABHL(TBBTD,SLULZ.K,.03,.10,.07)              12, A

TBBTD*=43.0E-3/17.5E-3 1/YR                           12A, C

      BBTDZ - BASIC BIRTH RATE-TEENAGR (1/YR)
      TBBTD - TABLE BASIC BIRTH RATE-TEENAGR
      SLULZ - SMOOTHED LOCAL UNEMPLOYMENT RATE (D)
```

The residual, which is calculated only at time equal to 0, is used to force the initial birth rate to equal its known value. Consequently, it is equal to the initial birth rate minus the basic birth rate.

```
RBTDZ=IBTDZ-BBTDZ                                     13, N

IBTDZ=15.4E-3 1/YR                                    13A, C

      RBTDZ - RESIDUAL IN BIRTH RT-TEENAGR (1/YR)
      IBTDZ - INITIAL BIRTH RATE TO TEENAGERS
      BBTDZ - BASIC BIRTH RATE-TEENAGR (1/YR)
```

The birth rate per person in the young adult and prime age classifications is computed similarly:

```
BRYDZ.K=(TRBRD.K)(BBYDZ.K+RBYDZ)                    14, A

     BRYDZ - BIRTH RATE TO YOUNG ADL(1/YR
     TRBRD - TREND IN BIRTH RATES (D)
     BBYDZ - BASIC BIRTH RATE-YNG ADL (1/YR)
     RBYDZ - RESIDUAL IN BIRTH RT-YNG ADL(1/YR)

BBYDZ.K=TABHL(TBBYD,SLULZ.K,.03,.10,.07)            15, A

TBBYD*=137.5E-3/106.E-3 1/YR                        15A, C

     BBYDZ - BASIC BIRTH RATE-YNG ADL (1/YR)
     TBBYD - TABLE BASIC BIRTH RATE-YNG ADL
     SLULZ - SMOOTHED LOCAL UNEMPLOYMENT RATE (D)

RBYDZ=IBYDZ-BBYDZ                                   16, N

IBYDZ=108.5E-3 1/YR                                 16A, C

     RBYDZ - RESIDUAL IN BIRTH RT-YNG ADL(1/YR)
     IBYDZ - INITIAL BIRTH RATE TO YOUNG ADULTS
     BBYDZ - BASIC BIRTH RATE-YNG ADL (1/YR)

BRPDZ.K=(TRBRD.K)(BBPDZ.K+RBPDZ)                    17, A

     BRPDZ - BIRTH RATE TO PRIME AGD(1/YR
     TRBRD - TREND IN BIRTH RATES (D)
     BBPDZ - BASIC BIRTH RATE-PRM AGD (1/YR)
     RBPDZ - RESIDUAL IN BIRTH RT-PRM AGD(1/YR)

BBPDZ.K=TABHL(TBBPD,SLULZ.K,.03,.10,.07)            18, A

TBBPD*=47.0E-3/40.5E-3 1/YR                         18A, C

     BBPDZ - BASIC BIRTH RATE-PRM AGD (1/YR)
     TBBPD - TABLE BASIC BIRTH RATE-PRM AGD
     SLULZ - SMOOTHED LOCAL UNEMPLOYMENT RATE (D)

RBPDZ=IBPDZ-BBPDZ                                   19, N

IBPDZ=43.8E-3 1/YR                                  19A, C

     RBPDZ - RESIDUAL IN BIRTH RT-PRM AGD(1/YR)
     IBPDZ - INITIAL BIRTH RATE TO PRM AGD
     BBPDZ - BASIC BIRTH RATE-PRM AGD (1/YR)
```

The birth rate of the middle-aged is so small that it is simply the product of the trend and a constant basic birth rate.

```
BRMDZ.K=(TRBRD.K)(BBMD)                          20, A

BBMD=.1E-3 1/YR                                  20A, C

    BRMDZ - BIRTH RATE TO MIDDL AGD(1/YR
    TRBRD - TREND IN BIRTH RATES (D)
    BBMD  - BASIC BIRTH RATE-MID AGD
```

Growing Rates. The rate of children growing out of the children class is the number of children in the class divided by the time spent in that class:

```
GCHDZ.K=CHLDZ.K/DCPD                             21, A

DCPD=14 YEARS                                    21A, C

    GCHDZ - GROWN CHILDREN (MEN/YR)
    CHLDZ - CHILDREN, AGES 0 TO 13 (MEN)
    DCPD  - DURATION OF CHILDHOOD PERIOD
```

The rates of growing out of the teenagers, young adults, and prime-aged and middle-aged classes are similar:

```
GTNDZ.K=TNDZ.K/DTPD                              22, A

DTPD=6 YEARS                                     22A, C

    GTNDZ - GROWN TEENAGERS (MEN/YR)
    TNDZ  - TEENAGERS, AGES 14 TO 19 (MEN)
    DTPD  - DURATION OF TEENAGE PERIOD

GYADZ.K=YADZ.K/DYPD                              23, A

DYPD=5 YEARS                                     23A, C

    GYADZ - GROWN YOUNG ADULTS (MEN/YR)
    YADZ  - YOUNG ADULTS, AGES 20 TO 24 (MEN)
    DYPD  - DURATION OF YOUNG ADULT PERIOD
```

```
GPMDZ.K=PMDZ.K/DPPD                                    24, A

DPPD=20 YEARS                                          24A, C

     GPMDZ - GROWN PRIME AGED (MEN/YR)
     PMDZ  - PRIME AGED, AGES 25 TO 44 (MEN)
     DPPD  - DURATION OF PRIME AGE PERIOD

GMADZ.K=MADZ.K/DMPD                                    25, A

DMPD=20 YEARS                                          25A, C

     GMADZ - GROWN MIDDLE AGED (MEN/YR)
     MADZ  - MIDDLE AGED, AGES 45 TO 64 (MEN)
     DMPD  - DURATION OF MIDDLE AGE PERIOD
```

Death Rates. The death rate of children during the first year is the product of the fractional death rate, the trend in that death rate, and the number of live births:

```
DNCDZ.K=(DRNCD)(TDRND.K)(LBCDZ.K)                      26, A

DRNCD=24E-03 D                                         26A, C

     DNCDZ - DEATHS OF NEW CHILDREN (MEN/YR)
     DRNCD - DEATH RATE PERCENTAGE OF NEW CHILDREN
     TDRND - TREND IN DEATH RATE PERCENTAGE OF
                NEW CHILDREN(D)
     LBCDZ - LIVE BIRTHS OF CHILDREN (MEN/YR)
```

The trend in this death rate is provided in a table:

```
TDRND.K=TABHL(TTDND,TIME.K,0,50,50)                    27, A

TTDND*=1/0.8                                           27A, C

     TDRND - TREND IN DEATH RATE PERCENTAGE OF
                NEW CHILDREN(D)
     TTDND - TABLE FOR TDRND (D)
     TIME  - TIME
```

The death rate of children depends on the fractional death rate of children, the trend in the death rate of children over time, and the number of children:

```
DCHDZ.K=(DRCHD)(TDRCD.K)(CHLDZ.K)              28, A

DRCHD=0.56E-03                                 28A, C

     DCHDZ - DEATHS OF CHILDREN (MEN/YR)
     DRCHD - DEATH RATE OF CHILDREN(MEN/MAN/YR)
     TDRCD - TREND IN DEATH RATE OF CHILDREN (D)
     CHLDZ - CHILDREN, AGES 0 TO 13 (MEN)
```

The trend in the death rate of children over time is simply a table function with time as the independent variable:

```
TDRCD.K=TABHL(TTDCD,TIME.K,0,50,50)            29, A

TTDCD*=1/.875                                  29A, C

     TDRCD - TREND IN DEATH RATE OF CHILDREN (D)
     TTDCD - TABLE FOR TDRCD (D)
     TIME  - TIME
```

The death rates of the other age classifications are similar:

```
DTNDZ.K=(DRTND)(TDRTD.K)(TNDZ.K)               30, A

DRTND=0.7E-03 1/YR                             30A, C

     DTNDZ - DEATHS OF TEENAGERS (MEN/YR)
     DRTND - DEATH RATE OF TEENAGERS
     TDRTD - TREND IN DEATH RATE OF TEENAGERS (D)
     TNDZ  - TEENAGERS, AGES 14 TO 19 (MEN)

TDRTD.K=TABHL(TTDTD,TIME.K,0,50,50)            31, A

TTDTD*=1/.8235 D                               31A, C

     TDRTD - TREND IN DEATH RATE OF TEENAGERS (D)
     TTDTD - TABLE FOR TDRTD
     TIME  - TIME
```

DYADZ.K=(DRYAD)(TDRYD.K)(YADZ.K)   32, A

DRYAD=1.0E-03 1/YR   32A, C

    DYADZ - DEATHS OF YOUNG ADULTS (MEN/YR
    DRYAD - DEATH RATE OF YOUNG ADULTS
    TDRYD - TREND IN DEATH RATE OF YOUNG ADULTS (D)
    YADZ   - YOUNG ADULTS, AGES 20 TO 24 (MEN)

TDRYD.K=TABHL(TTDYD,TIME.K,0,50,50)   33, A

TTDYD*=1/.8235 D   33A, C

    TDRYD - TREND IN DEATH RATE OF YOUNG ADULTS (D)
    TTDYD - TABLE FOR TDRYD
    TIME   - TIME

DPMDZ.K=(DRPMD)(TDRPD.K)(PMDZ.K)   34, A

DRPMD=1.9E-03 1/YR   34A, C

    DPMDZ - DEATHS OF PRIME AGED (MEN/YR)
    DRPMD - DEATH RATE OF PRIME AGED
    TDRPD - TREND IN DEATH RATE OF PRIME AGED (D)
    PMDZ   - PRIME AGED, AGES 25 TO 44 (MEN)

TDRPD.K=TABHL(TTDPD,TIME.K,0,50,50)   35, A

TTDPD*=1/.5263 D   35A, C

    TDRPD - TREND IN DEATH RATE OF PRIME AGED (D)
    TTDPD - TABLE FOR TDRPD
    TIME   - TIME

DMADZ.K=(DRMAD)(TDRMD.K)(MADZ.K)   36, A

DRMAD=12E-03 1/YR   36A, C

    DMADZ - DEATHS OF MIDDLE AGED(MEN/YR)
    DRMAD - DEATH RATE OF MIDDLE AGED
    TDRMD - TREND IN DEATH RATE OF MIDDLE AGED (D)
    MADZ   - MIDDLE AGED, AGES 45 TO 64 (MEN)

TDRMD.K=TABHL(TTDMD,TIME.K,0,50,50)   37, A

TTDMD*=1/.9167 D   37A, C

    TDRMD - TREND IN DEATH RATE OF MIDDLE AGED (D)
    TTDMD - TABLE FOR TDRMD
    TIME   - TIME

```
DOLDZ.K=(DROLD)(TDROD.K)(OLDZ.K)                    38, A

DROLD=95E-03                                        38A, C

    DOLDZ  -  DEATHS OF OLDSTERS (MEN/YR)
    DROLD  -  DEATH RATE OF OLDSTERS(MEN/MAN/YR)
    TDROD  -  TREND IN DEATH RATE OF OLDSTERS (D)
    OLDZ   -  OLDSTERS, OVER 65(MEN)

TDROD.K=TABHL(TTDOD,TIME.K,0,50,50)                 39, A

TTDOD*=1/.9091                                      39A, C

    TDROD  -  TREND IN DEATH RATE OF OLDSTERS (D)
    TTDOD  -  TABLE FOR TDROD (D)
    TIME   -  TIME
```

The death rate of all ages is the sum of the death rates of the six age classifications:

```
DTHDZ.K=DCHDZ.K+DTNDZ.K+DYADZ.K+DPMDZ.K+            40, S
    DMADZ.K+DOLDZ.K

    DTHDZ  -  DEATHS (MEN
    DCHDZ  -  DEATHS OF CHILDREN (MEN/YR)
    DTNDZ  -  DEATHS OF TEENAGERS (MEN/YR)
    DYADZ  -  DEATHS OF YOUNG ADULTS (MEN/YR
    DPMDZ  -  DEATHS OF PRIME AGED (MEN/YR)
    DMADZ  -  DEATHS OF MIDDLE AGED(MEN/YR)
    DOLDZ  -  DEATHS OF OLDSTERS (MEN/YR)
```

Migration Rates. Migration rates can be positive or negative; positive rates are understood to mean net movement into the area.

Children migrate with their parents. Consequently, the rate of migration of children depends on the number of children per individual in each of the fertile age classifications and the number of people in those classifications migrating. Because the number of children per adult can vary over time, a "normal" number of children migrating is first computed by summing the products of the "normal" number of children per individual in an age classification times the number of individuals in that age classification migrating:

```
MCHDZ.K=(NMCDZ.K)(CHLDZ.K)/TICDZ.K                    41, A

    MCHDZ - MIGRATING CHILDREN(MEN/YR)
    NMCDZ - NORMAL NUMBER OF MIGRATING CHILDREN(MEN/YR)
    CHLDZ - CHILDREN, AGES 0 TO 13 (MEN)
    TICDZ - TOTAL INDICATED NUMBER OF CHILDREN(MEN)
```

The actual migration rate is computed by multiplying the normal number of migrating children by the ratio of the actual number of children in the geographic subregion to the "normal" or indicated number of children:

```
NMCDZ.K=(0.090)(MTNDZ.K)+(.473)(MYADZ.K)+            42, A
   (.903)(MPMDZ.K)+(.0875)(MMADZ.K)

    NMCDZ - NORMAL NUMBER OF MIGRATING CHILDREN(MEN/YR)
    MTNDZ - MIGRATING TEENAGERS(MEN/YR)
    MYADZ - MIGRATING YOUNG ADULTS(MEN/YR)
    MPMDZ - MIGRATING PRIME AGED(MEN/YR)
    MMADZ - MIGRATING MIDDLE AGED(MEN/YR)
```

The normal or indicated number of children is simply the sum of the products of the number of children per individual in each age classification times the number of people in that classification:

```
TICDZ.K=(0.090)(TNDZ.K)+(.473)(YADZ.K)+             43, A
   (.858)(PMDZ.K)+(.061)(MADZ.K)

    TICDZ - TOTAL INDICATED NUMBER OF CHILDREN(MEN)
    TNDZ  - TEENAGERS, AGES 14 TO 19 (MEN)
    YADZ  - YOUNG ADULTS, AGES 20 TO 24 (MEN)
    PMDZ  - PRIME AGED, AGES 25 TO 44 (MEN)
    MADZ  - MIDDLE AGED, AGES 45 TO 64 (MEN)
```

Migration of an individual old enough to make his own decision depends upon two factors: the availability of jobs and the individual's willingness to migrate. A person's willingness to migrate, in turn, depends on his age and his skill level. Thus, the number of teenagers migrating is the product of three quantities: (1) the percent of teenagers migrating, (2) the total number of teenagers, and (3) the multiplier reflecting the effect of skill level on migration:

```
MTNDZ.K=(MPTDZ.K)(TNDZ.K)(ESMDZ.K)                    44, A

    MTNDZ  -  MIGRATING TEENAGERS(MEN/YR)
    MPTDZ  -  MIGRATING PERCENT OF TEENAGERS(1/YR
    TNDZ   -  TEENAGERS, AGES 14 TO 19 (MEN)
    ESMDZ  -  EFFECT OF SKILL LEVEL ON MIGRATION (D)
```

The percent of teenagers migrating is linearly related to two terms: (1) the delayed difference in unemployment rates and (2) the reciprocal of the number of teenagers:

```
MPTDZ.K=MITDZ.K+(MPBTD)(DDUDZ.K)                      45, A

MPBTD=-.499 1/YR                                      45A, C

MITDZ.K=(MPCTD/TNDZ.K)+MPATD                          45B, A

MPCTD=0 MEN/YR                                        45C, C

MPATD=-.00109 1/YR                                    45D, C

    MPTDZ  -  MIGRATING PERCENT OF TEENAGERS(1/YR
    MPBTD  -  MIGRATING PERCENT FACTOR B FOR TEENAGERS
    DDUDZ  -  DIFFERENCE IN UNEMPLOYMENT AS AFFECTS
                  MIGRATION (D)
    MPCTD  -  MIGRATING PERCENT FACTOR C FOR TEENAGERS
    TNDZ   -  TEENAGERS, AGES 14 TO 19 (MEN)
    MPATD  -  MIGRATING PERCENT FACTOR A FOR TEENAGERS
```

The percent of the other age classifications migrating is computed similarly:

```
MYADZ.K=(MPYDZ.K)(YADZ.K)(ESMDZ.K)                    46, A

    MYADZ  -  MIGRATING YOUNG ADULTS(MEN/YR)
    MPYDZ  -  MIGRATING PERCENT YOUNG ADULTS(1/YR
    YADZ   -  YOUNG ADULTS, AGES 20 TO 24 (MEN)
    ESMDZ  -  EFFECT OF SKILL LEVEL ON MIGRATION (D)

MPYDZ.K=M1YDZ.K+(MPBYD)(DDUDZ.K)                      47, A

MPBYD=-1.31 1/YR                                      47A, C
```

M1YDZ.K=(MPCYD/YADZ.K)+MPAYD   47B, A

MPCYD=0 MEN/YR   47C, C

MPAYD=-.00877 1/YR   47D, C

    MPYDZ - MIGRATING PERCENT YOUNG ADULTS(1/YR
    MPBYD - MIGRATING PERCENT FACTOR B FOR YOUNG
           ADULTS
    DDUDZ - DIFFERENCE IN UNEMPLOYMENT AS AFFECTS
           MIGRATION (D)
    MPCYD - MIGRATING PERCENT FACTOR C FOR YOUNG
           ADULTS
    YADZ   - YOUNG ADULTS, AGES 20 TO 24 (MEN)
    MPAYD - MIGRATING PERCENT FACTOR A FOR YOUNG
           ADULTS

MPMDZ.K=(MPPDZ.K)(PMDZ.K)(ESMDZ.K)   48, A

    MPMDZ - MIGRATING PRIME AGED(MEN/YR)
    MPPDZ - MIGRATING PERCENT PRIME AGED (1/YR
    PMDZ   - PRIME AGED, AGES 25 TO 44 (MEN)
    ESMDZ - EFFECT OF SKILL LEVEL ON MIGRATION (D)

MPPDZ.K=M1PDZ.K+(MPBPD)(DDUDZ.K)   49, A

MPBPD=-.308 1/YR   49A, C

M1PDZ.K=(MPCPD/PMDZ.K)+MPAPD   49B, A

MPCPD=171 MEN/YR   49C, C

MPAPD=-.00364 1/YR   49D, C

    MPPDZ - MIGRATING PERCENT PRIME AGED (1/YR
    MPBPD - MIGRATING PERCENT FACTOR B FOR PRIME
           AGED
    DDUDZ - DIFFERENCE IN UNEMPLOYMENT AS AFFECTS
           MIGRATION (D)
    MPCPD - MIGRATING PERCENT FACTOR C FOR PRIME
           AGED
    PMDZ   - PRIME AGED, AGES 25 TO 44 (MEN)
    MPAPD - MIGRATING PERCENT FACTOR A FOR PRIME
           AGED

```
MMADZ.K=(MPADZ.K)(MADZ.K)(ESMDZ.K)                    50, A

    MMADZ - MIGRATING MIDDLE AGED(MEN/YR)
    MPADZ - MIGRATING PERCENT MIDDLE AGED (1/YR
    MADZ  - MIDDLE AGED, AGES 45 TO 64 (MEN)
    ESMDZ - EFFECT OF SKILL LEVEL ON MIGRATION (D)

MPADZ.K=M1MDZ.K+(MPBMD)(DDUDZ.K)                      51, A

MPBMD=-.134 1/YR                                      51A, C

M1MDZ.K=(MPCMD/MADZ.K)+MPAMD                          51B, A

MPCMD=100 MEN/YR                                      51C, C

MPAMD=-.00292 1/YR                                    51D, C

    MPADZ - MIGRATING PERCENT MIDDLE AGED (1/YR
    MPBMD - MIGRATING PERCENT FACTOR B FOR MIDDLE
                AGED
    DDUDZ - DIFFERENCE IN UNEMPLOYMENT AS AFFECTS
                MIGRATION (D)
    MPCMD - MIGRATING PERCENT FACTOR C FOR MIDDLE
                AGED
    MADZ  - MIDDLE AGED, AGES 45 TO 64 (MEN)
    MPAMD - MIGRATING PERCENT FACTOR A FOR MIDDLE
                AGED
```

As oldsters are generally not in the labor market, their migration rate does not depend on the effect of skills:

```
MOLDZ.K=(MPODZ.K)(OLDZ.K)                             52, A

    MOLDZ - MIGRATING OLDSTERS(MEN/YR)
    MPODZ - MIGRATING PERCENT OLDSTERS (1/YR)
    OLDZ  - OLDSTERS, OVER 65(MEN)

MPODZ.K=M1ODZ.K+(MPBOD)(DDUDZ.K)                      53, A

MPBOD=-.080 1/YR                                      53A, C
```

```
M10DZ.K=(MPCOD/OLDZ.K)+MPAOD                    53B, A

MPAOD=-.00308 1/YR                              53C, C

MPCOD=37 MEN/YR                                 53D, C
```

```
    MPODZ - MIGRATING PERCENT OLDSTERS (1/YR)
    MPBOD - MIGRATING PERCENT FACTOR B FOR OLDSTERS
    DDUDZ - DIFFERENCE IN UNEMPLOYMENT AS AFFECTS
              MIGRATION (D)
    MPCOD - MIGRATING PERCENT FACTOR C FOR OLDSTERS
    OLDZ  - OLDSTERS, OVER 65(MEN)
    MPAOD - MIGRATING PERCENT FACTOR A FOR OLDSTERS
```

The effect of job availability on migration is represented as the lesser of two terms: (1) the difference between local and national unemployment rates and (2) the smoothed difference between the same rates. This means that emigration will not turn up as soon as jobs become scarce but will follow up after a delay. As jobs become available locally, emigration will turn down immediately.

```
DDUDZ.K=MIN(DURLZ.K,DUDDZ.K)                    54, A

    DDUDZ - DIFFERENCE IN UNEMPLOYMENT AS AFFECTS
              MIGRATION (D)
    DURLZ - DIFFERENCE BETWEEN LOCAL AND NATIONAL
              UNEMPLOYMENT RATES(D)
    DUDDZ - DIFFERENCE IN UNEMPLOYMENT DELAYED (D)
```

The smoothed difference in unemployment rates delayed is formed in a standard smoothing equation:[4]

[4] See J. W. Forrester, *Industrial Dynamics*, (Cambridge, Mass.: The M.I.T. Press and John Wiley & Sons, Inc., 1961), p. 406.

```
DUDDZ.K=DUDDZ.J+(DT)(1/DEDUD)(DURLZ.J-           55, L
    DUDDZ.J)

DUDDZ=DURLZ                                      55A, N

DEDUD=2 YEARS                                    55B, C
```

     DUDDZ - DIFFERENCE IN UNEMPLOYMENT DELAYED (D)
     DEDUD - DELAY IN EFFECT OF DIFFERENCE IN UNEMPLOYMENT
            (YEARS)
     DURLZ - DIFFERENCE BETWEEN LOCAL AND NATIONAL
            UNEMPLOYMENT RATES(D)

The effect of skill level on migration is provided in a table where the independent variable is the average skill level:

```
ESMDZ.K=TABLE(TESMD,AVSDZ.K,8,16,1)              56, A

TESMD*=1/1/1/1/1/1/1/1/1 (D)                     56A, C
```

     ESMDZ - EFFECT OF SKILL LEVEL ON MIGRATION (D)
     TESMD - TABLE OF SKILL EFFECT ON MIGRATION
     AVSDZ - AVG SKILL(MAN-YRS/MAN)

The net migration into this area is the sum of the migration rates for each of the age classifications:

```
NIMDZ.K=MCHDZ.K+MTNDZ.K+MYADZ.K+MPMDZ.K+         57, S
    MMADZ.K+MOLDZ.K
```

     NIMDZ - NET IN MIGRATION (MEN)
     MCHDZ - MIGRATING CHILDREN(MEN/YR)
     MTNDZ - MIGRATING TEENAGERS(MEN/YR)
     MYADZ - MIGRATING YOUNG ADULTS(MEN/YR)
     MPMDZ - MIGRATING PRIME AGED(MEN/YR)
     MMADZ - MIGRATING MIDDLE AGED(MEN/YR)
     MOLDZ - MIGRATING OLDSTERS(MEN/YR)

Skills. The availability of skills in a subregion may have considerable consequences for the growth of the subregion. To test this hypothesis, skills have been included in the model although the effect of skills was never fully implemented empirically due to budget constraints.

The average skill level is measured in man-years of education per man. It is the total skill level divided by the number of people in the working-age classifications:

```
AVSDZ.K=SKLDZ.K/EWDZ.K                              58, A

    AVSDZ  -  AVG SKILL(MAN-YRS/MAN)
    SKLDZ  -  TOTAL SKILL LEVEL(MAN-YRS OF EDUCATION)
    EWDZ   -  ELIGIBLE FOR WORK(MEN)
```

The number of people eligible to work is the sum of the teenagers, young adults, prime aged, and middle aged:

```
EWDZ.K=TNDZ.K+YADZ.K+PMDZ.K+MADZ.K                  59, A

    EWDZ   -  ELIGIBLE FOR WORK(MEN)
    TNDZ   -  TEENAGERS, AGES 14 TO 19 (MEN)
    YADZ   -  YOUNG ADULTS, AGES 20 TO 24 (MEN)
    PMDZ   -  PRIME AGED, AGES 25 TO 44 (MEN)
    MADZ   -  MIDDLE AGED, AGES 45 TO 64 (MEN)
```

The total skill level (measured in man-years of education) is a level formed by the difference between the rate of adding skills and the rate of losing skills. This level is initialized with the product of the initial average skill level times the sum of the age classifications in the labor force:

```
SKLDZ.K=SKLDZ.J+(DT)(ASKDZ.J-LSKDZ.J)               60, L

SKLDZ=(IASDZ)(TNDZ+YADZ+PMDZ+MADZ)                  60A, N

IASDZ=10 MAN-YRS/MAN                                60B, C

    SKLDZ  -  TOTAL SKILL LEVEL(MAN-YRS OF EDUCATION)
    ASKDZ  -  ADDED SKILLS(MAN-YRS/YR)
    LSKDZ  -  LOST SKILLS(MAN-YRS/YR)
    IASDZ  -  INITIAL AVERAGE SKILL LEVEL (MAN-YRS
                 OF EDUCATION)
    TNDZ   -  TEENAGERS, AGES 14 TO 19 (MEN)
    YADZ   -  YOUNG ADULTS, AGES 20 TO 24 (MEN)
    PMDZ   -  PRIME AGED, AGES 25 TO 44 (MEN)
    MADZ   -  MIDDLE AGED, AGES 45 TO 64 (MEN)
```

The rate of adding skills is the sum of the rates of adding skills due to migration, children growing up, and additional skills due to continuing education:

```
ASKDZ.K=ASMDZ.K+ASCDZ.K+ASEDZ.K                    61, A

    ASKDZ - ADDED SKILLS(MAN-YRS/YR)
    ASMDZ - ADDED SKILLS DUE TO MIGRATION (MAN-YRS/YR)
    ASCDZ - ADDED SKILLS DUE TO CHILDREN GROWING
              (MAN-YRS/YR)
    ASEDZ - ADDED SKILLS DUE TO CONTINUING EDUCATION
              (MAN-YRS/YR)
```

The added skills due to migration are the product of the average skills of migrants and the sum of the migration rates of the four working-age classes:

```
ASMDZ.K=(SMDZ.K)(MTNDZ.K+MYADZ.K+MPMDZ.K+          62, A
  MMADZ.K)

    ASMDZ - ADDED SKILLS DUE TO MIGRATION (MAN-YRS/YR)
    SMDZ  - SKILL OF MIGRANTS(MAN-YRS/MAN)
    MTNDZ - MIGRATING TEENAGERS(MEN/YR)
    MYADZ - MIGRATING YOUNG ADULTS(MEN/YR)
    MPMDZ - MIGRATING PRIME AGED(MEN/YR)
    MMADZ - MIGRATING MIDDLE AGED(MEN/YR)
```

The average skill of migrants is the average skill level times a bias factor. The bias factor reflects the fact that it is usually those with greater skills who migrate:

```
SMDZ.K=(AVSDZ.K)(BMSD)                             63, A

BMSD=1.20                                          63A, C

    SMDZ  - SKILL OF MIGRANTS(MAN-YRS/MAN)
    AVSDZ - AVG SKILL(MAN-YRS/MAN)
    BMSD  - BIAS FACTOR,MIGRATION OF SKILL(D)
```

The added skills due to children entering the teenage class are the product of the number of children growing up and the education level of those children:

```
ASCDZ.K=(EGCD)(GCHDZ.K)                             64, A

EGCD=8 MAN-YRS/MAN                                  64A, C

    ASCDZ - ADDED SKILLS DUE TO CHILDREN GROWING
              (MAN-YRS/YR)
    EGCD  - EDUCATION OF GROWN CHILDREN
    GCHDZ - GROWN CHILDREN (MEN/YR)
```

The added skills due to continuing education are the product of the number of teenagers and the fraction remaining in school:

```
ASEDZ.K=(ETND.K)(TNDZ.K)                          65, A

      ASEDZ - ADDED SKILLS DUE TO CONTINUING EDUCATION
                   (MAN-YRS/YR)
      ETND  - EDUCATION OF TEENAGERS (MAN-YRS/MAN/YR)
      TNDZ  - TEENAGERS, AGES 14 TO 19 (MEN)
```

The fraction remaining in school, here called the education of teenagers, is the product of the basic education of teenagers and a trend:

```
ETND.K=(BETND)(TETND.K)                           66, A

BETND=0.6 MAN-YRS/MAN-YR                           66A, C

      ETND  - EDUCATION OF TEENAGERS (MAN-YRS/MAN/YR)
      BETND - BASIC EDUCATION OF TEENAGERS
      TETND - TREND IN EDUCATION OF TEENS(D)
```

The trend in education of teens is provided in a table:

```
TETND.K=TABLE(TTETD,TIME.K,0,50,50)               67, A

TTETD*=1/1.66                                      67A, C

      TETND - TREND IN EDUCATION OF TEENS(D)
      TTETD - TABLE FOR TETND (D)
      TIME  - TIME
```

Skills are lost through death and retirement:

```
LSKDZ.K=LSDDZ.K+LSADZ.K                           68, A

      LSKDZ - LOST SKILLS(MAN-YRS/YR)
      LSDDZ - LOST SKILLS DUE TO DEATH (MAN-YRS/YR)
      LSADZ - LOST SKILLS DUE TO AGING (MAN-YRS/YR)
```

Skills lost through death are the product of the average skill level and the sum of the death rates of the working-age classes:

```
LSDDZ.K=(AVSDZ.K)(DTNDZ.K+DYADZ.K+DPMDZ.K+        69, A
  DMADZ.K)

   LSDDZ - LOST SKILLS DUE TO DEATH (MAN-YRS/YR)
   AVSDZ - AVG SKILL(MAN-YRS/MAN)
   DTNDZ - DEATHS OF TEENAGERS (MEN/YR)
   DYADZ - DEATHS OF YOUNG ADULTS (MEN/YR
   DPMDZ - DEATHS OF PRIME AGED (MEN/YR)
   DMADZ - DEATHS OF MIDDLE AGED(MEN/YR)
```

The skills lost due to retirement are the product of the average skill level, the rate of retirement, and a bias factor. The bias factor reflects the fact that older people on the average do not have as high a skill level as the younger people:

```
LSADZ.K=(BRSD)(AVSDZ.K)(GMADZ.K)                  70, A

BRSD=0.8                                          70A, C

   LSADZ - LOST SKILLS DUE TO AGING (MAN-YRS/YR)
   BRSD  - BIAS FACTOR ON RETIREMENT OF SKILLS (D)
   AVSDZ - AVG SKILL(MAN-YRS/MAN)
   GMADZ - GROWN MIDDLE AGED (MEN/YR)
```

Labor Force. The total labor force is the sum of the labor force provided by each age classification. Each term is therefore the product of the fraction of that age class in the labor force and the number of people in that age class available to work.

```
TLFLZ.K=LF1LZ.K+(FTLLZ.K)(NTNDZ.K)                71, A

LF1LZ.K=(FYLLZ.K)(NYADZ.K)+(FPLLZ.K)(NPMDZ.K)     71A, A
 +(FMLLZ.K)(NMADZ.K)+(FOLLZ.K)(NOLDZ.K)

   TLFLZ - TOTAL LABOR FORCE (MEN)
   FTLLZ - FRACT TEENAGERS IN LABOR FORCE (D)
   NTNDZ - NET TEENAGERS (MEN)
   FYLLZ - FRACT YNG ADULT IN LABOR FORCE (D)
   NYADZ - NET YOUNG ADULTS (MEN)
   FPLLZ - FRACT PRIME AGD IN LABOR FORCE (D)
   NPMDZ - NET PRIME AGED (MEN)
   FMLLZ - FRACT MIDDLE AG IN LABOR FORCE (D)
   NMADZ - NET MIDDLE AGED (MEN)
   FOLLZ - FRACT OLDSTERS   IN LABOR FORCE (D)
   NOLDZ - NET OLDSTERS (MEN)
```

The fraction of teenagers in the labor force is linearly related to the ratio of total employment to total working population and the ratio of the working population to the number of teenagers. The constant term sets this fraction equal to its actual value at time equal to 0.

```
FTLLZ.K=FTALZ+FT1LZ.K+FT2LZ.K                          72, A

FTALZ=FTILZ-FT1LZ-FT2LZ                                72A, N

FTILZ=.277 D                                           72B, C

FT1LZ.K=(FTLBL)(REPLZ.K)                               72C, A

FTLBL=.46 D                                            72D, C

FT2LZ.K=(FTLCL)(WPPLZ.K)/NTNDZ.K                       72E, A

FTLCL=-.02 D                                           72F, C

     FTLLZ - FRACT TEENAGERS IN LABOR FORCE (D)
     FTALZ - FACTOR A-TEENAGERS IN LABOR FORCE(D)
     FTILZ - FRACT TEENAGERS IN LABOR FORCE INITIALLY
     FTLBL - FRACT TEENAGERS IN LABOR FORCE FACTOR B
     REPLZ - RATIO OF EMPLOYMENT TO WORKNG POP(D)
     FTLCL - FRACT TEENAGERS IN LABOR FORCE FACTOR C
     WPPLZ - WORKING POP (MEN)
     NTNDZ - NET TEENAGERS (MEN)
```

The number of teenagers available for work is simply the total number less those that are not available.

```
NTNDZ.K=TNDZ.K-TNPDZ.K                                 73, A

     NTNDZ - NET TEENAGERS (MEN)
     TNDZ  - TEENAGERS, AGES 14 TO 19 (MEN)
     TNPDZ - TEENAGE NON-WORKER(MEN)
```

Teenagers not available for work are represented as the sum of those in institutions and in military service.

```
TNPDZ.K=(TNMRL)(INMLZ.K)+(TRMLZ)(WMSIZ.K)          74, A

TNMRL=.082 D                                       74A, C

TRMLZ=.20 D                                        74B, C
```

```
     TNPDZ - TEENAGE NON-WORKER(MEN)
     TNMRL - TEENAGER/INMATE RATIO (D)
     INMLZ - INMATES (MEN)
     TRMLZ - TEENAGE RATIO IN MILITARY
     WMSIZ - WORKERS IN MILITARY SERVICE
```

For each age classification, the fraction in the labor force and the number available for work are computed similarly.

```
FYLLZ.K=FYALZ+FY1LZ.K+FY2LZ.K                      75, A

FYALZ=FYILZ-FY1LZ-FY2LZ                            75A, N

FYILZ=.691 C                                       75B, C

FY1LZ.K=(FYLBL)(REPLZ.K)                           75C, A

FYLBL=1.09 D                                       75D, C

FY2LZ.K=(FYLCL)(WPPLZ.K)/NYADZ.K                   75E, A

FYLCL=.04 D                                        75F, C
```

```
     FYLLZ - FRACT YNG ADULT IN LABOR FORCE (D)
     FYALZ - FACTOR A-YOUNG ADL IN LABOR FORCE(D)
     FYILZ - FRACT YNG ADULT IN LABOR FORCE INITIALLY
     FYLBL - FRACT YNG ADULT IN LABOR FORCE FACTOR B
     REPLZ - RATIO OF EMPLOYMENT TO WORKNG POP(D)
     FYLCL - FRACT YNG ADULT IN LABOR FORCE FACTOR C
     WPPLZ - WORKING POP (MEN)
     NYADZ - NET YOUNG ADULTS (MEN)
```

```
NYADZ.K=YADZ.K-YNPDZ.K                              76, A

    NYADZ - NET YOUNG ADULTS (MEN)
    YADZ  - YOUNG ADULTS, AGES 20 TO 24 (MEN)
    YNPDZ - YOUNG ADULT NON-WRKR(MEN)

YNPDZ.K=(YNMRL)(INMLZ.K)+(YRMLZ)(WMSIZ.K)          77, A

YNMRL=.057 D                                       77A, C

YRMLZ=.35 D                                        77B, C

    YNPDZ - YOUNG ADULT NON-WRKR(MEN)
    YNMRL - YNG ADLT/INMATE RATIO (D)
    INMLZ - INMATES (MEN)
    YRMLZ - YNG ADLT FRACTION IN MILITARY
    WMSIZ - WORKERS IN MILITARY SERVICE


FPLLZ.K=FPALZ+FP1LZ.K+FP2LZ.K                      78, A

FPALZ=FPILZ-FP1LZ-FP2LZ                            78A, N

FPILZ=.659 D                                       78B, C

FP1LZ.K=(FPLBL)(REPLZ.K)                           78C, A

FPLBL=.707 D                                       78D, C

FP2LZ.K=(FPLCL)(WPPLZ.K)/NPMDZ.K                   78E, A

FPLCL=.07 D                                        78F, C

    FPLLZ - FRACT PRIME AGD IN LABOR FORCE (D)
    FPALZ - FACTOR A-PRIME AGD IN LABOR FORCE(D)
    FPILZ - FRACT PRIME AGD IN LABOR FORCE INITIALLY
    FPLBL - FRACT PRIME AGD IN LABOR FORCE FACTOR B
    REPLZ - RATIO OF EMPLOYMENT TO WORKNG POP(D)
    FPLCL - FRACT PRIME AGD IN LABOR FORCE FACTOR C
    WPPLZ - WORKING POP (MEN)
    NPMDZ - NET PRIME AGED (MEN)
```

```
NPMDZ.K=PMDZ.K-PNPDZ.K                                   79, A

     NPMDZ - NET PRIME AGED (MEN)
     PMDZ  - PRIME AGED, AGES 25 TO 44 (MEN)
     PNPDZ - PRIME AGED NON-WORKER(MEN)

PNPDZ.K=(PNMRL)(INMLZ.K)+(PRMLZ)(WMSIZ.K)                80, A

PNMRL=.234 D                                             80A, C

PRMLZ=.40 D                                              80B, C

     PNPDZ - PRIME AGED NON-WORKER(MEN)
     PNMRL - PRM AGED/INMATE RATIO (D)
     INMLZ - INMATES (MEN)
     PRMLZ - PRM AGED FRACTION IN MILITARY
     WMSIZ - WORKERS IN MILITARY SERVICE

FMLLZ.K=FMALZ+FM1LZ.K+FM2LZ.K                            81, A

FMALZ=FMILZ-FM1LZ-FM2LZ                                  81A, N

FMILZ=.597                                               81B, C

FM1LZ.K=(FMLBL)(REPLZ.K)                                 81C, A

FMLBL=.86                                                81D, C

FM2LZ.K=(FMLCL)(WPPLZ.K)/NMADZ.K                         81E, A

FMLCL=.07                                                81F, C

     FMLLZ - FRACT MIDDLE AG IN LABOR FORCE (D)
     FMALZ - FACTOR A-MIDDLE AG IN LABOR FORCE(D)
     FMILZ - FRACT MIDDLE AG IN LABOR FORCE INITIALLY
     FMLBL - FRACT MIDDLE AG IN LABOR FORCE FACTOR B
     REPLZ - RATIO OF EMPLOYMENT TO WORKNG POP(D)
     FMLCL - FRACT MIDDLE AG IN LABOR FORCE FACTOR C
     WPPLZ - WORKING POP (MEN)
     NMADZ - NET MIDDLE AGED (MEN)

NMADZ.K=MADZ.K-MNPDZ.K                                   82, A

     NMADZ - NET MIDDLE AGED (MEN)
     MADZ  - MIDDLE AGED, AGES 45 TO 64 (MEN)
     MNPDZ - MIDDLE AGED NON-WRKR(MEN)
```

```
MNPDZ.K=(MNMRL)(INMLZ.K)+(MRMLZ)(WMSIZ.K)          83, A

MNMRL=.229                                         83A, C

MRMLZ=.05 D                                        83B, C
```

```
    MNPDZ - MIDDLE AGED NON-WRKR(MEN)
    MNMRL - MDL AGED/INMATE RATIO (D)
    INMLZ - INMATES (MEN)
    MRMLZ - MDL AGED FRACT IN MILITARY
    WMSIZ - WORKERS IN MILITARY SERVICE
```

```
FOLLZ.K=FOALZ+FO1LZ.K+FO2LZ.K                      84, A

FOALZ=FOILZ-FO1LZ-FO2LZ                            84A, N

FOILZ=.150 D                                       84B, C

FO1LZ.K=(FOLBL)(REPLZ.K)                           84C, A

FOLBL=.65 D                                        84D, C

FO2LZ.K=(FOLCL)(WPPLZ.K)/NOLDZ.K                   84E, A

FOLCL=.004 D                                       84F, C
```

```
    FOLLZ - FRACT OLDSTERS  IN LABOR FORCE (D)
    FOALZ - FACTOR A-OLDSTERS  IN LABOR FORCE(D)
    FOILZ - FRACT OLDSTER IN LABOR FORCE INITIALLY
    FOLBL - FRACT OLDSTERS IN LABOR FORCE FACTOR B
    REPLZ - RATIO OF EMPLOYMENT TO WORKNG POP(D)
    FOLCL - FRACT OLDSTER IN LABOR FORCE FACTOR C
    WPPLZ - WORKING POP (MEN)
    NOLDZ - NET OLDSTERS (MEN)
```

```
NOLDZ.K=OLDZ.K-ONPDZ.K                             85, A
```

```
    NOLDZ - NET OLDSTERS (MEN)
    OLDZ  - OLDSTERS, OVER 65(MEN)
    ONPDZ - OLDSTER NON-WORKER(MEN)
```

```
ONPDZ.K=(ONMRL)(INMLZ.K)+(ORMLZ)(WMSIZ.K)          86, A

ONMRL=.323 D                                       86A, C

ORMLZ=0 D                                          86B, C
```

```
    ONPDZ - OLDSTER NON-WORKER(MEN)
    ONMRL - OLDSTERS/INMATE RATIO (D)
    INMLZ - INMATES (MEN)
    ORMLZ - OLDSTERS FRACT IN MILITARY
    WMSIZ - WORKERS IN MILITARY SERVICE
```

The ratio of employment to the working population is calculated as follows:

```
REPLZ.K=TWELZ.K/WPPLZ.K                              87, A

    REPLZ — RATIO OF EMPLOYMENT TO WORKNG POP(D)
    TWELZ — TOTAL WORKERS EMPLOYED (MEN)
    WPPLZ — WORKING POP (MEN)
```

The working population is simply the sum of the working population in each age classification:

```
WPPLZ.K=NTNDZ.K+NYADZ.K+NPMDZ.K+NMADZ.K+             88, A
  NOLDZ.K+0

    WPPLZ — WORKING POP (MEN)
    NTNDZ — NET TEENAGERS (MEN)
    NYADZ — NET YOUNG ADULTS (MEN)
    NPMDZ — NET PRIME AGED (MEN)
    NMADZ — NET MIDDLE AGED (MEN)
    NOLDZ — NET OLDSTERS (MEN)
```

The number of inmates is computed as a fraction of the total population:

```
INMLZ.K=(NMRLZ)(POPDZ.K)                             89, A

NMRLZ=.0118 D                                        89A, C

    INMLZ — INMATES (MEN)
    NMRLZ — INMATE/POPULATION RATIO
    POPDZ — POPULATION (MEN)
```

The total numbers of people employed is the sum of the number of workers in each of the industrial activities:

```
TWELZ.K=WDFIZ.K+WNFIZ.K+WTPIZ.K+WCPIZ.K+                90, A
    WXMIZ.K+WWCIZ.K+WAZ.K+WE1LZ.K

WE1LZ.K=WBSIZ.K+WHSIZ.K+WWRZ.K+WGEIZ.K+                  90A, A
    WMSIZ.K+0

      TWELZ - TOTAL WORKERS EMPLOYED (MEN)
      WDFIZ - WORKERS IN DURABLE FABRICATION(MEN)
      WNFIZ - WORKERS IN NONDURABLE FABRICATION (MEN)
      WTPIZ - WORKERS IN TRANSPORTATION-INTENSIVE
                 PROCESSING INDUSTRIES(MEN)
      WCPIZ - WORKERS IN CAP-INT PROC(MEN)
      WXMIZ - WORKERS IN EXPORT MINING (MEN)
      WWCIZ - WORKERS IN WATER WORKS CONST (MEN
      WAZ   - WORKERS IN AGRICULTURE (MEN)
      WBSIZ - WORKERS IN BUSINESS SERVING IND(MEN
      WHSIZ - WORKERS IN HOUSEHOLD SERVING IND(MEN
      WWRZ  - WORKERS IN EXPORT WATER BASED RECRTN
                 (MEN)
      WGEIZ - WORKERS IN GOV AND EDUCATION(MEN
      WMSIZ - WORKERS IN MILITARY SERVICE
```

The number unemployed is the difference between the labor force and those employed:

```
ULZ.K=TLFLZ.K-TWELZ.K                                    91, A

      ULZ   - NUMBER UNEMPLOYED (MEN)
      TLFLZ - TOTAL LABOR FORCE (MEN)
      TWELZ - TOTAL WORKERS EMPLOYED (MEN)
```

The local unemployment rate is the number unemployed divided by the total labor force:

```
LURLZ.K=ULZ.K/TLFLZ.K                                    92, A

      LURLZ - LOCAL UNEMPLOYMENT RATE (D)
      ULZ   - NUMBER UNEMPLOYED (MEN)
      TLFLZ - TOTAL LABOR FORCE (MEN)
```

The smoothed, local unemployment rate is calculated in the usual smoothing equation:

```
SLULZ.K=SLULZ.J+(DT)(1/DSLUL)(LURLZ.J-        93, L
    SLULZ.J)

SLULZ=LURLZ                                   93A, N

DSLUL=1 YR                                    93B, C

     SLULZ - SMOOTHED LOCAL UNEMPLOYMENT RATE (D)
     DSLUL - DELAY IN SMOOTHING LOCAL UNEMPLOYMENT
               RATE
     LURLZ - LOCAL UNEMPLOYMENT RATE (D)
```

The difference between local and national unemployment rates is calculated as one would expect:

```
DURLZ.K=LURLZ.K-NURL.K                        94, A

NURL=.05 D                                    94A, C

     DURLZ - DIFFERENCE BETWEEN LOCAL AND NATIONAL
               UNEMPLOYMENT RATES(D)
     LURLZ - LOCAL UNEMPLOYMENT RATE (D)
     NURL  - NATIONAL UNEMPLOYMENT RATE
```

Industry

Industry is divided into two broad classifications—export and local. Export industries are producing goods and services that are consumed by people in (or from) other areas while local industries produce for local consumption. The first four industries described below grow or decline, depending on local wages and proximity to markets. The growth of export mining, export government, and education is provided exogenously. The business- and household-serving industries grow according to the local demand.

Relative Wage Rates.[5] Relative wages are computed for both the high- and low-skill industries. Wage rates relative to the market area for the high-skill

[5] See Chapter 10.

industries are computed by smoothing a target relative wage with a long time constant:

```
RWIZ.K=RWIZ.J+(DT)(1/DRWI)(TRWIZ.J-RWIZ.J)        95, L

RWIZ=.948                                         95A, N

DRWI=10 YR                                        95B, C
```

```
    RWIZ  - RELATIVE WAGES (D)
    DRWI  - DELAY IN RELATIVE WAGES
    TRWIZ - TARGET RELATIVE WAGE (D)
```

The target relative wage is linearly related to the average wages by the following equations:

```
TRWIZ.K=TRWAI+(TRWBI)(AWGIZ.K)                    96, A

TRWAI=.4 D                                        96A, C

TRWBI=.3 1/$                                      96B, C
```

```
    TRWIZ - TARGET RELATIVE WAGE (D)
    TRWAI - TARGET RELATIVE WAGE FACTOR A
    TRWBI - TARGET RELATIVE WAGE FACTOR B
    AWGIZ - AVERAGE WAGE ($/MAN)
```

The average wage is computed by dividing the total wage bill by the total number of workers. The wage bill is the sum of the products of the wages in a particular industrial classification and the number of workers in that classification:

```
AWGIZ.K=(1/AW6IZ.K)(AW1IZ.K+AW2IZ.K)             97, A
```

```
    AWGIZ - AVERAGE WAGE ($/MAN)
    AW6IZ - CIVILIAN WORKERS
    AW1IZ - WAGES * WORKERS
    AW2IZ - WAGES * WORKERS - NO REL WAGE
```

The total number of workers in this case includes only the civilian workers:

```
AW6IZ.K=TWELZ.K-WMSIZ.K                           98, A
```

```
    AW6IZ - CIVILIAN WORKERS
    TWELZ - TOTAL WORKERS EMPLOYED (MEN)
    WMSIZ - WORKERS IN MILITARY SERVICE
```

Part of the total wage bill is itself the sum of the products of the relative wages and the sum of the products of the normal wages and number of workers in each industry:

```
AW1IZ.K=(RWIZ.K)(AW3IZ.K)+(RWLIZ.K)(AW5IZ.K)       99, A

     AW1IZ - WAGES * WORKERS
     RWIZ  - RELATIVE WAGES (D)
     AW3IZ - NORMAL WAGES * WORKERS
     RWLIZ - RELATIVE LOW WAGES(D)
     AW5IZ - NORMAL WAGES * WORKERS
```

The sum of the products of the normal wages and workers in the high-skill industries is given as follows:

```
AW3IZ.K=AW4IZ.K+(IWBXZ)(WBSIZ.K)                   100, A

AW4IZ.K=(IWDXZ)(WDFIZ.K)+(IWWXZ)(WWCIZ.K)+         100A, A
   (IWTXZ)(WTPIZ.K)+(IWCXZ)(WCPIZ.K)

     AW3IZ - NORMAL WAGES * WORKERS
     IWBXZ - INIT HOURLY WAGES IN BUS SRV
     WBSIZ - WORKERS IN BUSINESS SERVING IND(MEN
     IWDXZ - INIT HOURLY WAGES IN DUR FAB
     WDFIZ - WORKERS IN DURABLE FABRICATION(MEN)
     IWWXZ - INIT HOURLY WAGES IN WTR CNS
     WWCIZ - WORKERS IN WATER WORKS CONST (MEN
     IWTXZ - INIT HOURLY WAGES IN TRP PRC
     WTPIZ - WORKERS IN TRANSPORTATION-INTENSIVE
              PROCESSING INDUSTRIES(MEN)
     IWCXZ - INIT HOURLY WAGES IN CAP PRC
     WCPIZ - WORKERS IN CAP-INT PROC(MEN)
```

The only low-skill industrial classification is nondurable fabricating. Its normal wage bill is computed as follows:

```
AW5IZ.K=(IWNXZ)(WNFIZ.K)                           101, A

     AW5IZ - NORMAL WAGES * WORKERS
     IWNXZ - INIT HOURLY WAGES IN NDR FAB
     WNFIZ - WORKERS IN NONDURABLE FABRICATION (MEN)
```

The sum of the products of wages and workers in those industries without a specific relative wage is computed as follows:

```
AW2IZ.K=(IWMXZ)(WXMIZ.K)+(IWGXZ)(WGEIZ.K)+        102, A
  (NWHXZ)(WHRIZ.K)+(IWAXZ)(WAZ.K)

    AW2IZ - WAGES * WORKERS - NO REL WAGE
    IWMXZ - INIT HOURLY WAGES IN XPR MNG
    WXMIZ - WORKERS IN EXPORT MINING (MEN)
    IWGXZ - INIT HOURLY WAGES IN GOV + EDC
    WGEIZ - WORKERS IN GOV AND EDUCATION(MEN
    NWHXZ - NORMAL HRLY WGS HSH SRV
    WHRIZ - WORKERS IN HOUSHOLD SRVNG + RECREATION
    IWAXZ - INIT HOURLY WAGES IN AGRICLT
    WAZ   - WORKERS IN AGRICULTURE (MEN)
```

The total of workers in household serving and recreation is calculated as shown:

```
    WHRIZ.K=WHSIZ.K+WWRZ.K                         103, A

    WHRIZ - WORKERS IN HOUSHOLD SRVNG + RECREATION
    WHSIZ - WORKERS IN HOUSEHOLD SERVING IND(MEN)
    WWRZ  - WORKERS IN EXPORT WATER BASED RECRTN
              (MEN)
```

The relative wages in the low-skill industries are computed similarly to those in the high-skill industries:

```
RWLIZ.K=RWLIZ.J+(DT)(1/DRWI)(TLWIZ.J-RWLIZ.J)     104, L

RWLIZ=.843                                        104A, N

    RWLIZ - RELATIVE LOW WAGES(D)
    DRWI  - DELAY IN RELATIVE WAGES
    TLWIZ - TARGET LOW RELATIVE WAGE (D)
```

The target relative wage for low-skill industries is linearly related to the average wage and the smoothed local unemployment rate:

```
TLWIZ.K=TLWAI+TL1IZ.K                              105, A

TLWAI=.525                                         105A, C

TL1IZ.K=(TLWBI)(AWGIZ.K)+(TLWCI)(SLULZ.K)          105B, A

TLWBI=.3                                           105C, C

TLWCI=-2.5                                         105D, C

        TLWIZ - TARGET LOW RELATIVE WAGE (D)
        TLWAI - TARGET LOW WAGE FACTOR A
        TLWBI - TARGET LOW WAGE FACTOR B
        AWGIZ - AVERAGE WAGE ($/MAN)
        TLWCI - TARGET LOW WAGE FACTOR C
        SLULZ - SMOOTHED LOCAL UNEMPLOYMENT RATE (D)
```

Durable Fabricating Industries.[6] The number of workers in the durable fabricating industries is determined by a level equation depending on the change in durable fabricating employment:

```
WDFIZ.K=WDFIZ.J+(DT)(CDFIZ.J+0)                    106, L

WDFIZ=26954                                        106A, N

        WDFIZ - WORKERS IN DURABLE FABRICATION(MEN)
        CDFIZ - CHANGE IN DURABLE FABRICATION(MEN/YR)
```

The change in durable fabricating employment is the product of the percent change and the number of workers in durable fabricating industries:

```
CDFIZ.K=(PDFIZ.K)(WDFIZ.K)                         107, A

        CDFIZ - CHANGE IN DURABLE FABRICATION(MEN/YR)
        PDFIZ - PERCENT CHANGE IN, DURABLE FABRICATION(1/YR)
        WDFIZ - WORKERS IN DURABLE FABRICATION(MEN)
```

[6] See Chapter 10 for a discussion of the export industries.

The percent change depends on a basic growth in demand for labor for durable fabricating plus a coefficient of elasticity times the cost of manufacturing in this area relative to the national average:

```
PDFIZ.K=GDDIZ+(-CEDI)(RCDIZ.K)                    108, A

GDDIZ=.0121  1/YR                                 108A, C

CEDI=.4  1/YR                                     108B, C

     PDFIZ - PERCENT CHANGE IN DURABLE FABRICATION(1/YR)
     GDDIZ - GROWTH IN LABOR DEMAND DUR FAB
     CEDI  - COST ELASTICITY OF DURABLES
     RCDIZ - RELATIVE COST OF DURABLES MANUFACTURED(D)
```

The relative cost of manufacturing is the total cost index minus 1:

```
RCDIZ.K=TCDIZ.K-1                                 109, A

     RCDIZ - RELATIVE COST OF DURABLES MANUFACTURED(D)
     TCDIZ - TOTAL COST INDEX FOR DURABLE FABRICATION(D)
```

The total cost index is the weighted sum of constant costs, transportation costs, and labor costs. The weights depend on the relative importance of the different kinds of costs to the industry. Labor costs depend on the relative wage, while transportation costs depend on the access of industry to its market.

```
TCDIZ.K=(1)(WCDFI)+(WTDFI)(AMDIZ)+                110, A
  (WLDFI)(RWIZ.K)+(0)(0)

WCDFI=.7042  D                                    110A, C

WTDFI=.0220  D                                    110B, C

WLDFI=.2738  D                                    110C, C

     TCDIZ - TOTAL COST INDEX FOR DURABLE FABRICATION(D)
     WCDFI - WT,CONSTANT COSTS IN DUR FAB
     WTDFI - WT,TRANSPRT COSTS IN DUR FAB
     AMDIZ - ACCESS TO MARKET - DUR FAB (D)
     WLDFI - WT, LABOR COSTS IN DURABLE FABR (D)
     RWIZ  - RELATIVE WAGES (D)
```

The cost of access to market, as provided in a table, is declining over time:

```
AMDIZ.K=TABHL(TMDIZ,TIME.K,0,15,15)                    111, A

TMDIZ*=0.934/0.869 D                                   111A, C

    AMDIZ - ACCESS TO MARKET - DUR FAB (D)
    TMDIZ - TABLE OF ACCESS TO MARKET - DUR FAB
    TIME  - TIME
```

Nondurable Fabricating Industries. The growth of nondurable fabricating industries is calculated similarly to that of durable fabricating industries:

```
WNFIZ.K=WNFIZ.J+(DT)(CNFIZ.J+0)                        112, L

WNFIZ=40234                                            112A, N

    WNFIZ - WORKERS IN NONDURABLE FABRICATION (MEN)
    CNFIZ - CHANGE IN NONDURABLE FABRICATION(MEN/YR)

CNFIZ.K=(PNFIZ.K)(WNFIZ.K)                             113, A

    CNFIZ - CHANGE IN NONDURABLE FABRICATION(MEN/YR)
    PNFIZ - PERCENT CHANGE IN NONDURABLES(1/YR)
    WNFIZ - WORKERS IN NONDURABLE FABRICATION (MEN)

PNFIZ.K=GDNIZ+(-CENI)(RCNIZ.K)                         114, A

GDNIZ=-.0074 1/YR                                      114A, C

CENI=.4 1/YR                                           114B, C

    PNFIZ - PERCENT CHANGE IN NONDURABLES(1/YR)
    GDNIZ - GROWTH IN LABOR DEMAND NONDURABLE
                FABRICATION (1/YR)
    CENI  - COST ELASTICITY OF NON-DURABLES
    RCNIZ - RELATIVE COST OF NONDURABLE FABRICATING
                (D)
```

```
RCNIZ.K=TCNIZ.K-1                                    115, A

    RCNIZ - RELATIVE COST OF NONDURABLE FABRICATING
            (D)
    TCNIZ - TOTAL COST INDEX FOR NONDURABLE FABRICATION(D)

TCNIZ.K=(1)(WCNFI)+(WTNFI)(AMNIZ)+                   116, A
  (WLNFI)(RWLIZ.K)+(0)(0)

WCNFI=.7730 D                                        116A, C

WTNFI=.0237 D                                        116B, C

WLNFI=.2033 D                                        116C, C

    TCNIZ - TOTAL COST INDEX FOR NONDURABLE FABRICATION(D)
    WCNFI - WT,CONSTANT COSTS IN NDR FAB
    WTNFI - WT,TRANSPRT COSTS IN NDR FAB
    AMNIZ - ACCESS TO MARKET - NDR FAB
    WLNFI - WT, LABOR COSTS IN NDR FAB
    RWLIZ - RELATIVE LOW WAGES(D)

AMNIZ.K=TABHL(TMNIZ,TIME.K,0,15,15)                  117, A

TMNIZ*=0.976/0.902 D                                 117A, C

    AMNIZ - ACCESS TO MARKET - NDR FAB
    TMNIZ - TABLE OF ACCESS TO MARKET - NDR FAB
    TIME  - TIME
```

Processing Industries. The growth of labor-intensive and capital-intensive processing industries is similar to the fabricating industries except that access to resources is included in the total cost index as well as access to market:

```
WTPIZ.K=WTPIZ.J+(DT)(CTPIZ.J+0)                      118, L

WTPIZ=2522                                           118A, N

    WTPIZ - WORKERS IN TRANSPORTATION-INTENSIVE
            PROCESSING INDUSTRIES(MEN)
    CTPIZ - CHANGE IN TRANSPORTATION-INTENSIVE
            PROCESSING INDUSTRIES(MEN/YR)
```

```
CTPIZ.K=(PTPIZ.K)(WTPIZ.K)                    119, A
```

    CTPIZ - CHANGE IN TRANSPORTATION-INTENSIVE
          PROCESSING INDUSTRIES(MEN/YR)
    PTPIZ - PERCENT CHANGE IN TRANSPORTATION-
          INTENSIVE PROCESSING INDUSTRIES(1/YR)
    WTPIZ - WORKERS IN TRANSPORTATION-INTENSIVE
          PROCESSING INDUSTRIES(MEN)

```
PTPIZ.K=GDTIZ+(-CETI)(RCTIZ.K)                120, A

GDTIZ=-.0012 1/YR                             120A, C

CETI=.4 1/YR                                  120B, C
```

    PTPIZ - PERCENT CHANGE IN TRANSPORTATION-
          INTENSIVE PROCESSING INDUSTRIES(1/YR)
    GDTIZ - GROWTH IN LABOR DEMAND TRANSPORTATION
          INTENSIVE-PROCESSING INDUSTRIES(1/YEAR)
    CETI   - COST ELASTICITY OF TRANSPORTATION-INTENSIVE
          PROCESSING INDUSTRIES
    RCTIZ - RELATIVE COST OF TRANSPORTATION-INTENSIVE
          (D) PROCESSING INDUSTRIES(D)

```
RCTIZ.K=TCTIZ.K-1                             121, A
```

    RCTIZ - RELATIVE COST OF TRANSPORTATION-INTENSIVE
          (D) PROCESSING INDUSTRIES(D)
    TCTIZ - TOTAL COST INDEX FOR TRANSPORTATION
          INTENSIVE-PROCESSING IND (D)

```
TCTIZ.K=(1)(WCTPI)+(WSTPI)(AMTIZ)+              122, A
  (WLTPI)(RWIZ.K)+(WATPI)(ASTIZ)

WCTPI=.6621 D                                   122A, C

WSTPI=.0583 D                                   122B, C

WLTPI=.2390 D                                   122C, C

WATPI=.0406 D                                   122D, L

ASTIZ=1.45 D                                    122E, C

      TCTIZ - TOTAL COST INDEX FOR TRANSPORTATION
                INTENSIVE-PROCESSING IND (D)
      WCTPI - WT,CONSTANT COSTS IN TRP PRC
      WSTPI - WT,TRANSPRT COSTS IN TRP PRC
      AMTIZ - ACCESS TO MARKET - TRP PRC
      WLTPI - WT, LABOR COSTS IN DTRP PRC
      RWIZ  - RELATIVE WAGES (D)
      WATPI - WT,MAT ACQS COSTS IN TRP PRC
      ASTIZ - ACCESS TO SOURCES FOR TRANSPORTATION
                INTENSIVE PROCESSING INDUSTRIES(D)

AMTIZ.K=TABHL(TMTIZ,TIME.K,0,15,15)             123, A

TMTIZ*=0.747/0.692 D                            123A, C

      AMTIZ - ACCESS TO MARKET - TRP PRC
      TMTIZ - TABLE OF ACCESS TO MARKET - TRP PRC
      TIME  - TIME

WCPIZ.K=WCPIZ.J+(DT)(CCPIZ.J+0)                 124, L

WCPIZ=3893                                      124A, N

      WCPIZ - WORKERS IN CAP-INT PROC(MEN)
      CCPIZ - CHANGE IN CAP-INT PROC(MEN/YR)

CCPIZ.K=(PCPIZ.K)(WCPIZ.K)                       125, A

      CCPIZ - CHANGE IN CAP-INT PROC(MEN/YR)
      PCPIZ - PERCENT CHANGE IN CAP-INT PROC (1/YR)
      WCPIZ - WORKERS IN CAP-INT PROC(MEN)
```

```
PCPIZ.K=GDCIZ+(-CECI)(RCCIZ.K)                    126, A

GDCIZ=.0069 1/YR                                  126A, C

CECI=.4 1/YR                                      126B, C

     PCPIZ - PERCENT CHANGE IN CAP-INT PROC (1/YR)
     GDCIZ - GROWTH IN LABOR DEMAND - CAP PRC
     CECI  - COST ELASTICITY OF CAP-INT PROC
     RCCIZ - RELATIVE COST OF CAP-INT PROC (D)

RCCIZ.K=TCCIZ.K-1                                 127, A

     RCCIZ - RELATIVE COST OF CAP-INT PROC (D)
     TCCIZ - TOTAL COST INDEX FOR CAPITAL INTENSIVE
              PROCESSING (D)

TCCIZ.K=(1)(WCCPI)+(WSCPI)(AMCIZ)+                128, A
   (WLCPI)(RWIZ.K)+(WACPI)(ASCIZ)

WCCPI=.8012 D                                     128A, C

WSCPI=.0468 D                                     128B, C

WLCPI=.1141 D                                     128C, C

WACPI=.0379 D                                     128D, C

ASCIZ=1.29 D                                      128E, C

     TCCIZ - TOTAL COST INDEX FOR CAPITAL INTENSIVE
              PROCESSING (D)
     WCCPI - WT,CONSTANT COSTS IN CAP PRC
     WSCPI - WT,TRANSPRT COSTS IN CAP PRC
     AMCIZ - ACCESS TO MARKET - CAP PRC (D)
     WLCPI - WT, LABOR COSTS IN CAP PRC
     RWIZ  - RELATIVE WAGES (D)
     WACPI - WT,MAT ACQS COSTS IN CAP PRC
     ASCIZ - ACCESS TO SOURCES FOR CAP PRC

AMCIZ.K=TABHL(TMCIZ,TIME.K,0,15,15)               129, A

TMCIZ*=0.780/0.715 D                              129A, C

     AMCIZ - ACCESS TO MARKET - CAP PRC (D)
     TMCIZ - TABLE OF ACCESS TO MARKET - CAP PRC
     TIME  - TIME
```

Export Government and Education. The number of workers involved in export government and education is provided exogenously in a table:

```
WGEIZ.K=TABLE(TGEIZ,TIME.K,0,50,50)                    130, A

TGEIZ*=0/0 MEN                                         130A, C

    WGEIZ - WORKERS IN GOV AND EDUCATION(MEN
    TGEIZ - TABLE OF WORKERS IN EXPORT GOV AND
            EDUCATION
    TIME  - TIME
```

Export Mining. The number of workers in export mining is also provided exogenously in a table:

```
WXMIZ.K=TABLE(TWMIZ,TIME.K,0,50,5)                     131, A

TWMIZ*=8303/4450/2900/2080/1550/1170/900/              131A, C
    710/570/460/370 MEN

    WXMIZ - WORKERS IN EXPORT MINING (MEN)
    TWMIZ - TABLE OF WORKERS IN EXPORT MINING
    TIME  - TIME
```

Waterworks Construction Industry. Also the number of workers in the waterworks construction industry is provided exogenously in a table:

```
WWCIZ.K=TABLE(TWWIZ,TIME.K,0,50,5)                     132, A

TWWIZ*=0/0/0/0/0/0/0/0/0/0/0 (MEN)                     132A, C

    WWCIZ - WORKERS IN WATER WORKS CONST (MEN
    TWWIZ - TABLE OF WORKERS IN WATER WORKS
    TIME  - TIME
```

Business-Serving Industries.[7] The number of workers in business-serving industries is a level determined by the rate of growth of business-serving industries:

```
WBSIZ.K=WBSIZ.J+(DT)(BSGIZ.J+0)                        133, L

WBSIZ=24382                                            133A, N

    WBSIZ - WORKERS IN BUSINESS SERVING IND(MEN
    BSGIZ - BUSINESS SERVING IND GROWTH RATE(MEN/YR
```

[7] See Chapter 9 for a discussion of the local-serving industries.

The rate of growth of business-serving industries is the product of the labor availability multiplier and the desired business-serving industry growth rate:

```
BSGIZ.K=(LAMIZ.K)(DBGIZ.K)                        134, A

    BSGIZ - BUSINESS SERVING IND GROWTH RATE(MEN/YR
    LAMIZ - LABOR AVAILABILITY MULTIPLIER
    DBGIZ - DESIRED BUSINESS SERVING INDUSTRY
            GROWTH RATE (MEN/YR)
```

The labor availability multiplier depends on the local unemployment rate:

```
LAMIZ.K=TABHL(TLAMI,LURLZ.K,0,.1,.05)             135, A

TLAMI*=0/.8/1 D                                   135A, C

    LAMIZ - LABOR AVAILABILITY MULTIPLIER
    TLAMI - TABLE LABOR AVAILABILITY MULTIPLIER
    LURLZ - LOCAL UNEMPLOYMENT RATE (D)
```

The desired business-serving industry growth rate depends on the desired additional workers required. If the desired additional workers are greater than 0, the desired growth rate will be relatively slow, reflecting the need to find not only labor but also capital. On the other hand, when there is an excess of workers, this excess will be laid off quickly:

```
DBGIZ.K=TABLE(TDBGI,DABIZ.K,-1E5,1E5,1E5)         136, A

TDBGI*=-1E5/0/3E4 MEN/YR/MAN                      136A, C

    DBGIZ - DESIRED BUSINESS SERVING INDUSTRY
            GROWTH RATE (MEN/YR)
    TDBGI - TABLE OF DESIRED BUSINESS SERVING
            INDUSTRY GROWTH RATE (MEN/YR)
    DABIZ - DESIRED ADDITIONAL WORKERS IN BUSINESS
            SERVING INDUSTRIES (MEN)
```

The desired additional workers are equal to the desired number of workers less the actual workers minus a third term, the initial bias in desired workers in business-serving industries:

```
DABIZ.K=DWBIZ.K-WBSIZ.K-IBBIZ.K                    137, A

     DABIZ - DESIRED ADDITIONAL WORKERS IN BUSINESS
                SERVING INDUSTRIES (MEN)
     DWBIZ - DESIRED WORKERS IN BUSINESS SERVING
                INDUSTRIES (MEN)
     WBSIZ - WORKERS IN BUSINESS SERVING IND(MEN
     IBBIZ - INITIAL BIAS IN DESIRED WORKERS IN
                BUSINESS SERV IND(MEN)
```

The desired number of workers in business-serving industries is a function of the total number of workers in the businesses served:

```
DWBIZ.K=TABLE(TDWBI,TWBIZ.K,0,1.5E6,250E3)      138, A

TDWBI*=0/31E3/77E3/123E3/169E3/215E3/            138A, C
  261E3 MEN

     DWBIZ - DESIRED WORKERS IN BUSINESS SERVING
                INDUSTRIES (MEN)
     TDWBI - TABLE FOR DWBIZ
     TWBIZ - TOTAL WORKERS IN BUSINESSES SERVED
                (MEN)
```

The total number of workers in the businesses served is the total number of workers employed less those workers in business-serving industries:

```
TWBIZ.K=TWELZ.K-WBSIZ.K                          139, A

     TWBIZ - TOTAL WORKERS IN BUSINESSES SERVED
                (MEN)
     TWELZ - TOTAL WORKERS EMPLOYED (MEN)
     WBSIZ - WORKERS IN BUSINESS SERVING IND(MEN
```

The initial bias in desired workers is necessary to avoid a large initial transient that might otherwise arise from two slightly conflicting pieces of data. The first datum is the number of workers desired, given the total number of workers employed in the businesses served, which is derived from national figures. The other datum is the number of workers employed in this region, which is used to initialize the model. There is no reason to expect these two figures to agree exactly, nor would one expect the real world to correct this discrepancy in a great hurry. Consequently, this initial bias is chosen to set the desired additional workers equal to zero at time equal to 0. This initial bias decays to zero with a time constant of 20 years:

```
IBBIZ.K=IBBIZ.J+(DT).(1/TCIBI)(0-IBBIZ.J)          140, L

IBBIZ=DWBIZ-WBSIZ                                  140A, N

TCIBI=20 YRS                                       140B, C

     IBBIZ - INITIAL BIAS IN DESIRED WORKERS IN
             BUSINESS SERV IND(MEN)
     TCIBI - TIME CONSTANT OF INITIAL BIAS
     DWBIZ - DESIRED WORKERS IN BUSINESS SERVING
             INDUSTRIES (MEN)
     WBSIZ - WORKERS IN BUSINESS SERVING IND(MEN
```

Household-Serving Industries. The growth of household-serving industries is formulated similarly to business-serving industries except that the desired number of workers in household-serving industries depends on the population and a trend

```
WHSIZ.K=WHSIZ.J+(DT)(HSGIZ.J+0)                    141, L

WHSIZ=109193                                       141A, N

     WHSIZ - WORKERS IN HOUSEHOLD SERVING IND(MEN
     HSGIZ - HOUSEHOLD SERVING IND GROWTH RATE(MEN/YR

HSGIZ.K=(LAMIZ.K)(DHGIZ.K)                         142, A

     HSGIZ - HOUSEHOLD SERVING IND GROWTH RATE(MEN/YR
     LAMIZ - LABOR AVAILABILITY MULTIPLIER
     DHGIZ - DESIRED HOUSEHOLD SERVING INDUSTRY
             GROWTH RATE (MEN/YR)
```

DHGIZ.K=TABLE(TDHGI,DAHIZ.K,-1E5,1E5,1E5)   143, A

TDHGI*=-1E5/0/3E4 MEN/YR/MAN   143A, C

    DHGIZ — DESIRED HOUSEHOLD SERVING INDUSTRY
            GROWTH RATE (MEN/YR)
    TDHGI — TABLE OF DESIRED HOUSEHOLD SERVING
            INDUSTRY GROWTH RATE (MEN/YR)
    DAHIZ — DESIRED ADDITIONAL WORKERS IN HOUSEHOLD
            SERVING INDUSTRIES (MEN

DAHIZ.K=DWHIZ.K-WHSIZ.K-IBHIZ.K   144, A

    DAHIZ — DESIRED ADDITIONAL WORKERS IN HOUSEHOLD
            SERVING INDUSTRIES (MEN
    DWHIZ — DSRD WORKERS IN HOUSEHLD SRVNG IND
    WHSIZ — WORKERS IN HOUSEHOLD SERVING IND(MEN
    IBHIZ — INITIAL BIAS IN DESIRED WORKERS IN
            HOUSEHOLD SERVING INDUSTRIES(MEN)

DWHIZ.K=(TRHWI.K)(BWHIZ.K)   145, A

    DWHIZ — DSRD WORKERS IN HOUSEHLD SRVNG IND
    TRHWI — TREND IN HOUSEHOLD WORKERS (D)
    BWHIZ — BASE WORKERS — HOUSEHOLD SERVING INDUSTRIES
            (MEN)

TRHWI.K=TABLE(TTRHI,TIME.K,0,50,50)   146, A

TTRHI*=1/1 D   146A, C

    TRHWI — TREND IN HOUSEHOLD WORKERS (D)
    TTRHI — TABLE FOR TREND IN HOUSEHOLD WORKERS
    TIME — TIME

BWHIZ.K=TABLE(TDWHI,POPDZ.K,0,5E6,.5E6)   147, A

TDWHI*=-13770/84040/181900/279700/377500/   147A, C
  475300/573100/670900/768700/866500/
 964300 MEN

    BWHIZ — BASE WORKERS — HOUSEHOLD SERVING INDUSTRIES
            (MEN)
    TDWHI — TABLE FOR BASE WORKERS HSHLD SRV
    POPDZ — POPULATION (MEN)

```
IBHIZ.K=IBHIZ.J+(DT)(1/TCIBI)(0-IBHIZ.J)          148, L

IBHIZ=DWHIZ-WHSIZ                                 148A, N

    IBHIZ - INITIAL BIAS IN DESIRED WORKERS IN
                HOUSEHOLD SERVING INDUSTRIES(MEN)
    TCIBI - TIME CONSTANT OF INITIAL BIAS
    DWHIZ - DSRD WORKERS IN HOUSEHLD SRVNG IND
    WHSIZ - WORKERS IN HOUSEHOLD SERVING IND(MEN
```

Military Service. In this formulation, the number of workers in military service is set to 0:

```
WMSIZ=0 MEN                                       149, C

    WMSIZ - WORKERS IN MILITARY SERVICE
```

Agriculture. The number of workers in agriculture is a level depending on the rate of change of workers in agriculture:

```
WAZ.K=WAZ.J+(DT)(CWAZ.J+0)                        150, L

WAZ=5453                                          150A, N

    WAZ  - WORKERS IN AGRICULTURE (MEN)
    CWAZ - CHANGE OF WORKERS IN AGRICULTURE(MEN/YR)
```

The rate of change of workers in agriculture depends on the product of the percent change of workers in agriculture and the number of workers in agriculture:

```
CWAZ.K=(PCWA.K)(WAZ.K)                            151, A

    CWAZ - CHANGE OF WORKERS IN AGRICULTURE(MEN/YR)
    PCWA - PERCENT CHANGE OF WORKERS IN AGRICULTURE(1/YR)
    WAZ  - WORKERS IN AGRICULTURE (MEN)
```

The percent change of workers in agriculture is provided exogenously in a table:

```
PCWA.K=TABLE(TCWA,TIME.K,0,50,10)                 152, A

TCWA*=-0.025/-.025/-.025/-.008/-.008/-.008        152A, C

    PCWA - PERCENT CHANGE OF WORKERS IN AGRICULTURE(1/YR)
    TCWA - TABLE FOR PCWA (1/YR)
    TIME - TIME
```

Water Supply[8]

River Flow. River flow is calculated at two points in every geographic area. One point is the handover point to the downstream geographic area. The other is a critical point associated either with the lowest dissolved oxygen sag in the region or with a point of high water withdrawal.

The minimum river flow at the critical point is the minimum natural flow at that critical point plus the reservoir releases during minimum flow less the consumption that takes place above the critical point:

```
MRCWZ.K=MNCWZ+RRMWZ.K-CACWZ.K                    153, A

MNCWZ=95 CFS                                     153A, C
```

```
     MRCWZ - MINIMUM RIVER FLOW AT CRITICAL POINT
                 (CFS)
     MNCWZ - MINIMUM NATURAL FLOW AT CRITICAL POINT
     RRMWZ - RESERVOIR RELEASES DURING MINIMUM
                 FLOW (CFS)
     CACWZ - CONSUMPTION ABOVE CRITICAL PT (CFS)
```

The reservoir releases during minimum flow are provided exogenously in a table:

```
RRMWZ.K=TABLE(TRRWZ,TIME.K,0,50,5)               154, A

TRRWZ*=0/0/0/0/0/0/0/0/0/0/0 CFS                 154A, C
```

```
     RRMWZ - RESERVOIR RELEASES DURING MINIMUM
                 FLOW (CFS)
     TRRWZ - TABLE OF RESERVOIR RELEASES
     TIME  - TIME
```

The consumption above the critical point is the product of the fraction of the total consumption above the critical point and the additional consumption:

```
CACWZ.K=(FCCWZ)(ACWZ.K)                           155, A

FCCWZ=.30 D                                       155A, C
```

```
     CACWZ - CONSUMPTION ABOVE CRITICAL PT (CFS)
     FCCWZ - FRACTION OF CONSUMPTION ABOVE CRITICAL
                 POINT
     ACWZ  - ADDITIONAL CONSUMPTION (CFS)
```

[8] See Chapter 11.

The additional consumption is that which results from economic growth and increases in water consumption. The model is concerned with the additional consumption rather than with the total consumption because the data available for river flow already reflect the current consumption. The additional consumption is equal to the difference between the total consumption and the total initial consumption. The difference is converted from millions of gallons per day to cubic feet per second by multiplying by 1.55:

```
ACWZ.K=(1.55)(TCMWZ.K-TCIWZ)                    156, A

     ACWZ  - ADDITIONAL CONSUMPTION (CFS)
     TCMWZ - TOTAL CONSUMPTION IN MGD
     TCIWZ - TOTAL CONSUMPTION INITIALLY (MGD)
```

The total consumption initially is equal to the total consumption computed by an equation calculated only at time equal to 0:

```
TCIWZ=TCMWZ                                     157, N

     TCIWZ - TOTAL CONSUMPTION INITIALLY (MGD)
     TCMWZ - TOTAL CONSUMPTION IN MGD
```

The total consumption in millions of gallons per day is equal to the sum of the consumption by residence, fabricating industries, and processing industries. The consumption by each group is the product of the withdrawal and the fraction consumed:

```
TCMWZ.K=(FCRW)(RWWZ.K)+(FCFIW)(FIWWZ.K)+        158, A
  (FCPIW)(PIWWZ.K)+(0)(0)

FCRW=.09 D                                      158A, C

FCFIW=.04 D                                     158B, C

FCPIW=.08 D                                     158C, C

     TCMWZ - TOTAL CONSUMPTION IN MGD
     FCRW  - FRACTION OF WITHDRAWAL CONSUMED-RESIDENCES
     RWWZ  - RESIDENTIAL SUMMER WITHDRAWAL (MGD)
     FCFIW - FRACTION OF WITHDRAWAL CONSUMED-FABRICATING
             INDUSTRIES
     FIWWZ - FABRICATING IND. WITHDRAWAL (MGD)
     FCPIW - FRACTION OF WITHDRAWAL CONSUMED-PROCESSING
             INDUSTRIES
     PIWWZ - PROCESSING IND. WITHDRAWAL (MGD)
```

The residential summer withdrawal is equal to the per capita summer withdrawal times the urban population:

```
RWWZ.K=(PCWW.K)(UPWZ.K)                          159, A
```

```
    RWWZ  - RESIDENTIAL SUMMER WITHDRAWAL (MGD)
    PCWW  - PER CAPITA SUMMER WITHDRAWAL (MGD/MAN)
    UPWZ  - URBAN POPULATION (MEN)
```

The per capita summer withdrawal is provided exogenously in a table:

```
PCWW.K=TABLE(TPCWW,TIME.K,0,50,50)               160, A
```

```
TPCWW*=160E-6/340E-6 MGD/MAN                      160A, C
```

```
    PCWW  - PER CAPITA SUMMER WITHDRAWAL (MGD/MAN)
    TPCWW - TABLE OF PER CAPITA SUMMER WITHDRAWAL
    TIME  - TIME
```

The urban population is equal to the total population less the farm population:

```
UPWZ.K=POPDZ.K-FPWZ.K                             161, A
```

```
    UPWZ  - URBAN POPULATION (MEN)
    POPDZ - POPULATION (MEN)
    FPWZ  - FARM POPULATION (MEN)
```

The farm population is equal to the number of persons living on a farm per farm workers times the total number of farm workers:

```
FPWZ.K=(PPFWW)(WAZ.K)                             162, A
```

```
PPFWW=3.3 MEN/MAN                                 162A, C
```

```
    FPWZ  - FARM POPULATION (MEN)
    PPFWW - FARM DWELLERS PER FARM WORKER
    WAZ   - WORKERS IN AGRICULTURE (MEN)
```

The fabricating industry withdrawal is equal to the withdrawal per worker in the fabricating industries times the total number of workers in the two fabricating industry classifications:

```
FIWWZ.K=(PFWWW)(WDFIZ.K+WNFIZ.K)                  163, A
```

```
PFWWW=250E-6 MGD/MAN                              163A, C
```

```
    FIWWZ - FABRICATING IND. WITHDRAWAL (MGD)
    PFWWW - PER FABRICATING WORKER WITHDRAWAL
    WDFIZ - WORKERS IN DURABLE FABRICATION(MEN)
    WNFIZ - WORKERS IN NONDURABLE FABRICATION (MEN)
```

The processing industry withdrawal is calculated similarly:

```
PIWWZ.K=(PPWWW)(WTPIZ.K+WCPIZ.K)                    164, A

PPWWW=5700E-6 MGD/MAN                               164A, C

    PIWWZ - PROCESSING IND. WITHDRAWAL (MGD)
    PPWWW - PER PROCESSING WORKER WITHDRAWAL
    WTPIZ - WORKERS IN TRANSPORTATION-INTENSIVE
                PROCESSING INDUSTRIES(MEN)
    WCPIZ - WORKERS IN CAP-INT PROC(MEN)
```

The minimum river flow at the handover point is equal to the flow at the critical point plus the natural additions below the critical point minus the consumption below the critical point:

```
MRFWZ.K=MRCWZ.K+MNAWZ-CBCWZ.K                       165, A

MNAWZ=855 CFS                                       165A, C

    MRFWZ - MINIMUM RIVER FLOW AT HANDOVER(CFS)
    MRCWZ - MINIMUM RIVER FLOW AT CRITICAL POINT
                (CFS)
    MNAWZ - MIN NATURAL ADDITIONS BELOW CRITCL PT
    CBCWZ - CONUMPTION BELOW CRITICAL PT (CFS)
```

The consumption below the critical point is equal to the additional consumption minus the consumption above the critical point:

```
CBCWZ.K=ACWZ.K-CACWZ.K                              166, A

    CBCWZ - CONUMPTION BELOW CRITICAL PT (CFS)
    ACWZ  - ADDITIONAL CONSUMPTION (CFS)
    CACWZ - CONSUMPTION ABOVE CRITICAL PT (CFS)
```

In two subregions, there is the danger that a city withdrawing water from the river will try to withdraw more water than is flowing by the city. To study this possibility, a ratio of maximum withdrawal at one point to minimum flow is calculated. This ratio is equal to a geographic spread factor times the total withdrawal in the subsector divided by the minimum river flow at the critical point. The geographic spread factor is the fraction of the total withdrawal occurring at this critical point:

```
RWFWZ.K=(GSFWZ)(TWWZ.K)/MRCWZ.K                    167, A

GSFWZ=.13 D                                         167A, C

     RWFWZ - RATIO OF MAXIMUM WITHDRAWAL AT ONE
               POINT TO MINIMUM FLOW (D)
     GSFWZ - GEOGRAPHIC SPREAD FACTOR (D)
     TWWZ  - TOTAL WITHDRAWAL (CFS)
     MRCWZ - MINIMUM RIVER FLOW AT CRITICAL POINT
               (CFS)
```

The total withdrawal is equal to a factor converting millions of gallons a day into cubic feet per second, times the sum of the three withdrawals:

```
TWWZ.K=(1.548)(RWWZ.K+FIWWZ.K+PIWWZ.K+0)           168, A

     TWWZ  - TOTAL WITHDRAWAL (CFS)
     RWWZ  - RESIDENTIAL SUMMER WITHDRAWAL (MGD)
     FIWWZ - FABRICATING IND. WITHDRAWAL (MGD)
     PIWWZ - PROCESSING IND. WITHDRAWAL (MGD)
```

Pollution. Pollution is measured in terms of the lowest dissolved oxygen occurring within a subregion. The dissolved oxygen at this critical point is equal to 10 minus the dissolved oxygen deficit:

```
DOWZ.K=10-DODWZ.K                                   169, A

     DOWZ  - DISSOLVED OXYGEN (PPM)
     DODWZ - DISSOLVED OXYGEN DEFICIT (PPM)
```

The dissolved oxygen deficit is equal to the dissolved oxygen coefficient times the total BOD generated in the subregion divided by the minimum river flow at the critical point. The dissolved oxygen coefficient is calculated in the DO submodel:

```
DODWZ.K=(DOCWZ)(TBOWZ.K)/MRCWZ.K                    170, A

DOCWZ=8.9E-3 PPM*CFS/(LB/DAY)                       170A, C

     DODWZ - DISSOLVED OXYGEN DEFICIT (PPM)
     DOCWZ - DISSOLVED OXYGEN COEFFICIENT
     TBOWZ - TOTAL BOD POLLUTION (LB)
     MRCWZ - MINIMUM RIVER FLOW AT CRITICAL POINT
               (CFS)
```

The total BOD generated in the subregion is equal to the sum of the residential BOD and the industrial BOD:

```
TBOWZ.K=RBOWZ.K+IBOWZ.K                              171, A

    TBOWZ - TOTAL BOD POLLUTION (LB)
    RBOWZ - RESIDENTIAL BOD POLLUTION (LB)
    IBOWZ - INDUSTRIAL BOD POLLUTION (LB)
```

The residential BOD is equal to the per capita BOD times the population:

```
RBOWZ.K=(PCBWZ)(POPDZ.K)                             172, A

PCBWZ=.22 LB                                         172A, C

    RBOWZ - RESIDENTIAL BOD POLLUTION (LB)
    PCBWZ - PER CAPITA BOD POLLUTION
    POPDZ - POPULATION (MEN)
```

Industrial BOD is equal to the BOD generated per processing worker times the total number of workers in the processing industries:

```
IBOWZ.K=(PPWBW)(WTPIZ.K+WCPIZ.K)                     173, A

PPWBW=1.5 LB/MAN                                     173A, C

    IBOWZ - INDUSTRIAL BOD POLLUTION (LB)
    PPWBW - PER PROCESSING WORKER POLLUTION
    WTPIZ - WORKERS IN TRANSPORTATION-INTENSIVE
            PROCESSING INDUSTRIES(MEN)
    WCPIZ - WORKERS IN CAP-INT PROC(MEN)
```

Recreation[9]

The recreation subsector serves two purposes: it creates an estimate of the number of people employed in recreation and an estimate of the utilization of the facilities.

The number of workers in export water-based recreation is the product of the fraction of workers in export recreation, the workers needed per visitor-day and the total number of visitor-days:

```
WWRZ.K=(FWXRZ)(WNVDR)(TVDRZ.K)                        174, A

FWXRZ=.625 D                                          174A, C

WNVDR=142E-06 MEN/MAN-DAY                            , 174B, C

     WWRZ  - WORKERS IN EXPORT WATER BASED RECRTN
               (MEN)
     FWXRZ - FRACT OF WORKERS IN EXPORT RECRTN
     WNVDR - WORKERS NEEDED PER VISITOR-DAY(M/MD
     TVDRZ - TOTAL VISITOR DAYS (MAN-DAYS/YR)
```

The total number of visitor-days is the sum of the number of visitor-days at each site:

```
TVDRZ.K=VDARZ+VDBRZ+VDCRZ                              175, A

     TVDRZ - TOTAL VISITOR DAYS (MAN-DAYS/YR)
     VDARZ - VISITOR DAYS SITE A (MAN-DAYS/YR)
     VDBRZ - VISITOR DAYS (MAN-DAYS)
     VDCRZ - VISITOR DAYS SITE C (MAN-DAYS)
```

[9] See Chapter 11.

The number of visitor-days at Site A is the product of the visits per person at Site A, the trend in visitor-days, and the population:

```
VDARZ.K=(VPARZ)(TVDR.K)(POPDZ.K)                    176, A

      VDARZ - VISITOR DAYS SITE A (MAN-DAYS/YR)
      VPARZ - VISITS PER PERSON SITE A (MAN-DAYS/YR/
              MAN)
      TVDR  - TREND IN VISITOR DAYS (D)
      POPDZ - POPULATION (MEN)
```

The visits per person at Site A is a step that occurs when the site is completed. In this particular case the site has already been completed, so there is a positive initial value for the visits per person:

```
VPARZ.K=STEP(VBARZ,TBARZ)                           177, A

TBARZ=16                                            177A, C

VPARZ=VAARZ                                         177B, N

      VPARZ - VISITS PER PERSON SITE A (MAN-DAYS/YR/
              MAN)
      VBARZ - VISITS/PERSON WITH FINAL PARAMETERS
              (1960) (MAN-DAYS/YR/MAN)
      TBARZ - TIME OF ALTERATION SITE A
      VAARZ - VISITS/PERSON WITH INITIAL PARAMETERS
              (1960) (MAN-DAYS/YR/MAN)
```

The total number of visits is linearly related to an activity index, the square root of the number of acres of water, the park capacity, and the number of miles to the nearest major highway. This is then divided by the total population to get the number of visits per person:

```
VBARZ=(1/POPDZ)(987+VXARZ)                          178, N

VXARZ=(2940)(RAARZ)+(11900)(RWARZ)+                 178A, N
   (87.8)(RCARZ)+(-1990)(RMARZ)

RAARZ=70.5                                          178B, C

RWARZ=15.9                                          178C, C

RCARZ=150                                           178D, C

RMARZ=25                                            178E, C
```

```
     VBARZ - VISITS/PERSON WITH FINAL PARAMETERS
               (1960) (MAN-DAYS/YR/MAN)
     POPDZ - POPULATION (MEN)
     RAARZ - RECREATION ACTIVITIES INDEX SITE A
     RWARZ - RECREATION WATER ACRES INDEX SITE A
     RCARZ - RECREATION CAPACITY INDEX SITE A
     RMARZ - RECREATION MILES TO HIGHWAY INDEX
               SITE A
```

The visits per person with initial parameters is calculated similarly:

```
VAARZ=(1/POPDZ)(987+VYARZ)                          179, N

VYARZ=(2940)(IAARZ)+(11900)(IWARZ)+                 179A, N
   (87.8)(ICARZ)+(-1990)(IMARZ)

IAARZ=70.5                                          179B, C

IWARZ=15.9                                          179C, C

ICARZ=150                                           179D, C

IMARZ=31                                            179E, C
```

```
     VAARZ - VISITS/PERSON WITH INITIAL PARAMETERS
               (1960) (MAN-DAYS/YR/MAN)
     POPDZ - POPULATION (MEN)
     IAARZ - INITIAL ACTIVITIES INDEX SITE A
     IWARZ - INITIAL WATER ACRES INDEX SITE A
     ICARZ - INITIAL CAPACITY INDEX SITE A
     IMARZ - INITIAL MILES TO HIGHWAY INDEX SITE A
```

380   Appendix D

The visitor-days at the other two sites are computed similarly:

```
VDBRZ.K=(VPBRZ)(TVDR.K)(POPDZ.K)                    180, A

     VDBRZ - VISITOR DAYS (MAN-DAYS)
     VPBRZ - VISITS PER PERSON SITE B
     TVDR  - TREND IN VISITOR DAYS (D)
     POPDZ - POPULATION (MEN)

VPBRZ.K=STEP(VBBRZ,TBBRZ)                           181, A

TBBRZ=16                                            181A, C

VBBRZ=(1/POPDZ)(987+VXBRZ)                          181B, N

VXBRZ=(2940)(RABRZ)+(11900)(RWBRZ)+                 181C, N
   (87.8)(RCBRZ)+(-1990)(RMBRZ)

RABRZ=-.336                                         181D, C

RWBRZ=0                                             181E, C

RCBRZ=0                                             181F, C

RMBRZ=0                                             181G, C

     VPBRZ - VISITS PER PERSON SITE B
     VBBRZ - VISITS/PERSON WITH FINAL PARAMETERS(1960)
     TBBRZ - TIME OF COMPLETION SITE B
     POPDZ - POPULATION (MEN)
     RABRZ - RECREATION ACTIVITIES INDEX SITE B
     RWBRZ - RECREATION WATER ACRES INDEX SITE B
     RCBRZ - RECREATION CAPACITY INDEX SITE B
     RMBRZ - RECREATION MILES TO HIGHWAY INDEX
               SITE B


VDCRZ.K=(VPCRZ)(TVDR.K)(POPDZ.K)                    182, A

     VDCRZ - VISITOR DAYS SITE C (MAN-DAYS)
     TVDR  - TREND IN VISITOR DAYS (D)
     POPDZ - POPULATION (MEN)
```

```
VPCRZ.K=STEP(VBCRZ,TBCRZ)                            183, A

TBCRZ=18                                             183A, C

VBCRZ=(1/POPDZ)(987+VXCRZ)                           183B, N

VXCRZ=(2940)(RACRZ)+(11900)(RWCRZ)+                  183C, N
   (87.8)(RCCRZ)+(-1990)(RMCRZ)

RACRZ=-.336                                          183D, C

RWCRZ=0                                              183E, C

RCCRZ=0                                              183F, C

RMCRZ=0                                              183G, C

    VBCRZ - VISITS/PERSON WITH FINAL PARAMETERS(1960)
    TBCRZ - TIME OF COMPLETION SITE C
    POPDZ - POPULATION (MEN)
    RACRZ - RECREATION ACTIVITIES INDEX SITE C
    RWCRZ - RECREATION WATER ACRES INDEX SITE C
    RCCRZ - RECREATION CAPACITY INDEX SITE C
    RMCRZ - RECREATION MILES TO HIGHWAY INDEX
              SITE C
```

The trend in visitor-days is provided in a table:

```
TVDR.K=TABLE(TTVDR,TIME.K,0,50,50)                   184, A

TTVDR*=1.0/1.5 D                                     184A, C

    TVDR  - TREND IN VISITOR DAYS (D)
    TTVDR - TABLE OF TREND IN VISITOR DAYS
    TIME  - TIME
```

Income Sector

This model uses relative unemployment rate and relative wages rather than per capita income as key variables in a number of feedback loops. Nevertheless, many individuals are interested in the personal income figure, which this subsector calculates. The figure is not used in any of the feedback loops, therefore this sector is merely a calculating appendage.

The civilian per capita income is the sum of wages and transfer payments divided by the civilian population:

```
PCIXZ.K=(1/CPPDZ.K)(WGIXZ.K+TPIXZ.K)                    185, S

     PCIXZ - CIV. PER CAPITA INCOME($/MN/YR
     CPPDZ - CIVILIAN POPULATION
     WGIXZ - WAGE INCOME ($/YR)
     TPIXZ - TRANSFER PAYMENTS
```

The civilian population is calculated as expected:

```
CPPDZ.K=POPDZ.K-WMSIZ.K                                 186, S

     CPPDZ - CIVILIAN POPULATION
     POPDZ - POPULATION (MEN)
     WMSIZ - WORKERS IN MILITARY SERVICE
```

The wage income is the sum of the products of the annual wages in each industrial classification and the number of workers in that classification:

```
WGIXZ.K=WG1XZ.K+WG2XZ.K+WG3XZ.K                         187, S

WG1XZ.K=(WGDXZ.K)(WDFIZ.K)+(WGNXZ.K)(WNFIZ.K)          187A, S
 +(WGTXZ.K)(WTPIZ.K)+(WGCXZ.K)(WCPIZ.K)

WG2XZ.K=(WGMXZ.K)(WXMIZ.K)+(WGWXZ.K)(WWCIZ.K)          187B, S
 +(WGAXZ.K)(WAZ.K)+(WGBXZ.K)(WBSIZ.K)

     WGIXZ - WAGE INCOME ($/YR)
     WGDXZ - ANNUAL WAGE DUR FAB ($/MAN/YR)
     WDFIZ - WORKERS IN DURABLE FABRICATION(MEN)
     WGNXZ - ANNUAL WAGE NDR FAB ($/MAN/YR)
     WNFIZ - WORKERS IN NONDURABLE FABRICATION (MEN)
     WGTXZ - ANNUAL WAGE TRP PRC ($/MAN/YR)
     WTPIZ - WORKERS IN TRANSPORTATION-INTENSIVE
                    PROCESSING INDUSTRIES(MEN)
     WGCXZ - ANNUAL WAGE CAP PRC ($/MAN/YR)
     WCPIZ - WORKERS IN CAP-INT PROC(MEN)
     WGMXZ - ANNUAL WAGE XPR MNG ($/MAN/YR)
     WXMIZ - WORKERS IN EXPORT MINING (MEN)
     WGWXZ - ANNUAL WAGE WTR CNS ($/MAN/YR)
     WWCIZ - WORKERS IN WATER WORKS CONST (MEN
     WGAXZ - ANNUAL WAGE AGRICLT ($/MAN/YR)
     WAZ   - WORKERS IN AGRICULTURE (MEN)
     WGBXZ - ANNUAL WAGE BUS SRV ($/MAN/YR)
     WBSIZ - WORKERS IN BUSINESS SERVING IND(MEN
```

```
WG3XZ.K=WG4XZ.K+(WGGXZ.K)(WGEIZ.K)                    188, S

WG4XZ.K=(WGHXZ.K)(WHSIZ.K+WWRZ.K)                     188A, S

    WGGXZ - ANNUAL WAGE GOV + EDC  ($/MAN/YR)
    WGEIZ - WORKERS IN GOV AND EDUCATION(MEN
    WGHXZ - ANNUAL WAGE HSH SRV ($/MAN/YR)
    WHSIZ - WORKERS IN HOUSEHOLD SERVING IND(MEN
    WWRZ  - WORKERS IN EXPORT WATER BASED RECRTN
                (MEN)
```

The annual wage in the durable fabricating industry is the product of the initial hours in durable fabricating, the relative wage, and other factors affecting durable fabricating wages:

```
WGDXZ.K=(IHDXZ)(RWIZ.K)(FWDXZ.K)                      189, S

IHDXZ=1769 HR/YR                                      189A, C

    WGDXZ - ANNUAL WAGE DUR FAB ($/MAN/YR)
    IHDXZ - INIT HOURS IN DUR FAB
    RWIZ  - RELATIVE WAGES (D)
    FWDXZ - OTHER FACTORS IN DUR FAB WAGES ($/HR)
```

The other factors affecting durable fabrication wages is calculated as the product of the trend in wages and the initial hourly wage:

```
FWDXZ.K=(TRWGX.K)(IWDXZ)                               190, S

IWDXZ=2.34 $/HR                                       190A, C

    FWDXZ - OTHER FACTORS IN DUR FAB WAGES ($/HR)
    TRWGX - TREND IN WAGES (D)
    IWDXZ - INIT HOURLY WAGES IN DUR FAB
```

The trend in wages is simply a product of the trend in hours and the trend in hourly wages:

```
TRWGX.K=(TRHRX.K)(TRHWX.K)                             191, S

    TRWGX - TREND IN WAGES (D)
    TRHRX - TREND IN HOURS (D)
    TRHWX - TREND IN HOURLY WAGE (D)
```

These trends are provided in tables:

```
TRHRX.K=TABLE(TTHRX,TIME.K,0,50,50)                    192, S

TTHRX*=1/.75 D                                         192A, C

    TRHRX - TREND IN HOURS (D)
    TTHRX - TAB/OF TREND IN HOURS
    TIME  - TIME

TRHWX.K=TABLE(TTHWX,TIME.K,0,50,10)                    193, S

TTHWX*=1/1.34/1.81/2.43/3.26/4.38 D                    193A, C

    TRHWX - TREND IN HOURLY WAGE (D)
    TTHWX - TAB OF TRENT IN HOURLY WAGE
    TIME  - TIME
```

The annual wage in most of the remaining industrial classifications is computed similarly:

```
WGNXZ.K=(IHNXZ)(RWLIZ.K)(FWNXZ.K)                      194, S

IHNXZ=2187 HR/YR                                       194A, C

    WGNXZ - ANNUAL WAGE NDR FAB ($/MAN/YR)
    IHNXZ - INIT HOURS IN NDR FAB
    RWLIZ - RELATIVE LOW WAGES(D)
    FWNXZ - OTHER FACTORS IN HDR FAB WAGES ($/HR)

FWNXZ.K=(TRWGX.K)(IWNXZ)                                195, S

IWNXZ=1.60 $/HR                                        195A, C

    FWNXZ - OTHER FACTORS IN HDR FAB WAGES ($/HR)
    TRWGX - TREND IN WAGES (D)
    IWNXZ - INIT HOURLY WAGES IN NDR FAB

WGTXZ.K=(IHTXZ)(RWIZ.K)(FWTXZ.K)                       196, S

IHTXZ=1958 HR/YR                                       196A, C

    WGTXZ - ANNUAL WAGE TRP PRC ($/MAN/YR)
    IHTXZ - INIT HOURS IN TRP PRC
    RWIZ  - RELATIVE WAGES (D)
    FWTXZ - OTHER FACTORS IN TRP PRC WAGES ($/HR)
```

```
FWTXZ.K=(TRWGX.K)(IWTXZ)                              197, S

IWTXZ=2.36 $/HR                                      197A, C

     FWTXZ - OTHER FACTORS IN TRP PRC WAGES ($/HR)
     TRWGX - TREND IN WAGES (D)
     IWTXZ - INIT HOURLY WAGES IN TRP PRC

WGCXZ.K=(IHCXZ)(RWIZ.K)(FWCXZ.K)                     198, S

IHCXZ=1759 HR/YR                                     198A, C

     WGCXZ - ANNUAL WAGE CAP PRC ($/MAN/YR)
     IHCXZ - INIT HOURS IN CAP PRC
     RWIZ  - RELATIVE WAGES (D)
     FWCXZ - OTHER FACTORS IN CAP PRC WAGES ($/HR)

FWCXZ.K=(TRWGX.K)(IWCXZ)                              199, S

IWCXZ=2.23 $/HR                                      199A, C

     FWCXZ - OTHER FACTORS IN CAP PRC WAGES ($/HR)
     TRWGX - TREND IN WAGES (D)
     IWCXZ - INIT HOURLY WAGES IN CAP PRC

WGWXZ.K=(IHWXZ)(RWIZ.K)(FWWXZ.K)                     200, S

IHWXZ=2080 HR/YR                                     200A, C

     WGWXZ - ANNUAL WAGE WTR CNS ($/MAN/YR)
     IHWXZ - INITIAL HOURS IN WTR CNS
     RWIZ  - RELATIVE WAGES (D)
     FWWXZ - OTHER FACTORS IN WTR CNS WAGES ($/HR)

FWWXZ.K=(TRWGX.K)(IWWXZ)                              201, S

IWWXZ=3.08 $/HR                                      201A, C

     FWWXZ - OTHER FACTORS IN WTR CNS WAGES ($/HR)
     TRWGX - TREND IN WAGES (D)
     IWWXZ - INIT HOURLY WAGES IN WTR CNS

WGBXZ.K=(IHBXZ)(RWIZ.K)(FWBXZ.K)                     202, S

IHBXZ=1544 HR/YR                                     202A, C

     WGBXZ - ANNUAL WAGE BUS SRV ($/MAN/YR)
     IHBXZ - INIT HOURS IN BUS SRV
     RWIZ  - RELATIVE WAGES (D)
     FWBXZ - OTHER FACTORS IN BUS SRV WAGES ($/HR)
```

```
FWBXZ.K=(TRWGX.K)(IWBXZ)                              203, S

IWBXZ=2.34 $/HR                                      203A, C

    FWBXZ - OTHER FACTORS IN BUS SRV WAGES ($/HR)
    TRWGX - TREND IN WAGES (D)
    IWBXZ - INIT HOURLY WAGES IN BUS SRV
```

The annual wage in export mining is simply the product of the initial hours in export mining, the initial hourly wage, and the trend in wages:

```
WGMXZ.K=(IHMXZ)(IWMXZ)(TRWGX.K)                      204, S

IHMXZ=1548 HR/YR                                     204A, C

IWMXZ=2.76 $/HR                                      204B, C

    WGMXZ - ANNUAL WAGE XPR MNG ($/MAN/YR)
    IHMXZ - INIT HOURS IN XPR MNG
    IWMXZ - INIT HOURLY WAGES IN XPR MNG
    TRWGX - TREND IN WAGES (D)
```

This simpler form is also used in calculating the annual wages in government and education and agriculture:

```
WGGXZ.K=(IHGXZ)(IWGXZ)(TRWGX.K)                      205, S

IWGXZ=1.85 $/HR                                      205A, C

IHGXZ=2080 HR/YR                                     205B, C

    WGGXZ - ANNUAL WAGE GOV + EDC  ($/MAN/YR)
    IHGXZ - INIT HOURS IN GOV + EDC
    IWGXZ - INIT HOURLY WAGES IN GOV + EDC
    TRWGX - TREND IN WAGES (D)


WGAXZ.K=(IHAXZ)(IWAXZ)(TRWGX.K)                      206, S

IHAXZ=514 HR/YR                                      206A, C

IWAXZ=.89 $/HR                                       206B, C

    WGAXZ - ANNUAL WAGE AGRICLT ($/MAN/YR)
    IHAXZ - INIT HOURS IN AGRICLT
    IWAXZ - INIT HOURLY WAGES IN AGRICLT
    TRWGX - TREND IN WAGES (D)
```

The annual wage in household serving is computed as the product of the initial hours, the normal hourly wage, and the trend in wages:

```
WGHXZ.K=(IHHXZ)(NWHXZ.K)(TRHWX.K)                    207, S

IHHXZ=1595 HR/YR                                     207A, C

     WGHXZ  -  ANNUAL WAGE HSH SRV ($/MAN/YR)
     IHHXZ  -  INIT HOURS IN HSH SRV
     NWHXZ  -  NORMAL HRLY WGS HSH SRV
     TRHWX  -  TREND IN HOURLY WAGE (D)
```

The normal hourly wage in household serving depends on the population:

```
NWHXZ.K=TABHL(TNWHX,POPDZ.K,.2E6,2E6,.2E6)           208, A

TNWHX*=1.45/1.55/1.60/1.63/1.66/1.68/1.69/           208A, C
  1.70/1.71/1.73 TAB

     NWHXZ  -  NORMAL HRLY WGS HSH SRV
     TNWHX  -  OF NWHXZ
     POPDZ  -  POPULATION (MEN)
```

Transfer payments are computed as the sum of social security payments and unemployment compensation. This sum is then multiplied by a trend:

```
TPIXZ.K=(TRTPX.K)(SSPXZ.K+UNCXZ.K)                   209, S

     TPIXZ  -  TRANSFER PAYMENTS
     TRTPX  -  TREND IN TRANSFER PAYMENTS(D
     SSPXZ  -  SOCIAL SECURITY PAYMENTS
     UNCXZ  -  UNEMPLOYMENT COMPENSATION NORMAL HRLY
               WGS HSH SRV
```

The trend is provided in a table:

```
TRTPX.K=TABLE(TTTPX,TIME.K,0,50,50)                  210, A

TTTPX*=1/2 D                                         210A, C

     TRTPX  -  TREND IN TRANSFER PAYMENTS(D
     TTTPX  -  TAB OF TREND IN TRANSFER PAYMENTS
     TIME   -  TIME
```

Social security payments are calculated as the product of initial payments and the number of people 65 or older:

```
SSPXZ.K=(ISSPX)(OLDZ.K)                          211, S

ISSPX=1730                                       211A, C

    SSPXZ - SOCIAL SECURITY PAYMENTS
    ISSPX - INIT SOC SEC PAYMNTS ($/MAN)
    OLDZ  - OLDSTERS, OVER 65(MEN)
```

Similarly, unemployment compensation is the initial amount times the number of people unemployed:

```
UNCXZ.K=(IUEBX)(ULZ.K)                           212, S

IUEBX=960                                        212A, C

    UNCXZ - UNEMPLOYMENT COMPENSATION NORMAL HRLY
              WGS HSH SRV
    IUEBX - INIT UNEMPLOY COMPNS ($/MAN)
    ULZ   - NUMBER UNEMPLOYED (MEN)
```

Electric Power Requirements

The power-requirements subsector estimates the future requirements for electric power by estimating the residential consumption for heating and for other purposes along with the consumption by commerce and by industry. Similar to the income subsector, these results are not incorporated into the feedback structure of the model. Further, the work is very preliminary, only having been the subject of research during Phase II of the study.

The total consumption of electricity is equal to the sum of the products of the per household consumption times the number of households, the per household-serving worker consumption times the number of workers in household-serving industries, and the per industrial worker consumption times the number of industrial workers:

```
TCEZ.K=(PHEZ.K)(HEZ.K)+(PHWEZ.K)(WHSIZ.K)+        213, A
  (PIWEZ.K)(IWEZ.K)+(0)(0)

    TCEZ  - TOTAL CONSUMPTION (KWH/YR)
    PHEZ  - PER HOUSEHOLD CONSUMPTION(KWH/YR/HH
    HEZ   - HOUSEHOLDS (HH)
    PHWEZ - PER HOUSEHOLD SERVING WORKER CONSUMPTION
              (KWH/YR/MAN)
    WHSIZ - WORKERS IN HOUSEHOLD SERVING IND(MEN)
    PIWEZ - PER INDUSTRIAL WORKER CONSUMPTION
              (KWH/YR/MAN)
    IWEZ  - INDUSTRIAL WORKERS (MEN)
```

The per household consumption of electricity is equal to the sum of the per household consumption exclusive of space heating plus the average household consumption for heating:

```
PHEZ.K=PHXEZ.K+AHHEZ.K                             214, A

    PHEZ  - PER HOUSEHOLD CONSUMPTION(KWH/YR/HH
    PHXEZ - PER HOUSEHOLD CONSUMPTION EXCLUSIVE
              OF HEATING (KWH/YR/HH)
    AHHEZ - AVG HOUSHLD CONSMPTN FOR HEATING(KWH/YR/HH
```

The per household consumption of electricity exclusive of heating is a level determined by the growth rate of household consumption exclusive of heating:

```
PHXEZ.K=PHXEZ.J+(DT)(GHXEZ.J+0)                    215, L

PHXEZ=3400                                         215A, N

    PHXEZ - PER HOUSEHOLD CONSUMPTION EXCLUSIVE
              OF HEATING (KWH/YR/HH)
    GHXEZ - GROWTH RATE OF HOUSEHOLD CONSUMPTION
              EXCLUSIVE OF HEATING (KWH/YR/YR/HH)
```

The growth rate of household consumption exclusive of heating is equal to the fractional growth rate times the per household consumption of electricity exclusive of heating:

```
GHXEZ.K=(FHXEZ)(PHXEZ.K)                        216, A

FHXEZ=.03 1/YR                                  216A, C

    GHXEZ - GROWTH RATE OF HOUSEHOLD CONSUMPTION
              EXCLUSIVE OF HEATING (KWH/YR/YR/HH)
    FHXEZ - FRACTIONAL GROWTH RATE OF HOUSEHOLD
              CONSUMPTN EXCLUSIVE OF HEATING
    PHXEZ - PER HOUSEHOLD CONSUMPTION EXCLUSIVE
              OF HEATING (KWH/YR/HH)
```

The average household consumption for heating is equal to the per household consumption of electricity for heating times the fraction of households heated:

```
AHHEZ.K=(PHHEZ)(FHHEZ.K)                        217, A

PHHEZ=14E3 (KWH/YR)                             217A, C

    AHHEZ - AVG HOUSHLD CONSMPTN FOR HEATING(KWH/YR/HH
    PHHEZ - PER HOUSEHOLD CONSUMPTION FOR HEATING
    FHHEZ - FRACTION OF HOUSEHOLDS HEATED BY ELECTRICITY
              (D)
```

The fraction of households heated by electricity is provided exogenously in a table:

```
FHHEZ.K=TABLE(TFHEZ,TIME.K,0,50,10)             218, A

TFHEZ*=.001/.1/.25/.4/.6/.8 D                   218A, C

    FHHEZ - FRACTION OF HOUSEHOLDS HEATED BY ELECTRICITY
              (D)
    TFHEZ - TABLE OF FRACTION OF HOUSEHOLD HEATED
              BY ELECTRICITY
    TIME  - TIME
```

The number of households is the population divided by the number of people per household:

```
HEZ.K=POPDZ.K/PPHE                          219, A
```

```
PPHE=3.4 MEN/HH                             219A, C
```

```
    HEZ   - HOUSEHOLDS (HH)
    POPDZ - POPULATION (MEN)
    PPHE  - PERSONS PER HOUSEHOLD
```

The per household-serving worker consumption of electricity is a level determined by the growth rate of consumption by household-serving workers:

```
PHWEZ.K=PHWEZ.J+(DT)(GHWEZ.J+0)             220, L
```

```
PHWEZ=3400                                  220A, N
```

```
    PHWEZ - PER HOUSEHOLD SERVING WORKER CONSUMPTION
                (KWH/YR/MAN)
    GHWEZ - GROWTH RATE OF PER HOUSEHOLD SERVING
                WORKER CONSUMPTION (KWH/YR/YR/MAN)
```

The growth rate of consumption by household-serving workers is equal to the product of the fractional growth rate times the consumption per household worker:

```
GHWEZ.K=(FHWEZ)(PHWEZ.K)                     221, A
```

```
FHWEZ=.05 1/YR                               221A, C
```

```
    GHWEZ - GROWTH RATE OF PER HOUSEHOLD SERVING
                WORKER CONSUMPTION (KWH/YR/YR/MAN)
    FHWEZ - FRACTION GROWTH RATE OF PER HOUSEHOLD
                SERVING WORKER CONSUMPTION
    PHWEZ - PER HOUSEHOLD SERVING WORKER CONSUMPTION
                (KWH/YR/MAN)
```

The consumption per industrial worker is computed in the same manner as the consumption per household worker:

```
PIWEZ.K=PIWEZ.J+(DT)(GIWEZ.J+0)             222, L
```

```
PIWEZ=7E3                                   222A, N
```

```
    PIWEZ - PER INDUSTRIAL WORKER CONSUMPTION
                (KWH/YR/MAN)
    GIWEZ - GROWTH RATE OF PER INDUSTRIAL WORKER
                CONSUMPTION (KWH/YR/YR/MAN)
```

```
GIWEZ.K=(FIWEZ)(PIWEZ.K)                          223, A

FIWEZ=.04 1/YR                                    223A, C

     GIWEZ - GROWTH RATE OF PER INDUSTRIAL WORKER
                 CONSUMPTION (KWH/YR/YR/MAN)
     FIWEZ - FRACTIONAL GROWTH RATE OF PER INDUSTRIAL
                 WORKER CONSUMPTION
     PIWEZ - PER INDUSTRIAL WORKER CONSUMPTION
                 (KWH/YR/MAN)
```

The number of industrial workers is the total number of workers employed less those employed in household-serving industries and those employed in agriculture:

```
IWEZ.K=TWELZ.K-WHSIZ.K-WAZ.K                      224, A

     IWEZ  - INDUSTRIAL WORKERS (MEN)
     TWELZ - TOTAL WORKERS EMPLOYED (MEN)
     WHSIZ - WORKERS IN HOUSEHOLD SERVING IND(MEN
     WAZ   - WORKERS IN AGRICULTURE (MEN)
```

The ratio of total consumption of electricity to the initial total consumption of electricity is computed as one might expect:

```
ROIEZ.K=TCEZ.K/ITCEZ                              225, S

ITCEZ=TCEZ                                        225A, N

     ROIEZ - RATIO OF CURRENT TO INITIAL CONSUMPTION(D
     TCEZ  - TOTAL CONSUMPTION (KWH/YR)
     ITCEZ - INITIAL TOTAL CONSUMPTION (KWH/YR)
```

The total consumption by households in the subregions is the product of the number of households and the per household consumption:

```
SCHEZ.K=(HEZ.K)(PHEZ.K)                           226, S

     SCHEZ - SUBREGION CONSMPTN BY HOUSHLDS(KWH/YR
     HEZ   - HOUSEHOLDS (HH)
     PHEZ  - PER HOUSEHOLD CONSUMPTION(KWH/YR/HH
```

The subregion consumption by households for heating is equal to the number of households times the average household consumption for heating:

```
SHHEZ.K=(HEZ.K)(AHHEZ.K)                              227, S

    SHHEZ - SUBRGN CONSMPTN BY HH FOR HEATING
              (KWH/YR)
    HEZ   - HOUSEHOLDS (HH)
    AHHEZ - AVG HOUSHLD CONSMPTN FOR HEATING(KWH/YR/HH)
```

The total consumption exclusive of heating by households in a subregion is equal to the number of households times the per household consumption of electricity exclusive of heating:

```
SHXEZ.K=(HEZ.K)(PHXEZ.K)                              228, S

    SHXEZ - SUBRGN CONSMPTN BY HH EXCL OF HEAT(KWH/YR)
    HEZ   - HOUSEHOLDS (HH)
    PHXEZ - PER HOUSEHOLD CONSUMPTION EXCLUSIVE
              OF HEATING (KWH/YR/HH)
```

Index